SOCRATIC PUZZLES

SOCRATIC

PUZZLES

Robert Nozick

Harvard University Press

Cambridge, Massachusetts

London, England ❧ 1997

Designed by Marianne Perlak

Library of Congress Cataloging-in-Publication Data

Nozick, Robert.
  Socratic puzzles / Robert Nozick.
    p. cm.
  Includes bibliographical references and index.
  ISBN 0-674-81653-6 (alk. paper)
    1. Methodology. 2. Socrates. 3. Philosophy. 4. Political
science—Philosophy. 5. Ethics. I. Title.
B945.N683S63 1997
191—dc21   96-39221

To the memory of my parents,

Max Nozick (1906–1990)
and
Sophie Cohen Nozick (1908–1975)

CONTENTS

SOCRATIC PUZZLES

INTRODUCTION

It is disconcerting to be known primarily for an early work. Others have identified me as a "political philosopher," but I have never thought of myself in those terms. The vast majority of my writing and attention has focused on other subjects.

Anarchy, State, and Utopia was an accident. It was written during 1971–72, a year spent at the Center for Advanced Study in the Behavioral Sciences, adjacent to Stanford University, and my plan for that year was to write on the topic of free will. Social and political philosophy was a serious but not a predominant interest of mine. After several months of getting nowhere on the topic of free will, I was invited in early December to give a talk to a Stanford University student group, and I presented some thoughts on how a state would arise out of (individualist) anarchy. Those thoughts seemed worth writing up, and that was done by the beginning of January, when the mail from Cambridge brought John Rawls's long-awaited book, which I had read in manuscript and discussed extensively with Rawls. In lectures at Harvard, I had been developing the entitlement theory of justice, within a libertarian framework, and when I read the final version of *A Theory of Justice* that January, I was moved to write down the entitlement theory along with my critical thoughts on Rawls's theory, which had developed significantly since our last discussions. By the end of February, I had on my desk an essay on state-of-nature theory, an essay on distributive justice, and also an essay on utopia that I had delivered at a meeting of the American Philosophical Association and brought along with me to Stanford. These three pieces fit together and it seemed that with some integration and some additional material they might constitute a book. So, rather than returning to the intractable problem of free will, I set to intensive work to complete that book before my stay at Stanford would be up in July.

I have not responded to the sizable literature on *Anarchy, State, and Utopia,* or followed it closely. I did not want to spend my life writing "The Son of Anarchy, State, and Utopia," "The Return of the Son of . . . ," etc. I had other philosophical questions to think about: knowledge, the self, why there is something rather than nothing, and—of course—free will. Also, I believed that responding to criticisms of that book or reading them closely would not be a good way for me to gain any critical distance from its positions. My natural tendency would be to defend strongly those positions under attack—and *attack* it was!— and how could I learn that my views were mistaken if I thought about them always with defensive juices flowing? (I returned briefly to express reservations about some of *Anarchy, State, and Utopia*'s views in *The Examined Life*, pp. 30–32, 286–296.) I have not responded to the literature on my other writing either. I could say that any intellectual contribution I could make was likely to be greater in broaching new ideas on new subjects than in elaborating or defending my previous ideas, and that would be true, but also it is true that what pleases and excites me is to think new thoughts about new topics. I have learned much from philosophers who stay with one area or one theme, gaining deeper insight, but my bent is elsewhere.

Philosophers seek structures telling how things are related and constituted. They find complexity in what appears simple, and simplicity in what appears complex. Philosophy's understanding is structural, its method is clarity of thought and reasoning.

Socrates, at western philosophy's beginning, made critical thinking an explicit. methodical activity. The aim was to bring everything to conscious, explicit, and critical awareness: the definition of important concepts, the articulation of principles of conduct, the methods of reasoning themselves. Philosophers since then have been indebted to Socrates not only for his intellectual daring and incisive trains of thought, but for the vivid and inspiring way he embodies what a philosopher is. Medieval thinkers paid tribute to the scope and depth of Aristotle's theories by referring to him as "the philosopher." But when I think of "the" philosopher, I think of Socrates. Scholars have disagreed over central questions about this sharp and clear thinker. What did he mean when he said he did not know the answers to his questions, what does his method of critical discussion presuppose, and what is his concern in improving the souls of those he encounters? In "Socratic Puzzles" (Essay 6), I propose some answers.

The intellectual problems and puzzles in the other essays of this volume* are not all of them "Socratic," if that means focusing on the particular questions Socrates investigated. However, the writing here grows out of what Socrates did and is continuous with it. Sometimes an interesting question motivates analyzing a concept, sometimes a central notion leads to a new and puzzling question, and sometimes these links iterate to form a longer chain of reasoning. That is true of much of philosophy, of course, so while the title of this book marks it as philosophy, it does not specifically describe its contents. Rather, it pays Socrates homage.

One of philosophy's central tasks has been to formulate and justify rules, norms, and principles to help guide us through the welter of possibilities we face, different possibilities of action, of belief, of ways we could be. Let me indicate how the essays here fit within this philosophical task, and how they connect to my other writing. Normative principles of action will make actions depend upon our beliefs (about what is the case, and what will happen if we act a certain way) and upon our desires or evaluations (what we want to happen or value happening). But what normative rules or principles should our beliefs and desires satisfy? And, given (appropriate) beliefs and desires, what specific principle or rule should then select the action?

The most widely discussed rule mandates that our actions maximize expected utility. Along with normative conditions on the structure of preferences, this rule is part of a normative theory of decision that was formulated by economists and mathematicians in the mid-twentieth century. Philosophers, with their interest in explicit normative or rational rules, were not slow in taking up this theory. I was drawn seriously into the study of philosophy in Sidney Morgenbesser's philosophy classes at Columbia College, and there I first encountered these decision theories. I was led to Morgenbesser's classes in particular by my earlier experience in a section that he taught of a required general education course at Columbia on twentieth-century social and political thought. Every time I said something in that course, Morgenbesser raised an objection—I was overlooking a distinction or ignoring an objection or failing to consider how some structural feature of my point might generalize—and

*I am very grateful to Tamar Gendler for her persuasiveness in urging me to bring together a volume of essays and for her help in assembling this work for press.

his objection would convince me that I wasn't thinking clearly enough, and that there was a clearer way to think. Thus I was lured to take more courses in the hope of learning to think that clearly—soon I had amassed enough courses to "major in Morgenbesser." It was in graduate school at Princeton, studying with Carl Hempel, that I took a really close look at decision theory, and a projected dissertation (spurred initially by Hempel's writing) on the confirmation and acceptance of scientific hypotheses, after some months and some work, was transformed into "The Normative Theory of Individual Choice" (1963; published in 1990 by Garland Press). Here, I discussed normative conditions on preference, the theory of choice under certainty, risk and uncertainty, and some issues about game theory.

It was in the dissertation that I first discussed Newcomb's Problem, a problem in decision theory thought up by a physicist in California, William Newcomb, and told to me at a party by a mutual friend and physicist at Princeton, David Martin Kruskal. (It was, for me, the most consequential party I have attended.) This intriguing problem was first published in "Newcomb's Problem and Two Principles of Choice" (Essay 2); the treatment there differed from that in the dissertation. Martin Gardner wrote a "Mathematical Games" column on the problem in *Scientific American*, and he asked me to do a guest column (Essay 3) responding to the vast amount of mail he had received. I returned to the problem in *The Nature of Rationality* (pp. 40–50), where I propose the maximization of decision-value (a weighted sum of causally expected, evidentially expected, and symbolic utility). Although three distinct positions on Newcomb's Problem are a small fraction of the positions in the by-now vast literature, they are more than enough for one writer!

Decision theory ("rational choice theory") has received extensive application in the social sciences, and it provides the structure for some of my later philosophical work. It plays a role in *Anarchy, State, and Utopia*'s thoughts about how individual action would give rise to a state, and also in its game-theoretic analysis of utopia; in *The Nature of Rationality* I reformulate decision theory and apply it to issues of rational belief. Decision theory provides the implicit background structure in the essay on "Coercion" (Essay 1), and that part of decision theory concerned with the structure and measurement of preference (utility theory) is one of the models for the theory of moral structures, and the measurement of moral weight, presented in "Moral Complications and Moral Structures" (Essay 10).

Another model was Noam Chomsky's *Syntactic Structures*, and I meant "Moral Complications" to begin to uncover the structure underlying our moral judgments. The essay presents several possible structures (the maximization structure, the deductive structure, and the simple balancing structure) before discussing the more complicated moral balancing structure with its own special governing principles. I added a bit to the formulation and investigation of alternative moral structures in the presentation and discussion of "side-constraints" in *Anarchy, State, and Utopia* (pp. 26–42), but with rare exceptions, the task has not been pursued very extensively by philosophers since then.* One of the new principles in "Moral Complications" (Principle VII) is put to use in a review of Michael Walzer's *Just and Unjust Wars* (Essay 17) to sharpen his proposal about what risks should be incurred to protect civilians in warfare.

Utility theory, the component of decision theory concerning the structure of rational preferences and of their measurement, has been of interest to normative social theory, especially within the utilitarian tradition which mandates maximizing the total happiness or the aggregate sum of utility. That tradition's use of the utility notion, and some other uses as well (hence the interest of the problem, even for critics of utilitarianism), faces the well-known problem of interpersonal comparisons of utility: how can we systematically compare the strength of different people's preferences or desires? "Interpersonal Utility Theory" (Essay 4) presents a new strategy for attacking this problem and makes specific new proposals.

A normative concern about what conditions an individual's choices should satisfy fits in naturally with a concern about the range of choice a person should be free to make. Given my background view that coercion is justified only under very stringent conditions, I was led to investigate the notion of coercion directly (Essay 1). Philosophers had not previously looked closely at this notion, and it presented interesting problems, not simply of formulating an adequate definition that would handle a range of complicated cases, but of understanding why the contours of the notion of coercion take the particular form they do. Why should *threats* be an important component of coercion when offers also can establish a significant difference between the utility yielded by two actions? The answer went beyond the utilities involved in the actual

---

*However, the structure of "prima facie" principles, investigated in one direction in "Moral Complications," has been developed in other intricate and fruitful directions by writers in the field of artificial intelligence studying default structures; for instance, in John Holland, Keith Holyoak, Richard Nisbett, and Paul Thagard, *Induction: Processes of Inference, Learning, and Discovery* (Cambridge, MA: MIT Press, 1986).

choice situation (after the threat or offer has been made); it lay in the hypothetical choice of entering into those threat or offer situations. A person normally would be willing to be the recipient of an offer yet be unwilling to be the recipient of a threat. The difference in willingness to move *into* the situation makes a difference in the voluntariness of the action that is done *within* the situation. A moral evaluation must look beyond the immediate situation and beyond the agent's first-level desires within that situation. (The literature on coercion has grown greatly since my essay appeared. For a discussion, see Alan Wertheimer, *Coercion* [Princeton, NJ: Princeton University Press, 1987].)

The issue of how wide a range of factors must be considered by moral or evaluative principles recurs elsewhere. The moral treatment owed to a person who is mentally retarded, I claim in a review of Tom Regan's book where he discussed this topic (Essay 18), depends not only on the traits he or she possesses but also upon the typical and normal traits possessed by members of the human species, even when the particular person being treated lacks some of these traits. (The closest-continuer theory of identity over time, in *Philosophical Explanations*, pp. 29–70, also widens a context: to determine whether two entities are identical, one must look beyond the traits and relations of those two entities themselves.)

Another principle of normative evaluation is subject to examination in "Goodman, Nelson on Merit, Aesthetic" (Essay 13), where I criticize Goodman's view that a work has aesthetic merit if it is a work of art and changes the way we view the world. That essay contains my only published poem; readers will discover why I want them to think it is a poor poem. "The Characteristic Features of Extremism" (Essay 16) was written for a 1987 conference in Jerusalem (organized by the American Jewish Congress) on political extremism in the United States and Israel, and it was presented in a panel with Geula Cohen, a member of the Israeli Knesset. (Afterwards, some members of the audience asked how, without having met her beforehand, I could so accurately describe the other panelist!) The phenomenon of extremism has grown even more widespread and serious since then. A United States Supreme Court decision (*Baker v. Carr*) formulates the principle that every person's vote is to count equally, and Essay 12 applies formal apparatus to that decision (and in passing presents a counter-example to the Shapley-Shubik power index).

Preference and decision fall under normative rules, and so does belief. Rules encourage or mandate some beliefs, and they discourage or exclude others. Such rules also might be used to criticize the beliefs of other people—always a satisfying activity. (Surely that was part of the appeal of the verifiability criterion of meaning—now known to be defective—put forth by the logical positivists. Allied with the rule not to believe or pay attention to anything (cognitively) meaningless, it allowed one, without further thought, to dismiss whatever was not verifiable, and to criticize others for indulging in meaningless talk.) Rules of rational belief, and the justification of these rules, has been a—perhaps *the*—longtime interest of philosophers. (I investigated such rules recently in *The Nature of Rationality*.) One rule often proposed is to believe the simplest hypothesis compatible with the evidence. It has been a puzzle why the simplest hypothesis is most likely to be the true one. "Simplicity as Fall-Out" (Essay 8) shows how a procedure for fixing belief, without seeking simplicity, might lead one nevertheless to end up believing the simplest hypothesis compatible with the evidence. Thus it proposes an invisible-hand explanation of simplicity.

The reviews of Walzer and of Regan are the only two book reviews I have written. Perhaps this surprising paucity of book reviews is explained by my first attempt at one in the late 1960s. I agreed to review H. L. A. Hart's book of essays, *Punishment and Responsibility*, for the *Harvard Law Review*, and after reading this admirable work I set out with what seemed to me a reasonable plan: first, to develop the correct theory of punishment, and then, after doing so, to stand on that platform to state what was right and what was wrong with Hart's views. The review never got written. (The thinking done then, however, found its way into the discussions of punishment in *Anarchy, State, and Utopia* and *Philosophical Explanations*.)

My interest in the minimization of coercion led me to investigate "libertarian" views and arguments. "Who Would Choose Socialism?" (Essay 14) formulates one such argument, looking at the percentage of Israelis who choose life in a kibbutz. "Why Do Intellectuals Oppose Capitalism?" (Essay 15) considers why intellectuals are especially resistant to capitalism and to arguments in its favor, and it hypothesizes a new sociological law. The essay on Ayn Rand, "On the Randian Argument" (Essay 11), examines her moral arguments, which academic philosophers previously had neglected, but since it treated them with the standard critical tools of the trade, it brought me vituperation from some of Rand's followers. It is interesting to notice the themes of part I of *Anarchy, State, and Utopia* that are first adumbrated in this essay:

side-constraints and rights, whether the night-watchman state of classical liberal theory is redistributive, whether what matters is only people's *experiences*.

This aspect of early work holds true of other philosophers, as I discovered once while teaching a graduate seminar where the work of contemporary philosophers was looked at with the aim of understanding how they generated their ideas and theories. In addition to mature work, the seminar looked also at some early papers, where (I assumed) working methods of thought would be closer to the surface. What surprised me—in the early writing of Quine and Goodman, for example—was how many of these philosophers' later striking ideas were present already in these very early works, for those who had eyes to see.

The essay on Ayn Rand was written as a sidenote to my own independent thinking about topics in social philosophy and the moral foundations of capitalism. The essay on Quine, "Experience, Theory, and Language" (Essay 7), however, grew not from thinking independently about topics in the philosophy of language but from thinking about the ideas of Quine himself. Despite its particular points and its discussion of some new questions (such as why Duhem's thesis holds), I was struck, in rereading it soon after its writing, by the difference between thinking independently about a subject and thinking that is focused upon someone else's ideas. When you approach a topic through the route of someone's theories, that person's mode of structuring the issues limits how far you can stray and how much you can discover. You think within their "problematic."

Psychologists have investigated a phenomenon they call "anchoring and adjustment." For example, a subject is asked to estimate a person's height by estimating how far that height deviates from a fixed benchmark—from, say, five feet tall. If he thinks the person is five foot seven, he says "plus seven inches." The interesting fact is that the expressed estimates of a person's height will differ, depending upon the fixed benchmark. In theory, that particular benchmark should make no difference. If it is six feet instead of five feet, then the height of someone who is five foot seven can be said to deviate by "minus five inches" from that taller benchmark. Any given height can equally well be located by its distance from either benchmark. Nevertheless, the estimate of a given person's height by a group of judges who start with the five-foot benchmark will be less than the estimate by a group of judges who start with the benchmark of six feet. It is as though the benchmark exerts a gravitational attraction on the estimate, pulling that estimate toward itself. It is similar, I think, when you approach a topic through the thought of another. Even when your own conclusions do deviate, they are "gravitationally" pulled toward those of your source. I cannot say, however, that I have consciously refrained from writing extensively on historical figures in order to avoid being trapped within their mode of thinking. I simply have not felt the urge to do so—except in the case of Socrates.

I do not work within the framework of any one philosopher's thought but I do draw upon a kitbag of intellectual structures (in addition to the tools of mathematical logic which all contemporary philosophers use). Decision theory (and the associated material of utility theory, game theory, and social choice theory) is one structure I keep in mind, and use, and tinker with developing. There also is evolutionary theory, microeconomic theory, and inductive logic. I find such intellectual structures attractive and lovely, and I tend to scout other fields for already developed structures that might find philosophical application or might inspire the development of an analogous new philosophical structure.

Another structure I draw upon is presented in models of explanation, formulated by philosophers of science. Because of the presence of Carl Hempel at Princeton, the topic of explanation was central in the intellectual life of its philosophy graduate students. (And it was an admiration for Hempel's work, promulgated in classes at Columbia with Sidney Morgenbesser and with Ernest Nagel, that was the major factor leading me to do graduate study at Princeton.) Hempel's models of deductive-nomological and statistical explanation, their elaborations, difficulties, etc., was the *lingua franca* of study there. Everyone, no matter what his interests—unfortunately, there were no "hers" there then—felt obliged to keep current on that subject. It is no accident that my second book is entitled *Philosophical Explanations,* and that it focuses upon that notion, even though in ways different from Hempel. (*Anarchy, State, and Utopia* also was concerned with explanation: with fundamental explanation and with invisible-hand explanations of the state.)

Essays in the present volume also are concerned with explanation. "Invisible-Hand Explanations" (Essay 9) investigates that notion further, including new instances beyond those discussed and presented in *Anarchy, State, and Utopia.* "On Austrian Methodology" (Essay 5) sharpens and then examines the claim of "methodological individualism," made by economists in the Austrian tradition, that all of the institutional structures of a society can and must be explained in terms of the actions of individuals. It also contains a critical examination of their thesis that social science should be based upon an *a priori* theory of human choice. Thus the interests in theories of choice and in explanation come together.

A philosophical interest in explanation also is normative in part. We want to understand understanding, but we also seek explanations and therefore do not want to believe what could not be an adequate explanation. An account of what structure an explanation must possess thereby specifies our aim and guides us in our beliefs. "Experience, Theory, and Language" (Essay 7) pursues the theme of explanation in several directions: What explains why we cannot test isolated explanatory hypotheses but only large conjunctions of them? What is linguistics needed to explain?

The common intellectual interest in explanation was a fruitful stimulus for philosophical interchange at Princeton. At Columbia in the late 1950s, C. Wright Mills had just published *The Power Elite,* and no matter what their subject of study, students had to know what they thought about its thesis of a ruling elite in America. (In Essay 9, I speculate about an invisible-hand explanation of a ruling class.) Thomas Kuhn's *Structure of Scientific Revolutions* held this focal position at many universities in the 1970s, and perhaps sociobiology did for a while afterwards. I sometimes ask students whether there is any serious work of nonfiction which all (or most) of their friends have read or feel they have to read. For the past fifteen years or so, the answer has been *no.* I do not know why there now is no such common intellectual idea or book that students debate with interest and excitement—have films displaced books as students' common focus?—but it is unfortunate for students (and also for their teachers, who cannot take for granted the students' passion over any recent ideas).

Philosophers seek intellectual understanding but philosophy, and what propels it, is not solely intellectual. This volume closes with several philosophical fictions (selections 19–22) that bring forth the emotional content of philosophical problems and ideas. These different aspects of philosophy are explored more fully, and more personally, in *The Examined Life.*

Philosophy is endlessly interesting and ample; *anything* can be thought about philosophically. The philosopher's deepest urge, though, is to articulate and understand the ultimate basis and nature of things. What is the basis of our beliefs and our ethical principles, our standards of reasoning and of justification? What is the fundamental nature of mind, matter, identity over time, causality, knowledge, free will, truth, and consciousness? And how are all these to be put together into a meaningful whole? What could be more worth thinking about? And what could be more ennobling than thinking about these things? It is, Aristotle said, the most godlike of human activities.

Philosophy is not just thought. It is a way of life too, infused by thought and transformed by it. I wrote about these matters in *The Examined Life*. Ordinary speech takes "being philosophical" to mean being calm about setbacks, being dispassionate, balanced, and distant about tragedies and calamities. I certainly had no desire to cultivate that attitude when, excited by philosophy's intellectual methods and insights, I entered the subject. In late 1994, however, when stomach cancer led to serious surgery followed by months of chemotherapy and radiation treatments, along with dire statistics (never about the most relevant reference class, I thought, and in any case wasn't it an individual probabilistic propensity that I needed to know?), I found, even as I took vigorous steps to avoid what most probably would occur, that I had no complaints and felt no distress. My fifty-five-year lifespan already had been longer than that of most people in human history. (I maintain it was not a complaint when the first words I said to the surgeons upon coming up from anesthesia after seven hours were "I hope we don't have to do this again. I don't have the stomach for it.") And I had no urge to transform my life in whatever time remained. I harbored no hidden desire to run off to Tahiti, or to become an opera singer, or a racing car driver or a Dean. I wanted to continue loving my wife and my children, having fun with them, and doing exactly the things I had been: thinking, teaching, and writing. Only now I needed to do them better. And sooner. It has been simple to accept my own situation calmly; a danger to those I love, however, would prompt all-out warfare.

Nietzsche demanded that you should live a life you would be willing to repeat infinitely often. That seems a bit stringent. Philosophy, however, does constitute a way of life that is worth continuing to its end. As Socrates showed us at the beginning.

CHOICE
AND
UTILITY

1 | COERCION

⤙ ⤙ ⤙

This study of coercion is intended as a preliminary to a longer study of liberty, whose major concerns will be the reasons which justify making someone unfree to perform an action, and the reason why making someone unfree to perform an action needs justifying. Though coercion is intimately connected with liberty (some writers capsulize freedom as absence of coercion), it does not exhaust the range of nonliberty or unfreedom. In particular, being coerced into not doing an act is neither a necessary nor a sufficient condition for being unfree to do it. That it is not necessary is shown by the following examples:

(a) A person robs a bank and is caught and punished. If he knew for sure he would be caught and punished for robbing the bank, he would not do so, but he does not know this and so robs the bank. He was unfree to rob the bank, though he was not coerced into not doing so.

(b) I was not coerced into not murdering a member of the audience at Columbia when I read this paper, though I was unfree to do so.

(c) If I lure you into an escape-proof room in New York and leave you imprisoned there, I do not coerce you into not going to Chicago though I make you unfree to do so.

That being coerced into not doing act A is not a sufficient condition for being unfree to do A is shown by the following example: You threaten to get me fired from my job if I do A, and I refrain from doing A because of this threat and am coerced into not doing A. However, unbeknownst to me you are bluffing; you know you have absolutely no way to carry out this threat, and would not carry it out if you could. I was not unfree to do A (no doubt I thought I was), though I was coerced into not doing A. But though coercion does not exhaust the notion of unfreedom, it is obviously closely connected to it.[1]

This paper attempts to clarify the concept of coercion, and some related concepts. Though this is an interesting and intriguing task, I do not pursue it for its own sake. I am primarily interested in the uses to which such a clarification can be put; the questions one will be in a better position to answer given this clarification (*other* than questions like: what are the necessary and sufficient conditions for P's coercing Q into not doing A, or for P's threatening Q). I shall not be able here to get to these further questions, and shall be engaged largely in tool sharpening rather than in tool use.

One final preliminary remark, or warning, or apology. This study of coercion is an *exploratory* study, and is meant to raise questions and suggest problems. To many of these questions and problems I propose tentative answers and solutions, but some are left open. I would be happier if I could answer or solve them all. But in philosophy questions and problems often outlive specific proposed answers and solutions. Unfortunately, so it was in the course of writing this paper.

Conditions for Coercion

I shall begin by considering an account of coercion obtained from combining some things said on this subject in Hart and Honore's *Causation in the Law* with some remarks of Hart in his *The Concept of Law*.[2] According to this account, person P coerces person Q into not doing act A if and only if

(1) P threatens to do something if Q does A (and P knows he's making this threat).

(2)   This threat renders Q's doing A substantially less eligible as a course of conduct than not doing A.

(3) P makes this threat in order to get Q not to do A, intending that Q realize he's been threatened by P.

(4) Q does not do A.

(5) P's words or deeds are part of Q's reasons for not doing A.[3]

Conditions 1–5 do not appear to be sufficient for coercion. For example, P threatens Q, saying that if Q performs a particular action, a rock will fall and kill him. P thinks Q knows of his (P's) infamous procedure of murdering people, but Q thinks that P is telling him about some strange natural law that holds independently of human action, namely whenever someone performs this action, he gets killed by a falling rock. That is, Q understands what P says, not as a *threat* but as a *warning*. If Q refrains from performing the action, P has not coerced him into not doing it, even though the five conditions are satisfied. This suggests that we add as a further condition:

(6) Q knows that P has threatened to do the something mentioned in 1, if he, Q, does A.[4]

It is not clear that the conditions thus far listed are sufficient. You threaten to do something if I do A, thinking that I don't want this something done. But in fact, I don't mind it or even slightly want it. However, I realize that you must feel very strongly about my doing A, since you've threatened me, and that you will be very upset if I do A (*not* that you will *choose* to be upset to punish me for doing A). Since I don't want you to be upset, I refrain from doing A. You did not coerce me into not doing A, though it seems that the conditions listed are satisfied; in particular it seems that the relevant conditions 5 and 2 are satisfied. Or, if they can be so interpreted so that they're not satisfied, it would be well to make this interpretation explicit, replacing 5, 1, and 2 by:

(5′)   Part of Q's reasons for not doing A is to avoid (or lessen the likelihood of) the consequence[5] which P has threatened to bring about or have brought about.[6]

(1′) P threatens to bring about or have brought about some consequence if Q does A (and knows he's threatening to do this).

(2′) A with this threatened consequence is rendered substantially less eligible as a course of conduct for Q than A was without the threatened consequence.

Must P make the threat *in order* to get Q not to do A? Must condition 3 be satisfied? In normal situations it will be satisfied; e.g., a highwayman says "If you don't give me your money, I'll kill you," making this threat in order to get me to give him my money. But suppose that we are conducting an experiment for the Social Science Research Council, to study people's reactions in the highwayman situation. We don't care how he reacts to our threat (if he gives over the money we must turn it over to the SSRC; if he resists we are empowered to kill him and, let us suppose, have no moral scruples about doing so). We do not say "your money or your life" in order to get him to give us his money, but in order to gather data. We might even suppose that I think him very brave and have bet with you that he'll resist and be killed. After making the bet, I want him *not* to hand over the money, and I don't make the threat in order to get him to hand it over. In the grip of fear and trembling, he hands over the money. Surely we coerced him into doing so. This suggests replacing 3 by a more complicated condition:

> (Part of) P's reason for deciding to bring about the consequence or have it brought about, if Q does A, is that P believes this consequence worsens Q's alternative of doing A (i.e., that P believes that this consequence worsens Q's alternative of doing A, or that Q would believe it does).[7]

The SSRC example satisfies this condition, since (part of) the researchers' reason for deciding to kill Q if he doesn't turn over the money is that they believe this consequence worsens Q's alternative of not giving them the money.

But the condition formulated is not broad enough, for we want to cover cases where P has not decided to bring about the consequence if Q does A, but is bluffing instead, or neither intends nor intends not to bring it about if Q does A. This suggests disjoining another condition with the one above:

> If P has not decided to bring about the consequence, or have it brought about, if Q does A, then (part of) P's reason for saying he will bring about the consequence, or have it brought about, if Q does A is that (P believes) Q will believe this consequence worsens Q's alternative of doing A.[8]

One is tempted to say that this disjunctive condition is superfluous, because it is built into the notion of threatening, and hence follows from condition 1'. That is, one is tempted to say that if this condition is not satisfied, if *P*'s reasons or motives are not as described, then *P* has not *threatened Q*. I shall have more to say about this later.

The conditions listed still do not appear to be sufficient. Consider cases where *Q* wants to do *A* in order to bring about *x*, and *P* says that if *Q* does *A*, he (*P*) will do something which just prevents *A* from bringing about *x*. This makes *A* substantially less eligible as an alternative for *Q* (*Q* now, we may suppose, has no reason to do *A*), and the other conditions may well be satisfied. Yet, at least some cases of this sort ("If you say another word, I shall turn off my hearing aid") are not cases of coercion.[9]

Cases of this sort suggest the following condition:

(7)   *Q* believes that, and *P* believes that *Q* believes that, *P*'s threatened consequence[10] would leave *Q* worse off, having done *A*, than if *Q* didn't do *A* and *P* didn't bring about the consequence.[11]

In the application of this condition, in deciding how well or poorly off *Q* is having done *A* and having had his purpose *x* thwarted, one must ignore *Q*'s wasted effort, humiliation at having failed to bring about *x*, and (in some cases) *Q*'s forgone opportunities. Similarly in deciding how well or poorly off *Q* would be not doing *A* and not having *P* bring about the consequence, one must ignore any regret *Q* might feel at not doing *A*.[12]

According to our account of "*P* coerces *Q* into doing *A*," the following cases are *not* cases in which *P* coerces *Q* into doing *A*.

(1)   *Q* mishears *P* as having said "Your money or your life" and hands over his money, but *P* said something else, or said this as a question about something he thought *Q* said, etc.

(2)   *P* doesn't speak English, but has picked up the sentence "Your money or your life" from a movie, though he does not know what it means. To be friendly, *P* utters this one sentence to *Q* who is sitting next to him in a bar (perhaps while showing *Q* his unusual knife for *Q* to admire). *Q* hands over his money.

(3)   *Q* walks into a room, and unbeknownst to him there is a tape recorder in the next room playing part of the soundtrack of a movie. *Q* hears "Put all of your money on the table and then leave, or I'll kill you." *Q* puts his money on the table, and leaves.

I suggest that in these cases, though *Q* feels coerced and thinks he is coerced, *P* does not coerce *Q* into giving over the money. (In the third case there is no plausible person *P* to consider.) Those who refuse to accept this might hold the view that though P does not coerce Q into giving over the money, nonetheless Q is coerced into giving over the money. Such a person would reject the view that "Q is coerced into doing A" is equivalent to "there is a P who coerces Q into doing A," and perhaps suggest that Q is coerced into doing A if and only if

(1)   There is a P who coerces Q into doing A, or

(2) Q is justified in believing that there is a P who has threatened to bring about a consequence which significantly worsens his alternative of not doing A (and that P has the appropriate reasons and intentions), and (part of) Q's reasons for doing A is to avoid or lessen the likelihood of this consequence he believes was threatened.

I should mention that a threat need not be verbally expressed; it may be perfectly clear from actions performed what the threat is, or at least that something undesirable will occur if one doesn't perform some appropriate action. For example, members of a street gang capture a member of a rival gang and ask him where that gang's weapons are hidden. He refuses to tell, and they beat him up. They ask again, he refuses again, they beat him again. And so on until he tells. He was coerced into telling. His captors didn't have to *say,* "if you don't tell us we will continue to beat you up or perhaps eventually do something worse." This is perfectly clear to all involved in the situation. In many situations the infliction of violence is well understood by all parties to be a threat of further infliction of violence if there is noncompliance. Nothing need be *said.*[13] It may be for reasons such as this that some writers (e.g., Bay) say that all infliction of violence constitutes coercion. But this is, I think, a mistake. If a drunken group comes upon a stranger and beats him up or even kills him, this need not be coercion. For there need have been no implicit threat of further violence if the person didn't comply with their wishes, and it would indeed be difficult for this to be the case if they just come upon him and kill him.[14]

There is another type of situation very similar to the one we have thus far been concerned with, for which similar conditions can be offered. I have in mind cases where no one threatens to inflict some damage on Q if he does A, but someone sets things up so that damage is automatically inflicted if Q does A. It's not that if you do A, I will bring about a consequence which you consider to be bad, but rather that I now do something (the doing of which is not conditional upon your doing A)

which is such that if you do A after I have done this thing, there will be a consequence which you consider to be bad.[15] Though in such situations a person is deterred from doing something, it is not obvious to me that he is coerced into not doing it. If it is coercion then the account of coercion would say that P coerces Q into not doing A if and only if either of the two sets of conditions is satisfied.[16]

I suggest that it is as a case of this sort of situation, rather than the one discussed earlier, that we are to understand the following: some adult's mother says to him, "If you do A I'll have a heart attack, or the probability = p that I'll have a heart attack." I have in mind a case where the mother does not *choose* to have a heart attack if her son does A or to do something which will bring on or raise the probability of a heart attack. She just knows she will (or that the probability = p). It seems to me that the mother's statement is not plausibly construed as a threat to (choose to) do something or bring about a consequence if her son does A. To use a distinction which will be discussed later, what the mother issues is not a threat but rather a nonthreatening warning. If we look just at the first sort of situation, we will conclude that the mother did not coerce the son into not doing A. But this example can plausibly be viewed as a case of the second sort of situation, in which before Q does A, P does something, making this known to Q, which worsens Q's alternative of doing A. And if this counts as coercion, then the mother may coerce the son. We should look, in this case, at the mother's act, prior to her son's doing A, of telling him that she will or probably will have a heart attack if he does A. We may suppose that without her announcement the consequence of her son's doing A is some probability of her having a heart attack and some probability of his feeling guilty (a function of the probability of his realizing why she died and the probability that he will feel guilty anyway because he did something she didn't like and then she died) and some probability of A's having quite nice consequences. And we may suppose that after the mother's announcement the consequences of his doing A are changed significantly. For now there is some probability of her dying and his feeling *enormously* guilty (because he ignored her warning), and even if she won't die because of his doing A, if he does A he will worry over this possibility, feel guilty about doing something he knows upsets her, etc. Her act of making her announcement before he did A worsened the consequence of his doing A. If we suppose, furthermore, that one of her reasons for making the announcement was to worsen the consequences, and that one of his reasons for not doing A was *this* worsening of consequences, then we have a situation of the second sort. And if this sort of situation counts as coercion, the son was coerced into not doing A.[17]

Noncentral Cases of Coercion

I have thus far concentrated upon the central part or core of the notion of coercion, and, in order to avoid too many complications all at once, have spoken of necessary and sufficient conditions for coercion (period). However, I believe that there are further cases of coercion which do not themselves satisfy the conditions thus far discussed, but which are cases of coercion by virtue of standing in certain specifiable relations to central cases of coercion.[18] It is a task of some intricacy to get these relations just right. The statements which follow are meant to *indicate* areas in which principles must be formulated. It is *not* claimed that these statements are the formulations which one would eventually arrive at, nor is it claimed that the statements which follow exhaust the areas for which principles must be formulated. Let me repeat: the statements below are meant to indicate areas for which principles must be formulated and are *not* put forward as the correct formulation of principles in these areas. I would expect that, after such principles are adequately formulated, a recursive definition of "P coerces Q into doing A" would be offered, which would begin with the conditions for the central cases discussed earlier.

(1)   If P coerces Q into doing A, and "A" contains as a proper part the referring expression "r_1," and "B" is obtainable by substituting the referring expressions "r_2" for "r_1" in "A," and "r_2" and "r_1" have the same reference, and "r_1" occurs transparently in "Q does A," then P coerces Q into doing B.[19]

(2)   If P coerces Q into doing A, and it is a necessary truth that if anyone does A he does B, and it is not a necessary truth that if anyone does anything he does B, then P coerces Q into doing B.

(3)   If P coerces Q into doing A, and it is a nomological truth that if anyone does A he does B, and it is not a nomological truth that if anyone does anything he does B, then P coerces Q into doing B.

(4)   If P coerces Q into doing A, and if the only way anyone can do A is by doing either B_1 or B_2 or, . . . , or B_n, then P coerces Q into doing B_1 or B_2 or, . . . , B_n.[20]

(5)   If P coerces Q into doing A, and the only way in which Q can do A is by doing either B_1 or B_2 or, . . . , or B_n, then P coerces Q into doing B_1 or B_2 or, . . . , or B_n.[21]

(6)   If Q can do A only by doing B_1 or B_2 or, . . . , or B_n, and Q sets out to do A (intending to do it) because of P's threat of a harmful consequence if Q doesn't do A, and Q does one of the B_1 in order to do A, then Q is coerced into doing B_1 or B_2 or, . . . , or B_n, even if Q does not do A (whether because he's prevented from doing A or because he's changed his mind about doing it).

(7)   If P coerces Q into doing B_1 or B_2 or, . . . , or B_n, and B_1 is the best of the B_1's, the only one of the B_1's it would be reasonable to do, etc., and Q does B_1 for this reason, then P coerces Q into doing B_1.

(8)   If P coerces Q into doing A, and x is a consequence of Q's A, and ——, then P coerces Q into bringing about x. (What further conditions are needed in the blank?)[22]

In order to avoid concluding that Q was coerced into doing B when Q does A (partly) because of the threat, and does B (which stands in one of the stated relations to A) for some *other* reason, we must add to the antecedent of each of these statements the qualification that (part of) the reason Q does B (or, B_1, or B_2, or . . . , or B_n) is to avoid or lessen the likelihood of P's threatened consequence (if Q does A).

Threats and Offers

The notion of a threat has played a central role in what has been said thus far. In this section we shall consider the differences between threats and offers, and in the next section we shall consider the differences between threats and warnings.

If P offers Q substantially more money than Q is earning at his current job to come to work for P, and Q accepts because he wants to increase his income, has P coerced Q into working for him? Some writers (Hale, Bay) would say that P has; the threat being "come to work for me or I won't give you the money."[23] On this view, every employer coerces his employees, every employee his employer ("give me the money or I won't work for you"), every seller of an object coerces his customers ("give me the money or I won't give you the object"), and every customer the person from whom he buys. It seems clear that normally these aren't cases of coercion. Offers of inducements, incentives, rewards, bribes, consideration, remuneration, recompense, payment do not normally constitute threats, and the person who accepts them is not normally coerced.

As a first formulation, let us say that whether someone makes a threat against Q's doing an action or an offer to Q to do the action depends on how the consequence he says he will bring about changes the consequences of Q's action from what they would have been in the normal or natural or expected course of events. If it makes the consequences of Q's action worse than they would have been in the normal and expected course of events, it is a threat; if it makes the consequences better, it is an offer.[24] The term *expected* is meant to shift between or straddle *predicted* and *morally required*.[25] This handles pretty well the clear cases of threats and offers. Let us see how it fares with more difficult examples.

(a) P is Q's usual supplier of drugs, and today when he comes to Q he says that he will not sell them to Q, as he normally does, for $20, but rather will give them to Q if and only if Q beats up a certain person.

(b) P is a stranger who has been observing Q, and knows that Q is a drug addict. Both know that Q's usual supplier of drugs was arrested this morning and that P had nothing to do with his arrest. P approaches Q and says that he will give Q drugs if and only if Q beats up a certain person.

In the first case, where P is Q's usual supplier of drugs, P is *threatening* not to give Q the drugs. The normal course of events is one in which P supplies Q with drugs for money. P is threatening to *withhold* the supply, to *deprive* Q of his drugs, if Q does not beat up the person. In the second case, where P is a stranger to Q, P is not *threatening* not to supply Q with drugs; in the normal course of events P does not do so, nor is P expected to do so. If P does not give Q the drugs he is not *withholding* drugs from Q nor is he *depriving* Q of drugs. P is *offering* Q drugs as an inducement to beat up the person. Thus in the second case, P does not *coerce* Q into beating up the person, since P does not threaten Q. (But the fact that P did not coerce Q into beating up the person does not mean that it would not be true for Q to say, in some legitimate sense of the phrase: "I had no choice.")

There is a further point to be considered about the first case in which
P is Q's usual supplier of drugs. In addition to threatening to withhold
the drugs if Q doesn't beat up a certain person, hasn't P made Q an
offer? Since in the normal and expected course of events Q does not get
drugs for beating up the person, isn't this a case in which P then offers
Q drugs as an incentive to beat up the person? And if P *has* made this
offer, why do we view the overall situation as one in which P threatens
Q, rather than as one in which P makes Q an offer? We have here
a situation in which P takes a consequence viewed as desirable by Q
(receiving drugs) off one action (paying \$20) and puts it onto another
action (beating up the person). Since Q prefers and P believes that Q
prefers paying the money and receiving the drugs to beating up the
person and receiving the drugs, and since Q would rather not beat up
the person, P's statement is a threat to withhold the drugs if Q doesn't
beat up the person, and this threat predominates over any subsidiary
offer P makes for Q to beat up the person, making the whole situation
a threat situation.

But instead of subtracting a desirable consequence from one of Q's
actions and tagging the *same* consequence onto another of Q's actions,
P may subtract a desirable consequence C from one of Q's actions
A_1 and add a *more* desirable consequence C' onto another action A_2
available to Q. For example, the dope peddler might say to Q, "I will
not give you drugs if you just pay me money, but I will give you a
better grade of drugs, without monetary payment, if you beat up this
person." It seems plausible to think that as one increases the desirability
of C' to Q, at some point the situation changes from one predominantly
involving a threat to deprive Q of C if he does A_1 (doesn't do A_2) to
one which predominantly involves an offer to Q of C' if he does A_2.
And it seems plausible to claim that this turning point from threat to
offer, as one increases the value of C' for Q, comes at the point where Q
begins preferring A_2 and C' to A_1 and C (stops preferring the latter to
the former?).[26]

The following principle embodies this claim, and also covers the case
where it is the same consequence which is switched from one action to
another, as in the earlier example. It also is meant to apply to obvious
mixtures of threats and offers, e.g., "If you go to the movies I'll give you
\$10,000. If you don't go, I'll kill you."

> If P intentionally changes the consequences of two actions A_1 and
> A_2 available to Q so as to lessen the desirability of the consequences

of A_1, and so as to increase the desirability of the consequences of A_2, and part of P's reason for acting as he does is to so lessen and increase the desirabilities of the respective consequences, then

(a)   This resultant change predominantly involves a threat to Q if he does A_1 if Q prefers doing the old A_1 (without the worsened consequences) to doing the new A_2 (with the improved consequences).

(b)   This resultant change predominantly involves an offer to Q to do A_2 if Q prefers doing the new A_2 (with the improved consequences) to the old A_1 (without the worsened consequences).

This principle ties in nicely with something we shall say later. For when the change predominantly involves a threat, Q would normally not be willing to have this change made (since he'd rather do the old A_1 than either of the two alternatives after the change), whereas when the change predominantly involves an offer, Q would normally be willing to have the change made (since he'd rather do the new A_2 than the old A_1, and if he prefers doing one of the old alternatives (A_1) to doing the new A_2, he can still do it). I shall claim later that this willingness or unwillingness to make the change marks an important difference between offers and threats.[27]

If a statement's being a threat or an offer depends upon how the carrying out of the statement affects the normal or expected course of events, one would expect that there will be situations where it is unclear whether a person is making a threat or an offer because it is unclear what the normal and expected course of events is. And one would expect that people will disagree about whether something is a threat or an offer because they disagree about what the normal and expected course of events is, which is to be used as a baseline in assessing whether something is a threat or an offer. This is indeed the case.

Consider the following example. Q is in the water far from shore, nearing the end of his energy, and P comes close by in his boat. Both know there is no other hope of Q's rescue around, and P knows that Q is the soul of honesty and that if Q makes a promise he will keep it. P says to Q "I will take you in my boat and bring you to shore if and only if you first promise to pay me $10,000 within three days of reaching shore with my aid." Is P offering to take Q to shore if he makes the promise, or is he threatening to let Q drown if Q doesn't make the promise? If one views the normal or expected course of events as one in which Q drowns without P's intervention, then in saying that he will save Q if and only if Q makes the promise, P is *offering* to save Q. If one views the normal or expected course of events as one in which a person in a boat who comes by a drowning person, in a situation such as this, saves him, then in saying that he will save Q if and only if Q makes the promise, P is *threatening* not to save Q. Whether P's saying that he will save Q if and only if Q makes the promise is an *offer* to save Q or a *threat* not to save Q depends upon what the normal or expected course of events is.

Since it is likely to be clear to the reader which course of events he wants to pick out as normal and expected as the background against which to assess whether P's statement is an offer or a threat (namely, the one that makes it a threat) we should sharpen the example. Suppose in addition to the foregoing that P knows that Q has greatly wronged P (or others), but that Q cannot be legally punished for this (no law covered the wrong, a legal technicality, the statute of limitations has run out, or some such thing). Or P knows that Q will go on to do monstrous deeds if rescued. In some such situations it will be unclear what P is morally expected to do, and hence unclear whether his statement is a threat or an offer. For other such situations it will be clear that P is morally expected to let Q drown, and hence his statement will be an offer.[28]

Thus far we have considered threats as introducing certain deviations from the normal and expected course of events. The question arises as to whether the normal or expected course of events itself can be coercive. Suppose that usually a slave owner beats his slave each morning, for no reason connected with the slave's behavior. Today he says to his slave, "Tomorrow I will not beat you if and only if you now do A." One is tempted to view this as a threat, and one is also tempted to view this as an offer. I attribute these conflicting temptations to the divergence between the normal course of events, in which the slave is beaten each morning, and the (morally) expected course of events, in which he is not. And I suggest that we have here a situation of a threat, and that here the morally expected course of events takes precedence over the normal course of events in assessing whether we have a threat or an offer.[29]

One might think that in deciding whether something is a threat or an offer, the (morally) expected course of events always takes precedence over the normal or usual course of events, where these diverge. It is not obvious that this is so. I have in mind particularly the example mentioned earlier, where your normal supplier of dope says that he will continue to supply you if and only if you beat up a certain person. Here, let us suppose, the morally expected course of events is that he doesn't supply you with drugs, but the course of events which forms the background for deciding whether he has threatened you or made you an offer is the normal though not morally expected course of events (in which he supplies you with drugs for money); it is against this background that we can obtain the consequence that he's threatened you.

Thus, in both the slave and the addict examples the normal and morally expected courses of events diverge. Why do we pick one of these in one case, and the other in the other, as the background against which to assess whether we have a threat or an offer? The relevant difference between these cases seems to be that the slave himself would prefer the morally expected to the normal course of events whereas the addict prefers the normal to the morally expected course of events.[30] It may be that when the normal and morally expected courses of events diverge, the one of these which is to be used in deciding whether a conditional announcement of an action constitutes a threat or an offer is the course of events that the recipient of the action prefers.[31]

I have raised the question of whether the normal and expected course of events itself can be coercive, and was led to consider cases where the normal and (morally) expected courses of events diverged. I now would like to consider this question again, for cases where they do not diverge. Can P, by saying that he will bring about a consequence if Q does A (where this consequence is such that if Q does A, P would bring it about in the normal *and* (morally) expected course of events), coerce Q into not doing A? Suppose that in the normal *and* morally expected course of events, people get punished for theft. Aren't some people coerced into not stealing by the legal apparatus?

One might say that if a *type* of action or consequence is itself part of the normal and expected course of events if Q does A, one should use the normal and expected course of events minus this type of action or consequence as a background against which to assess whether a statement is a threat. If the consequences of an action would be worse, if the statement is carried out, than they would be in this *new* course of events (i.e., the normal and expected course of events without the type of action or consequence) then the statement is a threat. But who knows what the world would be like if there was no punishment for crimes? It might well be that things would be so bad that the institution of punishing crimes would improve the consequences of almost all actions, and hence count, according to this suggestion, as making offers to people.

An alternative procedure seems more reasonable; namely, to consider the normal and expected course of events, if Q does A, without P's particular act or without the particular consequence P will bring about, and against this background assess whether P's statement that if Q does A he will do a particular act or bring about a particular consequence constitutes a threat (i.e., whether P's statement, if carried out, makes Q's A worse than it would be in *this* new course of events).

There remain some problems about knowing what the course of events would be without this act, but these seem manageable. On this view, even though in the normal and expected course of events Q gets punished for theft, the statement that he will be punished for theft counts as a threat since the act of punishment, if Q steals, unfavorably affects the consequences of one act of Q's (stealing) against the background of the normal and expected course of events minus *this* act of punishment.[32]

According to the account offered earlier of (the first sort of) coercion, threats are necessary for coercion. One might extend the account to include some offers, if there were clear situations in which Q is coerced into doing A even though Q does A because P offered to do B if Q did A. Despite my inclination to say that one is never coerced when one does something because of an offer (unless in the case discussed earlier, the slave owner is making an offer to his slave), there is one sort of case, where the offer is closely tied to coercion or attempted coercion, which I find it difficult to decide about. Suppose that P knows that Q has committed a murder which the police are investigating, and knows of evidence sufficient to convict Q of this murder. P says to Q, "If you give me $10,000 I will not turn over the information I have to the police." Let us assume that were P unable to contact Q and present his proposal he would turn the information over to the police. Furthermore, in this situation P is (morally) expected to turn the information over to the police. So in the normal and expected course of events, P turns the information over to the police (whether or not Q gives him $10,000). It would seem, therefore, that P is *offering* not to turn the information over to the police, rather than *threatening* to turn it over. Yet one is strongly tempted to say, when Q pays P \$10,000 because he accepts the offer, that Q was coerced by P into paying the \$10,000.[33]

If the following principle were correct, then this would be a case of coercion:

> If P offers to refrain from aiding the threatener of a coercive consequence[34] for Q's A from bringing about this consequence, in exchange for Q's doing B, and if the credible threat of this consequence[35] if Q didn't perform B would coerce Q into doing B, then when Q does B because of the offer, Q was coerced into doing B.

A case similar to the previous one is one in which the police arrest Q for a crime, believing that he has committed it and having sufficient evidence to convict him of it. In the course of questioning Q, they come to believe that Q knows who has committed some other crime, and they say that Q will not be prosecuted if and only if he tells them who has committed this other crime. Since if the police did not think Q knew who committed the other crime they would have prosecuted, and since they are morally expected to have him prosecuted, the police have *offered* not to have Q prosecuted rather than *threatened* to have him prosecuted. If Q names the person who committed the other crime, in order to escape being prosecuted, some are strongly tempted to say that he was coerced into giving the information. The above principle would yield this consequence. Though I do not deny that one may say, in some legitimate sense of these expressions, "Q was forced to do what he did," "Q had no choice," I am unable to decide whether, in the above cases, Q was coerced into doing so, and I leave this an open question.

The two previous cases are cases where P is morally expected or required to do the act, and would normally do so (turn the murderer over to the police, have Q prosecuted). It is worth mentioning cases where P has a legal and moral right to do the act, but would not decide to do so (even if Q didn't do A) were he not trying to get Q to do A. For example, P has a right to build on his land blocking Q's view, or foreclose Q's mortgage, or bring legal action against Q (on a valid and enforceable claim) but would not decide to do so (it's not worth the trouble, P has no pressing need for funds, etc.) were it not for his wanting Q to do A. P tells Q that unless he does A, he (P) will build on his land, foreclose Q's mortgage, bring legal action against Q, etc. Since P's action is not part of the morally expected course of events (not that P is morally expected *not* to do it) and since in the normal course of events P wouldn't do it, the account yields the result that one would wish: In these cases P is threatening to perform his actions rather than offering not to do so.

Threats and Warnings

In the section on Conditions for Coercion, because of the example of the SSRC people saying "your money or your life," we rejected the condition that P says or does what he does *in order to* get Q not to perform some particular action A. We substituted instead a condition requiring that (part of) P's reason for deciding to bring about the consequence if Q does A (or, if he hasn't decided, saying that he has) is that (P believes that) this worsens Q's alternative of doing A (or that Q would believe it does). And we mentioned the view that this is part of the notion of making a threat. This view illuminates the fact that some statements about one's future actions if Q does A, are not threats even though the acts you've stated you would do if Q does A worsen Q's alternative of doing A.

Such statements about one's future actions I shall call nonthreatening warnings (for short, just "warnings"). The distinction between threats and nonthreatening warnings is crucial to some questions that arise in the law.[36] For example, an election is about to be held in a factory to determine whether the employees will be represented by a labor union. The owner of the factory announces to his employees that if the union wins the election, he will close his factory and go out of business. Has he *threatened* the employees with the loss of their jobs if the union wins, or merely *warned* them what will happen if the union wins? If a majority of the employees would have voted for the union if not for the announcement, and the union lost because of the announcement, were the employees *coerced* by their employer into rejecting the union?

We may view this situation as a game, represented by the following matrix:

	EMPLOYEES	
	I. Union wins	II. Union loses
A. Stays in business	(b)	(a)
B. Goes out of business	(c)	(d)

EMPLOYER

The employees make the first move (pick a column) and the employer makes the second (picks a row) knowing what move the employees have first made. That is, first the employees choose to be represented by the union or not, and then the employer, knowing what choice his employees have made, decides to stay in business or go out of business. I shall assume that each of the members of some particular majority of the employees preferentially ranks the outcomes as follows:

> (b)
> (a)
> (c)
> (d)

and shall call this the preference ordering of the employees.[37] There seem to me to be at least four cases worth considering,[38] corresponding to four different preference rankings of these alternatives by the employer. These are:

(1)	(2)	(3)	(4)
(a)	(a)	(a)	(c)–(a)
(b)	(c)–(b)	(c)	(b)
(c)	(d)	(b)	
(d)			

I assume, for each case, that the employer knows the preference ranking of the employees.

Case 1: The employer, if he were sure that the union would win the election, would not make his announcement, since he prefers continuing in business though the factory is unionized, to going out of business. That is, he prefers (b) to (c). However, he commits himself to going out of business if the factory is unionized, and announces this decision (that is, rules out (b)), in the hope that this will lead his employees to reject the union. By ruling out (b) beforehand he leaves his employees (a), (c), and (d) among which to choose, and since *of these* (a) is highest in the preference ranking of the employees, they will presumably then act so as to realize (a), and this is the alternative which the *employer* ranks most highly. The employer is committing himself beforehand, for strategic reasons, to do something (*B*) in a situation (*I*) such that had he not committed himself to this he would be better off doing something else (*A*) in that situation when and if it arose. It seems clear that in this case, when the employer announces that he will go out of business if the union wins the election he is *threatening* his employees.[39] For in the normal course of events, he does not go out of business, given his preferences, if the employees vote for the union. Hence he's announcing that he will depart from the normal course of events in a way to the detriment of his employees, if they elect the union.[40] And also (part of) his reason for deciding to go out of business if the union wins is that he believes that this worsens his employees' alternative of electing the union (and he thereby hopes to influence them to reject the union). Hence his announcement is a threat, and he has threatened to go out of business if the union wins the election.

Case 2: The employer announces that he will go out of business if the union wins the election, thus ruling out (b), and leaving the employees a choice between (a) and (c). He makes this announcement hoping that because of it, his employees will reject the union. Note that in this case, unlike the first one, there is not something the employer would *rather* do than go out of business if the union wins the election. (For he is indifferent between (c) and (b), whereas in the first case, the employer preferred (b) to (c).) Though there aren't exactly the same strategic considerations as in the first case, still strategic considerations are involved. And this employer, too, has threatened his employees. For in the normal or expected course of events he wouldn't have made his announcement, and would, being indifferent between (c) and (b), decide whether or not to stay in business if and when the union won the election. We may suppose that before he decides there is some nonzero probability of his deciding to close the factory, and some nonzero probability of his staying in business. This being what one would expect in the normal course of events, his announcement and commitment to going out of business, for sure, if the union wins the election changes the normal or expected course of events in the typical manner of a threat. For his being almost certain to go out of business is worse, from his employees' viewpoint, than there being some probability of his going out of business and some probability of his remaining in business. Since part of his reason for deciding to go out of business if the union wins is that (he believes) this worsens his employees' alternative of electing the union, this constitutes a threat.

But if in this case the employer does not announce that he will close if the union wins (which would be a threat), but instead announces truthfully that he is indifferent between closing and staying in business if the union wins and will decide what to do afterwards (and if his employees voting for the union in the face of this announcement would not anger him and yield a larger probability of his closing than if the announcement hadn't been made), then the case may be significantly different. This issue is also raised by case 3, and is treated in the discussion of it.

Case 4: The employer tells his employees what his preferences are, and that he will go out of business if the union wins. We may suppose that he doesn't make his decision or tell them this in order to get them to reject the union, since he doesn't care whether they reject it or not. For even if they elect it, he can go out of business, and there is nothing he *prefers* to that. No strategic considerations are involved. He makes his announcement solely to inform his employees of what will be the consequences of their action. It was no part of his reason for deciding to go out of business if the union won, that this worsened his employees' alternative of electing the union, and no part of his reason for making the announcement was to get his employees to reject the union. It seems clear that this is not a case of coercion, and that the employer has not made a threat (even though his employees might sorrowfully tell the union representative that they had no choice) but has rather issued a nonthreatening warning.

Case 3: I have left case 3 for last because it is the most difficult. In this case, the employer announces what his preference ranking is and says that he'll go out of business if the union wins the election. And indeed, unlike the employers in cases 1 and 2, but like the employer in case 4, he prefers going out of business if the union wins the election to staying in business with the union representing his employees. In the normal course of events, he would go out of business if the union wins, whether or not he has previously announced that he would do so. However, unlike the employer in case 4 but like the employers in cases 1 and 2, he prefers staying in business without the union to going out of business if the union wins the election, and makes his announcement in order to get his employees to reject the union. Has he threatened his employees, or just warned them? I am inclined to say that he has warned them rather than threatened them. (Note that a teacher can *warn* a student that he will fail unless his work improves, even if the teacher does so in order to get the student to work harder.) For he does not decide to close if the union wins in order to worsen the alternative of the union winning, and in making the announcement he does not worsen this alternative but rather makes known what its consequences will be. Furthermore, there seems to be no presumption against this employer's telling his employees that he will close if the union wins, whereas there is (normally) a presumption against making threats.[41]

These cases raise an interesting point relevant to the wider task of deciding what actions people should be free to do, and what actions they should be unfree to do. It may be that, even if one picks out a particular pattern of freedom and unfreedom as optimal, there is no acceptable institutional arrangement available to one which realizes this pattern. One may lack the institutional means to realize exactly the optimal pattern of freedom and unfreedom, or certain ways of realizing this pattern, and publicly distinguishing among persons, may be unacceptable to the society at large. So it may be that, given the available institutional means, the feasible patterns of freedom and unfreedom among which one must choose are suboptimal and nondominated patterns of the following forms:

(a)   Where some persons are unfree to do acts they should (according to the optimal pattern) be free to do.

(b)   Where some people are free to do acts they should be unfree to do.

(c)   Where some people are free to do acts they should be unfree to do, and some people are unfree to do acts they should be free to do.

A full theory of freedom would, as well as specifying the optimal pattern of freedom and unfreedom, concern itself with choices among such suboptimal patterns.

It may be that we have an example of such a choice here. For one may wish to make the case 1 and 2 employers unfree to make their announcements (threats) while leaving the case 3 and 4 employers free to make their announcements (warnings). However, it may be difficult to devise an institutional arrangement which accomplishes this, for it may be difficult to distinguish case 1 and 2 employers from case 3 and 4 employers. (Note that if one attempts to distinguish them, there will be reason for case 1 and 2 employers to lie when asked about their preferences.) The actual institutional choice one faces may be to forbid all such announcements, to allow all such announcements, or to use some condition almost coextensive with the suitable preferences and forbid and allow announcements on the basis of whether this condition is satisfied, regretfully admitting that one cannot handle *all* the cases in the way one would wish.[42]

Problems of choice among suboptimal patterns arise also and obviously for paternalistic legislation; legislation which, in order to prevent him from coming to harm, or to lessen the chance of this, or to enable him to realize some good, makes someone unfree to perform a particular act.[43] The feasible patterns will often require either making some persons, who do not need the paternalistic protection and might be better off without it, unfree to perform some acts, or leaving some people free to do acts they should be unfree to do (for their own protection). (I spare the reader examples.) One will often have to choose among such patterns because there is no realizable and acceptable institutional arrangement which divides people up just right (according to the optimal pattern) with respect to particular acts. An important point emerges from this discussion; namely, that the statement that a particular piece of legislation makes some persons unfree to perform some acts they should not be unfree to perform (according to the optimal pattern of freedom and unfreedom), even if true, is not by itself a *conclusive* objection to the legislation. For it may be that no feasible and acceptable pattern of freedom and unfreedom is more optimal (or all other realizable patterns are less optimal) than the one yielded by this legislation.

I might mention the statement, which we might call a tip, which stands to an offer as a nonthreatening warning stands to a threat; that is, P's statement which points out that P will bring about some consequence if Q does A which improves Q's alternative of doing A, though P's believing that it improves or that Q would believe it improves Q's doing A is not part of P's reason for deciding to bring about the consequence if Q does A.

Building into the notion of P's making Q an offer to do A the requirement that (part of) P's reason for bringing about the consequence if Q does A is to improve Q's alternative of doing A, illuminates the following example: P comes up to Q and says, "your money or your life." Q resists and beats P up. Had P not said what he did and had he not confronted Q with a gun, and had Q just beaten P up, Q would have been a bully and people would have scorned him. But now the consequences of beating P up are made far more attractive to Q; Q becomes a hero if he does so. But P hasn't made Q an offer to beat him up, because though what P did improved the consequences of some action of Q's, bringing about this improvement was not part of P's reason for acting as he did.[44] Has P tipped Q off to something? Highwaymen normally don't go on to say, "And if you resist and beat me up you'll be a hero," but if one did, he would have given his prospective victim a tip, however little appreciated. Note, incidentally, that one should not think for the case where Q beats P up after P makes his threat that Q was coerced into doing so, even though Q did so to avoid the threatened consequence. For not all of the other necessary conditions for coercion are satisfied.

Threats, Offers, and Choices

I have claimed that normally a person is not coerced into performing an action if he performs it because someone has offered him something to do it, though normally he is coerced into performing an action if he does so because of a threat that has been made against his not doing so. Writers who count offers as coercive do so, I suspect, because they accept something roughly like the following statement:

If Q has available to him the actions in a set A, and as a result of what P has done or will do

(a)   act A_1 is significantly higher in utility to Q than the other actions in A

(b)   act A_2 is significantly lower in utility to Q than the other actions in A

whereas it wasn't before, and Q

(a)   does A_1 because of this

(b)   refrains from A_2 because of this

then Q was coerced into

(a)   doing A_1

(b)   not doing A_2

According to this view, any action of P's which results in A_1's being significantly greater or A_2's being significantly less in utility than the other actions in A may coerce Q. It makes no difference, according to this view, how the difference in utility is brought about; whether in (a) A_1 is absolutely raised in utility or all the other members of A are absolutely lowered in utility, or whether in (b) A_2 is absolutely lowered in utility, or all the other members of A are absolutely raised in utility. It is only the resulting *relative* positions, however arrived at, which count. This view is mistaken, and I shall assume that we can all think of examples that show to our satisfaction that this is so. I now want to consider whether anything illuminating can be said about *why* the notion of coercion isn't so wide as to encompass all bringing about of actions by the bringing about of difference in relative position. The question I'm asking may seem bogus. After all, there will be some terms which apply both to getting someone to do something via threats, and to getting someone to do something via offers, e.g., "getting someone to do something." And there will be some terms which apply to one and not the other. Am I just asking why the word *coercion* is among those that apply to only one of these and not to both? And why expect the answer, presumably going back to the word's Latin roots, to be philosophically interesting? So let me state my task differently.

I would like to make sense of the following claims: when a person does something because of threats, the will of another is operating or predominant, whereas when he does something because of offers this is not so; a person who does something because of threats is subject to the will of another, whereas a person who acts because of an offer is not; a person who does something because of threats does not perform a fully voluntary action, whereas this is normally not the case with someone who does something because of offers; when someone does something because of offers it is his own choice, whereas when he does something because of threats it is not his own choice but someone else's, or not fully his own choice, or someone else has made his choice for him; when a person does something because of threats he does it unwillingly, whereas this is normally not the case when someone does something because of offers. (There are other ways to approach this area. One might ask why we say that we *accept* offers, but we go along with threats rather than accept them.)

I would like to make sense of these claims in the face of the following three roughly true statements, which seem to indicate that threat and offer situations are on a par so far as whose will operates, whether the act is fully voluntary, whose choice it is, and so forth.

(1)   A person can be gotten to do something which someone else wants him to do, which he otherwise wouldn't do, by offers as well as by threats.

(2)   A person can choose to do what there is a threat against his doing, just as a person can choose to do what there is an offer for him not to do. ("Just as"?)

(3)   Sometimes a threat is so great that a person cannot reasonably be expected not to go along with it, but also sometimes an offer is

so great that a person cannot reasonably be expected not to go along with it (that is, not to accept it).

I shall consider only a partially described person, whom I shall call the Rational Man, and unfortunately shall not get to us. The Rational Man, being able to resist those temptations which he thinks he should resist, will normally welcome credible offers,[45] or at any rate not be unwilling to have them be made. For he can always decline to accept the offer, and in this case he is no worse off than he would have been had the offer not been made. (Here I ignore the "costs" of making decisions, e.g., time spent in considering an offer.) Why *should* he be unwilling to be the recipient of an offer? On the other hand, the Rational Man will normally not welcome credible threats, will normally be unwilling to be threatened, even if he is able to resist going along with them. It is worth mentioning some cases which are or seem to be exceptions to this. A person might not mind threats if he was going to do the act anyway. But, since in this case he (probably) wasn't coerced, he needn't concern us here. A person might welcome threats which restrict the acts he can reasonably be expected to perform, and therefore improve his bargaining position with a third party, e.g., an employer negotiating with a labor union might welcome publicly known threats against raising wages by more than n percent. But what he welcomes is not his being coerced into not raising wages by more than n percent (he is not coerced), but its looking to others as though he is coerced. This needn't concern us here.

But there are other cases which are somewhat more difficult. For example, P tells Q that he'll give Q $10,000 if in the next week someone, without prompting, threatens Q. Someone does and Q welcomes the threat. Or, P is jealous of Q's receiving certain sorts of offers and tells Q that if he (Q) receives another offer before P does, then P will kill Q. Q cringes when the next offer comes. Or Q believes that having at least five threats (offers) made to one in one week brings good (bad) luck, and so is happy (unhappy) at the coming of the fifth threat (offer) in a week. Or for tax purposes Q welcomes a threat to illegally take some of his money. And so forth. I want to say that in such cases when threats are welcomed and offers shunned, they are done so for extraneous reasons, because of the special context. (One is tempted to say that in these contexts what would normally be a threat (offer) isn't really one.) I find it difficult to distinguish these special contexts from the others, but the claim that threats are normally unwelcome, whereas offers are not, is not meant to apply to contexts where some special if-then is believed to obtain, where it is believed to be the case that if a threat (offer) is made, resisted (accepted), or carried out then something good (bad) will happen to the recipient of the threat (offer) (where this good (bad) consequence is not "internal" to the threat (offer)), and this belief on the part of the recipient of the threat (offer) overrides other considerations. It is along such lines that I suggest viewing the person who welcomes a threat because it affords him the opportunity to prove to others or test for himself his courage. Finally, let me mention the case where a person is in an n-person prisoners' dilemma situation. In this case, he may most prefer everyone *else's* being coerced into performing a dominated action while he is left free to perform the dominant action. He may also prefer everyone's being coerced into performing a specific dominated action (e.g., paying taxes) to no one's being so coerced. And since he realizes that the policy he most prefers, which treats him specially, isn't a feasible alternative, he may welcome the threat to everyone including himself.[46] But though he welcomes the system which threatens everyone, he might still be coerced into performing his particular action (e.g., paying his taxes). This too seems to me not to be a counterexample to the claim that threats are unwelcome, but one of the special contexts, with special if-thens tagged onto the making of the threat, to which the claim is not meant to apply.

I have said that the Rational Man would normally be willing to have credible offers made to him, whereas he would not normally be willing to be the recipient of credible threats. Imagine that the Rational Man is given a choice about whether someone else makes him an offer (threatens him). For example, the Rational Man is asked, "Shall I threaten you (make you an offer)?" If he answers "yes," it is done. I am supposing that no offer is made the Rational Man to say "yes" to this question, and no threat is made against his not saying "yes"; i.e., that no threats of offers are involved in *this* choice about whether a threat (offer) is to be made. Let us call the situations before a threat or offer is made the presituation. (I shall speak of the prethreat and preoffer situations, in anticipation of what is to come.) And let us call the situations after a threat or offer is made the threat and the offer situations, respectively.

Looking first at offers:

(a)   The Rational Man is normally willing to go and would be willing to choose to go from the preoffer to the offer situation.

(b) In the preoffer situation, the Rational Man is normally willing to do A if placed in the offer situation.

(c) The Rational Man, in the preoffer situation, is unwilling to do A. (We're concerned with the case where he does A [partly] because of the offer.)

(d) The Rational Man, when placed in the offer situation, does not normally prefer being back in the preoffer situation.

Turning to threats:

(a) The Rational Man is normally unwilling to go and unwilling to choose to go from the prethreat situation to the threat situation.

(b) In the prethreat situation, the Rational Man is normally willing to do A if placed in the threat situation.

(c) The Rational Man, in the prethreat situation, is unwilling to do A, and would not choose to do it. (We're concerned with the case where he does the act [partly] because of the threat.)

(d) The Rational Man, when placed in the threat situation, would normally prefer being back in the prethreat situation, and would choose to move back.

The two significant differences between these two lists are:

(1) The Rational Man would be willing to move and to choose to move from the preoffer to the offer situation, whereas he would normally not be willing to move or to choose to move from the prethreat situation to the threat situation.

(2) The Rational Man, once in the offer situation, would not prefer being back in the preoffer situation, whereas the Rational Man in the threat situation would normally prefer being back in the prethreat situation.

If we concentrate solely on the choices made in the threat and offer situations, we shall be hard put to find a difference between these situations, which seems to make a difference as to whose will is operating, whose choice it is, whether the act is fully voluntary, done willingly or unwillingly, and so forth. If, however, we widen our focus and look not only at the choices made in the postsituations, but look *also* at the choice that would be made about moving from the presituation to the postsituation, then things look more promising. For now we face not just two choices but two pairs of choices:

(1)   To move from the preoffer to the offer situation, and to do *A* in the offer situation

(2)   To move from the prethreat to the threat situation, and to do *A* in the threat situation.

And the Rational Man would be (willing to) make both choices in (1), whereas he would not make both choices in (2). This difference in what choices are or would be made (when other factors are appropriately the same) seems to me to make the difference, when someone else intentionally moves you from the presituation to the postsituation, to whose choice it is, whose will operates, whether the act is willingly or unwillingly done, and to whether or not the act is fully voluntary.

One would like to formulate a principle that is built upon the preceding considerations, but I find it difficult to formulate one that I am confident is not open to very simple counter-examples. Very hesitantly and tentatively, I suggest the following plausible-looking principle:

> If the alternatives among which *Q* must choose are intentionally changed by *P*, and *P* made this change in order to get *Q* to do *A*, and before the change *Q* would not have chosen (and would have been unwilling to choose) to have the change made (and after it's made, *Q* would prefer that it hadn't been made), and before the change was made *Q* wouldn't have chosen to do *A*, and after the change is made *Q* does *A*, then *Q*'s choice to do *A* is not fully his own.

Notice that I have *not* said that the feature I am emphasizing which is mentioned in the principle, namely, being willing to choose to move from one situation to another, is by itself sufficient for a choice in the latter situation to be not fully one's own, but instead I have said that this feature, *in conjunction* with the other features listed in the antecedent of the principle, is sufficient.

Since this principle presents a sufficient condition for *Q*'s choice not being fully his own, it does not yield the consequence that in the offer situation, normally *Q*'s choice is fully his own. A detailed discussion of when choices *are* fully one's own, or fully voluntary, yielding this consequence, would take us far afield. Here I just wish to suggest that the crucial difference between acting because of an offer and acting because of a threat *vis-à-vis* whose choice it is, etc., is that in one case (the offer case) the Rational Man is normally willing to move or be moved from the presituation to the situation itself, whereas in the other case (the threat case) he is not. Put baldly and too simply, the Rational Man would normally (be willing to) choose to make the choice among the alternatives facing him in the offer situation, whereas normally he would not (be willing to) choose to make the choice among the alternatives facing him in the threat situation.

The principle seems to me to be on the right track in concentrating not *just* on the choice of whether or not to do A, but also on the choice to move into the threat or offer situation. But it is difficult to state a principle which gets all the details right and which is not trivial and unilluminating (as one would be which said: if P moves Q from S_1 to S_2 via threats then . . .). It seems that rather than speaking (just) of act A being fully one's own choice, one should speak of its being fully one's own choice to do A rather than B. I have in mind the following sort of case. P intentionally breaks Q's leg (intentionally moving him from S_1 [no broken leg] to S_2 [broken leg]). Q would prefer not making this move, and afterwards would prefer not having made it. But once Q has a broken leg, he chooses to have a decorated cast put on it, rather than a plain white one. If we just look at the act of wearing a decorated cast, we will have difficulties, for surely it is not Q's own choice (he was forced into a position where he had to wear a cast, etc.), yet in some sense it is. It seems to me more illuminating to say that wearing a cast rather than none was not fully Q's own choice, wearing a decorated cast rather than a plain one *was* fully Q's own choice, and wearing a decorated cast rather than none was not fully Q's own choice. It is not clear how to state a principle which takes this and similar complications into account, and is not open to obvious difficulties. I do, however, want to suggest that we shall not be able to understand why acts done because of threats are not normally fully voluntary, fully one's own choice, etc., whereas this is not normally the case with acts done in response to offers, if we attend only to the choice confronting the person in the threat and offer situations. We must look also at the (hypothetical) choice of getting (and willingness to get) into the threat and offer situations themselves.

We have said that if P coerces Q into not doing A then (part of) Q's reason for not doing A is to avoid or lessen the likelihood of P's threatened consequence. Assuming that all of the conditions in the first section of this paper are satisfied, then

(a)   In the case where Q's whole reason for not doing A is to avoid or lessen the likelihood of P's threatened consequence (ignoring his reasons for wanting to avoid this consequence), P coerces Q into not doing A.[47]

(b)   In the case where P's threatened consequence is not part of Q's reason for not doing A (even if it is a reason Q has for not doing A) then P does not coerce Q into not doing A.

But the case is more difficult when P's threatened consequence is part of Q's reason for not doing A, and other reasons which Q has for not doing A (which do not involve threats) are also part of his reason for not doing A. For in this case, Q contributes reasons of his own; it is not solely because of the threat that he refrains from doing A. If we had to say either that this situation was one of coercion or was not one of coercion we would, I think, term it coercion.[48] But, I think, for such cases one is inclined to want to switch from a classificatory notion of coercion to a quantitative one.[49]

Let me indulge in a bit of science fiction. Suppose that one were able to assign weights to the parts of Q's reasons for not doing A, which indicated what fraction of Q's total reason for not doing A any given part was.[50] One might then say, if P's threat was n/mth of Q's total reason for not doing A, that Q was n/m-coerced into not doing A. If P's threat is Q's whole reason for not doing A (no part of Q's reason for not doing A) then Q is 1-coerced (0-coerced) or, for short, coerced (not coerced). And, in the absence of precise weights, one might begin to speak of someone's being partially coerced, slightly coerced, almost fully coerced into doing something, and so forth.[51] Furthermore, without claiming that a person is *never* to be held responsible for an act he was coerced into doing, we might, for some cases in which his reasons (other than the threat) for doing an act aren't sufficient to get him to decide to do the act, be led to speak of a person's being (held) partially responsible for his act; not completely responsible because he did it partly because of the threat, and not complete absence of responsibility because he didn't do it solely because of the threat, but contributed some reasons of his own. I would end by saying that the consideration of such a view of responsibility, and the tracing of the modifications in what has been said thus far introduced by a thoroughgoing use of the notion of n/m-coerced, would require another paper—were it not for the thought that some readers might take this as a threat.

NEWCOMB'S PROBLEM AND TWO PRINCIPLES OF CHOICE

↝ ↝ ↝

Both it and its opposite must involve no mere artificial illusion such as at once vanishes upon detection, but a natural and unavoidable illusion, which even after it has ceased to beguile still continues to delude though not to deceive us, and which though thus capable of being rendered harmless can never be eradicated.

IMMANUEL KANT, *Critique of Pure Reason*, A422, B450

I

Suppose a being in whose power to predict your choices you have enormous confidence. (One might tell a science-fiction story about a being from another planet, with an advanced technology and science, whom you know to be friendly, etc.) You know that this being has often correctly predicted your choices in the past (and has never, so far as you know, made an incorrect prediction about your choices), and furthermore you know that this being has often correctly predicted the choices of other people, many of whom are similar to you, in the particular situation to be described below. One might tell a longer story, but all this leads you to believe that almost certainly this being's prediction about your choice in the situation to be discussed will be correct.

There are two boxes, (B1) and (B2). (B1) contains $1,000. (B2) contains either $1,000,000 ($M$), or nothing. What the content of (B2) depends upon will be described in a moment.

$$(\text{B1}) \quad \{\$1,000\} \quad (\text{B2}) \quad \left\{ \begin{array}{c} \$M \\ \text{or} \\ \$0 \end{array} \right\}$$

You have a choice between two actions:

(1)   taking what is in both boxes
(2)   taking only what is in the second box.

Furthermore, and you know this, the being knows that you know this, and so on:

(I)   If the being predicts you will take what is in both boxes, he does not put the M in the second box.
(II)   If the being predicts you will take only what is in the second box, he does put the M in the second box.[1]

The situation is as follows. First the being makes its prediction. Then it puts the M in the second box, or does not, depending upon what it has predicted. Then you make your choice. What do you do?

There are two plausible-looking and highly intuitive arguments which require different decisions. The problem is to explain why one of them is not legitimately applied to this choice situation. You might reason as follows:

First Argument: If I take what is in both boxes, the being, almost certainly, will have predicted this and will not have put the M in the second box, and so I will, almost certainly, get only $1,000. If I take only what is in the second box, the being, almost certainly, will have predicted this and will have put the M in the second box, and so I will, almost certainly, get M. Thus, if I take what is in both boxes, I, almost certainly, will get $1,000. If I take only what is in the second box, I, almost certainly, will get M. Therefore I should take only what is in the second box.

Second Argument: The being has already made his prediction, and has already either put the M in the second box, or has not. The M is either already sitting in the second box, or it is not, and which situation obtains is already fixed and determined. If the being has already put the M in the second box, and I take what is in both boxes I get $M + $1,000, whereas if I take only what is in the second box, I get only M. If the being has not put the M in the second box, and I take what is in both boxes I get $1,000, whereas if I take only what is in the second box, I get no money. Therefore, whether the money is there or not, and which it is already fixed and determined, I get $1,000 more by taking what is in both boxes rather than taking only what is in the second box. So I should take what is in both boxes.

Let me say a bit more to emphasize the pull of each of these arguments:

The First: You know that many persons like yourself, philosophy teachers and students, etc., have gone through this experiment. All those who took only what was in the second box, including those who knew of the second argument but did not follow it, ended up with M. And you know that all the shrewdies, all those who followed the second argument and took what was in both boxes, ended up with only $1,000. You have no reason to believe that you are any different, *vis-à-vis* predictability, than they are. Furthermore, since you know that I have all of the preceding information, you know that I would bet, giving high odds, and be rational in doing so, that if you were to take both boxes you would get only $1,000. And if you were to irrevocably take both boxes, and there were some delay in the results being announced, would not it be rational for you to then bet with some third party, giving high odds, that you will get only $1,000 from the previous transaction? Whereas if you were to take only what is in the second box, would not it be rational for you to make a side bet with some third party that you will get $M from the previous transaction? Knowing all this (though no one is actually available to bet with), do you really want to take what is in both boxes, acting against what you would rationally want to bet on?

The Second: The being has already made his prediction, placed the $M in the second box or not, and then left. This happened one week ago; this happened one year ago. Box (B1) is transparent. You can see the $1,000 sitting there. The $M is already either in the box (B2) or not (though you cannot see which). Are you going to take only what is in (B2)? To emphasize further, from your side, you cannot see through (B2), but from the other side it is transparent. I have been sitting on the other side of (B2), looking in and seeing what is there. Either I have already been looking at the $M for a week or I have already been looking at an empty box for a week. If the money is already there, it will stay there whatever you choose. It is not going to disappear. If it is not already there, if I am looking at an empty box, it is not going to suddenly appear if you choose only what is in the second box. Are you going to take only what is in the second box, passing up the additional $1,000 which you can plainly see? Furthermore, I have been sitting there looking at the boxes, hoping that you will perform a particular action. Internally, I am giving you advice. And, of course, you already know which advice I am silently giving to you. In either case (whether or not I see the $M in the second box) I am hoping that you will take what is in both boxes. You know that the person sitting and watching it all hopes that you will take the contents of both boxes. Are you going to take only what is in the second box, passing up the additional $1,000 which you can plainly see, and ignoring my internally given hope that you take both? Of course, my presence makes no difference. You are sitting there alone, but you know that if some friend having your interests at heart *were* observing from the other side, looking into both boxes, he *would* be hoping that you would take both. So will you take only what is in the second box, passing up the additional $1,000 which you can plainly see?

I should add that I have put this problem to a large number of people, both friends and students in class. To almost everyone it is perfectly clear and obvious what should be done. The difficulty is that these people seem to divide almost evenly on the problem, with large numbers thinking that the opposing half is just being silly.[2]

Given two such compelling opposing arguments, it will not do to rest content with one's belief that one knows what to do. Nor will it do to just repeat one of the arguments, loudly and slowly. One must also disarm the opposing argument; explain away its force while showing it due respect.

Now for an unusual suggestion. It might be a good idea for the reader to stop reading this paper at the end of this section (but do, please, return and finish it), mull over the problem for a while (several hours, days) and then return. It is not that I claim to solve the problem, and do not want you to miss the joy of puzzling over an unsolved problem. It is that I want you to understand my thrashing about.

II

My strategy in attacking this problem is ostrich-like; that is, I shall begin by ignoring it completely (except in occasional notes) and proceed to discuss contemporary decision theory. Though the problem is not, at first, explicitly discussed, the course my discussion takes is influenced by my knowledge of the problem. Later in the paper, I shall remove my head from the sand and face our problem directly, having advanced toward a solution, I hope, or at least having sharpened and isolated the problem.

Writers on decision theory state two principles to govern choices among alternative actions.

> *Expected-Utility Principle:* Among those actions available to a person, he should perform an action with maximal expected utility.

The expected utility of an action yielding the exclusive outcomes $O_1, \ldots,$ O_n with probabilities $p_1, \ldots, p_n$ respectively,

$$\left(\sum_{i=1}^{n} p_i = 1 \right) \text{ is } p_1 \times u(O_1) + p_2 \times u(O_2) + \cdots + p_n \times u(O_n),$$

i.e., $\sum_{i=1}^{n} p_i \times u(O_i).$

> *Dominance Principle:* If there is a partition of states of the world such that relative to it, action A weakly dominates action B, then A should be performed rather than B.

Action A weakly dominates action B for person P iff, for each state of the world, P either prefers the consequence of A to the consequence of B, or is indifferent between the two consequences, and for some state of the world, P prefers the consequence of A to the consequence of B.

There are many interesting questions and problems about the framework used or assumed by these principles and the conditions governing preference, indifference, and probability which suffice to yield the utility measure, and the exact way the principles should be formulated.[3] The problem I want to begin with is raised by the fact that for some situations, one of the principles listed above requires that one choose one action whereas the other principle requires that one choose another action. Which should one follow?

Consider the following situation, where A and B are actions, S_1 and S_2 are states of the world, and the numerical entries give the utility of the consequences, results, effects, outcomes, upshots, events, states of affairs, etc., that obtain, happen, hold, etc., if the action is done and the state of the world obtains.

	S_1	S_2
A:	10	4
B:	8	3

According to the dominance principle, the person should do A rather than B. (In this situation A strongly dominates B, that is, for each state of nature the person prefers the consequence of A to the consequence of B.) But suppose the person believes it very likely that if he does A, S_2 will obtain, and if he does B, S_1 will obtain. Then he believes it very likely that if he does A he will get 4, and if he does B he will get 8.

$$
\begin{array}{ccc}
 & S_1 & S_2 \\
A: & 10 & 4 \\
B: & 8 & 3
\end{array}
$$

The expected utility of $A = \text{prob}(S_1|A)10 + \text{prob}(S_2|A)4$. The expected utility of $B = \text{prob}(S_1|B)8 + \text{prob}(S_2|B)3$. If, for example,

$$\text{prob}(S_1|A) = .2$$
$$\text{prob}(S_2|A) = .8$$
$$\text{prob}(S_1|B) = .9$$
$$\text{prob}(S_2|B) = .1,$$

then the expected utility of $A = 5.2$, and the expected utility of $B = 7.5$. Thus the expected-utility principle requires the person to do B rather than A.[4]

The dominance principle as presented here speaks of dominance relative to a partition of the states of the world. This relativization is normally not made explicit, which perhaps accounts for the fact that writers did not mention that it may be that relative to one partition of the states of the world, one action A dominates another, whereas relative to another partition of the states of the world, it does not.

It will be helpful to have before us two facts:

First: Suppose a matrix is given, with states $S_1, \ldots, S_n$, in which action A does not dominate action B. If there is some rearrangement of the utility entries in the row for action A which gives a new row which dominates the row for action B, then there are states $T_1, \ldots, T_n$ such that in the matrix with these states, action A dominates action B.

Proof: I shall describe how one can get the appropriate states $T_1, \ldots, T_n$ in one case. It is obvious how this procedure can be used generally. Suppose that $a_1, \ldots, a_n$ and $b_1, \ldots, b_n$ are utility numbers such that, for all i, $a_i \geq b_i$, and for some i, $a_i > b_i$. We may suppose that a_i is the entry in the A row for the ith column, that is, for state S_i. We might, for example, have the following matrix:

$$
\begin{array}{cccccc}
 & S_1 & S_2 & S_3 & \ldots & S_n \\
A: & a_1 & a_2 & a_3 & \ldots & a_n \\
B: & b_{12} & b_3 & b_{19} & \ldots & b_6
\end{array}
$$

Let

$$T_1 = A \ \& \ S_{12} \text{ or } B \& S_1{}^5$$
$$T_2 = A \ \& \ S_3 \ \text{ or } B \& S_2$$
$$T_3 = A \ \& \ S_{19} \text{ or } B \ \& \ S_3$$
$$\vdots$$
$$T_n = A \ \& \ S_6 \ \text{ or } B \ \& \ S_n.$$

Thus we get the matrix,

	T_1	T_2	T_3	$\ldots$	T_n
A:	a_{12}	a_3	a_{19}	$\ldots$	a_6
B:	b_{12}	b_3	b_{19}	$\ldots$	b_6

In this matrix, action A dominates action B. Since the kind of procedure followed does not depend on any specific features of the example, the point is made.

Second: Suppose there is a matrix with states $S_1, \ldots, S_n$ such that action A dominates action B. If there is some rearrangement of the utility entries in the B row so that the rearranged row is not dominated by A, then there are states $T_1, \ldots, T_n$ such that if the matrix is set up with these states, B is not dominated by A.

Proof: Suppose that $a_i \geq b_i$, for all i; $a_i > b_i$ for some i; and that some B-row value is greater than some A-row value. (Given that there is some arrangement in which A dominates B, this last supposition follows from its being possible to rearrange the B row so that it is not dominated by the A row.) Suppose, without loss of generality that $b_{12} > a_2$. Thus we have the following matrix:

	S_1	S_2	S_3	$\ldots$	S_n
A:	a_1	a_2	a_3	$\ldots$	a_n
B:	b_1	b_2	b_3	$\ldots$	b_n

Let

$$T_1 = S_1$$
$$T_2 = S \ \& \ S_2 \text{ or } B \ \& \ S_{12}$$
$$T_3 = S_3$$
$$\vdots$$

$$T_{11} = S_{11}$$
$$T_{12} = A \,\&\, S_{12} \text{ or } B \,\&\, S_2$$
$$T_{13} = S_{13}$$
$$\vdots$$
$$T_n \ = S_n.$$

Thus we get the following matrix:

	T_1	T_2	T_3	$\ldots$	T_{12}	$\ldots$	T_n
A:	a_1	a_2	a_3	$\ldots$	a_{12}	$\ldots$	a_n
B:	b_1	b_{12}	b_3	$\ldots$	b_2	$\ldots$	b_n

Since $b_{12} > a_2$, A does not dominate B.

It may seem that the states $T_1, \ldots, T_n$ defined in terms of the actions A and B, and the states $S_1, \ldots, S_n$ are contrived states, which some general condition could exclude. It should be noted that—since the states $S_1, \ldots, S_n$ can be defined in terms of the actions A and B and the states $T_1, \ldots, T_n$ (I will give some examples below)—attempts to show that $T_1, \ldots, T_n$ are contrived will face many of the problems encountered in ruling out Goodman-style predicates. Furthermore, as we shall see soon, there are cases where the S states and the T states, which are interdefinable in this way, both seem perfectly natural and uncontrived.

The fact that whether one action dominates another or not may depend upon which particular partition of the states of the world is used would cause no difficulty if we were willing to apply the dominance principle to *any* partition of the states of the world. Since we are not, this raises the question of when the dominance principle is to be used. Let us look at some examples.

Suppose that I am about to bet on the outcome of a horse race in which only two horses, H_1 and H_2, are running. Let:

$S_1 = $ Horse H_1 wins the race.

$S_2 = $ Horse H_2 wins the race.

$A_1 = $ I bet on horse H_1.

$A_2 = $ I bet on horse H_2.

Suppose that I will definitely bet on one of the two horses, and can only bet on one of the two horses, and that the following matrix describes the situation. (I might have been offered the opportunity to enter this situation by a friend. Certainly no race track would offer it to me.)

	S_1	S_2
A_1:	I win \$50	I lose \$5
A_2:	I lose \$6	I win \$49

Suppose further that the personal probability for me that H_1 wins is .2, and the personal probability for me that H_2 wins is .8. Thus the expected utility of A_1 is $.2 \times u(\text{I win \$50}) + .8 \times u(\text{I lose \$5})$. The expected utility of A_2 is $.2 \times u(\text{I lose \$6}) + .8 \times u(\text{I win \$49})$. Given my utility assignment to these outcomes, the expected utility of A_2 is greater than that of A_1. Hence the expected-utility principle would have me do A_2 rather than A_1.

However, we may set the matrix up differently. Let:

$S_3 = $ I am lucky in my bet.

$S_4 = $ I am unlucky in my bet.

(Given that I am betting on only one horse today, we could let $S_3 = $ The only horse I bet on today wins. Similarly for S_4, with "loses" substituted for "wins.") Thus we have the following matrix:

	S_3	S_4
A_1:	I win \$50	I lose \$5
A_2:	I win \$49	I lose \$6

But when set up in this way, A_1 dominates A_2. Therefore the dominance principle would have me do A_1 rather than A_2.[6]

In this example, the states are logically independent of which action I perform; from the fact that I perform $A_1(A_2)$ one cannot deduce which state obtains, and from the fact that $S_1(S_2, S_3, S_4)$ obtains one cannot deduce which action I perform. However one pair of states was not probabilistically independent of my doing the actions.[7] Assuming that S_1 and S_2 are each probabilistically independent of both A_1 and A_2, $\text{prob}(S_3|\text{I do } A_1) = .2$; $\text{prob}(S_3|\text{I do } A_2) = .8$; $\text{prob}(S_4|\text{I do } A_1) = .8$; $\text{prob}(S_4|\text{I do } A_2) = .2$. Thus neither of the states S_3 or S_4 is probabilistically independent of each of the actions A_1 and A_2.[8]

In this example, it is clear that one does not wish to follow the recommendation of the dominance principle. And the explanation seems to hinge on the fact that the states are not probabilistically independent of the actions. Even though one can set up the situation so that one action dominates another, I believe that if I do A_1, the consequence will probably be the italicized consequence in its row, and I believe that if I do A_2, the consequence will probably be the italicized consequence in A_2's row.

And given my assignment of utilities in this case, and the probabilities I assign (the conditional probabilities of the states given the actions) it is clear why I prefer to do A_2, despite the fact that A_1 dominates A_2.

	S_3	S_4
A_1:	I win $50	*I lose $5*
A_2:	*I win $49*	I lose $6

Let us consider another example: Suppose that I am playing roulette on a rigged wheel, and that the owner of the casino offers me a chance to choose between actions A_1 and A_2 so that the following matrix describes the situation (where S_1 = black comes up on the next spin; S_2 = red comes up on the next spin):

	S_1	S_2
A_1:	I win $10	I win $100
A_2:	I win $5	I win $90

Finally suppose that I know that the owner's employee, who is overseeing the wheel and who I am confident is completely loyal to the owner, has been instructed to make black come up on the next spin if I choose A_1 and to make red come up on the next spin if I choose A_2. Clearly even though A_1 dominates A_2, given my knowledge of the situation I should choose A_2. I take it that this needs no argument. It seems that the reason that I should not be guided by dominance considerations is that the states S_1 and S_2 are not probabilistically independent of my actions A_1 and A_2. We can set up the situation so that the states are probabilistically independent of the actions. But when set up in this way, I am led, given my utility assignment to the outcomes, to do A_2.

Let S_3 = the fellow running the roulette wheel follows his boss's instructions; S_4 = the fellow running the roulette wheel disobeys his boss's instructions. (Note that $S_3 = A_1$, & S_1 or A_2 & S_2; $S_4 = A_1$ & S_2 or A_2 & S_1.) We then have the following matrix:

	S_3	S_4
A_1:	I win $10	I win $100
A_2:	I win $90	I win $5

Even if I am not sure that S_3 is true, so long as the personal probability of S_3 for me is sufficiently high, I will be led to do A_2, given my utility assignment to the outcomes.

These examples suggest that one should not apply the dominance principle to a situation where the states are not probabilistically independent of the actions. One wishes instead to maximize the expected utility. However, the probabilities that are to be used in determining the expected utility of an action must now be the conditional probabilities of the states given that the action is done. (This is true generally. However, when the states are probabilistically independent of the actions, the conditional probability of each state given that one of the actions is done will be equal to the probability of the state, so the latter may be used.) Thus in the roulette wheel example, we may still look at the first matrix given. However, one does not wish to apply the dominance principle but to find the expected utility of the actions, which in our example are:

$$\text{E.U.}(A_1) = \text{prob}(S_1|A_1) \times u(\text{I win \$10})$$
$$+ \text{prob}(S_2|A_1) \times u(\text{I win \$100})$$
$$\text{E.U.}(A_2) = \text{prob}(S_1|A_2) \times u(\text{I win \$5})$$
$$+ \text{prob}(S_2|A_2) \times u(\text{I win \$90}).[9]$$

The following position appropriately handles the examples given thus far (ignoring Newcomb's example with which the paper opens) and has intuitive appeal.[10]

(1) It is legitimate to apply dominance principles if and only if the states are probabilistically independent of the actions.

(2) If the states are not probabilistically independent of the actions, then apply the expected-utility principle, using as the probability-weights the conditional probabilities of the states given the actions.

Thus in the following matrix, where the entries in the matrix are utility numbers,

	S_1	S_2	...	S_n
A:	O_1	O_2	...	O_n
B:	U_1	U_2	...	U_n

the expected utility of A is $\sum_{i=1}^{n} \text{prob}(S_i|A)O_i$, and the expected utility of B is $\sum_{i=1}^{n} \text{prob}(S_i|B)U_i$.

III

Is this position satisfactory? Consider the following example: P knows that S or T is his father, but he does not know which one is. S died of some terrible inherited disease, and T did not. It is known that this disease is genetically dominant, and that P's mother did not have it, and that S did not have the recessive gene. If S is his father, P will die of this disease; if T is his father, P will not die of this disease. Furthermore, there is a well-confirmed theory available, let us imagine, about the genetic transmission of the tendency to decide to do acts which form part of an intellectual life. This tendency is genetically dominant. S had this tendency (and did not have the recessive gene), T did not, and P's mother did not. P is now deciding whether (a) to go to graduate school and then teach, or (b) to become a professional baseball player. He prefers (though not enormously) the life of an academic to that of a professional athlete.

	S is P's father	T is P's father
A:	x	y
B:	z	w

$x = P$ is an academic for a while, and then dies of the terrible disease; $z = P$ is a professional athlete for a while, and then dies of the terrible disease; $y = P$ is an academic and leads a normal academic life; $w = P$ is a professional athlete and leads the normal life of a professional athlete, though doing a bit more reading; and P prefers x to z, and y to w. However, the disease is so terrible that P greatly prefers w to x. The matrix might be as follows:

	S is P's father	T is P's father
A:	-20	100
B:	-25	95

Suppose that our well-confirmed theory tells us, and P, that if P chooses the academic life, then it is likely that he has the tendency to choose it; if he does not choose the academic life, then it is likely that he does not have the tendency. Specifically, prob(P has the tendency|P decides to do A) = .9

prob(P does not have the tendency|P decides to do A) = .1

prob(P has the tendency|P decides to do B) = .1

prob(P does not have the tendency|P decides to do B) = .9.

Since P has the tendency iff S is P's father, we have

prob(S is P's father|P decides to do A) = .9

prob(T is P's father|P decides to do A) = .1

prob(S is P's father|P decides to do B) = .1

prob(T is P's father|P decides to do B) = .9.

The dominance principle tells P to do A rather than B. But according to the position we are now considering, in situations in which the states are not probabilistically independent of the actions, the dominance principle is not to be used, but rather one is to use the expected-utility principle with the conditional probabilities as the weights. Using the above conditional probabilities and the above numerical assumptions about the utility values, we get:

The expected utility of $A = (.9 \times -20) + (.1 \times 100) = -8$

The expected utility of $B = (.1 \times -25) + (.9 \times 95) = 83$.

Since the expected utility of B is greater than that of A, the position we are considering would have P do B rather than A. But this recommendation is perfectly wild. Imagine P saying, "I am doing B because if I do it it is less likely that I will die of the dread disease." One wants to reply, "It is true that you have got the conditional probabilities correct. If you do A it is likely that S is your father, and hence likely that you will die of the disease, and if you do B it is likely that T is your father and hence unlikely that you will die of the disease. But which one of them is your father is already fixed and determined, and has been for a long time. The action you perform legitimately affects our estimate of the probabilities of the two states, but which state obtains does not depend on your action at all. By doing B you are not *making* it less likely that S is your father, and by doing B you are not making it less likely that you will die of the disease." I do not claim that this reply is without its problems.[11] Before considering another example, let us first state a principle not under attack:

> The dominance principle is legitimately applicable to situations in which the states are probabilistically independent of the actions.[12]

If the states are not probabilistically independent of the actions, it *seems* intuitive that the expected-utility principle is appropriate, and that it is not legitimate to use the dominance principle if it yields a different result from the expected-utility principle. However, in situations in which the states, though not probabilistically independent of the actions, are already fixed and determined, where the actions do not affect whether or not the states obtain, then it *seems* that it is legitimate to use the dominance principle, and illegitimate to follow the recommendation of the expected-utility principle if it differs from that of the dominance principle.

For such situations—where the states are not probabilistically independent of the actions, though which one obtains is already fixed and determined—persons may differ over what principle to use.

Of the twelve sorts of situation in which it is not the case both that none of the states are already fixed and determined and none of the states are probabilistically independent of the actions, I shall discuss only one; namely, where each of the states is already fixed and determined, and none of the states is probabilistically independent of the alternative actions.[13]

The question before us is: In this sort of situation, in which all of the states are already fixed and determined, and none of the states are probabilistically independent of the acts, and the dominance principle requires that one do one action, whereas the expected-utility principle requires that one do another, should one follow the recommendation of the dominance principle or of the expected-utility principle?

The question is difficult. Some may think one should follow the recommendation of the dominance principle; others may think one should follow the recommendation of the expected-utility principle in such situations.

Now for the example which introduces a bit of reflexivity, which I hope will soon serve us in good stead. Suppose that there are two inherited tendencies ("tendencies" because there is some small probability that it would not be followed in a specific situation):

(1)   an inherited tendency to think that the expected-utility principle should be used in such situations. (If P has this tendency, he is in state S_1.)

(2)   an inherited tendency to think that the dominance principle should be used in such situations. (If P has this tendency, he is in state S_2.)

It is known on the basis of *post mortem* genetic examinations that

(a) P's mother had two neutral genes. (A gene for either tendency genetically dominates a neutral gene. We need not here worry about the progeny who has a gene for each tendency.)

(b)   One of the men who may be P's father had two genes for the first tendency.

(c)   The other man who may be P's father had two genes for the second tendency.

So it is known that P has one of the tendencies, but it is not known which one he has. P is faced with the following choice:

	S_1	S_2
A:	10	4
B:	8	3

The choice matrix might have arisen as follows. A deadly disease is going around, and there are two effective vaccines against it. (If both are given, the person dies.) For each person, the side effects of vaccine B are worse than that of vaccine A, and each vaccine has worse side effects on persons in S_2 than either does on persons in S_1.

Now suppose that the theory about the inherited tendencies to choice tells us, and P knows this, that from a person's choice in *this* situation the probabilities of his having the two tendencies, given that he has one of the two, can be estimated, and in particular

$\text{prob}(S_1|A) = .1$

$\text{prob}(S_2|A) = .9$

$\text{prob}(S_1|B) = .9$

$\text{prob}(S_2|B) = .1.$

What should P do? What would you do in this situation?

P may reason as follows: if I do A, then very probably S_2 obtains, and I will get 4. If I do B, then very probably S_1 holds, and I will get 8. So I will do B rather than A.

One wants to reply: whether S_1 or S_2 obtains is already fixed and determined. What you decide to do would not bring about one or the other of them. To emphasize this, let us use the past tense. For you are in

S_1 iff you were in S_1 yesterday; you are in S_2 iff you were in S_2 yesterday. But to reason "If I do A then very probably I was in S_2 yesterday, and I will get 4. If I do B, then very probably I was in S_1 yesterday, and I will get 8. So I will now do B rather than A" is absurd. What you decide to do does not affect which state you were in yesterday. For either state, over which you have no control, you are better off doing A rather than B. To do B for reasons such as the above is no less absurd than someone who has already taken vaccine B yesterday doing some other act C today because the prob (He was in S_1 yesterday|He does C today) is very high, and he wants the (delayed) side effects of the vaccine he has already taken to be less severe.

If an explanation runs from x to y, a correct explanatory theory will speak of the conditional probability prob$(y|x)$. Thus the correct explanatory theory of P's choice in this situation will speak of

prob(P does $A|P$ is in S_1)

prob(P does $A|P$ is in S_2)

prob(P does $B|P$ is in S_1)

prob(P does $B|P$ is in S_2).

From these, the theory may enable us to determine

prob(P is in $S_1|P$ does A)

prob(P is in $S_2|P$ does A)

prob(P is in $S_1|P$ does B)

prob(P is in $S_2|P$ does B)

but these would not be the basic explanatory probabilities. Supposing that probabilistic explanation is legitimate, we could explain why P does A by having among our antecedent conditions the statement that P is in S_2, but we cannot *explain* why P is in S_2 by having among our antecedent conditions the statement that P does A (though P's doing A may be our reason for believing he is in S_2). Given that when the explanatory line runs from x to y (x is part of the explanation of y) and not from y to x, the theory will speak of and somehow distinguish the conditional probabilities prob$(y|x)$, then the probability prob$(x|y)$ will be a *likelihood* (as, I think, this term is used in the statistical literature). Looking at the likelihoods of the states given the actions may perhaps give one the illusion of control over the states. But I suggest that when the states are already fixed and determined, and the explanatory theory has the influence running from the states to the actions, so that the conditional probabilities of the states on the actions are likelihoods, then if the dominance principle applies, it should be applied.

If a state is part of the explanation of deciding to do an action (if the decision is made) and this state is already fixed and determined, then the decision, which has not yet been made, cannot be part of the explanation of the state's obtaining. So we need not consider the case where prob (state|action) is in the basic explanatory theory, for an already fixed state.[14] What other possibilities are there for already fixed and determinded states? One possibility would be a situation in which the states are not part of the explanation of the decision, and the decision is not part of the explanation of which state obtains, but some third thing is part of the explanation of the states obtaining and the decision's being made. Hence neither prob(state of the matrix obtaining| P does a specific action) nor prob(P does a specific action|state of the matrix obtains) would be part of the basic explanatory theory (which has conditional probabilities from antecedent to consequent going in the direction of explanation).

Let us consider a case like this, whose matrix exemplifies the structure of the prisoners' dilemma situation, much discussed by game theorists.[15] There are two people, (I) and (II), and the following matrix describes their situation (where the first entry in each box represents the payoff to person (I) and the second entry represents the payoff to person (II)). The situation arises just once, and the persons cannot get together to agree upon a joint plan of action.

$$
\begin{array}{cccc}
 & & \text{(II)} & \\
 & & C & D \\
\text{(I)} \quad A: & 10, 3 & 4, 4 \\
\quad B: & 8, 8 & 3, 10
\end{array}
$$

Notice that for person (I), action A dominates action B, and for person (II), action D dominates action C. Hence if each performs his dominant action, each ends up with 4. But if each performs the nondominant action, each ends up with 8. So, in this situation, both persons' following the dominance principle leaves each worse off than if both did not follow the dominance principle.

People may differ over what should be done in this situation. Let us, once again, suppose that there are two inherited tendencies, one to perform the dominant action in this situation, and one to perform the other action. Either tendency is genetically dominant over a possible third inherited trait. Persons (I) and (II) are identical twins, who care only about their own payoffs as represented in this matrix, and know that their mother had the neutral gene, one of their two possible fathers had only the gene to perform the dominant action, and the other had only the gene not to perform the dominant action. Neither knows which man was their father, nor which of the genes they have. Each knows, given the genetic theory, that it is almost certain that if he performs the dominant (dominated) action his brother will also. We must also suppose that the theory tells us and them that given all this information upon which they base their choice, the correlation between their actions holds as almost certain, and also given *this* additional information, it holds as almost certain, etc.

I do not wish here to discuss whether one should or should not perform the dominant action in prisoners' dilemma situations. I wish merely to consider the following argument for not performing the dominant action in the situation I have just described. Suppose brother I argues: "If I perform the dominant action then it is almost certain$_1$ that I have that gene, and therefore that my brother does also, and so it is almost certain$_2$[16] that he will also perform the dominant action and so it is almost certain$_2$ that I will get 4. Whereas if I perform the dominated action, for similar reasons, it is almost certain that my brother will also, and hence it is almost certain that I will get 8. So I should perform the dominated action."

Here one surely wishes to reply that *this* argument is not a good argument for performing the dominated action. For what this brother does will not affect what the other brother does. (To emphasize this, suppose that brother II has already acted, though brother I does not yet know what he has done.) Perhaps in prisoners' dilemma situations one should perform the dominated action, but *this* argument does not show that one should in this situation.

The examples thus far considered lead me to believe that if the actions or decisions to do the actions do not affect, help bring about, influence, etc., *which* state obtains, then whatever the conditional probabilities (so long as they do not indicate an influence), one should perform the dominant action.

If the considerations thus far adduced are convincing, then it is clear that one should also choose the dominant action in the following situations, having the same structure (matrix) as Newcomb's, and differing only in that:

(1)   The being makes his prediction and sets the process going whereby the $M gets placed in the second box, or not. You then make your choice, and *after* you do, the (long) process terminates and the $M gets in the box, or not. So while you are deciding, the $M is not already there, though at this time he has already decided whether it will be or not.

(2)   The being gathers his data on the basis of which he makes his prediction. You make your choice (e.g., press one of two buttons which will open one or both boxes later by delayed action), and he then makes his prediction, on the basis of the data previously gathered, and puts the $M in, or not.

This suggests that the crucial fact is *not* whether the states are already fixed and determined but whether the actions *influence* or *affect* which state obtains.

Setting up a simple matrix,[17] we have the following possibilities (with the matrix entries being recommended decision policies for the situation).

	A dominant action is available	No dominant action is available
The actions influence which state obtains. The conditional probabilities differ.	(I) Maximize expected utility	(II) Maximize expected utility
No influence of actions on states. However, conditional probabilities differ.	(III)	(IV)
No influence of actions on states. The conditional probabilities are all the same.	(V) Do dominant action (or, equivalently, maximize expected utility)	(VI) Maximize expected utility

The standard theories make the recommendations in (V) and (VI). They do not consider (I) and (II), but (ignoring other difficulties there might be with the policy) maximizing expected utility seems reasonable here. The difficulties come in the middle row. (III) is the situation exemplified by Newcomb's situation and the other examples we have listed from the person choosing whether to lead the academic life, onwards. I have argued that in these situations one should choose the dominant action and ignore the conditional probabilities which do not indicate an influence. What then should one do in situation (IV), where which action is done does not influence which state obtains, where the conditional probabilities of the states given the actions differ, and where *no* dominant action is available. If the lesson of case (III) is that one should ignore conditional probabilities which do not indicate an influence, must not one ignore them completely in case (IV) as well?

Not exactly. What one should do, in a choice between two actions A and B, is the following.[18] Let $p_1, \ldots, p_n$ be the conditional probability distribution of action A over the n states; let $q_1, \ldots, q_n$ be the conditional probability distribution of action B over the n states. A probability distribution $r_1, \ldots, r_n$, summing to 1, is between $p_1, \ldots, p_n$ and $q_1, \ldots, q_n$ iff for each i, r_1 is in the closed interval $[p_i, q_i]$ or $[q_i, p_i]$. (Note that according to this account, $p_1, \ldots, p_n$ and $q_1, \ldots, q_n$ are each between $p_1, \ldots, p_n$ and $q_1, \ldots, q_n$.) Now for a recommendation: If relative to each probability distribution between $p_1, \ldots, p_n$ and $q_1, \ldots, q_n$, action A has a higher expected utility than action B, then do action A. The expected utility of A and B is computed with respect to the same probability distribution. It will not, of course, be the case that relative to every possible probability distribution A has a higher expected utility than B. For, by hypothesis, A does not dominate B. However, it may be that relative to each probability distribution between $p_1, \ldots, p_n$ and $q_1, \ldots, q_n$, A has a higher expected utility than B. If, on the other hand, it is not the case that relative to each probability distribution between $p_1, \ldots, p_n$ and $q_1, \ldots, q_n$, A has a higher expected utility than B (and it is not the case that relative to each, B has a higher expected utility than A), then we are faced with a problem of decision under constrained uncertainty (the constraints being the end probability distributions), on which kind of problem there is not, so far as I know, agreement in the literature.[19] Since consideration of the issues raised by such problems would take us far afield, we thankfully leave them.

To talk more objectively than some would like,' though more intuitively than we otherwise could, since the actions do not affect or influence which state obtains, there is some one probability distribution, which we do not know, relative to which we would like to compare the action A and B. Since we do not know the distribution, we cannot proceed as in cases (V) and (VI). But since there is *one* unknown correct distribution "out there," unaffected by what we do, we must, in the procedure we use, compare each action with respect to the *same* distribution. Thus it is, at this point, an irrelevant fact that one action's expected utility computed with respect to one probability distribution is higher than another action's expected utility computed with respect to *another* probability distribution. It may seem strange that for case (IV) we bring in the probabilities in some way (even though they do not indicate an influence) whereas in case (III) we do not. This difference is only apparent, since we could bring in the probabilities in case (III) in exactly the same way. The reason why we need not do this, and need only note that A dominates B, is that if A dominates B, then relative to each probability distribution (and therefore for each one between the conditional ones established by the two actions) A has a higher expected utility than B.[20]

Now, at last, to return to Newcomb's example of the predictor. If one believes, for this case, that there is backwards causality, that your choice causes the money to be there or not, that it causes him to have made the prediction that he made, then there is no problem. One takes only what is in the second box. Or if one believes that the way the predictor works is by looking into the future; he, in some sense, sees what you are doing, and hence is no more likely to be wrong about what you do than someone else who is standing there at the time and watching you, and would normally see you, say, open only one box, then there is no problem. You take only what is in the second box. But suppose we establish or take as given that there is no backwards causality, that what you actually decide to do does not affect what he did in the past, that what you actually decide to do is not part of the explanation of why he made the prediction he made. So let us agree that the predictor works as follows: He observes you sometime before you are faced with the choice, examines you with complicated apparatus, etc., and then uses his theory to predict on the basis of this state you were in, what choice you would make later when faced with the choice. Your deciding to do as you do is not part of the explanation of why he makes the prediction he does, though your being in a certain state earlier is part of the explanation of why he makes the prediction he does, and why you decide as you do.

I believe that one should take what is in both boxes. I fear that the considerations I have adduced thus far will not convince those proponents of taking only what is in the second box. Furthermore, I suspect that an adequate solution to this problem will go much deeper than I have yet gone or shall go in this paper. So I want to pose one question.

I assume that it is clear that in the vaccine example, the person should not be convinced by the probability argument, and should choose the dominant action. I assume also that it is clear that in the case of the two brothers, the brother should not be convinced by the probability argument offered. The question I should like to put to proponents of taking only what is in the second box in Newcomb's example (and hence not performing the dominant action) is: what is the difference between Newcomb's example and the other two examples which make the difference between not following the dominance principle and following it?

If no such difference is produced, one should not rush to conclude that one should perform the dominant action in Newcomb's example. For it must be granted that, at the very least, it is not *as clear* that one should perform the dominant action in Newcomb's example, as in the other two examples. And one should be wary of attempting to force a decision in an unclear case by producing a similar case where the decision is clear, and challenging one to find a difference between the cases which makes a difference to the decision. For suppose the undecided person, or the proponent of another decision, cannot find such a difference. Does not the forcer, now, have to find a difference between the cases which explains why one is clear and the other is not? And might not *this* difference then be produced by the other person as that which perhaps should yield different decisions in the two cases? Sometimes this will be implausible; e.g., if the difference is that one case is relatively simple, and the other has much additional detail, individually irrelevant, which prevents the other case from being taken in as a whole. But it does seem that someone arguing as I do about a case must not only: (a) describe a similar case which is clear, and challenge the other to state a difference between them which should make a difference to how they are handled, but must also (b) describe a difference between the cases which explains why though one case is clear, the other is not, or one is tempted to handle the other case differently. And, assuming that all accept the difference stated in (b) as explaining what it is supposed to explain,

(I)   The simplest situation is that in which all agree that the difference mentioned in (b) is not a reason for different decisions in the two cases.

(II)   However, if the forcer says it is not a reason for different decisions in the two cases, and the other person says it is or may be, difficult questions arise about upon whom, if anyone, the burden of further argument falls.

What then is the difference that makes some cases clear and Newcomb's example unclear, yet does not make a difference to how the cases should be decided? Given my account of what the crucial factors are (influence, etc.), my answer to this question will have to claim that the clear cases are clear cases of no influence (or, to recall the cases which we considered at the beginning, of influence), and that in Newcomb's example there is the *illusion* of influence. The task is to explain in a sufficiently forceful way what gives rise to this illusion so that, even as we experience it, we will not be deceived by it.

I have said that if the action is referred to in an explanation of the state's obtaining, so that the doing of the action affects or influences which state obtains, then the dominance principle should not be applied. And if the explanation of the states' obtaining does not make reference to the action, the action does not influence which state obtains, does not (partly) bring it about that a state obtains, then the dominance principle should be applied to such situations where a dominant action is available. But if this is so, where is there room for unclarity about a case? What other possibility is there? Either the action is referred to in the explanation of the state's obtaining, or it is not. How does the temptation to take only what is in the second box arise in the Newcomb example, and why does it linger?

The possibility to which I wish to call attention can be described differently, depending upon other views which one holds. (I describe the possibility specifically with Newcomb's example in mind.) (1) The action *is* referred to in the explanation of the state's obtaining, but the term which refers to the action occurs in the explanation, in a nonextensional belief context. Thus it does not follow from the fact that the action is referred to, in this way, in the explanation of the state's obtaining, that the doing of the action affects which state obtains. (2) The action is not referred to in the explanation of the state's obtaining. What is brought in by the explanation of the state's obtaining is some being's well-founded beliefs about the person's doing the action. Since the person's doing the action is not part of the explanation of the state's obtaining, it does not affect or influence which state obtains.

In Newcomb's example, the predictor makes his prediction on the basis of determining what state the person is in, and what his theory tells him about what such a person will do in the choice situation.

Believing his theory accurate, he puts the money in or not, according to his belief about the person's future actions, where this belief depends upon his finding out what initial state the person is in, and what his theory tells him about a person in such an initial state. Thus, if the predictor puts the $M in the second box, part of the explanation of this is his belief that the person will take only what is in the second box. If he does not put the $M in the second box, part of the explanation of this is his belief that the person will take what is in both boxes. Thus the explanation of the money's being in the second box (or not) refers to the person's action only in a nonextensional belief context (or does not refer to it at all but only to the predictor's beliefs about it).

It is apparently a persistent temptation for people to believe, when an explanation of something x brings in terms referring to y in a nonextensional belief context (or brings in beliefs about y), that y, in some way, influences or affects x. Thus one finds writers on teleological explanation having to state that in the simple case where someone goes to the refrigerator to get an apple, it is not the apple's being there when he gets there which caused him to go, or which (partly) explains his actions, but rather his beliefs about an apple's being there. But this cannot be the whole story about Newcomb's example. For there are many persons not at all tempted to say that the apple's being there when he gets there influenced his action of going there, who do want to or are tempted to take only what is in the second box.

Let us return to the writers on teleology. To show that the apple's being there does not influence the person's actions, but rather it is his beliefs about the apple's being there that do, they usually argue that even if the apple were not there, so long as the person had the beliefs, he would act in the same way. The relevant feature of nonextensional belief contexts here is that from P believes that . . . x . . . , it does not follow that x exists, from P believes that p, it does not follow that p is true. So, the argument runs, he *could* have his beliefs without there being an apple there, and this shows that the apple does not influence his actions in this case. And surely the explanation of his action should be the same, in the case where the apple is in the refrigerator, as in the case where it is not though he believes it is. The parallel argument for Newcomb's example would run: The predictor could believe that you will take only the second even if you do not. This shows that your action does not influence whether or not the money is there, but rather the predictor's beliefs about your action has this influence. But by the conditions of the problem, the predictor is almost certain to predict correctly, so that it is not clear that the predictor could believe that you will take only the second even if you do not. Thus, the condition of the problem which has the predictor's predictions almost certainly being correct tends to get us to treat the predictor's beliefs as though they do not have these nonextensional features. For if his predictions are almost certainly correct, then almost certainly: if he believes you will do A then you will do A.

One further thing should be mentioned. It is a reasonably intuitive principle that if R brings it about that p, and if p if and only if q (for some "iff" stronger than the material biconditional), then R brings it about that q. Or, if it is up to R whether p, and p iff q (for some strong "iff"), then it is up to R whether q. Thus one finds writers arguing that if there are necessary and sufficient causal conditions for our actions, which conditions go back to a time before we were born, then what we do is not up to us. For, so the argument runs, those conditions obtaining before we were born clearly were not up to us, and so what they are necessary and sufficient for is not up to us either. I do not wish here to discuss whether this principle is correct. All that is required for my purposes is that the principle have intuitive appeal, and be a hard one to escape.

This would also reinforce the feeling that as choosers in Newcomb's example, we can, somehow, influence what the predictor did. For, one might argue, Newcomb's problem is a problem for the chooser only if what he does is up to him. And if one assumes this, and the principle is operating, then it will be difficult to escape the feeling that what the predictor did is up to you, the chooser.

I do not claim that this last principle alone creates the problem. For the problem does not arise in e.g., the vaccine case.[21] But it does, I believe, contribute to it.

Thus I wish to claim that Newcomb's example is less clear than the others because

(a)   in it the explanation of the state's obtaining refers to the action (though this reference occurs in a nonextensional belief context)

and that

(b)   the conditions of the problem prevent one obvious way of refuting the teleologist's view in this case (which view depends upon the truth that generally if y is part of the explanation of x, then y influences x).

This leads to the feeling that, somehow, you as chooser can influence what the predictor did, and this feeling is perhaps reinforced by the operation of the intuitive principle. All this leads to the lurking feeling that one can now choose to take only what is in the second box, and so make oneself the sort of person who does so, and so, somehow, influence what the predictor did. I hope you find this explanation of why some cases are clear and Newcomb's is not clear acceptable, and that it is clear that this difference between the cases should not make a difference to how they are decided.[22]

At this point one perhaps wants to say, "If you produce a case having the features you say distinguish Newcomb's example from the others, where it is clear that the dominant action should be performed, then I will be convinced that the dominant action should be performed in Newcomb's example. But not until." If I am right about the role of similar examples, then this cannot be done; an answer to Newcomb's example cannot be forced in this way. Or rather, if it can be done, then it will show that I have not picked out the right difference. For if one case that fits my description is clear, and another which fits it is not clear, then we still have to produce features to explain why one is clear and the other is not. And perhaps *those* features should make a difference between the decisions in the two cases. At some point, given an acceptable explanation of why one case is clear and another is not, one just has to see that the explanatory features do not make a difference to what should be decided in the two cases. Or, at any rate, the point that the explanatory features do not make a difference to what should be decided can itself be forced by a clear case only at the cost of the claim that those very features explain why some cases are clear and others are not.

In closing this paper, I must muddy up the waters a bit (more?).

(1) Though Newcomb's example suggests much about when to apply the dominance principle, and when to apply the expected-utility principle (and hence is relevant to formal decision theory), it is not the expected-utility principle which leads some people to choose only what is in the second box. For suppose the probability of the being's predicting correctly was just .6.

Then the expected utility of taking what is in both boxes = prob(he predicts correctly|I take both)×u(I receive \$1,000)

+ prob(he predicts correctly|I take only second)×u(I receive $1,001,000) = .6 × u($1,000) + .4 × u($1,001,000).

The expected utility of taking only what is in the second box = .6 × u($1,000,000) + .4 × u($0).

And given the utility I assume each of my readers assigns to obtaining these various monetary amounts, the expected utility of taking only what is in the second box is greater than the expected utility of taking what is in both boxes. Yet, I presume, if the probability of the being's predicting correctly were only .6, each of us would choose to take what is in both boxes.

So it is not (just) the expected-utility argument that operates here to create the problem in Newcomb's example. It is crucial that the predictor is almost certain to be correct. I refrain from asking a proponent of taking only what is in the second box in Newcomb's example: if .6 is not a high enough probability to lead you to take only what is in the second box, and almost certainty of correct predictions leads you to take only the second, what is the minimum probability of correct prediction which leads you to take only what is in the second box? I refrain from asking this question because I am very unsure about the force of drawing-the-line arguments, and also because the person who wishes to take what is in both boxes may also face a problem of drawing the line, as we shall see in a moment.

(2) If the fact that it is almost certain that the predictor will be correct is crucial to Newcomb's example, this suggests that we consider the case where it *is* certain, where you know the prediction is correct (though you do not know what the prediction is). Here one naturally argues: I know that if I take both, I will get $1,000. I know that if I take only what is in the second, I get M. So, of course, I will take only what is in the second. And does a proponent of taking what is in both boxes in Newcomb's example (e.g., me) really wish to argue that it is the probability, however minute, of the predictor's being mistaken which makes the difference? Does he really wish to argue that if he knows the prediction will be correct, he will take only the second, but that if he knows someone using the predictor's theory will be wrong once in every 20 billion cases, he will take what is in both boxes? Could the difference between one in n, and none in n, for arbitrarily large finite n, make this difference? And how exactly does the fact that

the predictor is certain to have been correct dissolve the force of the dominance argument?

To get the mind to really boggle, consider the following:

	S_1	S_2
A:	10	4
B:	8	3

Suppose that you know that either S_1 or S_2 already obtains, but you do not know which, and you know that S_1 will cause you to do B, and S_2 will cause you to do A. Now choose! ("Choose?")

To connect up again with a causalized version of Newcomb's example, suppose you know that there are two boxes, (B1) and (B2). (B1) contains $1,000. (B2) contains either a valuable diamond or nothing. You have to choose between taking what is in both boxes and taking only what is in the second. You know that there are two states: S_1 and S_2. You do not know which obtains, but you know that whichever does, it has obtained for the past week. If S_2 obtains, it causes you to take only what is in the second, and it has already caused a diamond to be produced in box (B2). If S_1 obtains, it causes you to take what is in both boxes, and does not cause a diamond to be produced in the second box. You know all this. What do you choose to do?

While we are at it, consider the following case where what you decide (and why) either (1) does affect which future state will obtain, upon which consequences depend, or (though this would not be the same problem for the view I have proposed, it might be for yours) even if it does not affect which state obtains, the conditional probabilities of the states, given what you do and why, differ.

	S_1	S_2
A:	live	die
B:	die	live

(1) Apart from your decisions (if you do not know of this matrix, or know of it and cannot reach a decision), prob S_1 > prob S_2

(2) prob(S_1|do A with (1) as reason) < prob(S_2|do A with (1) as reason)

(3) prob(S_1|do B with (2) as reason) > prob(S_2|do B with (2) as reason)

$\vdots$

even (n) prob$(S_1|$do A with $n-1$ as reason$) <$ prob$(S_2|$do A with $n-1$ as reason$)$

odd (n) prob$(S_1|$do B with $n-1$ as reason$) >$ prob$(S_2|$do B with $n-1$ as reason$)$

$\vdots$

Also: prob$(S_1|$you do what you do because indifferent between A and $B) >$ prob$(S_2|$you do what you do because indifferent between A and $B)$

prob$(S_1|$doing A with all of the above as reason$) <$
prob$(S_2|$doing A with all of the above as reason$)$

and

prob$(S_1|$doing B with all of the above as reason$) >$
prob$(S_2|$doing B with all of the above as reason$)$.

Finally, where "all this" refers to all of what is above this place and, reflexively, to the next two, in which it appears:

prob$(S_1|$doing A with all this as reason$) <$
prob$(S_2|$doing A with all this as reason$)$

and

prob$(S_1|$doing B with all this as reason$) >$
prob$(S_2|$doing B with all this as reason$)$.

What do you do?

3 REFLECTIONS
ON NEWCOMB'S
PROBLEM

↩ ↩ ↩

This essay originally appeared as a guest column in Martin Gardner's series, "Mathematical Games," in *Scientific American*. Gardner's column on Newcomb's Problem, published in July 1973, "produced an enormous outpouring of letters." This correspondence was forwarded to Nozick, who responded with the following comments. (Copyright ©1974 by Scientific American, Inc. All rights reserved.)

Newcomb's problem involves a being who has the ability to predict the choices you will make. You have enormous confidence in the being's predictive ability. He has already correctly predicted your choices in many other situations and the choices of many other people in the situation to be described. We may imagine that the being is a graduate student from another planet, checking a theory of terrestrial psychology, who first takes measurements of the state of our brains before making his predictions. (Or we may imagine that the being is God.) There are two boxes. Box 1 contains $1,000. Box 2 contains either $1 million or no money.

You have a choice between two actions: taking what is in both boxes or taking only what is in the second box. If the being predicts you will take what is in both boxes, he does not put the $1 million in the second box. If he predicts you will take only what is in the second box, he puts the million in the second box. (If he predicts you will base your choice on some random event, he does not put the money in the second box.) You know these facts, he knows you know them, and so on. The being makes his prediction of your choice, puts the $1 million in the second box or not, and then you choose. What do you do?

There are plausible arguments for reaching two different decisions:

1. *The expected-utility argument.* If you take what is in both boxes, the being almost certainly will have predicted this and will not have put

the $1 million in the second box. Almost certainly you will get only $1,000. If you take only what is in the second box, the being almost certainly will have predicted this and put the money there. Almost certainly you will get $1 million. Therefore (on plausible assumptions about the utility of the money for you) you should take only what is in the second box.

	He predicts your choice correctly	He predicts your choice incorrectly
Take both	$1,000	$1,001,000
Take only second	$1,000,000	$0

2. *The dominance argument.* The being has already made his prediction and has either put the $1 million in the second box or has not. The money is either sitting in the second box or it is not. The situation, whichever it is, is fixed and determined. If the being put the million in the second box, you will get $1,001,000 if you take both boxes and only $1 million if you take only the second box. If the being did not put the money in the second box, you will get $1,000 if you take both boxes and no money if you take only the second box. In either case you will do better by $1,000 if you take what is in both boxes rather than only what is in the second box.

	He put $1,000,000 into box 2	He did not put $1,000,000 into box 2
Take both	$1,001,000	$1,000
Take only second	$1,000,000	$0

Each argument is powerful. The problem is to explain why one is defective. Of the first 148 letters to *Scientific American* from readers who tried to resolve the paradox, a large majority accepted the problem as being meaningful and favored one of the two alternatives. Eighty-nine believed one should take only what is in the second box, 37 believed one should take what is in both boxes—a proportion of about 2.5 to one. Five people recommended cheating in one way or another, 13 believed the problem's conditions to be impossible or inconsistent and four maintained that the predictor cannot exist because the assumption that he does leads to a logical contradiction.

Those who favored taking only the second box tried in various ways to undercut the force of the dominance argument. Many pointed out that if you thought of that argument and were convinced by it, the predictor would (almost certainly) have predicted it and you would end up with only $1,000. They interpreted the dominance argument as an attempt to outwit the predictor. This position makes things too simple. The proponent of the dominance argument does believe he will end up with only $1,000, yet nevertheless he thinks it is best to take both boxes. Several proponents of the dominance principle bemoaned the fact that rational individuals would do worse than irrational ones, but that did not sway them.

Stephen E. Weiss of Morgantown, West Virginia, tried to reconcile the two views. He suggested that following the expected-utility argument maximizes expectation, whereas following the dominance argument maximizes correct decision. Unfortunately that leaves unexplained why the correct decision is not the one that maximizes expectation.

The assumptions underlying the dominance argument, that the $1 million is already in the second box or it is not and that the situation is fixed and determined, were questioned by Mohan S. Kalelkar, a physicist at the Nevis Laboratories of Columbia University, who wrote: "Perhaps it is false to say that the being has definitely made one choice or the other, just as it is false to say that the electron [in the two-slit experiment] went through one slit or the other. Perhaps we can only say that there is some amplitude that B2 [second box] has $1 million and some other amplitude that it is empty. These amplitudes interfere unless and until we make our move and open up the box . . . To assert that 'either B2 contains $1 million or else it is empty' is an intuitive argument for which there is no evidence unless we open the box. Admittedly the intuitive evidence is strong, but as in the case of the double-slit electron diffraction our intuition can sometimes prove to be wrong."

Kalelkar's argument makes a version of the problem, in which the second box is transparent on the other side and someone has been staring into it for a week before we make our choice, a significantly different decision problem. It seems not to be. Erwin Schrödinger, in a famous thought experiment, imagined a cat left alone in a closed room with a vial of cyanide that breaks if a radioactive atom in a detector decays.

Must a disciple of Niels Bohr's assert that the cat is neither alive nor dead, Schrödinger asked, until measurements have been made to decide the case? Even if one accepts the Bohr interpretation of quantum mechanics, however, what choice *does* one make, in Newcomb's problem, when one knows that others can see into the box from the other side and observe whether it is filled or empty?

Many who wrote asserted that the dominance argument assumes the states to be probabilistically independent of the actions and pointed out that this is not true for the two states "The $1 million is in Box 2" and "The $1 million is not in Box 2." The states would be probabilistically independent of the actions (let us assume) in the matrix for the utility argument, which has the states "He predicts correctly" and "He predicts incorrectly." Here, however, there is no longer dominance. Therefore it appears that the force of dominance principles is undercut. "It is legitimate to apply dominance principles if and only if the states are probabilistically independent of the actions. If the states are not probabilistically independent of the actions, then apply the expected-utility principle, using as the probability-weights the conditional probabilities of the states given in the actions." The quotation is from my original 1970 essay, which formulated this position, then went on to reject it as unsatisfactory for the following reasons.

Suppose a person knows that either man S or man T is his father but he does not know which. S died of some very painful inherited disease that strikes in one's middle thirties and T did not. The disease is genetically dominant. S carried only the dominant gene. T did not have the gene. If S is his father, the person will die of the dread disease. If T is his father, he will not. Furthermore, suppose there is a well-confirmed theory that states a person who inherits this gene will also inherit a tendency toward behavior that is characteristic of intellectuals and scholars. S had this tendency. Neither T nor the person's mother had such a tendency. The person is now deciding whether to go to graduate school or to become a professional baseball player. He prefers (although not enormously) the life of an academic to that of a professional athlete. Regardless of whether or not he will die in his middle thirties, he would be happier as an academic. The choice of the academic life would thus appear to be his best choice.

Now suppose he reasons that if he decides to be an academic, the decision will show that he has such a tendency and therefore it will be likely that he carries the gene for the disease and so will die in his middle thirties, whereas if he chooses to become a baseball player, it will be likely that T is his father, therefore he is not likely to die of the disease. Since he very much prefers not dying of the disease (as a baseball player) to dying early from the disease (as an academic), he decides to pursue the career of an athlete. Surely everyone would agree that this reasoning is perfectly wild. It is true that the conditional probabilities of the states "S is his father" and "T is his father" are not independent of the actions "becoming an academic" and "becoming a professional athlete." If he does the first, it is very likely that S is his father and that he will die of the disease; if he does the second, it is very likely that T is his father and therefore unlikely that he will die of the disease. But who his father is cannot be changed. It is fixed and determined and has been for a long time. His choice of how to act legitimately affects our (and his) estimate of the probabilities of the two states, but which state obtains (which person is his father) does not depend on his action at all. By becoming a professional baseball player he is not making it less likely that S is his father, therefore he is not making it less likely that he will die of the disease.

This case, and others more clearly including a self-reference that this case may seem to lack, led me to think probabilistic nonindependence was not sufficient to reject the dominance principle. It depends on whether the actions influence or affect the states; it is not enough merely that they affect our judgments about whether the states obtain. How do those who reject the dominance principle for Newcomb's problem distinguish it from those other cases where dominance principles obviously apply even though there is probabilistic nonindependence?

But one must move carefully here. One cannot force a decision in a difficult case merely by finding another similar case where the decision is clear, then challenging someone to show why the decision should be different in the two cases. There is always the possibility that whatever makes one case difficult and the other clear will also make a difference as to how they should be decided. The person who produces the parallel example must not only issue his challenge; he must also offer an explanation of why the difficult case is less clear, an explanation that does not involve any reason why the cases might diverge in how they should be decided. Interested readers can find my additional parallel examples where dominance is appropriate, plus an attempt to explain why Newcomb's case, although less clear, is still subject to dominance principles, in my original essay, "Newcomb's Problem and Two Principles of Choice" (Essay 2).

This obligation to explain differences in the clarity of parallel examples in order to show that no different decision should be made also rests on those who argued in their letters for taking only what is in the second box. For example, it rests on Robert Heppe of Fairfax, Virginia, who said that the situation "is isomorphic with one in which the human moves first and openly," and on A. S. Gilbert of the National Research Council of Canada, who called the Newcomb case "effectually the same as" one where you act first and an observer attempts to communicate with a "mindreader" in the next room who then guesses your choice, using a payoff matrix identical with Newcomb's.

A large number of those who recommended taking only the second box performed the expected-value calculation and concluded that, provided the probability that the being was correct was at least .5005, they would take only the second box. Not only did they see no problem at all; they either maximized expected monetary value or made utility linear with money in the range of the problem. Otherwise the cutoff probability would be different. William H. Riker of the department of political science at the University of Rochester suggested that people making different decisions merely differed in their utility curves for money. Such persons, however, need not differ in their choices among probability mixtures of monetary amounts in the standard situations in order to calibrate their utilities.

Those who favored taking both boxes made almost no attempt to diagnose the mistakes of the others. An exception is William Bamberger, an economist at Wayne State University. He wrote that the proponent of choosing only the second box "computes not the alternative payoffs of choosing one or two boxes for a given individual, but the average payoff of those who choose two as opposed to the average observed payoff of those who choose one." The problem, of course, is how to compute the probability for a given individual of his payoff for each choice. Should one use the differing conditional probabilities, or ignore them because dominance applies only when the states are probabilistically independent of the action (and so when for each state its conditional probabilities on each act is the same), or ignore them since the conditional probabilities of the state on the acts are to be used only when they represent some process of the act's influencing or affecting which state obtains?

A number of respondents said their choice would depend on whether the predictor made his prediction after they had at least started to consider the problem. If so, they would do their best to decide to take only the second box (so that this data would be available to the predictor), and some added that they hoped they would change their mind at the last minute and take both boxes. (They gave the predictor too little credit.) On the other hand, if the predictor made his prediction before they even considered the problem, these writers believed they would take both boxes, since there was no possibility of their deliberations affecting the prediction that had been made.

Several respondents maintained that if the conditions of the problem could be realized, we might be forced to revise our views about the impossibility of backward causality. Newcomb himself seems to think that special difficulties arise for proponents of backward causality if the predictor writes some term designating an integer on a slip of paper in the second box, with the understanding that you get $1 million only if that integer is a prime. Of course, the predictor writes a prime if, and only if, he predicts that you will take the second box. How can your choice determine whether a number is prime or composite? The advocate of backward causality need not think it does. What your choice affects, in his view, is what term the predictor writes down (or wrote down earlier), not whether the integer it designates is prime or composite.

The reasoning of some of the letters indicates it would be useful to specify precisely the conditions whereby we could discover in which time-direction causality operates. Might one even say that some conditions universally preceding certain decisions are part of the effects of the decision (by backward causality) rather than part of the cause?

Not everyone was willing to choose one or the other action. Among the five respondents who suggested some form of cheating, Robert B. Pitkin, editor of *American Legion Magazine*, speculated that Dr. Matrix, the numerologist, would walk in with a device to scan the contents of the boxes, take the boxes with the money in them and never open an empty box. "He quite naturally succeeded in getting all the money, for the rule of bridge that one peek is worth two finesses applies here too . . . By introducing a choice which the being has not anticipated, and is not permitted to take into account, he achieves a stunning victory for free will." (What prevents the being from taking this into account?)

Other letter writers also struck blows for free will. Nathan Whiting of New York would take both boxes but would open only the first one, leaving the second box unopened. Ralph D. Goodrich, Jr., of Castle Rock, Colorado, would take only the first box. Richard B. Miles of

Los Altos, California, also recommended a "creative" solution: Turn to another person before you make your choice and offer to sell him for $10,000 the contents of whatever box or boxes you choose.

Isaac Asimov wrote: "I would, without hesitation, take both boxes . . . I am myself a determinist but it is perfectly clear to me that any human being worthy of being considered a human being (including most certainly myself) would prefer free will, if such a thing could exist . . . Now, then, suppose you take both boxes and it turns out (as it almost certainly will) that God has foreseen this and placed nothing in the second box. You will then, at least, have expressed your willingness to gamble on his nonomniscience and on your own free will and will have willingly given up a million dollars for the sake of that willingness—itself a snap of the finger in the face of the Almighty and a vote, however futile, for free will . . . And, of course, if God has muffed and left a million dollars in the box, then not only will you have gained that million but *far more important* you will have demonstrated God's nonomniscience. If you take only the second box, however, you get your damned million and not only are you a slave but also you have demonstrated your willingness to be a slave for that million and you are not someone I recognize as human." (No one wrote to argue for taking only the second box on the grounds that either it results in getting $1 million or it demonstrates the being's fallibility, either of which is desirable.)

Those who held that the conditions of the problem could not be realized were of two types. There were those who believed the situation to be physically impossible because the being could not predict all the information input of every light signal that would arrive at your eyes in the appropriate time interval. ("To gain such knowledge the being must have a physical agency for collecting information that travels faster than the speed of light." wrote George Fredericks, a physicist at the University of Texas.) And there were those who argued that if the room is closed, the problem reduces to that of Maxwell's demon—a suggestion made by Fredericks and by John A. Ball of the Harvard College Observatory.

Those who believed the conditions of the problem to be inconsistent as well as physically impossible said that the almost certain predictability of decisions was inconsistent with free will, and therefore with making choices, yet the problem assumed that genuine choices could be made. This is a hard argument to drive through because it appears to be the choices that are predicted. The relevant connections are difficult to get straight. Predictability of decisions does not logically imply determinism under which the decisions are caused (for example, the possibility of backward causality, where an uncaused decision causes an earlier prediction, or "seeing ahead" in time in a block universe).

Nor, we should note in passing, does determinism entail predictability, even in principle. Events could be fixed in accordance with scientific laws that are not recursive. Is determinism incompatible with free will? It seems to many to be so, yet the argument that determinism is incompatible with responsibility for action, which free will implies, depends on a notion of responsibility insufficiently worked out to show precisely how the connections go. Some say merely that a free act is an uncaused one. Yet being uncaused obviously is not sufficient for an act to be free; one surely would not be responsible for such an action. What other conditions, then, must be satisfied by an uncaused act if it is to be a free one? The literature on free will lacks a satisfactory specification of what a free action would be like (given that "uncaused" is not enough). Perhaps if we were given this specification of additional conditions, they would turn out to be sufficient apart from the action's being uncaused.

Another problem will help to exhibit some complicated relations between free will and determinism. It has been asserted (by C. S. Lewis, for instance) that no determinist rationally can believe in determinism, for if determinism is true, his beliefs were caused, including his belief in determinism. The idea seems to be that the causes of belief, perhaps chemical happenings in the brain, might be unconnected with any reasons for thinking determinism true. They might be, but they need not be. The causes might "go through" reasons and be effective only to the extent that they are good reasons. In the same way it might be a causal truth about someone that he is convinced only by arguments that constitute specified types of good reasons (deductive, inductive, explanatory, and so on).

Some philosophers have argued recently that we know some statement p only if part of the cause (or more broadly the explanation) of our believing p is, if we pursue the story far enough, the fact that p is true. You know this magazine is before you now only if its being there is part of the explanation of why you believe it is there. If psychologists are stimulating your brain to create the illusion that you are seeing a magazine, you would not really know there is a magazine before you even if a psychologist happened to have left one on the table in front of you. The magazine's being there would not play the proper causal role in the story of your belief. If we do not mind our beliefs being caused by the facts, and indeed find it somewhat plausible to think we have knowledge only to the extent that they are, then we may also find it less disturbing that our actions are caused by certain types of facts holding in the world, for example, the fact that it would be better to do one thing rather than another. To say this, of course, is not to present a theory of free action; it is merely to hint that it may be possible to remove the sting of determinism. This approach is a comfortable one when we act correctly, but it is difficult to see how it can be extended plausibly to wrong acts where questions of responsibility are paticularly pressing.

Proponents of the C. S. Lewis position might reply that the determinist should not feel so comfortable. Even though he says he is caused to believe in determinism (and anything else) by what are good reasons, he must also maintain that he is caused to believe that such reasons are good reasons. He may have a second set of reasons for believing the first set of reasons are good. Now, however, his opponent can raise the same question as before. Why does he believe the second set of reasons? The determinist must end either by finding self-supporting reasons (which say of themselves that they are good reasons) or by admitting that the best explanation of why he believes they are good reasons is that they are. This surely leaves his opponent unsatisfied, and the match seems to be a draw.

Those who believe in free will find themselves in similar dilemmas. Kurt Rosenwald of Washington wrote: "When I was 19 or 20, I thought about the free-will problem . . . and I came to this conclusion: If we make an exhaustive study of that problem, and finally arrive at the result that our will is free, we still will not know whether our will is indeed free or our mind is of such a nature that we have to find our will to be free, although it is not, in fact, free. This became one of my reasons for studying not philosophy but the natural sciences. Thinking about it now, 50+ years later, it still seems to me that I was right." But does not the possibility that we are caused to believe in false conclusions apply also to conclusions in the natural sciences? And to the verdict of 50+ years later?

I published my original essay after thinking about Newcomb's problem intermittently for five years. In that essay I expressed the hope that someone would come forth with a solution to the problem that would enable me to stop returning to it. It is not surprising that no one did, yet it is surprising (to me) that the mere act of publishing Newcomb's problem, and sending my thoughts on it into the world, rid me of it. That is, I was rid of it until the problem was presented in *Scientific American* and I was invited to read more than 650 pages of letters about it. Unfortunately the letters do not, in my opinion, lay the problem to rest. And they have started me thinking about it again! You can't win.

4   INTERPERSONAL
UTILITY THEORY

✎   ✎   ✎

How might the topic of interpersonal comparisons of utility be brought within the domain of positive economic science as part of a testable and disconfirmable empirical theory? This essay sketches how we could develop such a testable theory of interpersonal comparisons if we already possessed other theories. We do not currently possess these other theories but we do have their beginnings and it is reasonable to think they will be developed adequately in the future. This essay, then, describes only the last part of this route to interpersonal utility theory, the part that builds upon these other theories yet to be developed. To show how it is *possible* for there to be an empirical theory of interpersonal comparisons leaves the nontrivial task of actually carrying through this project but, believing in the division of intellectual labor, I am content to leave that to economists.

No satisfactory general procedure has thus far been devised for making interpersonal comparisons of utility, and many doubt its feasibility despite the fact that we make such comparisons every day on an *ad hoc* and intuitive basis. It would be surprising if our ordinary (and often apparently obvious) judgments were completely built on sand. Yet even the general accuracy of most of our intuitive judgments of interpersonal comparisons does not guarantee the existence of a simple systematic procedure that would explicitly yield these judgments. We seek an explicit systematic procedure that would match those intuitive judgments (or at least delineate those distorting factors which make our judgments differ from the more accurate ones yielded by the procedure) and so sometimes serve as a substitute for intuition, a surrogate. However, this systematic procedure need not replicate the intuitive process we follow; our aim is not an accurate psychological theory of how the judgments get made but a procedure that, by whatever process, yields those judgments.

The central difficulty in devising a systematic procedure is that interpersonal differences in utility (such as the fact that you want something, or prefer one thing to another, more than I do) do not have direct empirical effects, unmediated by people's judgments of them. Such interpersonal differences do not *by themselves* cause any phenomena, or explain any phenomena, except insofar as these differences are recognized by people who act on their discernments. (No single interpersonal difference in utility has a direct effect in the world, but combinations of them might. If I want something more than you do *and* hours of labor have the same disutility for each of us, then I will (be willing to) work for it longer than you do. Hence, one interpersonal difference, that I want something more than you do, has an effect relative to another interpersonal comparison, that labor has the same disutility for us. However, there seems to be no way to separately fix one such interpersonal fact so as to thereby isolate the effect of others, nor is there any obvious way to amass many such joint effects of conjunctions of interpersonal comparisons so as to "triangulate" and fix one single interpersonal comparison.) For example, an explanation of certain redistributive activities might involve people acting on their judgments of interpersonal comparisons (in accordance with a norm which they accept mandating redistribution) while the explanation of their making these judgments might be that they are *true*; the facts are that way and are recognized to be so. In this way, an interpersonal difference in utility might have effects in the world.

These effects, however, do not help us very much, since they are mediated by people's unsystematic and intuitive judgments. A procedure utilizing effects based upon judgments seems shaky. Yet it might be that such intuitive judgments concatenate together in a manner from which system can be extracted, system which can be used to regiment such judgments, correct them and even test them. The analogy is inexact, but compare how preferences, including preferences among probability mixtures, hang together so that the conditions describing their concatenation suffice to yield the existence of a real-valued utility function unique up to a positive linear transformation. From no one particular preference could such information be extracted, only from the pattern they form together. In unity there is strength.

However, even one such procedure, with interpersonal comparisons, will leave us doubtful of its validity. What we need to do, instead, is to *triangulate* interpersonal comparisons, to formulate independent procedures, each with its own virtues as a candidate for grasping interpersonal comparisons. If these independently motivated procedures converge to the same results, to the same judgments of interpersonal comparison, then each procedure will receive additional support and confirmation from the other. Moreover, in concert the procedures may be testable, and falsifiable. One procedure can be used to specify aspects of the utility functions of two people, thereby constraining the range of data compatible with the other procedure. Together, then, the procedures can constitute a theory with empirical consequences and predictive power, hence a testable and falsifiable theory. If the conjoint theory passes such a test, it will receive empirical support. To be sure, like any other theory it will not be thereby *proven* to be true, but we justifiably will gain increased confidence in its accuracy.

A procedure for making interpersonal comparisons of utility will bring together and calibrate the separate utility scales of different individuals. Supposing that we have individual measurements of utility for persons I and II on a Von Neumann–Morgenstern interval scale, a procedure for interpersonal comparisons will fix a common zero point and unit or will fix two common points. It will equate the utility of x for person number I ($u_I(x)$) with the utility of z for person number II and it will equate the utility of y for person number I with the utility of w for person number II.

Suppose that each of those individuals satisfies the Archimedean axiom, so that if a is preferred to b is preferred to c then there is a probability $p (0 < p < 1)$ such that the person is indifferent between b for sure and the option of a with probability p and c with probability $(1 - p)$. Then, given the fixing of two interpersonal points between them, we can bring together the rest of their utility scales. Suppose person I is indifferent between r and a probability p_1 of x and $(1 - p_1)$ of y. Then for any alternatives s on person II's utility scale, $u_1(r) = u_{II}(s)$ if and only if person II is indifferent between s and a probability p_1 of z and $(1 - p_1)$

of w. (It is obvious how to proceed with alternatives not preferentially between the two original interpersonal comparison points.)

The procedure for making interpersonal comparisons can thus calibrate the two scales together, utilizing the Archimedean axiom. However, its ability to do so does not show its interpersonal comparisons are correct. Provided each individual satisfies the Von Neumann–Morgenstern or similar axioms for the existence of utility on an interval scale, the procedure of interpersonal comparisons will not notice anything awry, however it fixes its original points of comparison. For all other points on the scales are equated by their relationships to the two original points and so these later equatings will systematically show the same mistakes, if any, which infected the original comparisons. If "really" $u_I(x)$ is double that of $u_{II}(z)$ and $u_I(y)$ is double that of $u_{II}(w)$ then the $u_I(r)$ that the procedure equated to $u_{II}(s)$ will really be double it. I have here used an example of a ratio distortion but all we know really, solely from the procedure's going smoothly, is that its equatings either are accurate or are systematically distorted in accordance with some linear transformation. To be sure, whatever intuitive reason we had for thinking the procedure plausible will be reason for thinking there is no such systematic distortion. But nevertheless the worry haunts proposals about interpersonal comparisons that although it equates two scales, one is really double the other, or 5 times the other (or more generally, some positive linear transformation of the other). If one was the other writ large, but maintaining the same internal proportions, how could we tell the difference? Previous proposals about interpersonal comparisons, in addition to their own intrinsic defects, have all stumbled on this structural difficulty.

This difficulty can be avoided when we have two distinct independently motivated and independently plausible procedures, P_1 amd P_2, for making interpersonal comparisons. The conjunction of these two proposals constitutes a testable theory. When procedure P_1 is used to equate the two individuals' scales, this establishes predictions about what equatings between the two scales will be made by the operation of the independent procedure P_2. When these predictions are borne out, when the two procedures do mesh in this way, then (the rationale and intuitive power of) each supports the other. The predictions are empirical and need not be borne out. If they are not then the conjunction of the two proposals is disconfirmed—they cannot both be right. But if the predictions are confirmed, this, while it does not *prove* the joint accuracy of the procedures, will legitimately give us increased confidence that some real phenomenon is being described and delineated.

But don't we face the same structural difficulty as before? Mightn't the procedures still yield not accurate equatings but ratio (or positive linear) distortions? With procedure P_1 there is the possibility of such a distorting, and there also is the possibility that procedure P_2 distorts. However, when the two procedures are independent, it is unlikely that they will distort by exactly the same ratio or positive linear transform. Perhaps person II's utility is really double what procedure P_1 says, and perhaps person II's utility is really 9 times what procedure P_2 says. But it would be too much of a coincidence if these two independent procedures, while failing to be accurate, each failed in the same way, each happened to equate their separate units for the two people in the same mistaken ratio (or positive linear) relationship.

When the two independent procedures mesh in their result (and so in their predictions) we need some explanation of this agreement. One explanation is that the two theories are giving accurate renditions of the phenomenon that is out there and so agree. Another explanation is that both are inaccurate and just happen, by a coincidence, to distort by exactly the same factor. However, this "coincidence" will be implausible, especially if the two procedures differ greatly in their intuitive rationale and angle of approach. Third, it might be said that there is a "universal distorting force" which distorts all (otherwise accurate) procedures in exactly the same way. Such issues are familiar in discussions of the special theory of relativity and the extent to which conventional elements enter there. Economists need not worry unduly, I think, if their theory is on the same footing as other well-established parts of empirical science, facing the same philosophical possibilities of universal distorting forces. Finally, failing alternative explanations of the meshing of the two procedures, their independence might be placed into question; whether this is plausible will depend on the details of those procedures.

The structural problem of a procedure's being distorted is avoided by a conjunctive theory which proposes more than one procedure. (Ideally, it would be better to have more than just two independent procedures.) But if this avoidance strategy is to work, it must yield success early. If over the years researchers investigate many procedures and find that two mesh in their predictions, we cannot then conclude that they are accurate. For it is not unlikely, in that case of investigating many procedures, that we will encounter two inaccurate ones which, coincidentally, happen to distort by the same ratio. When large numbers of procedures are investigated, coincidence becomes a perfectly plausible explanation of the agreement of some two of them. Therefore, if our strategy is to work, we need to investigate accurate procedures early. The strategy, I think, is a promising one but the two procedures I propose later may well be inadequate (either not plausible or not independently motivated). I cannot, though, offer a general genial invitation to others to join in the effort and make their own proposals about procedures. You will understand if I invite only those with *good* ideas and good intuitions about interpersonal comparison procedures to make proposals so that the number investigated will not become too large too soon. (Once early success is achieved other, sleeker procedures, agreeing with the first established ones, can enter the field. It would raise interesting questions, of course, if two groups of proposals were found, each group's members meshing but the two groups differing.)

I have said the separate procedures, jointly testable, would be independently motivated. What sort of motivation can such a procedure have? It can yield some of the particular judgments of interpersonal comparison we make with confidence. Also it can yield some of the summary generalizations and maxims we have confidence in as holding *ceteris paribus*. For example, just about everyone finds it intuitive and plausible that a given additional amount of money will have less utility for a rich person than for a poor one. (To repeat, when all other things are equal; the amount might enable some particularly important threshold to be passed by the rich person, while not doing anything comparably important for the poor person.)

If a given procedure for making interpersonal comparisons yields this as a consequence, without simply building it in as an *ad hoc* feature, then the procedure will gain credibility. Yielding that intuitive result, one we have much confidence in, is from the point of view of evidential support like yielding some observable consequences. A theory that yields what any correct theory in that area must yield, whether this be observable consequences or intuitively correct generalizations, thereby reveals its mettle.

In addition, there are some metaconditions on proposals. For example, a proposal about interpersonal comparisons should, when applicable, be plausible as a proposal about intrapersonal intertemporal comparisons of utility. It should be plausible that it yields correct utility comparisons for the *same* person at different times (when it applies to yield any comparisons of that sort). A proposal that obviously fell down for one person over time could not be correct for two people. This metacondition is not empty, since we may have firmer intuitions about intrapersonal intertemporal comparisons than about interpersonal ones, and so we may filter out in this way some proposals about interpersonal comparisons.

My suggestion of how to proceed on the topic of interpersonal comparisons, then, is to formulate plausible and independently motivated procedures and check to see whether they converge to (approximately) the same results (and are plausible, when applicable, for intrapersonal intertemporal comparisons). When these independent proposals converge, bringing along their own supporting struts, then it will be rational to believe there is a real phenomenon "out there" they are delineating and demarcating. (Compare the situation in logic where three separate important notions which arose independently, general recursiveness, lambda-definability, and computability, turned out to delimit exactly the same functions.) What otherwise explains the convergence?

This seems a sensible way to proceed on the topic, unbefuddled by the philosophical problem of "other minds." This "other minds" problem also would apply to specifying a utility function for another person, apart from any issues about interpersonal comparisons. Though there is behavior, how do we know a *preference* is exhibited, or that a *choice* is made, or that the person is *aware* of the different alternatives available, or how the person *conceives* of the alternative selected, or what probability *judgments* the person makes, and so on. Since the procedure for interpersonal comparisons is to be a systematized surrogate for our ordinary intuitive judgments, not a solution to the philosophical problem of other minds, it is permissible for that procedure to utilize psychological predicates (not involving interpersonal comparisons) which apply to other people. It would be real progress, even, to somehow get from the existence claim that some procedure or other for interpersonal comparisons exists to a particular determinate procedure. Must our procedures avoid other "circles," though? Would it be all right to use a procedure whose very operation and application involved utilizing particular intuitive judgments of interpersonal comparisons? Not if the purpose is to justify making interpersonal comparisons, to show that there can be correct ones, but it would be permissible if the purpose is to find an efficient surrogate for the mess of our intuitive judgments. A procedure that utilized only a few such intuitive judgments might constitute a great advance in systematization. Intermediate purposes will raise more delicate questions about the legitimacy of circularities.

The triangulation strategy can yield genuine progress and illumination, even though it does not *prove* its hypotheses, by making "interpersonal comparisons" a topic *within* empirical social science. Within this framework, the difficulties which remain have a familiar character; they are the ones attendant upon any endeavor to fit a theory to data, thereby tentatively supporting the theory. After procedures are found which can be shown to work, there will be the task of discovering the deeper explanation of why they, in particular, do so.

Utility, as we are concerned with it here, is a measure of how much someone wants/desires a particular situation to obtain or continue. (More accurately, it is concerned with the magnitude of the desire/want as expressed in choice and other behavior, verbal reports of preference, etc. These may reveal, as the psychoanalysts tell us, only a portion of the magnitude of what's there in the unconscious yet reveals itself more deviously in compromise formations. It would be a very different sort of theory than utility theory as currently investigated that could get to desires partially masked in these and other ways.) The utility we discuss here is not a measure of the resulting *level* of want-satisfaction or felt well-being. If I want an additional \$1,000 exactly as much as David Rockefeller wants an additional \$55,000, this does not mean that when each of us gains our desire we end up at an equal level of overall satisfaction or felt well-being or wealth. We are equally satisfied *by* gaining our wish but we need not be equally satisfied in result of gaining our wish. The increment we each gain is equal but the resulting level we attain will not be equal if we do not start from equal levels to begin with.

Interpersonal comparisons of increments rather than levels may not be useful for purposes of redistribution according to some theories. It will serve, however, for retribution where, roughly, we compare how much this victim diswants the change inflicted on him with how much this wrongdoer diswants the change involved in a candidate punishment. (For more details, including discounting punishment by the wrongdoer's degree of responsibility, see Nozick, 1981, chap. 5, part III.) We don't try to put the wrongdoer at the same absolute level as where his victim ends up. A person who does mild harm to an already miserable person does not deserve to end up as totally miserable as his victim, nor does someone who mildly injures someone much happier than himself thereby deserve to have his own level *raised* significantly to become on a par with his victim's. It is sometimes said that in meting out retributive punishment we are "playing God"; however, our retribution is designed only to achieve certain incremental changes while divine justice, if it existed, presumably would focus upon a person's resulting absolute level. (Different kinds of interpersonal comparisons are distinguished in Sen, 1979.)

Zero Point

Utility functions measured on an interval scale, such as those of Von Neumann and Morgenstern, are unique up to a positive linear transformation. Like the familiar Fahrenheit and Centigrade scales of temperature, they have an arbitrary zero point and an arbitrary unit. (In the familiar formula, Fahrenheit equals (9/5) Centigrade +32; the 9/5 scales from one arbitrary unit to another, while the +32 moves from one arbitrary zero point to another.) The problem of interpersonal comparisons is to specify, for two persons' utility functions which are given, a common unit and a common zero point, to calibrate their utility functions so that the unit on each represents the same difference of utility for each, and the zero point on each represents the same degree of wanting.

Most people, learning the utility lingo, fall quite naturally into speaking of positive and negative utility, although this has no basis within the Von Neumann–Morgenstern mode of measurement, where the zero point might fall anywhere. It seems plausible that things (situations, states of affairs, etc.) that are wanted or desired have positive utility for the person while things that are diswanted, that are desired-not, have negative utility for the person. Zero utility, then, would apply to things, situations, changes that are neither wanted nor diswanted, to things the person is indifferent about.

My preference would be to specify zero utility directly in terms of indifference. While for some purposes it may be more desirable to proceed with a zero defined in this way, I am not sure it is necessary or appropriate here. Indeed, since we are not attempting interpersonal comparisons of resulting utility *levels* perhaps the issue of the zero can be avoided altogether and we need only pursue the task of finding a common unit. (Some economists, I know, will think me quixotic or confused in focussing any attention upon the zero point when level comparisons are not at stake. I prefer to think I persist because there is some presupposition of the economist's approach which I am denying, but my case would be stronger, I admit, if I could explicitly identify that presupposition which, once denied, necessitates my approach.) Therefore, readers who object to the words of this section can minimize their irritation by proceeding directly to the next section on the unit.

Since we are not attempting to make interpersonal comparisons of utility levels but rather of utility differences or units, the fixing of the zero point may appear, if it is necessary at all, trivial. Economists may simply want to say that something has zero utility if it has zero marginal utility. (Is there room, though, for the question of whether this provides an *interpersonal* zero? Must what has zero marginal utility for you be wanted the same by you as I want what has zero marginal utility for me?)

My preference, I have said, is to specify zero utility directly in terms of the notion of being indifferent about something, neither wanting it nor diswanting it. To be indifferent about an alternative x is to be indifferent between x and not-x. Something x has zero utility for a person if and only if $x I$ not-x; if and only if he is indifferent between having x and not, between x's occurring and not. It makes no difference to the person whether x or not-x, no difference he cares anything about. Similarly, we can understand x's having positive utility for a person as the person's preferring x to not-x; x has negative utility for the person if he prefers not-x to x.

In one way this is more general than the economist's usual way of proceeding, in another less general. We are not restricted, as with marginal utility, only to repeatable units; however, in the notation here, the variables $x, y, \ldots$ range not over total states but over partial ones, or aspects of total states. Thus, when we speak of preferences between (partial) alternatives, these are conditional on implicit things. It is a mistake, I think, to believe one has actually specified everything the preference depends upon; for each purported full description one can always find further factors, left out, whose variation affects the preference. This is no reason not to make these even more explicit but it is a reason not to use a theoretical structure which supposes that everything relevant already has been made explicit.

It seems plausible to use indifference between x and not-x as a criterion of x's having zero utility. But this use, even in the case of one person, depends upon a further empirical fact. It must also be the case that:

> If a person is indifferent between x and not-x, and that person also is indifferent between y and not-y, then the person is indifferent between x and y.

(And also indifferent between x and not-y, and also between not-x and y. However, since indifference is an equivalence relation, we needn't state these as additions.) There has to be indifference all around. For if the person preferred x to y, the utility function, assigning zero to everything, would not mirror preference. The above indented condition is an empirical precondition for using indifference between something's obtaining and not in order to specify a zero point on the person's utility scale. (Sometimes, though, it's not being satisfied will indicate that the alternatives were illegitimately specified, that they were contrary but not contradictory alternatives, relative but not absolute complements.)

Proceeding in this way, there is room to raise the question of whether this procedure serves to fix a *common* zero point for the two people. If one person is generally enthusiastic or even manic, mightn't his being indifferent between x and not-x represent a more positive state of wanting each than is represented by a depressed person's attitude toward y when he is indifferent between y and not-y? However, by utility we refer to strength of want, not to hedonic tone. Even if everything about life feels better to a manic person, an alternative he's indifferent about when manic isn't wanted more by him than an alternative someone else is indifferent about when depressed. What may be true, though, is that a depressed person has far more indifferences than average; getting depressed is a process in which many preferences are replaced by indifferences.

Unit: Bargaining

Facts of interpersonal differences in utility, I have said, do not have direct empirical consequences unmediated by people's discernings of those differences. I mean interpersonal differences as embodied in different magnitudes on the *same* side of the zero point. Of course, if x has positive utility for me but negative utility for you, then this difference alone, unmediated by people's discerning of the differences, may give rise to the fact that I seek x while you shun it.

To establish an interpersonal unit, we turn to consider consequences of interpersonal differences mediated by people's (apparent) discerning of these. One way would be simply to survey people's opinions about particular comparisons but, given the low motivation people will have to provide accurate (and checkable) answers, such survey material would be most unreliable; moreover, its particular results would not find a place in any systematic context. Far better to examine people's behavior, what we might call their revealed beliefs, about interpersonal comparisons. Some will be shown in situations involving redistributive activities but these activities will be a compound product of *normative* beliefs, actual interpersonal comparisons and self-interested distortions of these which feed into the normative beliefs to one's own benefit. Though a positive theory someday will need to be offered of people's normative behavior, that area is far too undeveloped to build upon even programatically now. It will be more fruitful to consider behavior which, though mediated by people's judgments of interpersonal comparisons, is not also mediated through their *normative* beliefs.

We therefore turn to an area already lying within positive economic science, for which (positive) economists already have proposed explanatory theories: bargaining and threat situations. When two of us stand to gain by reaching a mutual agreement or bargain, as compared to the situation of our not agreeing, yet various different agreements can be reached about which we have divergent preferences, what determines which (if any) agreement will be reached? What determines which party will get more of what he wants? A particular case of this is the one of bilateral monopoly; between the highest price one party is willing to pay and the lowest the other is willing to accept lie a range of mutually beneficial agreements, about which the parties have conflicting preferences. It is well known that we lack a fully adequate theory, for these cases, of where on the contract curve a bargain will be struck.

The formulated theories of bargaining mention many factors which might enter here, such as bargaining skill. It seems plausible that one factor will play an especially crucial role, namely, which party will be hurt more by no agreement. And here, as before, we do not refer to absolute levels of illfare when there is no agreement but rather increment in (what may be already existing) hurt due to nonagreement. The question is: who diswants no agreement more? (I am aware that not all theories of bargaining include such an interpersonal comparison, for example the theory (following Zeuthen) of John Harsanyi. Others already have criticized its mechanism of concessions. We might note that, within such a framework, it would be more plausible to develop a stochastic theory, where the parties' maximum tolerable probabilities of no agreement do not determine which one concedes, but only fix their respective probabilities of making the next concession.)

On our view here, bargaining (and not merely arbitration) theories will utilize interpersonal comparisons of utility. The party that stands to *lose* more if there is failure to reach agreement is (particularly) vulnerable to a threat by the other to leave. Here lies a great incentive for the more vulnerable party, if not to accept the other's most preferred terms, at least to make some concession, to be the one to give a little in the process of negotiations. George Homans, following others, incorporates within his theory of social exchange *the principle of least interest*: That person is able to dictate the conditions of association whose interest in the continuation of the affair is least; the party to the exchange who gets the lesser reward from it is less likely to change his behavior in favor of the other than is the party who gets the greater; the person who is perceived by the other as the less interested, the more indifferent to the exchange, is apt to have the greater power (Homans, 1974, pp. 73–74).

What is the appropriate baseline from which to measure each person's gains from the agreement? The theories of bargaining differ on this point. In Nash's model, followed by Harsanyi, this baseline is the no-agreement situation wherein both parties carry out their threats. Others have suggested the baseline is what the parties would receive if they treated the situation as a noncooperative game and maximized their security level, employing their minimax strategy. Or should the (shifting) baseline be the utility one party would receive from the other party's last offer?

It is not our purpose to present a specific theory of bargaining situations here. We shall proceed as though one such is available, presupposing interpersonal comparisons; but our purposes here would equally well be served if a theory utilized different baselines for different types of bargaining situations. Let us imagine the following, described vaguely. Each offer by one party establishes a new *status quo* point for the other party, replacing (the previous one offered which replaced . . .) the original baseline point (whether no agreement at all or the security level). The cost to the other party of breaking off the negotiations and leaving is now what he would have received under this most recent offer. If no agreement is reached, each of the parties stands to lose the difference between the last best offer they received and the baseline situation. The party that stands to lose the most makes the next concession. And he must concede enough to transform the situation into one where the other party stands to lose the most; otherwise the first one simply will have to make another concession immediately. Whether he makes the *least* concession sufficient to put the next move up to the other party, or he makes a larger concession in an attempt to reach agreement right then, may well depend upon other factors. (Notice that, starting with the *status quo* point, this theory holds that the one worst off under this, or forgoing the most under this, will make the first concession, one sizable enough to pass the new vulnerability to threat over to the other party. Compare how the Zeuthen-Harsanyi theory makes the identity of the concession maker dependent on who is willing to bear the greater probability of no agreement, where the concession is of a magnitude to shift this burden.)

Be the details as they may, the important point for us is that the process of bargaining, and the final result, will be importantly determined by the interpersonal comparisons the parties make. Each considers who gets hurt more, the other party or himself, and acts accordingly. Notice that each *wants* it to be the case that the other party will be hurt more, so when one party does make the concession, this reflects a particular interpersonal comparison he makes, and concedes, only reluctantly. It is in his interests not to acknowledge the fact that he is the one who will be hurt more, as it also is in his interests, if he *is* the one who will be hurt more by no agreement, to make a concession in order to reach agreement. So when he *does* make this concession, when both parties know *he* must make the concession, then both are agreeing in the interpersonal comparison they make. One happily and the other sorrowfully, they both agree which one will be hurt more.

What accounts for this agreement, so reluctantly wrung from one and acknowledged by him? One possible explanation is that he *is* the one who will be hurt more, and both discern this fact, and also the other's discernment of their knowledge, etc. To be sure, the other party may be a skillful faker, dissembler, actor, or liar, yet the first party has much incentive to see through this. Often, when both believe one will suffer more, and that one concedes, this is because they both know it is true and act accordingly on their knowledge.

Might not who concedes depend, not upon who will suffer the greater increment of hurt if there is no agreement, but upon who will suffer the greatest relative hurt as indicated by the ratio of hurt-increment to some measure of overall well-being? Might not the conceder be he who suffers the greatest percentage hurt, so that the bargaining situation cannot provide us with an interpersonal comparison of increment in utility? (I am indebted to Benjamin Friedman for raising these questions.) The intuition is that the percentage the hurt represents is what is important and will guide behavior. But Von Neumann–Morgenstern utility is a measure of preference, of how much someone wants or cares about something, not of intensity of pleasurable sensations. Perhaps it is a certain ratio that people do care about in their choices. If so, that is what is reflected in their utility functions and that is what is to be compared interpersonally. Such interpersonal comparisons of Von Neumann–Morgenstern utility are not designed to capture some notion of "equivalent well-being" but only of "equally wanting." (A similar point applies to a ratio-relativized treatment, rather than an absolute one, of the vertical axis in the utility curve for money.)

We are encouraged by the shared judgment of interpersonal differences by the participants in the bargaining situation, especially since it arises in a context devoid of normative desires to redistribute. The reluctant concessions are the solidest rock on which to build. But can we make something of this shared judgment, can we elaborate it into a systematic procedure for making interpersonal comparisons?

One procedure would involve overlap in separate bargaining situations. Two people, B and C, bargain separately with A, who is in the same situation both times with respect to *his* own potential gains and losses. If A concedes to B but does not concede to C (who instead concedes to him), then we can tentatively conclude that A would be hurt more than B would if no agreement were reached in their bargaining situation, while A would be hurt less than C would if no agreement were reached in *their* bargaining situation. We thereby can conclude that B is hurt less in the first situation than C is in the second, even though B and C do not interact together. We can test this result by putting B and C in a joint bargaining situation together where their stakes are exactly what they were in the previous separate situations with A. If the prediction that C will concede to B is borne out, then this provides reinforcing confirmation of that earlier interpersonal comparison.

This theory will utilize situations where the party's relationships are impersonal enough so that A can be in the very same situation, with respect to his own potential gains and losses, with B and C. Moreover, A in interacting with B doesn't know or take into account the fact that C will come. (His likelihood of external alternatives is the same in the AB and the AC situations.) Just as these factors have to be controlled, so might others. Ideally, we would want to utilize a bargaining theory which took account of all factors affecting bargaining behavior so that our mini-test bargaining situations (between A and B, and A and C) would hold constant all relevant factors other than who gets hurt more by no agreement, so that this alone could be isolated and determined. Alternatively, with a full and explicit theory, the other parameters might be allowed to vary in known ways while still one could determine which party gets hurt more by no agreement.

By chaining together people in a multiple network of bargaining, we may hope to determine (and test) an interpersonal fixing of the unit. Notice that this chaining together of different people in a network of bargaining situations need not provide sufficient information for full and general measurement of utility. That can be done by a standard Von Neumann–Morgenstern procedure. Given this individual utility measurement, our network of bargaining situations need only bring the different individuals into mutual interpersonal comparison.

Unit: Utility of Money

The discussion of bargaining describes how interpersonal comparison points might be extracted from people's behavior in bargaining situations, from their actions based upon their (implicit) judgment of interpersonal comparisons as they act self-interestedly. It would be desirable to have a procedure that directly establishes interpersonal comparisons, without going through people's judgments of such comparisons, even when the judgments are implicit and self-interested. (Such comparisons that do not go through people's judgment, we have said, are not needed for positive explanatory purposes.)

Supposing interpersonal comparisons *are* possible, what would we expect a comparison procedure to look like? It is not likely that some particular item, say oreo ice cream, will have the same utility for everyone and thereby demarcate an interpersonal comparison. What we should expect, instead, is that some *structural* fact will pick out the same utility for everyone, some salient structural feature of a utility curve. Again, it seems hardly likely that this will be a structural feature of the utility curve for a particular item, such as oreo ice cream, for it seems likely that here people will show the widest variation.

The more general the item, the more widespread it is in a common role in people's lives and the less specific its purposes, the more promising it is as a candidate to exhibit structural features that will serve to peg interpersonal comparisons. If a general procedure for making direct interpersonal comparisons is possible, it will be based upon salient structural features of the utility curves for something thusly general. For example, money. It is to the utility curve for money (or someplace similar), if anywhere, that we should look to base our direct theory.

The St. Petersburg paradox and its generalizations led theorists to assert that the utility of money is not linear with its amount or with the log of its amount and there is a finite upper bound to the utility of (any amount of) money. However, theorists have proposed different hypotheses about the shape of the utility curve for money.

In 1948, M. Friedman and L. J. Savage considered how the shape of the utility curve for money was related to willingness to undergo risk, in particular how the convexity or concavity of the curve was related to willingness to gamble, or to buy insurance. Let money or wealth be measured along the horizontal axis, and the utility of the amount be measured, by a Von Neumann–Morgenstern procedure, along the vertical axis. A gamble between two amounts of money M_1 and M_2 is a prospect of receiving M_1 with probability p and M_2 with probability $(1 - p)$. When amounts M_1 and M_2 have utilities $u(M_1)$ and $u(M_2)$, we graph these facts as points a and b. A gamble between M_1 and M_2 will be located somewhere along the straight line between a and b. (See Figure 4.1.) Its precise location will depend upon the particular probability p (of M_1) involved in the gamble. Note that it is not a trivial fact that the gamble falls along the straight line. The expected monetary value of the gamble, $p \times M_1 + (1 - p) \times M_2$, will fix its x-coordinate and its vertical location places it along the straight line because, within the Von Neumann–Morgenstern procedure for measuring utility, the utility of a gamble is its expected utility. Thus, the utility of this gamble is $p \times u(M_1) + (1 - p) \times u(M_2)$.

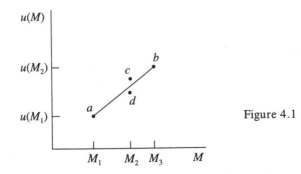

Figure 4.1

We now can ask which the person would prefer, the gamble or receiving (for sure) the expected monetary value of the gamble. Which does the person prefer (or is he indifferent): the gamble of receiving M_1 with probability p and M_2 with probability $(1 - p)$, or definitely receiving an amount of money M_3 which is equal to $p \times M_1 + (1 - p) \times M_2$? If the person prefers the expected monetary amount M_3 for sure to the gamble, then M_3 has a higher utility to him than the gamble, and therefore the utility of M_3 is *above* the straight line connecting points a and b, for instance at point c. If, however, the person prefers the gamble to M_3 for sure, then the utility of amount M_3 is below the straight line connecting a and b, for instance at point d.

Therefore a person will not gamble if or where his utility curve for money (around his present income) is convex from below, and so above the straight line connecting the endpoints. However, preferring sure things to gambles, he will insure within this range. If the utility curve (around his present income) is concave from below, and so below the straight line connecting the endpoints, the person will not insure but will gamble.

Friedman and Savage (1948) proposed that the utility curve for money was first convex, then concave, and then convex again, with two inflection points (see Figure 4.2). According to their hypothesis, if the person's present income is within the first convexity, at M_1 say, he will not gamble, and similarly for the last convexity at M_3, while if it is at M_2, within the concavity, he will gamble rather than insure.

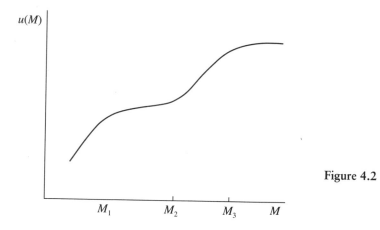

Figure 4.2

Soon afterwards, Harry Markowitz (1952) proposed a modification of the Friedman-Savage hypothesis. Markowitz pointed out that individuals at all income levels may choose *both* to gamble and to insure. Moreover, according to the Friedman-Savage hypothesis, people whose current income is in the middle concave range should like large symmetric bets giving them a 1/2 chance of great wealth and a 1/2 chance of poverty; and also people "almost" at the height of the rightmost convexity should like a fair bet that either moves him to that or (if he loses) lowers him to the height of the first convexity. To avoid these Friedman-Savage consequences, neither of which is observed, Markowitz proposes another curve. The utility function for levels of wealth above current wealth is first concave and then convex. The utility function going from present wealth downward is first convex, then concave. Putting these two together, we get the Markowitz hypothesis (Figure 4.3). There are three inflection points, with the middle inflection point being present (or "customary") wealth. The function is concave immediately above present wealth and convex immediately below it. (Markowitz also suggests that people avoid symmetric bets, so that the curve will fall faster to the left of the origin than it rises to the right.)

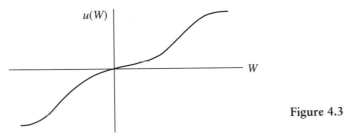

Figure 4.3

So things stood for many years, with the Friedman-Savage and Markowitz hypotheses receiving major attention and minor wrinkles. Recently two psychologists, Amos Tversky and Daniel Kahneman (1979), made yet another proposal, where the origin is a neutral reference point. (Tversky and Kahneman also present hypotheses about the "framing" of a decision, to account for where that neutral reference point will be placed.) Their curve is S-shaped, concave about the reference point and convex below it, with response to losses more extreme than response to gains.

Notice that each of these proposals concerns the general shape of the curve. It is not suggested that we each exhibit exactly the same curve, with dollar amounts filled in. Ten thousand dollars may be worth more to you than to David Rockefeller. What has been suggested is that different people's utility curves for money have the same general structure, though they will differ at which amounts along the x-axis the inflection points come. No doubt, other theorists will propose curves in addition to these, and we may hope someday to possess an adequate detailed theory of the contours of the utility curve for money. Perhaps it will be discovered that not everyone fits the same-shaped curve, or that the shapes change during the life cycle. I leave these complications aside for now.

To proceed to a particular procedure for interpersonal comparisons, we would need to utilize a particular curve, accepted as descriptively adequate. We can, however, say *how* we *would* proceed, even though we lack a final theory. Our procedure, we hope, is robust enough to take account of future advances in the fields of bargaining theory, utility theory and the utility curves for money. It is reasonable for our sketch of a program for interpersonal comparisons to build on the best extant theories, even while recognizing their inadequacies. When we know the details of fully adequate theories we then can check whether the program is indeed feasible. These remarks clearly apply to our use of utility curves for money but also to our use of Von Neumann–Morgenstern utility theory. If following a similar program with a mathematically restrictive non–Von Neumann–Morgenstern utility theory and its salient structural features led to different and incompatible comparisons, then we would have to check which best fit other features (intuitive judgments, general maxims, etc.). If both jibed equally well with different portions of the rest of our beliefs, we might conclude we had discovered *two* distinct real phenomena out there. Which each approach demarcates would depend, of course, on the details of those two theories.

If everyone does conform to the same-shaped Von Neumann–Morgenstern utility curve for money, this is a striking fact. Though located differently, each person's curve will exhibit the same structural features. We may utilize some of these salient structural features as (proposed) points of interpersonal comparison. The measurement of utility for an individual is unique only up to a positive linear transformation. Therefore, only those structural features (of the utility curve for money) that are invariant under positive linear transformations are candidates for interpersonal comparison points. The rest aren't even starters in the contest, e.g., being an amount of money where the curve has a slope of 1/2. That amount will shift for one person, depending upon how we scale his utilities. Only those structural points that are fixed stably for one person, being invariant under positive linear transformations, possess the stability needed to possibly mark points of interpersonal comparison.

An especially salient feature of the curves proposed by Friedman-Savage, and by Markowitz, are their inflection points. These points of inflection are invariant under positive linear transformations, and it seems plausible to propose these as pegs for interpersonal comparisons. (Those more sophisticated mathematically than I might focus upon other features which are invariant under positive linear transformations, and consider their intuitive suitability as pegs for interpersonal comparisons.) Supposing the Friedman-Savage hypothesis, for the moment, we equate in utility that amount of money M_1 where your curve first inflects with that possibly different amount M_2 where my curve first inflects. The utility of M_1 for you is the same as the utility of M_2 for me. Similarly for the second inflection points N_1 and N_2; these too contribute a point of interpersonal comparison. The Markowitz hypothesis involves three inflection points, but these are not all equally plausible as pegs for interpersonal unit comparison. (His middle point represents current income, which we would not want to hold must represent the same utility level for everyone. If it represents instead the same difference in utility for different people, that difference will be zero.) Thus, we propose Markowitz's first and third inflection points as interpersonal comparison points. The Tversky-Kahneman proposals about the curves, thus far only roughly formulated, present no inflection points as candidates for interpersonal comparison pegs. If further refinement of their proposal incorporates salient structural features, invariant under positive linear transformations, then these might be utilized in a proposal about interpersonal comparisons.

Earlier we mentioned the possibility that the different-shaped curves might fit different folks. Our proposal about interpersonal comparisons thus far have concerned only intrashaped comparisons, not intershaped comparison. When precise specifications of the different curves are available, perhaps intershape comparison points (or mappings) then will suggest themselves; if curves vary also in a systematic way within the person's life cycle, then intrapersonal intertemporal comparisons, if they could be made, might then be used to suggest interpersonal intershape comparison points.

Some may think it not really plausible to pick inflection points on the utility curves for money as interpersonal comparison points, even though these are salient structural features invariant under positive linear transformations and they are the type of peg there would be if there is any interpersonal comparison peg at all. For it may seem that the only thing the location of these points reflect is people's attitudes toward risk.

But people's attitudes toward risking money may well depend upon the utility of that amount of money to them. Using (comparative) behavior in a risky situation to indicate the (comparative) utility of money is not *in principle* more objectionable than using one person's preferences among risky alternatives, probability mixtures, to indicate the strength of his preferences among simple nonrisky alternatives.

To be sure, the Von Neumann–Morgenstern procedures for individual utility measurement, if they are infected by attitudes toward risk, are infected by each person's own attitudes and presumably hold that somewhat constant in their scaling of that individual. The interpersonal case is more hazardous. Yet the Von Neumann–Morgenstern procedure does not allow attitudes toward risk free leeway; certain attitudes are eliminated by the axiomatic conditions themselves, upon which the utility measurement is based. For example, the condition that if xIy then $px, (1 - p)zIpy, (1 - p)z$ rules out giving special weight to possible failure to get anything. If a person were indifferent between \$2,000 for sure and 1/2 (\$8,000), 1/2 (\$0) only because he's *sure* to get something good in the first case, this feature will be altered when both alternatives are embedded in yet another gamble, for example 1/10 (\$2,000), 9/10 (\$0) vs. 1/10 [1/2(\$8,000), 1/2 (\$0)], 9/10 (\$0), where now he's not sure to get something good on either alternative. The above Von Neumann–Morgenstern condition excludes preferences based on attitudes about risk insofar as the relevant risky feature or distinction can vary or disappear when the alternatives are uniformly embedded in yet wider gambles. *If* the Friedman-Savage and Markowitz curves are indeed Von Neumann–Morgenstern utility curves for money, then many differing attitudes about risk already are excluded in the individual case and so cannot later arise to contaminate the interpersonal comparison. Nonetheless, one would welcome an adequate theory of individual choice that explicitly builds in parameters representing attitude toward risk. If this were obtained, our proposal about interpersonal comparison pegs could control for varying risk attitudes, as independently specified and measured in separate individual choice situations. Alternatively, one could allow these attitudes toward risk to vary yet utilize the theory to take full account of how this known variation affects where the inflection points on the utility curves for money will fall and introduce interpersonal comparison pegs only after first correcting for any distortion in the inflection point's position that was introduced by attitudes toward risk.

Utilizing inflection points of the utility curves for money seems especially well suited (though not guaranteed) to yield another intuitive consequence. It should turn out that, *ceteris paribus*, for positive amounts of money or gains, the rightmost inflection points for wealthy people will occur at greater amounts of money than the structurally corresponding inflection points for poor people. We should, that is, discover it to be a consequence of the proposal about interpersonal comparisons, that a given fixed amount of money will have *less* utility for a wealthy person (since his inflection points come higher up) than for a poor person. Yielding this intuitive consequence supports the proposal about interpersonal comparisons whereas having the opposite consequence, or the one that there is no difference in the utility of money between the wealthy and the poor, would disconfirm a proposal about interpersonal comparisons. (If the rich and poor person's utility curves for money crossed somewhere in the upper right quadrant, we then might have to refine our simply put intuitive maxim.) The philosopher David Gordon has suggested to me a further prediction, using both bargaining and monetary situations, namely, given a plausible measure of bargaining power intrinsic to the structure of bargaining situations and their outcomes, that generally a poor person will have less bargaining power than a rich person—either than a rich person with whom he bargains or than a rich person would if he were in that situation.

We now have before us, given the proposal about a common zero point, two routes towards a common unit: one based upon concessions in bargaining situations and the other upon the utility curve for money. These routes are independent of each other; neither depends upon the rationale for, or the results of, the other. When both proposals are made, as stated earlier, their conjunction has empirical and testable consequences. When the bargaining procedure specifies as interpersonal comparison points P_1 for the first person and P_2 for the second, we can empirically determine where the first person's inflection point M_1 on the utility curve for money is in relation to his point P_1. Then we can check whether the second person's corresponding inflection point M_2 stands in that very same relation to his own P_2. For example, using the zero point and the Archimedean condition we can discover what particular probability mixture of the outside alternatives, with probability r, is indifferent to the preferentially middle one as a sure thing. With that particular probability in hand, we can now predict the relationship of the second person's corresponding inflection point M_2 to the zero point and his interpersonal comparison point P_2 from the bargaining situation. For that second relationship will involve the very same probability r that was observed in the earlier case.

If we use the bargaining procedure more fully, along with standard Von Neumann–Morgenstern individual utility measurement, to fully calibrate each individual's utility scales and bring them into comparison, then we can make a prediction, knowing one individual's inflection points on his utility curve for money, about the monetary amounts at which the other person's curve will inflect. The failure of this prediction would refute the conjunction of the two proposals, while the prediction's success would confirm (though not definitely prove) the conjunctive theory. When they mesh, there is reason to believe both theories demarcate the same real external phenomenon. To be sure, there remains the theoretical possibility that though they each portray some real-world phenomenon, they do so in a distorted way and in the same distorted way, distorted by the *same* ratio or positive linear transformation. However, this will be an implausible coincidence if the two theories are independent in their motivation and angle of approach.

This, then, is the appropriate time to mention one worry about the independence of the two particular procedures I have discussed. The money utility curve procedure is direct, not based upon anyone's judgments of interpersonal comparison (other than our own in proposing the procedure, but these judgments aren't utilized *within* the procedure). The bargaining procedure is indirect, based upon people's concessions due to implicit and self-interested judgments of interpersonal comparison. Mightn't the bargainers themselves make these judgments as estimates of the first procedure's direct facts? If these bargainers choose to concede or not depending upon their (implicit) beliefs about each other's utility curves for money and where they inflect, then the jibing of the two procedures will not indicate that an independently existing phenomenon is demarcated. To be sure, the bargaining situations often will involve not monetary amounts but other objects or joint activities and projects. (Who will be hurt more if we can't agree about what movie to go to see and instead go our separate ways?) But if these too are implicitly calibrated by being equated with monetary amounts, *and judged by relationship to inflection points,* then the indirect procedure will have been contaminated by our particular direct procedure and hence not be independent of it.

Clearly, it would be desirable to have a conjoint theory of interpersonal comparisons which utilizes two direct independently motivated and mutually supportive procedures. I have no other direct procedure to propose now. Perhaps the extension of economic analysis to topics outside its traditional domain, such as education and family behavior, will uncover still other general utility curves displaying salient structural features suitable to peg interpersonal comparisons.

This essay has not presented a specific procedure for making interpersonal comparisons, but only sketched a program toward that goal. We now can see how it is possible to have an empirical theory of interpersonal comparisons. Others (in accordance with our earlier warning, perceptive others!) will have to formulate the necessary prerequisite theories of bargaining and the utility curves for money, fill in the details, propose still other independent procedures, and perform the empirical tests. When the topic of interpersonal comparisons is thereby brought within the domain of empirical theory, I hope it will please us all, equally.

5 | ON AUSTRIAN METHODOLOGY

The major figures of the Austrian tradition in economic theory are Carl Menger and Frederick von Weiser, originators of marginal utility theory, Eugen von Böhm-Bawerk, and in this century Ludwig von Mises and the co-winner of the 1974 Nobel Prize in Economics, Frederick Hayek.[1]

A framework of methodological principles and assumptions, which economists in other traditions either do not accept or do not adhere to, shapes and informs the substantive theory of Austrian economics. I shall focus on the most fundamental features of this framework, the principle of methodological individualism and the claim that economics is an *a priori* science of human action, and upon two issues at the foundation of Austrian theory within this framework: the nature of preference and its relationship to action, and the basis of time-preference. I shall be forced to neglect the farthest reaches of the theory, for example, the Austrian theory of the business cycle, where still the fundamental methodological theses intertwine. I also shall leave untouched other illuminating distinctive emphases and approaches of Austrian theory, e.g., the constant awareness of and attention to processes occurring in and through time, the study of the coordination of actions and projects when information is decentralized, the realistic theory of competitive processes. Nor shall I be able to detail the intricate interconnections of the different Austrian themes.

I. Methodological Individualism

The methodological individualist claims that all true theories of social science are *reducible* to theories of individual human action, plus boundary conditions specifying the conditions under which persons act.[2]

Methodological individualists are reductionists to the extent of their claim that true theories of social science are reducible to theories of individual human action, but typically Austrians *oppose* other reductionist claims, e.g., that theories of human action are reducible to neurophysiology, chemistry, and physics, or that social science is reducible to these in a way which *bypasses* human action. This raises the question, which I shall not discuss here, of whether the *anti-reductionist* arguments which Austrian methodological individualists wish to use against the possibility of reduction from below (physics and neurophysiology) also can be wielded against methodological individualism itself, by nonindividualist social scientists who doubt the reducibility of social science to the level of individual human action.

We now must state the thesis of methodological individualism somewhat more precisely. Consider the question of whether we can reduce the theory of two-person interaction to the theory of individual human action. Economists who discuss individual human action often use the example of Robinson Crusoe, so we might call the theory of such individual action "Robinson Crusoe theory." Our question then is whether the theory of the interaction of Crusoe and Friday can be reduced to Crusoe theory.

Crusoe theory is the theory of Crusoe's interaction with the inanimate and nonhuman animate environment. Crusoe faces scarcity, allocates time and resources to some uses and forgoes others, does what he prefers, satisfies the principle of diminishing marginal utility, exhibits time-preference, saves from current consumption to increase future consumption, and so on. Crusoe theory will include the theory of individual decision under risk and uncertainty.[3] It will talk of various dimensions, such as actions, alternatives, expected consequences, estimates of likelihoods of expected consequences, and, I believe, expected utility, but nothing need be made of this now.

Does the theory of two-person interaction merely *specify* the previous Crusoe theory and apply it in particular circumstances, or does it introduce something new and irreducible? This question is interesting, and it is *not* clear what the answer is. Before discussing it further, I must contrast it with a trivial and uninteresting question and answer. Suppose it is asked whether the theory of two-person interaction is reducible to the theory comprised of all psychological truths about *individuals*, and that an affirmative answer is proposed, on the grounds that it *is* a psychological truth about Crusoe that when he interacts with another in a certain situation he behaves in a certain specified way.[4] This *is* a truth about Crusoe, but what kind of truth is it? In particular, is it a truth that *follows* from or is a specification of *the truths about Crusoe in noninteracting situations?*

Having distinguished the interesting from the trivial question, let us notice why the answer is not obvious. Crusoe can't just treat Friday's actions as events of inanimate nature, form certain expectations about them, estimate the probabilities of the different things which Friday might do, and act accordingly and rationally. The problem is that what Friday will do in some situations depends upon *his* estimate of the probabilities of what Crusoe will do, where Friday does *not* merely treat Crusoe as an inanimate object, but as someone who also is estimating what he (Friday) will do. Each treats the other as a rational agent whose action depends upon (his estimate of) the rational course of action of the other, mutually realizing that the other's act depends upon his own in this way. Such situations are treated in the literature of game theory.[5]

Is the theory of action in game-theoretic situations reducible to, that is, derivable from the general theory of isolated action (Crusoe theory) *plus* a statement that the people are in, and (mutually) realize they're in, a game-theoretic situation? Or, is the theory which is true of people in game-theoretic situations a new and irreducible theory? We cannot say merely that people will do what they think is best in this situation, taking this claim from Crusoe theory. The question is whether what they think best in *this* situation is determined by the Crusoe truths as applied to this situation. The answer to this question is not obvious, and we should note that theorists who work within game theory develop concepts (e.g., "equilibrium strategy") which do not seem merely to be specifications of some notion(s) within the Robinson Crusoe theory. (That is, they do not seem to be merely notions of Crusoe theory restricted by parameters of two-person interaction.) To say that since all there is are individual people, the Robinson Crusoe theory *must* be sufficient, would be to answer the *trivial* question. ("It's true of him that in a game-theoretic situation he does such and such.") The interesting one would remain.

However, I do not wish to deny that the inanimate environment might mimic game-theoretic situations. For example, suppose Crusoe interacts with a mechanism whose states causally depend upon the actual reasoning Crusoe goes through. Crusoe's reasoning is mirrored in the states of his brain, and these states causally influence the mechanism whose motions then affect Crusoe. If Robinson Crusoe theory includes the theory of Crusoe's interactions with *this* bit of inanimate nature, it may well include game theory. Or perhaps without such a mechanism a person may (consider himself to) be in a choice situation wherein he must anticipate and perhaps thwart the choices of his future self (who will not remember the earlier choice). So, again, the theory of one individual's behavior may come to include game-theoretic or similar principles.

It is plausible to try to demarcate such situations S as involving an agent's belief that outcomes are contingent (in a way which must be specified) upon how his environment reacts to his own actions. Given this demarcation, Robinson Crusoe theory would be the theory of an isolated individual's behavior in non-S situations. On the other hand, if the demarcation cannot be drawn, so that by this route the theory of an individual's behavior includes game theory, Kantian moral considerations, etc., then the present epicycle about n-person interactions will not be needed in order to state the methodological individualist position.

Is the theory of 3-person interactions reducible to Crusoe theory *plus* the theory of 2-person interactions? Three-person situations involve the possibility of coalitions of two against one, of a member of the majority coalition being lured away into a new coalition with the outsider, and so forth. Suppose, for example, that $10 is to be divided up among three persons so that if (at least) two of the three stay agreed to a particular division, it gets instituted. Crusoe and Friday say, "Let's each take $5, and freeze Defoe out." Defoe says to Crusoe, "I'll give you $6 and take only $4 for myself, so you're better off in a coalition with me than with Friday." Crusoe agrees. Friday then says to Defoe, "Let's divide the $10 by giving $5 to each of us, and freeze Crusoe out. That way we both benefit." And so on.[6] Once again, it is not obvious whether 3-person theory *is* reducible to 1- and 2-person theory, or whether instead new principles emerge which govern the new phenomena that are possible.

Our questions have been of the form: are the laws of $n + 1$–person interactions reducible to the laws of n-person (inter-)actions? The methodological individualist is committed, I believe, to saying

(a)   that there is an n above which there is no change in the laws; all laws about interactions are reducible to the theory of n (or fewer)-person interactions; all social science is reducible to the laws ($\leq n$) of human interaction *plus* a specification of the situation (to which the laws are applied)[7]

and

(b)   that n is *small*.

I admit that "small" is an imprecise way of delimiting the claim. How small must n be, if methodological individualism is to hold true? Three? Anything less than ten? However, such imprecision does not undermine the contrast of methodological individualism with the view that, for example, a new theory (as opposed to a specification and application of the previous theory) is needed for the explanation of behavior of (and in) *crowds*.[8] The methodological individualist denies that there are specialized and irreducible psychological truths to the effect that a person in a *revolutionary* situation and conditions C does A, etc. It *is* logically possible that there be such emergent truths, irreducible to the *general* theory of n-person interaction.[9] (In this case, the completely general claim of the methodological individualist would be incorrect.)

How does the methodological individualist treat *institutions*? Let us take as an example (admittedly a favorable one) the institution of money. Menger offers us the following account.[10] To avoid the disadvantages which direct barter involves of not being able to trade for something you want from Crusoe who wants nothing you have, and therefore having to search for an intermediate Friday who has what Crusoe wants and wants what you have, people will tend to hold, trade for, and be willing to accept in exchange those goods they know others are (more) likely to accept in exchange; the more this is known, the more will such goods be traded for, and so there will be convergence upon a small number of goods which will, for obvious reasons, be initially valuable, portable, easily divisible in varying quantities, and homogeneous. Thus a medium of exchange precipitates out of the exchanges of individuals in a barter situation, each attempting to improve his own situation while taking account of the likely actions of others. Menger thus provides us with an explanation of the *creation* and of the *maintenance* via individual actions of a particular institution.[11]

Existing institutions also shape and affect the actions of individuals. They affect the opportunities available to people, and they shape people's utility functions. Furthermore, institutions are transformed and altered into different ones, and sometimes they are overthrown; this, too, is the result of individual actions. These statements are not very controversial. The methodological individualist adds that in explaining each such transition and affecting, it is a *general* theory (of $\leq n$-person interaction) which is specified and applied, and not some specialized theory which fits only that social situation. Our construal of the thesis of methodological individualism has several virtues: under this construal, the thesis is an interesting one, it has real content, and could be false (emergence *could* be true), and at present its truth (I believe) is unknown. Furthermore, the explanations which methodological individualists offer, and view as satisfying their thesis, all fit the thesis so construed.[12]

Must methodological individualists speak of *institutions* at all? Rather, won't they view institutions merely as the *sum* of the actual acts done within them, so that any institution is nothing more than actual acts done by particular people (who occupy particular institutional roles but are otherwise identified)? However, institutions are not merely sums of particular act tokens, when if the person hadn't done those particular act tokens, he would have done other similar ones, or when if this person didn't occupy an office or role, another would have who would have acted similarly. In such a situation, the *subjunctives* must be explained also, not merely the indicative facts of which tokens were done when. It is the existence of such subjunctive facts which prevents the identification of an institution with the particular act tokens done (as we say) under it. But though this identification is blocked, the methodological individualist can proceed to (try to) explain the subjunctives as well as the act tokens on the basis of previous act tokens, and so nothing about institutions need be left unexplained.[13]

Let us glance further at the patterns whereby actions create and maintain institutions which shape actions (see Figure 5.1). An institution is self-sustaining if it shapes actions which maintain *it* (and are sufficient to overcome actions which tend to alter it). An institution is self-destructive if it shapes actions which alter and transform it.[14] There will be a regularity wherein Institution 1 is followed by Institution 2 if 1 shapes actions which create 2. Seeing this explanation will suggest what type of exceptions to the generalization there will be. The methodological individualist denies there is a law that Institution 2 must follow Institution 1, and that *because* of the law Institution 1 will willy-nilly shape some actions or other which lead to Institution 2. To explain the current situation of institutions and actions, we would show how current actions are shaped by yesterday's institutions and actions, and how today's institutions are yesterday's institutions altered by intervening actions (and maintained by some), with a cultural lag. Institutions don't disappear overnight, for they are embodied in modes of behavior which don't alter overnight.

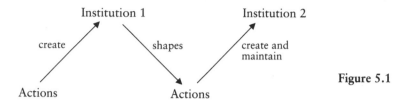

Figure 5.1

If each time we explain the current situation as arising from previous actions *in* a certain institutional setting, then why are actions *prior?* In this apparent chicken and egg situation, why aren't we equally methodological institutionalists? Why think in terms of Figure 5.1 rather than Figure 5.2? Do we eventually get back to a starting point of actions and *no* institutions?

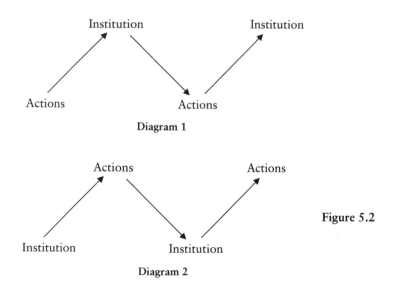

Figure 5.2

The first people came from organisms with mating patterns, group relations, territorial patterns, and so on. We have no need to press the term *institution*. Perhaps institutions are (by definition) transmitted and maintained *culturally*, whereas these far-past patterns were (initially) passed on *biologically*, as a result of evolutionary selection.[15] Given these facts, does the methodological individualist win or lose? He wins, I think, if he can explain all with the theory of human action plus evolutionary biology. *Institutions* are then, initially, a dependent variable.

However, the process of evolution may have instilled desires which themselves refer to institutional or particular social situations. In this case, even though non-macro-social explanations can be offered *from the beginning*, social scientific explanations of current behavior would have to admit (innate) desires or reinforcers for which macro-social reference would be needed to specify either what is desired or the conditions under which the desire is operative. The strongest and most general thesis of methodological individualism would then be false, and though the facts mentioned would surely not greatly perturb the methodological individualist, it is difficult to see how to modify his thesis so as to make it compatible with such biological facts and similar ones as yet unknown, while still avoiding the *trivial* thesis discussed earlier.[16]

We haven't yet focussed upon the part of the scheme where institutions shape actions. The methodological individualist, we have seen, is distinguished by his claim that it is a *general* theory of action which gets applied, not particular theories which are irreducible to general laws of action. But what are the general laws whereby institutions shape actions, what are the general laws of the shaping of utility functions? The Austrian tradition has devoted little attention to this question, perhaps because it was thought that all substantive features of utility functions (or preferences) were matters either of biology or of free choice. If methodological individualism is true, there will not be irreducible laws of the form: people brought up under institution I (tend to) have such-and-such a type of utility function. The fundamental laws will not mention a *particular* kind of institution; rather, there will be general laws of utility shaping, which are then applied to the situation of a particular institution, in order to show how *it* shapes. Institutions (the stable patterns of others' actions) provide opportunities for doing various things, and a certain patterning of rewards and punishments for actions. One general theory of the shaping of utility functions might state how opportunities, rewards and punishments, and contingencies of reinforcement combine to shape utility functions and preferences. The framework of *this* sort of theory is provided by the theory of operant conditioning.[17] This theory has been much attacked by libertarian writers, but it is important to see that methodological individualism requires *some general* theory (it need not be this one) of how utility functions are shaped in institutional environments.

Supposing the thesis of methodological individualism is true, what are its consequences for the practice of social science? The fact that all true theories of social science are reducible to general theories of human action and interaction ($\leq n$) does *not* mean that all true theories already will have been reduced, or that it will be obvious how the reduction is to be carried through. Therefore, a social scientific theory formulated at the macrolevel *cannot* be condemned merely because it is (as yet) unreduced. It could be condemned (supposing the thesis of methodological individualism were known to be true) if it were known that it was *impossible* to reduce it to theories of human action. But it is doubtful in the area of social science that a proof of the irreducibility of some theory will be forthcoming. (Though perhaps one could show that a *contrary* theory at the macrolevel follows from a specific consistent theory of human action.) Does it *follow* from the thesis of methodological individualism that the *proper* way to construct a social theory is to *start* with the theory of human action, and to work one's way up *from it*? (This is the procedure of the Austrians.) Compare the situation of someone who believes that the true theories of biology are (ultimately) reducible to physics and chemistry. He will not condemn the biologist for failing to do physics and chemistry, and he will not condemn biological theories which have not yet been reduced (even though he does believe that whatever true biological theories are discovered *will* be reduced to physics and chemistry *eventually*). Social scientists should be the last to claim that there cannot be a similar division of labor in *their* intellectual world. Thus, it appears that no consequences *need* follow from the thesis of methodological individualism about what our attitude should be to any given as-yet-unreduced macrotheory of social science. Methodological individualists, like everyone else, will have to assess the truth of such theories by examining the evidence and arguments for and against them. This conclusion is so much at variance with the usual Austrian methodological individualist view that it suggests an attempt be made to formulate the thesis of methodological individualism so that it is *not* merely about the reducibility of theories. If I knew how else to formulate it, I would.

II. The *A Priori* Science of Human Action and Its Applications

One branch of Austrian theorists (Mises, Rothbard) holds that (many of) the most important general laws of human n-person interaction are derived within (as they term it) an *a priori* science of human action. This science, it is held, begins with an examination of the essence of action (that is, purposeful behavior) and, in elaborating what is contained in this essence, is led to a body of necessary truths holding of human action as such.

Note that holding there is this *a priori* science of human action is logically independent of accepting the thesis of methodological individualism. For a methodological individualist might hold that all true social scientific theories are reducible to laws of human action, but that *none* of these latter laws are necessary truths. And someone might hold that there is a body of necessary truths about human action, but that these do *not* suffice to reduce and explain all true theories of social science.[18]

The idea of elaborating what is contained in the essence of human action is certainly an interesting and challenging one. Such a project, involving as it does synthetic necessary truths, would have been ruled out by the logical positivists as impossible and empty. But the positivist position and arguments on synthetic necessary statements, as much else within the positivist position (for example, the verifiability criterion of meaning), has fallen upon hard times. Recently, there has been a resurgence of interest in such statements, and it is fair to say, I think, that there are no arguments generally acknowledged to be compelling against the possibility of such synthetic necessary truths.[19]

This is not the appropriate occasion to investigate the general possibility of such truths. Instead, we shall consider the implications for the practice of economics if there were such a body of truths. Later sections of this essay will consider particular such (purported) truths. I shall consider only some of the (purported) derivations from the essence of action, but I should mention that there is a need for a clear, precise, and consistent statement of the content of the (a priori) theory within a specified vocabulary of primitive terms and with explicit definitions and axioms. Such a statement should make clear whether preference is initially over actions or outcomes; it would fix one notion (preference, satisfaction, desire) as primitive and define the others in terms of it; it would be sophisticated enough to take account of the considerations of the theory of choice under uncertainty and consistently distinguish in the presentation of the theory what it is expected *will* happen from what it is thought *might* happen; and it would avoid Mises' unfortunate tendency to speak as if the outcome of an action is preferred to the current situation (it need not be) rather than to what *would* obtain if the action weren't done. More care also is needed in stating the future orientation of action, for the point of an act may merely be to do it, or to be continuing a previously started plan, or to be following a previous commitment. Thus, it is a mistake, I think, to speak as Mises does of acting man necessarily ignoring sunk costs. It may be *irrational* to consider them, but people in restaurants, for example, whose food has come and turned out to be poor-tasting certainly often *speak* as though the reason they're going ahead to eat it is that money already has been committed to it. True, one might explain their sticking with this food rather than ordering another (preprepared) dish in the same way we explain why the newest, most modern equipment is not immediately installed in every factory. But, on the other hand, it is not *impossible* that letting something he's paid for go uneaten has disutility for that person. Economic theory *can* assume entrepreneurs ignore sunk costs, not because doing so is part of the essence of human action, but because the market tends to filter out entrepreneurs who take account of sunk costs. Finally, I would want the theory to be formulated so that even though preferring is a subjective psychological state, the ultimate things which are preferred one to another *need not* themselves be subjective psychological states (such as felt satisfactions or dissatisfactions, or removals of such things). This, I realize, is a more complicated question, but I need not linger over it here, since I have stated relevant considerations elsewhere.[20]

I must make only these brief remarks about formulating the theory, since I wish to examine in somewhat more detail the connection of preference, choice, and action, and the theory of time-preference. But first, in this section, consideration must be given to the *application* of a body of necessary truths about action. Actions are a certain type of behavior, namely, purposive behavior. Not all behavior is purposive. There is caused bodily movement which is not even behavior, such as the movement of a body when dropped unconscious from a height. There is behavior which is not action; for example, simple unconditioned reflexes. By training, such behavior might come under the control of choice, but if such training didn't take place, the reflex behavior wasn't action (though the earlier "nontraining" may have been). What about the conditional reflexes of classical Pavlovian conditioning? The ringing of the bell has been paired with food, and now (with no food present) the bell rings, and the dog, or the human being, salivates. Is this salivating behavior an action? I do not recall a discussion specifically on this point in the writings of the Austrians, but their answer, I believe, would be that such Pavlovian reflexes are not actions.

More interesting and difficult is *operant* behavior. Is behavior which falls under the principles of operant conditioning, action? Processes of operant conditioning by use of rewards and punishments, positive and negative reinforcements, on various contingencies of reinforcement, raise and lower the probability of various behaviors, and introduce various patterns of extinction.[21] Is such behavior, which is subject to and shaped by reinforcement, action? Austrians might quarrel with applying principles of operant conditioning to people and to theorizing about people in this way, for the behavior the Skinnerian psychologist applies his principles to is the very behavior the Austrian theorist would call "purposeful," that is, "action." The Skinnerian psychologist applies his principles to animals as well, which raises the question of whether the Austrian theorist counts operant behavior done by, e.g., rats and pigeons as action. Again, I do not recall a specific discussion of this question by an Austrian theorist, but I would think they would be reluctant to apply to animals many of the categories that go with actions, e.g., expectations, plans, images of a desired end. Recall that principles of operant conditioning have been observed to operate quite low on the evolutionary scale.

If such operant behavior of these other organisms is not action, then we have an interesting example of a type of behavior to which the categories of human action do not apply. The principles of operant conditioning, let us assume, apply to these other organisms. (Note that there is an evolutionary account of the adaptive advantage of operant conditioning; being operantly conditionable would be selected for in the process of evolution among organisms that were merely subject to classical conditioning.) Might those principles also be true of us, of large segments of the behavior of human beings, as an *a posteriori* theory? Do we know *a priori* that its categories and statements don't apply to much of human behavior?

There *is* this alternative, relatively elaborate conceptual scheme which does not appear to talk of or within the Misesian categories, yet whether it is true of people or not appears to be an empirical question, to be decided *a posteriori*. (Did these principles just stop being true at a certain point on the evolutionary scale? Does human consciousness and intelligence provide new means through which these principles work, or instead an area in which they don't work at all?) It may be that Skinnerian theory and human action theory are compatible, and can both be true of the same behavior. If so, even if human action theory *is* known *a priori,* it may be that it is not the best theory, for the Skinnerian theory actually may explain more, enable us to predict more, and so forth. In this case, the possession of an *a priori* theory would *not* stop us from pursuing and developing, formulating and testing, a body of contingent truths about behavior. Possession of an *a priori* theory cannot tell us that there won't also be a better, more predictive, wider-ranging *a posteriori* theory, and so *cannot* bar the pursuit of empirical science. (This point, obviously, does not depend on anything about Skinnerian theory, but it seemed useful to make it by considering an actual alternative framework, very different from Mises', which functions within an *a posteriori* theory currently under active investigation.)

On the other hand, it may be that the two theories cannot both be true of the same behavior, that the truth of one excludes the truth of the other. Many Austrians write as though there is *no* set of concepts, other than theirs, via which one conceivably might understand much of human behavior. The existence of Skinnerian theory casts this in doubt, and supposing this theory to be incompatible with human action theory, it raises the delicate question of which of the two bodies of theory is true of most of our behavior in the world. (In Austrian terms, it raises the question of whether that behavior *is* action.)

Note the importance for the Austrian view that there be nothing *else* close to action, nothing very similar to it. On that assumption, human behavior which isn't action can easily be distinguished. It would not be a delicate matter involving much observation and testing to decide *which* theory holds true of some behavior which appears to be action. On the other hand, suppose there were behaviors similar enough to human actions so that they could not be distinguished at one or even two glances. Suppose further that such nonaction behavior occurred frequently, often intermixed with the actions of persons. The nonaction behavior *does* obey different laws, though, e.g., the laws of operant conditioning. Even if there were an *a priori* theory of human action, the question of whether this theory fit a particular situation would have to be determined by detailed empirical investigation, complicated statistical procedures, etc. That is, the claim that the theory of human action fits a situation would require as much evidence as the claim that some other *a posteriori* theory fits a situation. The *a priori* character of the theory of human action would be of *no help* in deciding whether it was true of a behavioral situation, and economics would be carried on in as empirical a manner as any other science. (Even if somehow in this situation someone could know *a priori* that it was an action he was performing, others couldn't know this *a priori*.)

Thus, it is important for the Austrian view of how economics is to be carried on to add to their claim that there is an *a priori* science of human action, the claim that there is a great enough gulf between human action and other human behaviors to make it easy to identify which behavior is action. Otherwise, the only way to determine whether or not behavior is action might be to determine which laws it satisfies. And this might require as much empirical investigation as goes on in an *a posteriori* science of human behavior. Can the existence of such a gulf be known *a priori*; is it a necessary truth that no behavior mimics action closely enough to require detailed investigation to separate them? I do not see that it is, and the existence of an *a posteriori* theory of this sort (e.g., Skinnerian theory) has the consequence that the science of human behavior must, to a great extent, be carried on as an empirical science. Even if it were known *a priori* that actions satisfied certain laws, it would be an empirical question whether particular bits of behavior are actions and, hence, whether they satisfied those laws.[22]

Does the method of *verstehen* give us knowledge of which conceptual structure applies to people's behavior?[23] Critics of *verstehen* have claimed that it is at best a route to thinking up hypotheses, and not a way of coming to know which hypotheses are true.[24] Current views on the testing of hypotheses describe a role other than the suggesting of hypotheses or the showing of which one is true, namely, the assignment of plausibilities to hypotheses or (on the Bayesian view of statistics) of prior probabilities to these hypotheses. Such plausibilities or prior probabilities will affect what it takes to show a hypothesis is true or false. In an unpublished essay, Hilary Putnam makes the interesting suggestion that the process of *verstehen* comes into this prior assignment, and so legitimately plays a role (though not a *conclusive* one) in the process of accepting and rejecting hypotheses.

Even if we grant Putnam's point, we should step back to examine what might underlie the use of *verstehen*. Consider the enterprise of what, following Quine's use of the term *radical translation*,[25] we might call *radical verstehen*, the understanding of the behavior of organisms of another species or with whom we have *no* biological links since they evolved on another planet. Can we *verstehen* such organisms? Empathetic understanding might suggest hypotheses about their behavior, but these would have to be tested further. The *general hypothesis* that we are *able* to *verstehen* their behavior would be tested in the process of testing the specific hypotheses about them which empathetic understanding suggests.[26] What is clear is that we could not know *a priori* that we have the ability to empathetically understand the behavior of these organisms. If we do have this ability for those organisms, we will have to come to know this *a posteriori,* presumably by appropriate procedures of psychological science. It might turn out that we have this ability with only *some* types of their behavior; though empathetic understanding suggests with equal plausibility hypotheses about other types of their behavior, further testing might show our success rate with these latter hypotheses to be no better than random. Our reliability with different types of their behavior will be determined *a posteriori.*

Closer to home, consider the claim that *you* can *verstehen* the behavior of other persons. That, too, it seems, is not known *a priori.* Presumably, you will have confidence (if you do) in your ability to so understand the behavior of others because those of your everyday attempts to do so which had further predictive consequences have borne up pretty well. But such a nonrigorous test of the hypothesis cannot show that an alternative conceptual scheme is inapplicable when this alternative scheme often would have roughly the same further predictive consequences about the behavior of others in the situations of everyday life. In that case, the apparent success of our episodes of empathetic understanding might be only apparent.

But can't we know, without intricate testing, which concepts apply to our *own behavior,* that is, can't I know which apply to mine, and you know which apply to yours? We each certainly do apply a particular conceptual scheme to our own behavior with great confidence.[27] But on what basis do you do so and, in particular, do you know *a priori* that this scheme applies to you? Perhaps one wants to say that you know which concepts apply to your behavior since you're *doing* it, after all, and doing it in a way which *infuses* those concepts into the behavior which you produce, and which also leads you to know that those concepts are so infused. You know you're making it happen *as an action.* As it stands, this is too murky to be helpful. Clarifying it is unlikely to show that the way the concepts get infused into behavior you produce while under the sway of the concepts, makes the theory utilizing *those* concepts the best explanatory theory of your behavior. (And there still would remain the problem of knowing what concepts to apply to the behavior of *other* persons.)

Still, there is the fact that we *do* apply, with confidence, the categories of human action. Another theory, e.g., the Skinnerian theory, will fail to generally undermine this confidence until it is combined with a theory of concept formation so as, from its own perspective, to explain the (cross-cultural) fact that people confidentially hold to the usual (non-Skinnerian) categories. If the Skinnerian theory could explain why, though the usual theory is (as it claims) false, almost all people adhere to it, this would make it more difficult to retain undiminished confidence in either the usual theory or in the process of *verstehen,* which uses its categories. However, even in this case it would not be impossible to continue to believe the usual theory, and the Skinnerian theory itself may predict this will happen, since belief in the usual theory was reinforced on a schedule which makes it highly resistant to extinction. Indeed, we may question how faithfully operant conditioning theorists adhere to their own theory when they try to argue the public away from the product of long and varied processes of reinforcement!

Verstehen cannot, we have seen, help to eliminate all empirical questions about the application of Mises' or any other theory of human action. However, we should not leave the subject of *verstehen* without remarking that it *is* possible that people (or some people) do possess the capacity of empathetic understanding, for at least some types of behavior, and that this capacity might be trained so as to become even more reliable. Whether this is so or not is an empirical question. Suppose that investigation by the procedures of empirical science identifies some persons as especially reliable *verstehers* of at least some types of behavior; as it turns out, they rarely or never are inaccurate. Even if we did not possess a theory of *how* this capacity operated, we might use such reliable *verstehers* as *instruments* by which to learn various things, even as we use nonhuman detectors of facts. Tests might yield the result that particular *verstehers* had a reliability as high as that we attribute to our usual empirical procedures of theory construction and testing, and in that case we would no more hesitate to say that *verstehen* has given us knowledge than to say that the rest of science has. The standard procedures of the rest of science would be what established the reliability of *verstehen,* but once this *were* shown, there is the possibility that social science might then be carried on very differently.

One final remark about the applicability of *a priori* laws. Questions about this arise due to considerations *within* the theory as well, for example, for the principle of diminishing marginal utility. It is often objected to this principle that an additional unit of X (say, the sixth) may have *increased* utility since, now, along with the previous five units, the person is able to acquire something previously unavailable. The Austrian reply points out that in this case the relevant size of the unit is $6X$; the principle is meant to apply to situations where each additional unit of X can acquire only those things which previous units also were able to bring (and together with the others can bring only a larger conjunction of previously available things).[28] The *size* of the units must be chosen so this condition is satisfied. Now, it is logically possible, of course, that for *any* choice of a finite size of the unit X, *whenever* a new nth unit of X becomes available, there is also a new *total* use of the nX's (that is, of the new X and the previous ones together) which ranks higher in the person's preferences than the sum of any n of the previously available things (and than the sum of the conjunction of something obtainable with one X along with anything obtainable with $n-1$ X's together, etc.). Let us call such a situation an *expanding universe*. A person's universe is *locally expanding* if it is an expanding universe over as many units as he has; that is, for any choice of the size of unit, so that he has at least one. The principle of diminishing marginal utility is not *false* of a person in a locally expanding universe; it just doesn't *apply* to him. The combination of his preferences and the opportunities available to him does not satisfy the condition of application of the principle. Since whether or not a person is in a locally expanding universe is an empirical question, it is an empirical question whether or not the principle of diminishing marginal utility *applies* to a particular person in a particular situation.

III. Preference, Choice, and Action

Austrian writers put forward a number of interconnected theses about the relations of preference, choice, and action:

(1)   If a person does an action A, then that person preferred doing A to doing any other act which (he believed) was available to him at the time.

(2)   No evidence can establish that a person prefers A to B in the face of a choice of B when A was available to the person.

(3)   The notion of preference makes no sense apart from an actual choice made.[29]

Does all action show preference? (That is, is 1 above true?) Mightn't the person be *indifferent* between what he did and some other alternative available to him? We might have the following picture: of the acts available to a person, some he is willing to do, and others he is unwilling to do. He prefers A to B if and only if in a choice between A and B he is willing to do A and unwilling to do B. Let us grant that if he does A, this shows he was willing to do A. But doing A does *not* show he was unwilling to do B. He might have been willing to do B also. Thus, doing A does not show the person preferred doing it to doing B.

Writers sometimes speak of *weak preference,* of the person weakly preferring doing one act to doing another. We can understand "the person weakly prefers doing A to doing B" as: the person prefers doing A to doing B, or the person is indifferent between doing A and doing B. In terms of this relation of weak preference, a person is *indifferent* between doing A and doing B if and only if he weakly prefers A to B, *and* he weakly prefers B to A. A person *strongly* prefers A to B if and only if he weakly prefers A to B and he does not weakly prefer B to A. Choosing an act may well be a sufficient condition for weakly preferring doing it to doing one of its alternatives. But it is not a necessary condition for that and, hence, it is not a sufficient condition for *strong* preference. There are other indications of indifference; for example, the person flips a coin between doing A and doing B and acts on the outcome of the flip; or, the person uses a random device to choose between doing A, doing B, and flipping a coin to decide between doing A and doing B, and so forth.

Indeed, the Austrian theorists *need* the notion of indifference to explain and mark off the notion of a commodity, and of a *unit* of a commodity. If everyone or one person prefers one homogeneous batch of stuff to another homogeneous batch of the same shape of the same stuff (perhaps they like to choose the left-hand one, or the one mined first), these are *not* the *same* commodity. They will have different prices. Particular things x and y will be the *same* commodity (belong to the same commodity class) only if all persons are indifferent between x and y. Without the notion of indifference, and, hence, of an equivalence class of things, we cannot have the notion of a commodity, or of a unit of a commodity; without the notion of a unit ("an interchangeable unit") of a commodity, we have no way to state the law of (diminishing) marginal utility.[30]

Does the existence of behavior, when a choice was made, show *what* was chosen and what was preferred? The behavior done does not show *to what* something was preferred, for it does not show what behavior was *rejected*. That depends upon the person's *beliefs* about what alternatives were available to him, and these are not shown by his actual behavior. We might think it is shown by his talk, but why can talk show beliefs about the alternatives available yet not show preferences? We should not answer, "because beliefs issue in talk and preferences issue in action." For, don't beliefs sometimes issue in action, and preferences in talk? Rather, aren't talk and action each the product of beliefs *and* preferences *both*?

Do we at least know *what* was the preferred alternative? Note that the behavior performed can be described differently, e.g., "travelling to the first floor," "stepping in this particular place," "exerting a certain pressure." *What* did the person prefer doing to something else? Preference, it seems, does not apply to things directly, but applies only via *descriptions*, via something linguistic-like. We cannot just say *"that* behavior," and point. For *which* is that? We might try to narrow things down by noting that what he preferred was something he *knew* about; hence, the description has to be one he knew of at the time he was acting or choosing. But which of these descriptions he knows of is connected with his preference? Perhaps the answer is, *all* that he knows of: he prefers the combination of all the descriptions he knows of for the behavior he does, to the combination of all the descriptions he knows of for each of the alternative behaviors he doesn't do. But he may have *neglected* and even repressed many descriptions he knows of. He knows of many he didn't consciously think of at any point in the process of deciding; he thought of some which he forgot, but could recall with effort, and so forth.

It might be suggested, instead, that he prefers the combination of descriptions that (he thought) fit the behavior done which he was actually thinking of, as he decided, to the combination he was then actually thinking of which (he thought) fit the behavior rejected. But mightn't he then have been thinking only of the *worst* description, and then decided, "I'll do it nonetheless"? Need he have been thinking then of a description at all? Couldn't he have gone through deliberations, and then when the time came, just acted without consciously thinking about it?

What is preferred, it seems, is hidden from an observer. The most an observer can say, for sure, is that when action takes place something or other is (weakly) preferred to something or other else; more fully, something or other connected with the behavior done was (weakly) preferred to something or other else not connected (as closely) with the behavior done. It is often said that an external observer cannot *predict* behavior on the basis of preference. Here we see that he cannot retrospectively *describe* preference, even on the basis of the *behavior* done!

Must it be, at least, that the person who acts knows what he himself preferred? Can't he say, "I thought about many things about what to do, and then just acted later without thinking about it then. I don't know what about it I preferred"? Is this impossible? or just rare? "But he knows he preferred doing it!" Need he *know* what the *it* is which he preferred? "Well, he *did* it!" True, but who is denying that?

Let us now turn to the strongest of the above statements about the connection of preference and action, viz. (3): the notion of preference does not make sense apart from an *actual action* which exhibits it. Notice that this is stronger than saying that preference is *somehow* connected to choices, to what a person *would* choose under certain circumstances. It says the notion is inextricably tied to *actual* choices.

It is not clear that the Austrians can consistently maintain this strong thesis. Consider, for example, Mises' view of action as exchange.[31] An action A is done instead of another act B. What is not done, B, is the *price* of doing A. The value of B is the *cost* of doing A. Mises then goes on to talk of the profit of an act, and also of the (I assume, *ex post*) loss. Now the cost of doing act A cannot be the value of *everything* forgone, that is, it cannot be the *sum* of everything forgone. If it were, we almost never would have profit. Suppose there are five alternative acts, closely bunched, and you do the one act, A, which is the best. The cost of A is not the *sum* of the values of the other four. (This would greatly outweigh the value of A.) The cost of A is the value of the *best one* of the rejected alternatives. The best one of the rejected alternatives is the one you strongly prefer to all the others, or (if there's a tie at the top of the rejected alternatives) one you weakly prefer to each other rejected alternative. Notice that we are speaking of a person's preference apart from any *actual choice* of the preferred alternative. The next best alternative to A, call it B, is preferred to any of the others C, D, E, *though B itself is not chosen*. If we are to speak of the cost of A, when there is more than one other alternative rejected, it must *make sense* to speak of preference apart from an actual choice or doing of the preferred alternative. If *that* doesn't make sense, then neither does the notion of the *cost* of the action which was actually chosen.[32]

How *can* it make sense to speak of preference without an actual choice? Granting that the Austrians are wrong in denying that it makes sense, how is it possible? Let me present a sketch of a plausible account. Preference is connected with a *subjunctive*: to say a person prefers A to B at a time is to say he *would choose* A over B if he *were* given a choice between (only) A and B at that time. There's something about him in virtue of which he would choose A over B. It is not, for example, a random event.

That an event actually happens does not show that a subjunctive is true. Consider photons emitted toward a screen with two slits, and suppose that it is truly a random event which slit any photon goes through. If two people bet on which the next photon *will* go through, one saying it's one slit and the other saying the other, the winner is the one who picked the slit which turned out to be correct. The indicative statement is shown true by the event. In contrast, if someone says, "if a photon *were* emitted in the next second, it *would* go through the right-hand slit," and one is emitted, and does go through the right-hand slit, this does not show he was right. The *subjunctive* statement is *not* shown true by the event.

Perhaps this can be made intuitively more obvious via a recent account of subjunctives. Under this account, a subjunctive of the form "if p were true, q would be true" is itself true if and only if in all those possible worlds where p holds true which are *closest* to the actual world, q also holds true. The minimal change from the actual world necessary to make p true brings the truth of q along with it (in those closest worlds).[33]

Now it might turn out that those closest worlds in which p is true are neither uniformly q nor uniformly not-q. In that case, in the actual world neither of the subjunctives "if p were true q would be true" and "if p were true, not-q would be true" will hold true. If it is truly a random matter which slit the photon goes through, then before the photon is emitted, for each possible world in which a photon is emitted and goes through the right (left) slit there is another possible world, equally close to the actual one, in which a photon is emitted and goes through the left (right) slit. More precisely, the "photon is emitted"–neighborhood of the actual world contains worlds where the photon goes through the right slit, and it contains worlds where the photon goes through the left slit. The subjunctive "if a photon were emitted it would go through that slit" is not true.

To say a person did *A* rather than *B* because he preferred *A* to *B* is to say he did *A* rather than *B* because it's true of him that he *would* choose *A* over *B*. This is not a very potent explanation, but it does put the action in a pattern; it says the action flows from some underlying *disposition* (which might be very fleeting) to choose *A* over *B*. The occurrence of an action does not demonstrate that the subjunctive is true; also the person might have been indifferent. But often an action will stem from an underlying preference and will indicate that there is such a preference.

On this view of preference as constituted by the subjunctive to the effect that a person *would* choose *A* over *B* if he *were* given a choice between the two, we can see how to make sense of preference without an actual choice of the preferred act. It might be that a person would choose *A* over *B* in a choice between the two, but since he didn't have to make a choice between the two, that preference was not exercised; he did not actually choose *A* over *B*, and he didn't do *A*.

A substance is *soluble* in water if it *would dissolve* if placed in water. Substances which are never placed in water may yet be water-soluble, even though they never actually dissolve. "Prefers *A* to *B*" is like "soluble"; "chooses *A* over *B*" is like "dissolves." The claim that it makes no sense to say a person prefers *A* to *B* unless he's actually chosen *A* over *B* is like the claim that it makes no sense to say something is soluble unless it already has actually dissolved. Both claims are mistaken.[34]

The cost of an action, we saw, is the value of the most preferred alternative not chosen. To say that some unchosen alternative is preferred to every other one is to say it *would* be chosen over each other one in pairwise choices. And this might well be true. If the Austrians were correct in talking of scales of values as existing only in actual choices, there couldn't be a particular cost of a choice.

Subjunctives give us the possibility of making sense of *rationality* conditions on preference, e.g., the condition that preference be transitive. To say that preference is transitive at a time *t* is to say that for any three acts *X*, *Y*, and *Z* if

(1)   it's true that the person would choose *X* over *Y* if given a choice at time *t* between (only) *X* and *Y*

and

(2)　it's true that the person would choose Y over Z if given a choice at time t between (only) Y and Z

then

(3)　it's true that the person would choose X over Z if given a choice at time t between (only) X and Z.

It is possible that (1) and (2) are both true for some X, Y, and Z, yet (3) is not; rather, (4) might hold:

(4)　it's true that the person would choose Z over X if given a choice at time t between (only) X and Z.

Also, it is possible that *no* subjunctive, neither (3) nor (4), is true of the choice between X and Z. In this case, also, preference fails to be transitive. It is possible that (4) is true along with (1) and (2), because each of these subjunctives talks about different hypothetical circumstances. Since (1) and (2) do not talk about a choice between (only) X and Z, they don't, even together, settle what *would* happen under that condition. However, they arguably do settle what should happen, and so we have room for a rationality condition.[35]

Mises considers and objects to the requirement that preference be transitive (*Human Action*, p. 103):

> The attempt has been made to attain the notion of a nonrational action by this reasoning: If a is preferred to b and b to c, logically a should be preferred to c. But if actually c is preferred to a, we are faced with a mode of acting to which we cannot ascribe consistency and rationality. This reasoning disregards the fact that two acts of an individual can never be synchronous. If in one action a is preferred to b and in another action b to c, it is, however short the interval between the two actions may be, not permissible to construct a uniform scale of value in which a precedes b and b precedes c. Nor is it permissible to consider a later third action as coincident with the two previous actions. All that the example proves is that value judgments are not immutable and that therefore a scale of value, which is abstracted from various, necessarily nonsynchronous actions of an individual, may be self-contradictory.

The acts cannot be synchronous, but the subjunctives *can* hold true at the same time. So we can make sense of nontransitive preferences at a time. (Still, it does not follow that the *action* is irrational, only that the structure consisting of that action *plus* those preferences violates a normative requirement. *Which* should be changed is left open.) Leaving preferences aside, what are we to say about the corresponding nontransitive subjunctives? Isn't someone irrational of whom (1), (3) and (4) hold true?[36]

If preference is specified by choices that would be made in pairwise choice situations, there is room for normative conditions in addition to the transivity one. For there will be conditions connecting pairwise choices with nonpairwise choices. For example,

> If, if there were a choice only between X and Y, X would be chosen, then if there were a choice between X, Y and some other alternatives, Y would not be chosen.

and

> If in a choice among the members of set S, X would be chosen then in a choice among the members of a subset T of S of which X is a member, X would also be chosen.[37]

Why does Mises think it so important to argue that the structure of preferences cannot be irrational? Perhaps because he doesn't want anyone interfering with choices on the grounds that they arise from irrationally structured preferences. That, however, is another issue, and one might think it possible for people to have irrationally structured preferences and also hold that this is within their rights, so that they may not be interfered with on the grounds that their preferences are irrationally structured (unless they have explicitly contracted into such a scheme of interference). I should not neglect to mention that the view of preferences as embodying (and embodied in) subjunctives about choice opens up the possibility of formulating further conditions on preference among probability mixtures of outcomes (in the manner of Von Neumann and Morgenstern) or among uncertain actions (mappings of states of the world onto consequences, in the manner of L. J. Savage) so as to yield measurement of utility on an interval scale.[38]

Of the three statements connecting preference, choice, and action which we listed above, we have argued that the first and third are incorrect. What about the second? Can evidence establish a preference of A over B in the face of an opposite choice of B, when A was available to the person? Can there be indirect evidence that a person would choose A over B if given a choice (only) between A and B, so that we conclude he *does* prefer A to B, despite the fact that he has chosen B when A was available? The person might have chosen B over A and over lots of other things, over so many things, in fact, that he lost sight of A. Here would be a case where he would choose A in a choice (only) among A and B, yet in a choice among A, B, and many other things, he would choose B, because he would lose track of A. Or perhaps there's no "would" about the matter; he just gets confused and acts; no *subjunctive* is true of the wide choice. The person actually chose and did B (violating one of the rationality conditions listed earlier), yet this doesn't show he didn't prefer A to B. We might stand by the claim that he does prefer A to B, offering a special explanation of why he chose B that time.

These examples, which are designed to cast doubt on (2) above, involve choice among a large number of alternatives. There cannot be a similar counter-example which involves only a pairwise choice, if preference goes with a subjunctive involving "would *always* do A rather than B." If, however, preference goes with a subjunctive involving "would . . . unless . . . " then there is the possibility of a pairwise counter-example to (2). There remains, however, another difficulty with (2)'s claim that no evidence can establish that a person prefers A to B in the face of a choice of B when A was available to him. From a person's doing B, we cannot know he believed A was available to him, or how he conceived the rejected alternatives. If our earlier discussion of whether we can know *to what* something was preferred was correct, we cannot possibly, no matter what we conclude, fly in the face of a choice of B over A. For that is never a fact which *faces* us.

Rationality conditions are conditions which it is possible to violate. In contrast, it is difficult to see how preference *could* fail to be irreflexive and asymmetric. These seem to be part of the notion of preference, and it is a virtue of the subjunctive account that it makes no sense of instances where preference is reflexive or symmetric. However, though (in contrast to constitutive conditions) rationality conditions *are* conditions it is possible to violate, they had better not be violated *too much,* without special explanation. For if some organism violated them just about always, it would be unclear that it was *preferences* which the organism possessed, even though the binary subjunctives did hold of it. (If alpha-centurions always have an intransitive structure of subjunctives hold true of them, is it *preferences* that they have?) An organism has preferences, it seems, not merely because and when binary subjunctives are true of it. The binary subjunctives which hold true of it must hang together in a reasonable fashion. The organism must show some modicum of rationality to be counted as having preferences at all. Given a being whose subjunctives usually and normally fail to rationally cohere (with no special explanation of this failure), it is doubtful that it is *preferences* which the being has.[39]

IV. Time-Preference

Time-preference plays such a central role in the Austrian approach (to interest, capital theory, the business cycle, etc.) that we cannot close without giving it a brief examination. Böhm-Bawerk's famous three reasons for time-preference have frequently been examined,[40] and we turn to more recent views.

We can deal briefly with an argument of Rothbard's (*Man, Economy, and State*, p. 13, his italics):

> A fundamental and constant truth about human action is that *man prefers his end to be achieved in the shortest time.* Given the specific satisfaction, the sooner it arrives, the better. This results from the fact that time is always scarce, and a means to be economized. The sooner any end is attained, the better. Thus, with any *given end* to be attained, the shorter the period of action, i.e., production, the more preferable for the actor. *This is the universal fact of time preference.*

This argument does *not* demonstrate time-preference on the basis of the scarcity of time. Time is scarce, and we want to economize it, to use less of it in achieving our goals. Given a way of achieving our goal that takes two minutes, and another way that takes five minutes, we will choose the two-minute way, thereby leaving the three extra minutes for the pursuit of some other goal. However, time-preference is not the same thing as economizing time. Suppose there are two acts A and B, which each take five minutes to do, and yield the same goal, but one delivers its goal earlier than the other. Suppose A delivers seven minutes after it's done, and B delivers one year after *it's* done. However, each taking five minutes to do economizes time equally. Time-preference, therefore, cannot be derived from economizing time. It also may conflict with it, as when the action which delivers its goal sooner takes longer to perform than the action which delivers the goal later.

Mises connects time preference with action in a different and more striking way (*Human Action*, p. 484):

> Time preference is a categorial requisite of human action. No mode of action can be thought of in which satisfaction within a nearer period of the future is not—other things being equal—preferred to that in a later period. The very act of gratifying a desire implies that gratification

at the present instant is preferred to that at a later instant. He who consumes a nonperishable good instead of postponing consumption for an indefinite later moment thereby reveals a higher valuation of present satisfaction as compared with later satisfaction. If he were not to prefer satisfaction in a nearer period of the future to that in a remoter period, he would never consume and so satisfy wants. He would always accumulate; he would never consume and enjoy. He would not consume today, but he would not consume tomorrow either, as the morrow would confront him with the same alternative.

On this view, an action shows time-preference because if the person didn't prefer doing it now, he wouldn't do it now. Furthermore, if the person never preferred doing it at a time rather than at a later time, he would never act at that time, and so would never act at all.

Let us scrutinize this argument more closely. First, a person might be indifferent between doing some act now and doing it later, and do it now. ("Why not do it now?")[41] So action now can show time-(weak) preference, but it need not show time-(strong) preference. Second, a person might act now to get a particular satisfaction, without caring whether it comes sooner or later. He acts now because the option of getting the satisfaction is a fleeting one which will not be available later. Thus, a person can have a reason, other than time-preference, to act now; to prefer satisfaction sooner rather than later is not necessary in order to act now. Third, the fact that we act constantly cannot show that we *always* have time-preference for *all* goods. *At most,* it shows that when a person acts (and the option also is available later) he has time-preference *then* for the *particular* good he then acts to get. This is compatible with an alternation of periods of time-preference for good G, and periods of *no* time-preference for good G. The person acts to get G during one of the periods of time-preference for G. This is considerably weaker than general time-preference, as might be seen by considering what the theory of interest would look like if there were only this weak form of time-preference. Finally, even if Mises' approach yielded the strong conclusion he envisages (which, I believe, it does not), it would leave time-preference mysterious. Action shows time-preference; but why is there time-preference? Time-preference would still stand in need of *explanation.*[42]

Let us approach time-preference by considering apparently unrelated propositions, which Austrian theorists usually list as additional (non-*a priori*) assumptions, viz., leisure is a consumer's good, and labor has disutility.[43] It should be possible, I think, to derive the first of these from other deeper facts (which will not themselves be necessary truths, though). Note first that leisure *need not* be a consumer good, for each person. It depends what the person's *labor* is like. For example, suppose you have *no* desire for privacy, and a psychologist wants to study someone's life. He wishes to watch you from afar, unobtrusively, and he will pay you a fixed salary per hour. There is no limit to the amount of time you will gainfully labor, doing as thou wilt. Do not say that this is not *labor*, because it has no disutility, for that *would* make it a necessary truth that labor has disutility. Mustn't labor, at least, be an activity? The hired person is always acting. What he sells is a right; the right to watch him. It might even be more particular labor he does; his employment might require him *not* to do some trivial act A he cares nothing for.

Notice how the particular labor I have described differs from almost all other labor. It is a feature of almost all labor that it is incompatible with the simultaneous doing of other activities which the person wishes to do and which have some value for the person. Some consumption takes time, and cannot be done simultaneously with some other activities; for example, listening to Beethoven quartets and working a steam drill, lolling on the beach and teaching a philosophy class. Therefore, a person with multiple desires, some of which cannot be satisfied simultaneously with the particular labor he does, will want leisure time in which to satisfy these other desires. The value of an hour of leisure to the person will be the value to him of satisfying the most highly ranked of his desires or combinations of desires which can be satisfied in an hour, whose satisfaction is incompatible with the simultaneous doing of his particular form of labor. We do not need the additional assumption that labor has disutility. Even if labor is a good, we can still have tradeoffs of labor and leisure; that is, tradeoffs of labor with the other goods that can be had only in that person's nonlaboring time. (Thus, Austrian writers need not deny that work may itself have intrinsic satisfying quality.)

These are empirical facts of a high level of generality:

(a)   there are multiple goods;
(b)   most people's labor (what others will pay them for) is incompatible with their simultaneously achieving some other goods (as they judge them). These other goods cannot be achieved (*as well*) simultaneously with the labor;
(c)   in this area, beneficial tradeoffs are possible.

Now consider time-preference in the light of these.[44] If a person knew the moment of his death, and knew each of the desires that he could satisfy, then the incompatibility of various desires (the impossibility of their simultaneous satisfaction) would require him, if all the desires are to be satisfied, to stack desires back from the last moment, far enough so that they would all fit in. This, however, will not constitute time-preference.

Suppose uncertainty is introduced; the uncertainty usually mentioned in this context is uncertainty about the moment of one's death ("eat, drink, and be merry for tomorrow we *might* die"), and about whether a currently possible consumption will *continue* to be possible in the future. But it is another uncertainty I wish to emphasize here (if only because it is generally ignored), that concerning which *other* current desires (or which desires to be acquired in the future) you may come to be in a position to satisfy in the future. This uncertainty will lead a person to prefer satisfying some desire or other *now* rather than postponing *all* their satisfactions until later. For it might turn out later that another stronger desire can only be satisfied then, which is incompatible with the satisfaction then of any of the desires which it is currently possible to satisfy. And this might be true for all the "laters." (Add to this the uncertainty about whether it will remain possible to satisfy one of the current desires.) If you don't satisfy one of the desires now, you might *never* do so, for later it might be outranked by an incompatible desire. In these terms, there is nothing to *gain* by postponing the satisfaction of a desire, and there is something which *might* be lost. Satisfying some desire now, therefore, *weakly dominates* (in the sense of decision theory) postponing the satisfaction of all desires until later. Hence we have the rationality of an analogue of Mises' time-preference, though not of that which involves a preference of greater current consumption and less future consumption over uniform consumption (summing to the same as the previous alternative) throughout time.

The opportunity cost of failing to satisfy any desire now is the value of that desire, if any, current or future, which gets crowded out later. Since there might be such a crowded-out desire, there might be this opportunity cost. Given two desires which can be satisfied now or later, the greater need not be satisfied first; the opportunity costs of satisfying it first might be larger than those of satisfying it second. The opportunity cost analysis explains the *sequencing* of the satisfaction of desires. There is no opportunity cost to satisfying a particular desire now rather than

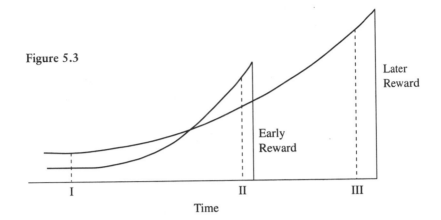

Figure 5.3

Later Reward

Early Reward

I   II   III

Time

none, unless we imagine a reason to want it later rather than now. But starting, as we suppose, with no such preference either way, dominance considerations give us a time-preference.

But this does not appear to be the whole story about time-preference. Such preference has been discovered in *animal* experiments, where the effectiveness of a reward declines with its distance forward in time in accordance with some concave curve. If the curve is more concave than an exponential one, for example, if it is a hyperbola, then we have the possibility of two such curves *crossing*. (See Figure 5.3.) The height of a curve at each point in time represents how valuable the later reward is to the organism at *that* point in time. At each time an organism chooses to occupy the highest curve. Thus, in the diagram drawn, at time I a person would choose to wait for the larger later reward rather than take the earlier smaller one which excludes getting the larger one, at time II the organism would choose the earlier smaller reward even though if it forgoes this and waits, the larger one will become available, and if the organism can somehow get beyond the time of the smaller reward, it will choose and reap the larger one. Thus, hyperbolic curves which cross are able to explain in an illuminating fashion the making and later breaking of resolutions (the first at time I and the second at time II), problems of self-control (at time II), etc.[45]

The time-preference found in animal experiments is not, I assume, to be explained by their performing rational calculations, even implicitly. How is it to be explained? If my earlier dominance argument about satisfying some desire or other in the present is correct, then an organism which does this and exhibits that sort of time-preference will, on the average, satisfy more of its desires. There would be other arguments as well which show that in a wide range of situations, time-preference would lead to greater total desire satisfaction. In an uncertain world, where contingencies frequently interfere with obtaining particular future satisfactions, time-preference enables organisms unable to reason about such contingencies to satisfy many of their desires.

Supposing such a time-preference tendency arose by random mutation and was transmitted genetically, and that the desires involved themselves were connected with survival to reproductive age, ability to protect progeny, etc., then time-preference would be evolutionarily adaptive, and would be selected for in the process of evolution, once it appeared. If some such explanation accounts for its presence in lower organisms, it is reasonable to think that we too have some genetically based time-preference. The evolutionary process has built time-preference into us, for within that process the rationality of time-preference is reflected as adaptive value.

My account here has been very sketchy, but some evolutionary account of time-preference in lower organisms must be given, and presumably we will be, in these ways, continuous with these other organisms. Economists should no more hesitate to use this biologically based fact about people than Mises hesitated to incorporate the general (non-*a priori*) statement that labor has disutility. However, it does leave us with a puzzle. The evolutionary process builds time-preference into organisms who do not calculate, as a (rough) rule of thumb to approximate what calculation would lead to. Discounting of future goods is a surrogate for the calculations of the dominance argument (plus perhaps other maximizing arguments). Let us now consider the situation of organisms who do calculate, and who can in their deliberations take into account various future contingencies. If these organisms (call them people) do such explicit calculation, and *also* feed into these calculations magnitudes of (future) desires which have been discounted to take such calculative considerations into account already, then isn't there *double-counting,* or rather, *double-discounting?* Time-preference first discounts, and our later calculations explicitly take into account factors and lead, in effect, to explicit discounting. When we ourselves can take various contingencies explicitly into account, do we want to be bound by the type of discounting found adaptive as an average rule of thumb in the evolutionary history of the species? Shouldn't we try to correct for such discounting as is built into us, and put *all* discounting into our calculations? Or should we instead eliminate all such discounting from our *calculations*?

The problem of double-discounting arises when our calculations utilize the current value to us of the future goods, which value we explicitly discount in order to take account of the uncertainties of the goods' being realized. The discounting is *double* because the current value to us of the future good exhibits time-preference, an implicit discounting of the future selected for in the evolutionary process because of the adaptive advantage of discounting for future uncertainties and other such factors.

This problem of double-discounting would be avoided if our calculations, instead of utilizing the current value to us of future goods, utilized some measure of how much the good would be worth to us at that time in the future when it would be realized. There would be no double-counting in explicitly discounting such future values which have not yet been discounted even implicitly, for uncertainties.

However, a measure according to your preferences now of how valuable a future good will be to you *then* does not fit well with Austrian theory's close typing of preference to actual choices, or even to the loosening in terms of subjunctives which we suggested earlier.[46] So the problem of double-discounting is an especially pressing one for Austrian theory. Having built-in time-preference and also realizing what the evolutionary explanation of such time-preference is, how should we, as rational beings, behave?

PHILOSOPHY
AND
METHODOLOGY

SOCRATIC PUZZLES

∽ ∽ ∽

Ignorance

Socrates claims he does not know the answers to the questions he puts, and that if he is superior in wisdom this lies only in the fact that, unlike others, *he* is aware that he does not know. Yet he does have doctrines he recurs to (that it is better to suffer injustice than to do it, that no one does wrong voluntarily but only from ignorance,[1] that a doer of injustice is better off being punished for it), and he shows great confidence in these judgments. When Polus says it is easy to refute the view that the unpunished unjust man is more wretched than the punished one, Socrates replies that it is "impossible. For the truth is never refuted" (*Gorgias*, 473b). And Socrates tells Callicles that the doctrine that it is more evil, ugly and shameful to do injustice than to undergo it "is secured and bound fast . . . with arguments of adamant and iron" (508e–509a). Is this supremely confident Socrates merely being ironic when he elsewhere denies that he knows? How are we to understand what Gregory Vlastos terms "Socrates' central paradox,"[2] his profession of ignorance?

Socrates does not (generally) deny knowledge of the Socratic doctrines (it is better to suffer injustice than to do it, etc.) but of the answers to the "What is F?" questions he pursues with others. His superior wisdom then resides in his knowing that he doesn't know, and cannot produce, the correct answer to these "What is F?" questions. Not knowing these things is compatible with his knowing other things. There is no contradiction in his saying he *knows* he does not know the nature of the relevant F's, for that knowledge he has is not itself the answer to one of his "What is F?" questions.

This limits the scope of Socrates' claim not to know, but what precisely does he mean by this profession of ignorance? It has been suggested that Socrates does believe he has true beliefs about the matters he discusses, but that he lacks something in addition to true belief that (he thinks) is necessary for knowledge or for a certain kind of knowledge. Terence Irwin holds that Socrates claims only true belief.[3] Vlastos objects (didn't Socrates think some of his beliefs justified?), and he proposes instead a distinction between two kinds of knowledge: elenctic knowledge, which one has when one's (true) belief has survived repeated testing in the process of elenctic inquiry; and certain-knowledge, which one has only if one knows with infallibility and certainty. Socrates (says Vlastos) is consistent: when he claims knowledge, he is claiming only the first kind; when he denies he has knowledge he is denying he has the second.[4] Those who heard Socrates say that he doesn't know the answer would have taken him to mean that he doesn't know the *truth*, whereas Irwin and Vlastos interpret him as saying that he doesn't *know* the truth. Their interpretations might rescue the literal truth of Socrates' denial but they leave him generating misleading implicatures.

I suggest that when Socrates says he himself doesn't know the answers to these questions, he means not just that he doesn't know the truth but that he doesn't *have* the truth; he doesn't even have true belief.

One instance where commentators have suggested a particular what-is-F truth that Socrates possesses concerns piety.[5] Socrates leads Euthyphro to the suggestion that piety is performing a service to the gods. Vlastos suggests that Socrates would have gone on to speak of a service to the gods that the gods want done and would do by themselves if they could. What specifically is this service? Vlastos suggests that Socrates would say it is improving our own souls, and helping to improve the souls of our fellows.[6] (Vlastos states that Socrates has arrived at a new and religiously revolutionary, nonritualistic conception of piety.) We can add that a pious act would be one that does this improving not by accident or solely for some different reason but (in part) *because* it is desired by the Gods. This would make Socrates, pursuing his ordained mission, the most pious person in Athens. Should we call it another paradox of Socrates that he, the most pious person, was prosecuted for impiety? (The first paradox is that the founder of Western rationality was set upon his course by an *oracle's* statement.) Or is *this* Socratic irony?

Can Socrates offer a satisfactory account[7] to answer the question: what is piety? We already have suggested one component in addition to the ones Socrates mentions or hints at: doing the pious act because it is desired by the gods. But the investigation into the nature of piety cannot stop here. Further questions will arise. (How precisely do we delineate the needed connection between our doing the act and its being desired by the gods? Will any desire by the gods for something excellent do, or does it matter why the gods have this desire? Would it nevertheless be pious if the gods desired something bad of us? What is the nature of the good to which the gods adhere? Must a pious act concern what the gods literally cannot do for (or accomplish by) themselves? Precisely what counts as an improvement in the soul's state? And so on.) In the same paragraph where he credits Socrates with reaching (and leading Euthyphro up to) a new conception of piety, Vlastos says (pp. 175–176):

> To derive from this a definition of piety, Euthyphro would then have had to generalize, contriving a formula that would apply, not only in Socrates' case, but in every possible case of pious conduct. This is a tall order, and it is by no means clear that Socrates himself would have been able to fill it. But this technical failure would not shake— would scarcely touch the central insight into the nature of piety . . . Whether or not a formula could be devised to encapsulate this insight in an elenctically foolproof definition . . .

Let us consider another concept, that of knowledge, a concept not discussed in the early dialogues but one which (as we have seen) the recent commentators lean upon. The history I shall rehearse is familiar but this particular example will serve us later.

Is knowledge true belief? No, says Plato in the *Theaetetus*. Is it true belief with an account or true belief with adequate reasons or justified true belief? No, shows the Gettier counterexample. Is it a true belief that *p* that is caused (or explained in part) by the fact that *p*? No, in view of the example of the person floating in a tank brought by psychologists to believe he is floating in that tank. Is knowledge belief that tracks the truth, that is, (1) a belief that *p*, where (2) *p* is true, (3) if *p* were not true the person would not believe it, and (4) if *p* were true the person would believe it? Leaving aside additional complications about methods and ways of knowing, I said *yes* in *Philosophical Explanations,* but others have raised objections.[8]

So what is knowledge, what are the necessary and sufficient conditions for knowledge that *p*? A reasonable philosopher today might say that, in view of the difficulties thus far encountered, he just does not know. And by this he means not that he is prepared to put forward conditions that he *believes* are correct without being certain that they are, but that there are not conditions he is prepared to put forth, not conditions he believes will not succumb to further counterexamples and complications. This reasonable philosopher may believe, on inductive grounds, that since all previous accounts have fallen so will any one he can formulate, or he may already know of examples or objections that he cannot yet handle. He knows that he cannot yet formulate "an elenctically foolproof definition."

He does know something else that more naive people do not; he knows that knowledge is not just true belief, or justified true belief, or . . . Moreover, he may know more than they do, in the sense that the account he would put forward if forced to mention the most adequate one he knows of, while itself false and inadequate, is more adequate, is closer to the truth (whatever that true account is) than the earlier accounts or than the general accounts that would be proposed by those who do not know the history of successive accounts.

Socrates himself, I suggest, was in this position with regard to the topics he discussed. I do not claim, anachronistically and absurdly, that he knew all of the difficulties revealed in the future discussions of knowledge or of any other topic. But I do claim that he was more thoughtful and more acute than his Athenian contemporaries in probing various topics. He knew more than his fellows, he knew precisely where their accounts failed, and he could formulate a more adequate account that did not fall to *those* objections. However, he also knew of or believed there were objections that would show his current best account to be inadequate, that is, *false.* He didn't know what piety, courage, justice, etc., were. He didn't have a completely adequate true belief about any of these topics. He didn't have accurate necessary and sufficient conditions for any of these notions, much less a completely accurate understanding of how all of these notions were interrelated. Hence, Socrates was not being ironic when he denied knowing the answers. He did not know. And he knew he did not.

Elenchus

In his discussions with others (and presumably in his own internal thinking) Socrates uses the method of *elenchus*. Inconsistencies in belief are uncovered, thus impelling the person to modify his beliefs. An inconsistency reveals that we *must* have some false belief, but we *do* have many false beliefs anyway—few of us believe all of our beliefs are true—so why is inconsistency especially bad? Provided we are careful not to deduce any consequences by forms of inference that depend upon the beliefs being inconsistent, why should inconsistency trouble us especially?

An inconsistency or mistake about the important (evaluative) concepts Socrates discusses is dangerous, either because it itself constitutes a defect in the state of one's soul, or because it easily can lead to one. Other apparently good things (wealth, power, etc.), without guidance by a correct knowledge of the good, can lead to one's harm.[9]

The Socratic search for the definition of a concept F is a search for necessary and sufficient conditions that provide a standard that can be utilized to decide whether F applies in any given case. However, when people often are able to apply the concept F to particular cases, judging whether or not it applies, why is an *explicit* standard necessary? An explicit standard can help to judge difficult cases or borderline ones. Moreover, explicit understanding of what makes something F can prevent being thrown into confusion by arguments that seem to show that F is impossible or never applies. Even someone who by and large can classify cases correctly as being knowledge or not, when faced with the skeptical argument, "you cannot know that you are not floating in a tank that generates all the experiences you have had; therefore you know almost nothing," might conclude that indeed he does not know most of what he thought he knew. An explicit understanding of what constitutes knowledge (or F) makes your beliefs about knowledge (or F) more stable and less prone to being upset by inadequate arguments. About the important evaluative concepts, connected with the nature of the good and the best state of one's soul, it is especially important not to be misled, given Socrates' view that knowledge is virtue. Morover, the stability of one's correct belief might itself be a component of a well-ordered soul.

What makes Socrates' method of *elenchus* a method of reaching the truth? What must hold true if *elenchus* is to be an effective way of reaching the truth? In "The Socratic Elenchus,"[10] Vlastos offers a very illuminating discussion of this matter. First, it is possible that I hold a false belief about some matter though my beliefs are not inconsistent. I believe that a particular undergraduate student comes from Seattle. *Elenchus* will not help here, in the absence of further information which I don't yet have. (For example, I might also believe that that student does know what city he comes from. If you now tell me, and I believe this, that the student believes he comes from Minneapolis, then my beliefs will form an inconsistent trio.)

Socratic *elenchus* doesn't get a grip to impel a change in belief unless there are inconsistencies. Or so the commentators tell us. We can imagine that a questioning procedure also is able to impel changes because of tensions, disharmonies, and complications that it uncovers, even when these do not constitute strict inconsistencies. A person can be made uncomfortable if his beliefs in combination are very improbable, or if to harmonize them he has to assume some other very improbable (or inordinately complex) further group of statements, etc. The discussion and probing of issues can utilize norms of belief, in addition to the norm of avoiding inconsistency, to impel change in belief.

What must hold, though, for the stringent *elenchus* that works only upon inconsistencies to do its work? When a person holds a false belief, what guarantees there will be inconsistencies? Socrates assumes (suggests Vlastos) that about the evaluative matters he discusses, the person will hold some true beliefs inconsistent with the falsehood.

(B)   For any person and for any false belief q about the requisite subject matter, the person entering into *elenchus* also will hold some true belief p, inconsistent with q.[11]

(How did he acquire these true beliefs? By recollection?)

An inconsistency is enough to get the elenctic process of change going, but what points that process toward the truth?[12] When an inconsistency is discovered among a person's beliefs p and q, he can remove that inconsistency by denying the true one p or by denying the false one q. What stops him from denying the true statement p?[13] If the belief that p and the belief that q are each merely beliefs, they seem on a par. What, then, prevents *elenchus* from leading him further from the truth?

I suggest the following. (Here, perhaps, I trespass upon Plato's topics rather than Socrates' assumptions.) *Elenchus* is a reliable vehicle for getting toward the truth when a person *knows* (and doesn't merely hold as true beliefs) truths about the subject matter sufficient to introduce inconsistency with any false beliefs he holds. So we strengthen Vlastos' assumption B to:

(K) For any person and for any false belief q about the requisite subject matter, the person entering into *elenchus* also will *know* some truth p, inconsistent with q.

But why does this knowledge make (it more likely that) the process of removing inconsistencies (will) move toward the truth, and not further in the direction of consistently false beliefs? The former will happen if knowledge has more stability (tenacity, stickiness) than belief, true or false. What this means is the following.

(R) When a person is faced with an inconsistency among statements, and resolves this inconsistency by giving up one statement, he will (tend to) give up a false statement that he believes rather than a true one that he knows.

When beliefs conflict, something about knowledge makes the person adhere more to what is known than to a false belief.[14]

If this is so, then the *elenctic* process will (tend to) lead someone toward the truth. Even if he just is more likely to give up a false belief rather than something known, and so sometimes does not do that, still, provided he has enough of such knowledge so that conflicts with his false beliefs will continue, the higher stickiness of knowledge will (tend to) win out in the end. In this *elenctic* competition, knowledge is more fit than false belief, and so tends to be selected for.

Do the necessary and sufficient conditions for knowledge guarantee its greater stability or stickiness, or is that just knowledge's fortunate concomitant? In the tracking account of knowledge described earlier, the fourth condition states that if p were true, the person would believe it. The belief that p is stable under small enough perturbations. In terms of the modelling of subjunctives by possible worlds, he continues to believe p in those p-worlds, the p-band of worlds, closest to the actual world. These include the worlds where p comes into conflict with a false belief in q; even there the person believes that p. Thus this fourth tracking condition gives us (a portion of) the requisite stability and stickiness of knowledge. I do not want to insist that this particular tracking condition is a part of the (correct) analysis of knowledge. But if it is, or if some modification is, or if some different condition is that gives knowledge greater stability than merely false belief, then the crucial condition will hold that makes *elenchus* an effective route toward the truth.

I have said that Socratic ignorance consists in not knowing (and not having a true belief stating) the answer to the "What is F?" question. And I have not denied that Socrates believes that he *has* reached the truth about some evaluative matters, e.g., concerning the doctrines that it is better to suffer injustice than to do it, that no one does wrong voluntarily but only out of ignorance, that it is better for someone that he be punished for an injustice he has committed. Elenchus is an effective route to reaching such evaluative truths, on this account, only for persons who satisfy conditions (K) and (R), that is, only for people who already do have *some* knowledge about these evaluative matters. So *elenchus* (if it is reliably effective) cannot be the only route to knowledge about these matters.

Why is elenchus not also an effective route to reaching a correct answer to "What is F?" Is it that we do not have the requisite knowledge concerning the nature of F to satisfy condition (K)? We will have *some* knowledge about F, though, for those concepts F that are involved in Socratic doctrines that *elenchus* can yield. Another possible answer would be that elenchus *is* able, in principle, to reach such a correct answer after a finite number of humanly takable steps (proposals, objections, modifications, etc.), but that number is so large the process is so long and arduous, that no one has yet reached that resultant stage.[15] Particular evaluative truths are less complex than the complete truth about the nature of the evaluative concepts; they can be reached early in the elenctic process, whenceforth they remain stable. Why are the answers to the what-is-F questions so complex? Analytic philosophers should not tax Socrates with these questions when they themselves lack a satisfactory explanation for why their own stock of correct analyses is so meager.

Improving Souls

In "The Paradox of Socrates," Gregory Vlastos accuses Socrates of being so strongly wedded to his method of *elenchus* as to evidence "a failure of love."

> I have already argued that he does care for the souls of his fellows. But the care is limited and conditional. If men's souls are to be saved,

they must be saved his way. And when he sees they cannot, he watches them go down the road to perdition with regret but without anguish. Jesus wept for Jerusalem. Socrates warns Athens, scolds, exhorts it, condemns it. But he has no tears for it . . . One feels there is a last zone of frigidity in the soul of the great erotic; had he loved his fellows more, he could hardly have laid on them the burdens of his "despotic logic," impossible to be borne.[16]

Does Socrates know of (or at least, believe there is) some other way souls can be improved? If not, then in adhering to his way he is, at worst, making a mistake due to ignorance. Indeed, it is not enough for Vlastos's charge that Socrates know of another way to improve souls. That other way must fit Socrates' particular talents and skills, it must be one that Socrates can follow (whether exclusively or in mixture with his own way) with at least equal success and effect. That Buddha too had a way of improving people—suppose that Socrates knew of this way—does not mean that Socrates willfully follows his own.

Of course, Vlastos is aware that firm Socratic doctrines seem to leave Socrates (or anyone else) no other way.[17] To improve the state of someone's soul is to make him more virtuous. That requires (and requires only) bringing him into a state of greater knowledge of the good. (Knowledge is virtue; virtue is knowledge.) True belief about the good is not sufficient. Perhaps knowledge of the good is an intrinsic part of a virtuous soul. In any case, true belief is unstable, hence an insufficient guide and gyroscope. Moreover, Socrates cannot simply tell people the truth; they cannot reach a knowledge of the good through the say-so and authority of anyone else. At best, that will give them an unstable true belief, open to upsetting by the next contrary "authority." The only way to aid their knowledge of the good is to get them to think through issues about the nature of the good and its relation to other things, that is, to engage them (or to get them to engage themselves) in *elenchus* concerning these matters. Socrates can give others a method of inquiry only by showing it to them in action; thereby he launches them upon their own path of inquiry. Given his doctrines and views, Socrates is not insisting upon saving his fellow citizens *his way*. There is no other way.

Inquiry arises because of puzzlement, John Dewey said. People who are quite confident of the truth of their very extensive views are unlikely to engage in probing inquiry about these matters. The first step for Socrates, then, must be to show these others that they *need* to think about these matters, that is, to show them that what they already are thinking (or unthinkingly assuming) is quite definitely wrong. Why will someone who is confident of his views enter such discussions? Travelling teachers may do so to show their wares. Others may have to be shamed or bulldozed into such discussions, for their own good (and the good of the onlookers). Even apart from its further effects, Socrates may hold that it is better for a person with false views about these matters to be refuted, just as it is better for someone who has committed injustice to be punished.[18] To improve people's souls, then, Socrates will have to make a *pest* of himself, buttonholing unwilling conversants, forcing them into physical and then intellectual corners.[19] Being a pest, an expression of his caring, puts Socrates into danger, or increases the danger he already is in.

Socrates has doctrines but what he teaches is not a doctrine but a method of inquiry. (He does think or hope that sustained inquiry will lead others closer to his doctrines.) He teaches the method of inquiry by involving others in it, by exhibiting it. Their job is to catch on, and to go on.

Socrates shows something more: the kind of person that such sustained inquiry produces. It is not his method alone that teaches us but rather that method (and those doctrines it has led him to) *as embodied in* Socrates. We see Socrates *within* his inquiries and his inquiring interactions with others; we see the way his inquiries shape and infuse his life, and his death. Socrates teaches with his person. Buddha and Jesus did as well. Socrates is unique among philosophers in doing this.

Socrates teaches us beyond the arguments he offers. The arguments presented in the *Crito* are weak, after all.[20] They are insufficient, individually and jointly, to show that Socrates has an *obligation* to the city not to escape. Yet who would say that Socrates should have accepted Crito's offer? Socrates is right that scurrying off to another city to gain a few more years would be the wrong thing *for him* to do. To escape would show an unseemly concern with death. It would not improve the state of his soul. The unflinching courage and integrity and calmness and clarity with which Socrates faces and meets death teach us how death is to be faced. This incarnation of rationality and courage and justice uplifts and ennobles our souls; we are the better for admiring and loving him.

About the best state of the soul, too, Socrates shows us more than he says. Arguments are presented in the *Gorgias* that it is better to suffer injustice than to do it, but these involve an *aesthetic* component. The unjust soul is disordered and unlovely; it is ugly. Socrates invokes here (without explicitly developing) a general notion of value within which the moral and the aesthetic fit. According to this general conception, souls can be more or less lovely, more or less beautiful.

We learn what this beauty of soul is, as did his hearers, not by being presented with an explicit theory but by encountering Socrates.[21] Socrates' teaching and its convincingness depend significantly upon the embodiment Socrates is, and the way in which this is displayed.

That is not something that Socrates himself would have said or believed. His reasoning and arguments were supposed to bear the full weight, at least when combined in elenchus with what the other person already knew or believed. This additional way that Socrates teaches us—call it the method of embodiment—stands alongside his method of elenchus, and also is worthy of sustained attention.

7 | EXPERIENCE, THEORY, AND LANGUAGE

ↅ ↅ ↅ

For the past twenty-five years Quine's powerful and deep philosophical views have been, deservedly, the focus of more attention, discussion, and controversy than those of any other philosopher in the English-speaking world. His powerful reductionist philosophy attracts those who wish to fit things into a sleek, limited, tight framework (quantification theory, loved by Quine and central to his philosophizing, also exemplifies the virtues he seeks in his philosophy as a whole), while it repels those who think it excludes much that is important about our intellectual lives or ourselves. I myself, strongly subject to *both* the attraction and the repulsion, am ambivalent about his view, and about such reductionist views. The basis of these contrasting pulls and pushes is itself an interesting and different topic, but to metaphilosophize on the sources of our (my?) philosophical ambivalence would be inappropriate on this occasion. Instead, I shall discuss some of Quine's themes, sometimes critically assessing his positions, and sometimes sympathetically defending or extending them. This will result in a clouding of rhetorical force, as perhaps befits an essay written out of ambivalence.

Quine is the theorist of slack.* Data underdetermine theory, there is leeway about which component to modify when data conflict with a theory, and translation is indeterminate. Also, theory underdetermines the world (the doctrine of ontological relativity).

These particular theses ramify throughout philosophy, and the fact of slack itself is of great philosophical interest.

> We cannot strip away the conceptual trappings sentence by sentence and leave a description of the objective world, but we can investigate the world, and man as a part of it, and thus find out what cues he could have of what goes on around him. Subtracting his cues from his world view, we get man's net contribution as the difference. This difference marks the extent of man's net conceptual sovereignty—the domain within which he can revise theory while saving the data.[1]

I. Experience and Language

Duhem and Experiential Meaning

What explains why, vide Duhem, our statements don't face the tribunal of experience singly? (Is it cowardice?) Would a language whose statements did this, a non-Duhemian language, be impossible for us? If not, in what ways would such a language be inferior? I do not ask these questions from the standpoint of what Quine calls first philosophy. *Within* our current theory, what explains Duhem's facts?

Our experiences are dependent upon the state and condition of our sensory apparatus, on our orientations in the world, and on what the world is like, including those aspects of the world which are distinguished as conditions of observation. Furthermore (one is tempted to continue), our experiences of the world depend upon many interconnected facts about the world. Since experiences are dependent upon so many things, which may vary independently, a being would have to know enormous amounts to have any hope of formulating statements with individual experiential content.

But this purported explanation dissolves when we notice that we have no clear language-independent notion of number of facts. We count facts in our language. Our view that our experiences depend upon many

---

* Quine's view countenances slack galore; how then can some have held it to be rigid? It excludes what on other views fixes things in determinate place. (Apparently, there is not enough slack to admit, as compatible with the data, a theory of fixed meanings.)

facts derives from our not having single statements with individual experiential content. We cannot explain why our statements do not singly connect with experience by the multiplicity of facts upon which experiences depend. Nor can we appeal to how complicated the facts are. For if we measure the degree of complicatedness of a sentence, language-independently, by the nature of its connection to experience, then long conjunctions which uniquely map onto experience will come out as quite *un*complicated.

The statements (in English, complicated conjunctions) which (arguably) singly have experiential content run athwart those which are important to us, and have been in the course of evolution. The precise experiential content of "there is an unrestrained tiger in front of me" is less important than avoiding knowledge of the experiential content of "I am being eaten by a tiger," a content which once known is unlikely, in any event, to be conveyed to others. About such dangers as there being a tiger present, type-two errors (accepting an hypothesis when it is false) were preferred to type-one errors (rejecting an hypothesis when it is true) and were selected for. Better to flee unnecessarily than to stand and refine the experiential content of one's statement!

The interest of many other statements stems from the diverse ways they fit into people's plans. Trees before you can be walked around, hid behind, climbed up, and cut down. What one wants to know is whether there is a tree there. That multi-purpose statement does not have the separable experiential content had by conjunctions about trees and lighting conditions and the state of one's eyes and lack of non-transparent obstruction between you and it, and so forth. What it has is utility.

The facts that evolution selects for attentiveness to, facts which have multi-purpose utility in our lives, lie athwart those with specific experiential content. If language is geared to the former facts, and its component sentences state them, then these sentences will not have (be exhausted in) separate experiential content. Relative to the grid set by our evolutionary past and activities, sentences with separate experiential content will be very complex, and our experiences will depend upon the conjunction of many (language-identified) facts.

Since language is geared, for evolutionary reasons and reasons of practical activity, to facts which lie athwart (those facts which correlate with) experiences (as represented perhaps by firings of nerve endings), it would be surprising if some significant unit of language was marked off via experiential content. In particular, it would be very surprising if the *unit of meaning* of the language were those entities (whatever they might be) with separate experiential content. Why should something have evolved or been formulated or come to be, whose units were *that*? If we were designing a language to be taught to organisms who had not developed their own, in order to aid them in surviving and acting in the world, would it be organized around units of distinguishable experiential content? Would distinguishable experiential content be a theoretically significant notion for a language with that purpose?

The claim that something with separate meaning must have separate experiential content is a philosophical imposition which rests on considerations about learning a language, to which I turn below, and on the question "how else *can* something have meaning?," which I take to be a symptom of being trapped by a picture. The explanation of why Duhem's thesis holds, makes implausible the view that the units of meaning are the units with separate experiential content. That the facts that language is geared to state lie athwart those with separate experiential content is understandable and explicable; that the sentences stating those facts which language is geared to state should lie athwart the language's units of meaning is not to be believed.

Not only are our individual sentences without separate experiential content;[2] there is no reason to think our total scientific theory has it either. Given the range of factors (as counted by our current partitioning of the world) upon which our experiences depend, including the facts of sensory psychology, one would have to know all of these (and that they were all), as well as the theory which connected them to our experiences, in order to know that one's total theory had experiential content. (And would there be open *ceteris paribus* clauses in one's body of theory?)[3] In the history of mankind, when did we reach the point of having theories extensive enough to have separate experiential content? Before then were all sentences without meaning? Through assuming separate experiential content must be *somewhere* in the language if language is to be meaningful, and not finding it in individual sentences, one might think it *must* lurk in the total set of sentences we would assert. Not there either.

If our total theory *did* have separate experiential content, we might think to assign experiential content to its *individual* sentences as follows. Consider the set of sentences of the language of length $\leq n$ (setting n high enough so that we don't exclude as too long any sentences we are interested in), and take the power set of this set. Within each set in the power set order the sentences alphabetically, and then order these sets alphabetically. For any sentence S and any set X within the ordered power set, we may consider the experiential content (observational consequences) of $\{S\} \cup X$. (S may already be contained in X, or its denial may be, or there may be no observational consequences of this particular union.) Against the structure provided by the ordered power set, we may now specify the experiential content (observational consequences) of any sentence S as $O_s = \langle \{T_1\}, \{T_2\}, \ldots, \{T_n\} \rangle$, where T_i the observational consequences of $\{S\} \cup$ the ith member of the ordered power set. The observational consequences of S would be specified as its observational consequences relative to all other sentences, and translation between languages would depend upon isomorphism between the components of such structures.

Is this then a way to formulate separately the experiential content of individual sentences? Actually not all (or even many) possible sets of sentences are conditioned to experience; instead only one evolving set is (that is, a sequence of sets). Since it is this actual process of conditioning to experience which, on Quine's view, gives the tie to experience, we *cannot* assume that *other* large conjunctions do have this tie to experience. For this assumes the conjuncts come already with their own individual (relative) observational content and that the content of the conjunction results from fitting together the individual contents. (How else would a conjunction, itself unconditioned to experience, have experiential content?) Quine, therefore, would reject this method whereby the individual observational content of the sentences we accept is to be specified relative to an ordering of all other sets of sentences, I conjecture. For these total sets (all but one) will not, on his view, have observational content since they will not have been actually conditioned to observation.

Duhem and Determinate Content

Since those facts we are interested in, for evolutionary reasons, lie athwart facts with specific experiential consequences, a language limited to stating these latter facts would fail to serve our purposes. But what would such a language be like? Would this be a non-Duhemian language: the applied lower functional calculus with one atomic predicate 'n fires at t,' where n ranges over nerve endings and t over instants (or intervals) of time? Label all nerve endings and specify the person. This language is suggested by Quine's remarks about information (*Philosophy of Logic*, p. 5), directed to showing that we cannot specify the meanings of our English sentences individually in this language. All sentences in this language have determinate informational content (*Philosophy of Logic,* pp. 4–5). But, whether in the first or the third person, these are highly theoretical statements of sensory psychology which are themselves subject to Duhem's thesis. (Is this very sophisticated language of psychological theory also the observation language? With community-wide agreement about its sentences?) These sentences may perform for the "naturalistically inclined" epistemologist *some* of the functions of introspectible sense data, in that their obtaining underlies a person's observation sentences; but they are unlike sense data statements in not being incorrigible. being theoretical, and being subject to Duhem's thesis. Being subject to Duhem's thesis does not, apparently, insure lack of determinate informational content or failure to state a separate fact of the matter. Therefore, Duhemian considerations do not show that sentences do not have separate meaning. (Such considerations would do so only along with a verification theory of separate meaning, but that theory would be difficult to square with Quine's remarks on the objective information of sentences.)

Quine also considers the possibility of specifying the content of sentences by specifying which distributions of elementary particles they are true in, and notes that we cannot do this (*Philosophy of Logic,* pp. 4–5). But there *are* sentences which are already, without analysis, sentences about the distribution of elementary particles. These sentences of physics would have determinate informational (factual) content surely, for if it were possible to translate other sentences into these, this (Quine says) would show that *the others* had determinate content. Yet still these sentences are subject to Duhem's thesis. For the statement that a certain distribution of particles obtained could be tested only in conjunction with many other sentences.

Let us say that a language's sentences have *uniform determinate content* if and only if there is some matrix of alternatives into which all the sentences are uniquely translatable. (The *one* matrix provides the uniformity, the uniqueness provides the determinateness.) Failing this, will the sentences of a language lack individual meaning? That would be too stringent a criterion. For even if two languages each satisfy the criterion (relative to two different matrices which do not "interfere"), it would exclude their union as containing individually meaningful sentences. Yet to admit any language which was the sum of languages which did satisfy the condition would exclude no language, without some constraint upon admissible matrices to prevent every atomic fragment of the language from providing its own matrix.

It might be objected that when Quine says that some statement S about distributions of elementary particles or firings of nerve endings does have separate content, he is speaking from within a theory which contains and utilizes a sub-theory about particles, nerve-ending firings, etc.; the sentences of this theory, when viewed from the outside, however, have no separate content and are subject to Duhem's thesis. But from *within* a theory *each* of its statements (excluding the ambiguous) has a determinate content. Yet Quine does not merely say (leaving us to realize he's speaking from within a theory) that *every* sentence has a determinate content.

"We can never hope to arrive at a technique for so analyzing out ordinary sentences as to reveal their implications in respect of the distribution of particles" (*Philosophy of Logic*, pp. 4–5). Our ordinary sentences are not geared to talk of what may micro-reduce what actually is their subject matter. Our interests lie elsewhere. (Would we know what someone who spoke such analyses of ordinary sentences *meant?*) The distributions of particles does not constitute a privileged matrix into which we must translate our ordinary sentences. It is notable, though, that Quine thinks that sentences would have determinate meaning ("objective information") if we *could* analyze their implications in respect of the distribution of particles. One might think that determinateness is the crucial criterion of separate meaning, rather than separate experiential content, which the particle statements lack. But Quine, I think, is concerned with and favors two distinguishable things, determinate content and experiential content. So he would view with some favor a particle language whose individual sentences separately have the first though not the second. Since separate experiential content is *one* way of providing uniform determinate meaning, his concerns converge in his treatment of determinate experiential content. But he has not yet given us a rationale or motivation for being concerned with uniform determinate content.

We have no argument for a sharp criterion connecting meaning with experiences. (Why is Quine so sanguine about holistic verificationism? "Epistemology Naturalized," p. 81.) Quine grants, moreover, that some sentences have separate informational content even though they are subject to Duhem's thesis and are not separately testable, and we would expect the unit of meaning not to be connected with experiential content anyway. Hence, it seems unlikely that any interesting conclusion about the theory of meaning will emerge from Duhemian considerations.[4] But something interesting *might* emerge from asking how we would expect a language to be organized, given the considerations adduced above to explain why Duhem's thesis holds.

Language Learning and Indeterminacy

One might think that considerations about language learning *do* show that the matrix of nerve-ending firings constitutes a privileged matrix into which our ordinary sentences must be translated. For it is through such firings that we learn language; how can what we learn transcend how we learn? And if meanings are artifacts shaped by us, will they not be fired in the kiln of our nerve endings?

Comfort for viewing meanings as going beyond stimuli might seem to come from a much studied phenomenon: on the basis of a few firings we generalize along pre-existing lines in quality space, thereby transcending the stimuli from which we learn. (Psychologists speak of generalization gradients; these vary from species to species.) However, we do not thereby transcend that type of stimulus, which can be used to check that we do generalize along the same paths. It is striking that we do generalize alike past particular data in those cases we can check with other data. One might speculate that we move similarly beyond the data in other uncheckable cases, but unlike the former case, direct evolutionary selective pressure would not explain the latter.

Another way to detach (partially) meaning from stimuli offers more promise. Consider specifying (not *defining*) X as that thing or mechanism which actually explains data D.[5] Here the reference of X is fixed by D and by the world. D may have separate experiential content, or it may have been originally explained, as X here is, but in terms of data with separate experiential content, and so on. Let us suppose that X stands in the ancestral of the explains-relation to something with separate experiential content. Cannot the meaning of X be fixed in this way, has it not been given separate meaning, even though clearly it itself does not have separate experiential content?

It might be said that if we fix the reference of X in this way, we can't *know* what X means or refers to. And it might seem as if the whole truth about the meaning or mechanism of reference of our terms must be exhausted by psychological truths about us. How can there be more to what *I* mean, to the meaning of the term as I use it, than is contained in my intentions, beliefs, etc.? There are numerous counter-examples to this apparently compelling view, e.g., Wittgenstein's on how what the person means by chess is fixed outside of *his* intentions and beliefs, Kripke's causal story about proper names, Quine on dispositions; and recently Putnam, in his illuminating talk about division of linguistic labor, has shown how unintuitive it is, how inefficient it would be, if we each had to carry around with us the complete meaning of what we say.[6]

One might think to use the way in which external facts fix meaning to resolve Quinean indeterminacies. But before looking at details, note how such views *undermine* one objection to Quine on indeterminacy. Many who object to Quine think it's perfectly certain what *they* mean, treating this as some incorrigible psychological fact about themselves. On the external determination view, of course, they *can* be wrong. (Add to this Wittgenstein's erosion of viewing meanings and intentions as internal psychological pellets, thereby undercutting a platform on which one might think to stand in confidently attacking Quine.) So how can they be so certain about what their fixed meaning is?

A tale will be useful here, which also will serve to combat the view that within neurology lies determinacy of translation. Suppose we send two ships off in opposite directions, containing infant children and teachers. One group of teachers will teach the children English, speaking it to them. The other group of teachers on the other ship will speak stage-English, which is the stage-language of English. (This is the language, described by Quine, whose terms denote temporal stages of enduring objects. It has nothing special to do with the theater!) The words of stage-English are some trivial phonetic transformation of the corresponding English words, "Blegg" instead of "egg," etc. Locked in a safe in the captain's cabin is a dictionary which states the meaning of stage-English words and sentences in English. Now suppose almost exactly the same things happen on the two ships; for each sentence heard on an occasion on the English-speaking ship, a corresponding sentence will be heard on the stage-English ship on the parallel occasion. (They are almost parallel worlds.) The children on the first ship will learn to speak English, and the children on the second will learn to speak a language which, let us suppose, is stage-English. The only neurological differences between a child on one ship and a corresponding child on the other ship will be due to the trivial phonetic differences; otherwise they are neurologically identical.

Indeed, it was not necessary that the children on the stage-English ship be taught a phonetically different language. If the phonetically different stage-language was somewhat longer, couldn't they be taught an abbreviation of it (recorded also in the captain's cabin), and mightn't this abbreviation be phonetically identical to English? So their neurology would be *identical* to that of English speakers, though of course there would remain the separate dictionaries in the different captain's cabins (and perhaps interested social scientists telemonitoring from afar).

Whatever neurological configuration realizes one of the languages will also realize the other; any neurological model of English will also be a neurological model of stage-English. Given the formal relations between the two languages, how could it be otherwise? Perhaps we can reduce the psychology of a speaker of English to neurology, identifying his believing there is a table before him (believing that semantic content) with a particular neurological state N. But there can be a parallel identification of his believing this corresponding stage-English sentence with the very *same* neurological state N. We can parallel one reduction by another; no determinacy lurks in neurological reduction.

But did the children on the second ship learn, as we supposed, stage-English? Though an attempt was made to teach them that language (perhaps their teachers even silently translated into English whenever they spoke, or silently said "that was stage-English; in English it means . . . "), perhaps the children really learned English, for perhaps a stage-language is unlearnable as a first language. But we have seen that the grounds for saying this cannot lie in neurology; what then can they be?

The view that the children on the second ship learn stage-English fits in very well with theories of the fixing of meaning by external facts. Here, the central external facts are the setting up of the experiment and the book in the captain's safe. Suppose these children are taken to an island, settle, have children, etc., and two hundred years later the misplaced captain's safe is discovered and opened. Would what the descendants learn then be important? What would they have to do to change their language to a non-stage language? Suppose instead that the children on the two ships were settled on the same island. Would the differences between them, as they fluently spoke together, be linguistically or semantically important? The children grow up, intermarry with those from the other ship, and raise their children who learn language from their parents and from others around them in the normal way. These latter children have learned language equally from persons from each of the ships who themselves were unaware of any linguistic differences among them. Do these children speak English or stage-English? *Is* there a fact of the matter about which *they* speak?

The mingling together of two distinct external sources produces an example of "no fact of the matter" about which language they speak. They just . . . speak. Someone who thought there *couldn't* be a case of "no fact of the matter" can, via the external fixing view, be brought to accept the possibility as making sense. Now, how *important* are our differences from those people for whom there is no fact of the matter? (And are you *sure* that we *are* different, that our language wasn't such a commingling of different streams?) How important a fact is it about us that we are in our group and not the one in which there is no determinate propositional content? Should we stop our children from intermarrying with theirs, so that our descendants will speak determinately, so that there will be a fact of the matter about which they mean? Whatever differences there are seem trivial, hardly worth making central to a philosophical position.

We have supposed, until now, that the fixing of meaning by external facts would fix determinate meaning. (Even on that supposition, we were led to conclude that the differences between determinate meaning and no determinate meaning were trivial.) But how will the intentions of people in the initial fixing situation have gained determinacy? And for any factual relation R between y (data, things, use of a word, etc.) and the x which is "fixed" by standing in that relation R to y, there will be an x' and R' such that $x'R'y$, or a y' such that $x'R'y'$, and there will be no apparent way to resolve the indeterminancy between terms denoting R and those denoting R' (or between those denoting y and those denoting y').

The topic of the relationship of language acquisition to meaning has led us to discuss introducing a term X to denote what explains data D. This mode of term introduction clearly does not attach the meaning of X to firings of nerve endings. (On the other hand, we have argued, it also does not fix X so as to narrow Quinean indeterminacies.) We *cannot* get a cogent argument for experiential content being what fixes the unit of meaning from considerations about language learning. The example of introducing terms via the explanation-relation which shows this also provides a special explanation of why Duhem's thesis holds for some sentences. Introduced via the notion of 'explanation,' the term X

will live for us upon the notion of 'best explanation,' which is a non-local notion, looking at large portions of theory.

Stimulus Meaning

Quine's own positive account of the relationship of meaning and experiential content centers on the notion of stimulus meaning; "stimulus meaning . . . may be properly looked upon still as the objective reality that the linguist has to probe" (*Word and Object*, p. 39). The stimulus meaning is the ordered pair of affirmative and negative stimulus meanings, and these meanings "of a sentence (for a given speaker at a given time) are mutually exclusive" (p. 33).

> A stimulation σ belongs to the affirmative stimulus meaning of a sentence S for a given speaker if and only if there is a stimulation σ' such that if the speaker were given σ', then were asked S, then were given σ and then were asked S again, he would dissent the first time and assent the second.
>   A stimulation σ belongs to the negative stimulus meaning of a sentence S for a given speaker if and only if there is a stimulation σ' such that if the speaker were given σ', then were asked S, then were given σ, and then were asked S again, he would assent the first time and dissent the second.   (*Word and Object*, p. 32)

The immediate difficulty is that since each of these definitions uses an existential quantifier ("there is a stimulation σ'"), it is left open that for the same σ and S there are two different stimulations σ' and σ'' which serve to place σ both in the affirmative and in the negative stimulus meaning of S. To have these be disjoint, we would need the truth of $(\exists\sigma')$(if the speaker were given σ' then were asked S, then were given σ and then were asked S again, he would dissent the first time and assent the second) $\supset \sim (\exists\sigma'')$(if the speaker were given σ'' then were asked S, then were given σ and then were asked S again, he would assent the first time and dissent the second), and also of the statement which is gotten from this by interchanging "assent" and "dissent." We have been given no argument for these very strong statements, and they appear to be false. First, an intuitive case. Let σ' be the auditory stimulation "Please say 'no' to the first question and 'yes' to the second." If this is an admissible stimulation, then $(\sigma) (S) (\sigma$ belongs to the affirmative stimulus meaning of $S)$; and we can proceed similarly with negative stimulus meaning. Excluding such stimulations[7] would make it difficult to ascertain (or define) the stimulus meanings of sentences like "He has just spoken well" or "He has just spoken loudly."

For any σ which would appear to fit S, let σ' be a stimulation which fits S and which leads the person to believe that though σ occurs, not-S; e.g., the evolving ocular radiation which occurs when he sees people construct and place a brown papier-mâché rabbit alongside a white rabbit. σ is the ocular radiation of seeing a brown rabbit with no white rabbit around. He assents to "gavagai" the first time and dissents the second (because he thinks he's still looking at the papier-mâché rabbit), so that, according to Quine's criterion, σ is in the *negative* stimulus meaning of "gavagai." And so on. Intuitively, what one will assent to on the basis of stimulation depends upon one's other beliefs, and even though Quine means to include this by speaking of stimulus meaning for a particular person at a particular time, different preliminary stimulations σ' can change the person's beliefs in different ways.

Can the tasks Quine sees for the (as we have seen, defective) notion of stimulus meaning be accomplished without its use? Quine adduces two areas of use: for the philosophy of science, to demarcate the intersubjective tribunal of evidence for science (see "Epistemology Naturalized," pp. 86–89) and for linguistics, within the theory of a child's (or scientist's) language learning and within the theory of translation. (We shall consider linguistics in the next section, after taking up here the use in the philosophy of science.)

The widespread agreement among scientists, Quine holds, stems from there being sentences (the observation sentences) "on which all members of the community will agree under uniform stimulation" ("Epistemology Naturalized," p. 87). This notion gets Quine into problems about intersubjectively uniform stimulation, the homology of nerve endings, etc. Why not focus instead upon those sentences for which each person can arrange (or have arranged) circumstances (or stimulations, if you wish) to prompt him to assent? There is no need that the circumstances or the stimulations be intersubjectively *the same*. There is agreement enough for science to proceed if everyone can be brought to assent; there is no need for them to follow exactly the same path to this agreement. The explanation of why each assents in some arrangeable situation, for Quine, will speak of each individual's history of conditioning of language to situations. To be sure, there must be enough perceived similarity in the circumstances so that they all think they're *agreeing* (rather than merely using homonyms) and hence supporting each other. Such would be the case if each sees the circumstance in which another assents as one in which, with some slight modifications, he also would be led to assent to the sentence. Each need only see the situations of the others as (modifiable into) ones which present a discriminative stimulus for himself to utter *S*.

It is fortunate that the concept of stimulus meaning is not necessary for the philosophy of science, for, in addition to the difficulties with Quine's definition, there is further trouble. What a linguist treats as assent and dissent (and a query also?) is underdetermined, not merely inductively but "on a par with the analytical hypotheses of translation that he adopts at later stages of his enterprise" ("Replies [to Critics]," in *Words and Objections*, edited by Donald Davidson and Jaakko Hintikka, p. 312; does *this* indeterminacy about assent and dissent also begin at each of our homes?). Even if the "on a par" puts it too strongly, it would seem there is strictly speaking no fact of the matter about whether something is assent (or dissent) or something else, and hence, strictly speaking, no fact of the matter even about stimulus meanings.[8]

II. Language and Theory

Why Linguists?

If "stimulus meaning by whatever name may be properly looked upon still as the objective reality that the linguist has to probe."[9] and stimulus meaning crumbles, why do we need linguists? What is it that linguists are trying to do, and what is their subject matter? Let us consider some possible answers, and criticisms of these answers of a sort that would appear to be congenial to Quine. Later we shall face the question of whether similar criticisms don't apply to Quine's own answer.

(a)   The job of the linguist is to produce a theory that explains the linguistic facts about the sentences of the language: grammatical facts, and semantic facts,[10] e.g., that some phrases and sentences are synonymous, that some words are semantically similar to each other in a respect in which other words aren't, that some words are antonyms (have incompatible meanings), that some expressions are meaningful and others are semantically anomalous, that words or sentences have multiple senses, that some phrases have senses that contain superfluous information, that some sentences are true by virtue of the fact that the meaning of the subject contains the property expressed by the predicate, that some sentences are false just by virtue of the fact that the meaning of the subject contains information incompatible with what is attributed to it in the predicate, that some sentences are neither true nor false on the basis of meaning alone, that some pairs of sentences are inconsistent, that a sentence sometimes follows necessarily from another one by virtue of a certain semantic relation between them, that some interrogatives presuppose the truth of some declaratives, that some sentences are possible answers to a question whereas others are not, that some questions answer themselves.

The 'facts' in this list are heavily *theoretical*; they are not what, in the first place, a linguist has to explain, though in explaining what he must he might be led (or forced) to a theory which countenances such facts, and so have to explain them also. But what is it that the linguist must explain in the first place, what sets him his original task?

(b)   The job of the linguist is to explain how we communicate to each other via language, how one person transmits his inner thoughts to another by encoding them in the form of external observable acoustic events which the other decodes thereby obtaining for himself his own inner representation of the speaker's thoughts.[11]

Once again, this can hardly be the data which the linguist starts out to explain, though he might be led to such a theoretical picture in the course of explaining, e.g., people's talking to each other.

(c)   The job of the linguist is to explain linguistic performance, that is, how someone utilizes his linguistic competence to communicate with his fellow speakers in actual speech situations, that is, how someone utilizes what an ideal speaker knows about the grammatical structure of his language, stated as the system of rules that formally represents the ideal linguistic structure of natural speech, abstracting from memory limitations, noise, what situation the person is (interested) in, etc., to communicate with his fellow speakers in actual speech situations.

Again we have a heavily theoretical description of the linguist's task. Linguistic performance is what is to be explained. The *hypothesis* is that a theory explaining this performance will incorporate and attribute to the speaker-hearer linguistic competence in the form of (tacit knowledge of) an internalized system of rules which describe (or perhaps constitute) the language. "In general, it seems that the study of performance models incorporating generative grammars may be a fruitful study; furthermore, it is difficult to imagine any other basis on which a theory of performance might develop" (Noam Chomsky, *Aspects of the Theory of Syntax*, p. 15). Can it turn out that the power of this internalized set of rules is beyond the power of the organism who internalizes it? "A model of the speaker's knowledge of his language may generate a set so complex that no finite device [models which represent actual performance, Chomsky holds, must necessarily be strictly finite] could identify or produce all of its members. In other words, we cannot conclude, on the basis of the fact that the rules of the grammar represented in the brain are finite, that the set of grammatical structures generated must be of the special type that can be handled by a strictly finite device."[12] Thus, it is mistaken to think (as is often done) that the results of formal linguistics are supposed to apply directly to psychology, by showing how powerful a psychological model of us must be, on the assumption that we must be at least as powerful as the language we speak. We should be wary of concluding that our language (*our* language) is more powerful than we are, solely because such a more powerful language is most elegantly described. ("In general, the assumption that languages are infinite is made to simplify the description of these languages"; Noam Chomsky, *Syntactic Structures*, p. 23.) Since we have no need to attribute to the organism itself knowledge of the description of its linguistic output (and so need not worry about *its* handling such complexities), we may choose the less elegant but psychologically more realistic description, striving for theoretical elegance in our psychological theory of what produces its speakings (and other behavior).[13] In any case, it is puzzling to encounter the confidence that a psychological theory of our speaking and acting on heard speech will incorporate the *more powerful* abstract structures (admitted to be beyond our power) that linguists present.

(d)   The job of the linguist is to (help) explain linguistic performance, which is "the actual use of language in concrete situations."[14]

Do we now, at last, have a sufficiently theoretically low-key statement of the initial task of the linguist? What could be more down to earth than trying to explain the actual use of language in concrete situations? The use of *what*? If on this view language *is* the internalized rules, physically realized, or (to avoid having the language transformed when its speakers die) an abstract entity of some sort,[15] then we are back to case (c) above. We do not want to interpret 'the actual use of language in concrete situations' as committing us to '$(\exists x) (\exists y) (\exists z)$ (x is a person, *y* is a language, and *z* is a situation, and *x* used *y* in *z*)'. In particular, we don't want to be committed to quantifying over entities which are languages in explaining the *task* of the linguist, in explaining why there's a job for him to do. Instead, we want the task to be something like helping to explain those events in the world which are people's talkings and their behavior before and after producing or hearing talkings. I am indebted to conversations with Burton Dreben for suggesting that Quine would criticize these specifications of the linguist's task which are offered by Katz and Chomsky in the above ways, as being heavily laden with philosophical assumptions and theories, and would favor instead descriptions of the task and data of linguistics which were less theoretically committed.

Quine on the Linguist's Task

However, cannot this line of criticism be turned against Quine's own description? Even if there can be no wholly neutral description of the data, isn't Quine's description also more laden with theory and assumptions than need be, especially as assessed from a more minimalist standpoint Quine should find congenial, that of Skinnerian psychology? Quine offers the following:

(e)   The job of the grammarian is to demarcate the class of all the strings of phonemes that get uttered or could get uttered within the community as normal speech without a bizarreness reaction.[16]

Why does the grammarian try to demarcate the class of all strings of phonemes that *could* get uttered?[17] Perhaps the picture is as follows: the grammarian wants to (help) explain what *does* get uttered. The meta-hypothesis is that the explanation of a particular utterance will have two parts or components: first, a component which specifies everything that could be uttered (by anyone, anytime, under any conditions), and secondly a selective component which operates on the specification of the set of all possible sentences (on the first component) to select the one which actually gets uttered. This meta-hypothesis that the explanation of the actual utterance of a particular sentence will refer to the set of all possible utterances is a very strong hypothesis. Will the explanation of a particular home run by Hank Aaron (that particular swing, trajectory, landing place, and number of RBI's) involve a specification of all possible home runs by him, and some further bit of theory which explains

why he hit a (that) particular one *of those?* Nor is there any reason to
think that the explanation of any particular home run will *refer to* the
set of all *actual* home runs he hits during his baseball career. The explanation of a particular knockout by Joe Louis does not incorporate
reference to the set of all knockouts he could have made or did make,
or to the set of all punches he could have thrown or did throw. It is
certainly *not* generally true that the explanation of a particular activity
will refer to and utilize a specification of all possible (or actual) activities
of that sort. An explanation of a particular activity may, however, *yield*
(as opposed to utilize) a specification of all actual or possible activities
of that sort. From the story of how a particular one was (or all the actual ones were) produced we may be able to see which ones *could be*
produced; a specification of that set might drop out of the theory. But
the explanatory task would not be to produce that specification, and
the specifications need play no explanatory role in the explanations one
does give.[18]

Thinking the primary task of the linguist is to demarcate and study
the set of sentences of the language, the set of sentences that *could* be
uttered, fits in nicely with the un-Quinean conception of language as an
existent entity to be studied, knowledge of the totality of which plays a
role in the production of individual sentences. But there is also another
route to thinking the linguist must specify the set of all sentences which
could be produced, that on the face of it might be more congenial to
Quine. This route runs as follows.

For sentence *S* a person does utter, it might be said, evidences a
disposition to utter it in some circumstances *C* and perhaps in other
circumstances as well. This disposition will be an internal (neurological)
condition of the organism, in virtue of which the person utters *S* in *C*.
Had the person not been in circumstances *C* he still would have had the
disposition to utter *S* in *C*. There is something about him which makes
him an *S*-utterer-in-*C*. The set of sentences a person is disposed to utter
under some circumstances or other will be the sentences he *could* utter,
and will correspond to facts about his internal neurological condition.
The job of the grammarian, on this conception, is to specify this set
of sentences, as an aid to specifying these occurrent neurological facts.
However, this view encounters difficulties.[19]

The set of all circumstances a person could be under is ill-specified.
Does it include someone's saying "repeat after me," in which case the
set of sentences will include all sound combinations the person can (be
taught to) produce?[20] Does it include the application of instruments of

torture? The meeting of extra-galactic visitors and all they might tell us? Does it include thinking for years and coining new terminology to deal with theoretical problems, e.g., "category," "muon," "stimulus meaning"? A child of ten will not be disposed to utter "I am twenty years old" until approximately ten more years have passed. Shall we count it as disposed at ten to utter "I am twenty years old" under the circumstance of ten years passing? For at age ten, it seems there is something about the child which, when ten years pass, eventuates in its saying "I am twenty years old." But then an infant would be disposed to utter all the sentences of English which it can learn. For isn't its internal state such that under certain circumstances it will utter those sentences of English? Also, which language you speak depends on how you were raised; did you as an infant have the disposition to utter all sentences of *every* language? Would the grammarian aid the student of your behavior by specifying the set of sentences of every actual, and possible, language?[21]

Consider a uniform homogeneous pinball about to be launched on a stationary pinball machine without flippers. The path the ball will follow will depend on the force applied and the surface of the machine, its frictional forces, placement of obstacles, their elasticity, its placement of holes, etc. Of course, even given all this, the path also will depend upon the nature (mass, shape, elasticity) of the ball. In virtue of these facts about the ball, it will follow the path it does in those circumstances. It has the disposition, we might say, to follow that path in those circumstances. Similarly it has another disposition to follow another path in other circumstances (on another machine, say); this disposition (as internal structure and properties of the ball) though distinct from the first disposition is not discrete from it,[22] for it is the same physical state as the first.

Suppose now it were suggested that since the ball does behave as it does, and lawfully, and could behave differently under other circumstances and lawfully, the theorist of the ball has the job of listing its possible paths, the different ones it is disposed to follow under different circumstances. After all, these all correspond to facts about the ball, being (internal) states of it. Yet it does not follow that this is the theorist's task. Listing of dispositions would be a central task for the theorist only if it were thought that (usually or often) distinct dispositions are discrete. Otherwise, the theorist should give a statement of the one or few states of the entity, and the laws governing its behavior.

Linguists and Psychologists

An alternative conception of the linguist's task is that of aiding the psychologist in the construction of a theory of verbal behavior,[23] with no initial commitment to the theoretical centrality of language as an entity or even to sentences as entities. It is not obvious that to say "there is not language, there are not sentences" is to be entwined in pragmatic contradiction. Quine has already rejected one traditional explanation of talking behavior and the changes in behavior it leads to, *viz.,* the explanation that uses the idea idea, the myth of the mental museum, etc. The *language story* is another theoretical story, also open to scrutiny. If it is an old story, so is the museum myth; if the theorists who treat language as a structural entity trace elaborate patterns among its parts, so do the theorists of relations among ideas or semantic markers. Why then does Quine not begin with the Skinner of *Verbal Behavior,* what leads him to a more traditionally oriented *language*-position? My aim here is *not* to endorse Skinner's view, but to show how close it is to Quine's views, and so to press the question of whether it isn't really his view.

This explanation of each individual's behavior would be an individual explanation; other persons and their actions would occupy the position of external conditions.[24] This is compatible with everything that Quine says about language being a "social art." If we view the linguist as aiding in the explanation of an individual's behavior, treating other individuals merely as sources of input for the individual in question, we avoid problems about the homology of nerve endings and worries about being "unable even to negotiate the A-B-Cs of behavioristic psychology."[25]

What explanatory task is the "intersubjective equating of stimulations" needed for? (Defining some (surrogates for) notions of traditional semantics; but what explanatory function do these latter notions have?) Compare the situation in economics, where no notion of interpersonal comparisons of utility is needed for the explanatory tasks of positive economics. Each individual's behavior is explained by his own utility function, joint behavior as the aggregate of individual behavior, perhaps coordinated, but the explanation of this needs no interpersonal comparisons. Sometimes a person may act on a belief about interpersonal comparisons (e.g., he might make a threat only if he believes its realization will hurt another person more than it will hurt himself), but to explain his actions we only need a theory about how *he* makes such comparisons. The situation of psychology would seem to be the same, with interpersonal comparisons of stimulations serving no useful function.

"But how can we make translations without interpersonal comparisons of stimulations or of something?" And Quine tells us that he is in favor of translation.[26] But what are translations *for?* Will translations aid in the task of psychological explanation of another's behavior including verbal behavior? To the extent that we explain people's actions and speech by attributing to them (in indirect discourse) beliefs and intentions, and we take what they say as indicating and sometimes stating their beliefs and intentions, then psychological explanation will involve translating. Our everyday psychological explanations do proceed by such attributions.[27] But such explanations are not offered or endorsed by Quine. Presumably he hopes they can be dispensed with. If they can, then insofar as translation rides on their back, it can be dispensed with also. The fundamental story of behavior and speech, for Quine, talks of conditioning, innate distances, and stimulation of nerve endings. Sentences attributing beliefs and intentions are rough and ready *summaries* of these more fundamental facts. A translation of S tells us that S stands to stimulations of its believer or to discriminative stimuli for him *roughly* as that which translates it does to our stimulations or discriminative stimuli. A translation *abbreviates* fact, and is only roughly accurate. It serves the purposes of psychological explanation when its inaccuracies or distortions do not matter, when the relevant portions of our theory of behavior do not cut so finely as to be perturbed by the roughness. Explaining by using translations is like navigating a ship on the geocentric theory; the distortions due to placing ourselves at the center don't matter for our purposes, but the simplifications do.

Within psychology, translations are convenient summaries; not only do they feed into a theory, the grain of the theory determines what is convenient and will not mislead. So a summary of facts about discriminative stimuli or stimulation of nerve endings, as presented in translations, need be only as fine, and accurate, as the theory connecting behavior to stimuli can make use of. Furthermore, we should expect that in using our everyday theory of belief, intention, and action, our psychological theory would, given its latitude, allow a great range to attributions of propositional attitudes.

Psychology remains a theory of individuals' behavior. It need not provide a notion of same or similar stimulation so as to provide the foundation for linguistics or the theory of translation. Instead, translating is the handmaiden of psychology, helping it conveniently to describe facts about discriminative stimuli and stimulations. Whatever rough and ready similarity translating brings will help the psychologist describe how it is with that particular person ("it's like . . . "); no fact of stimulation-similarity is used as an explanation, there is nothing for *it* to explain.

Other more practical purposes of translation, e.g., to enable us to have fluent interchange, social relations, economic relations with others, raise no new issues of principle that need concern us, especially since "going native" will be the best route and need involve no translating at all. The fact that we read literary and scientific works in translation and learn much from them raises no new problems of explanation special to translation; it presumably will be explained by judiciously combining our existing theories of learning from speech in your own language, and responding to writing in your own language, with our theories about the author's behavior. We may learn differently from different translations of the same text, and the question "which did the author mean?" will either be rejected or be transformed into the question of the psychological explanation of the author's behavior. Still, translations *are* made, read, and enjoyed. The theory of translators' behavior will be a part of psychology. Translators themselves will lean on learned aids, maxims, traditional equatings, etc. to carry out their task to the satisfaction, instruction, and delight of their readers, but in all this there is no *subject matter.*

Why might one think that the concept of stimulus meanings aids the psychologist (even when it is limited to intrapersonal use, thus avoiding problems of homology)? Perhaps one hypothesizes that a theory of linguistic performance, a theory of speakings (and changes in behavior from hearings?), will be based upon stimulus meanings, in that:

(a)   Some speakings just are assentings after σ which itself is after σ'' and dissenting; that is, just are the speakings in Quine's 'judicious experiment' ("Replies [to Critics]," p. 308).

(b)   Some speakings are sayings of S after σ which is in the affirmative stimulus meaning of S. Though it does not logically follow that a person will say S when σ-stimulated if he will assent if stimulated (σ', S? and then) σ, S?, it may be assumed that a small bit of psychological theory will fill in here.

However, if S is a standing sentence which the person believes, it will have a null affirmative stimulus meaning, as Quine defines this, for there will be no sequence of σ', S? to which the person will dissent. If we drop the initial setting σ', S?, altering Quine's notion to let σ into the affirmative stimulus meaning of S if the person merely assents to S? after σ, then every stimulation (which doesn't get him to give up believing S) will be in the affirmative stimulus meaning of a standing sentence he accepts. In either case, as Quine is well aware, the notion of stimulus meaning would seem to have little use in explaining utterances of a standing sentence, except perhaps in the situation of being asked S?.

Just as for the hypothesis that a theory of linguistic performance is to be based upon one of linguistic competence, we might interpret the concern with stimulus meanings as based upon the particular hypothesis that a theory of speaking is to be based upon stimulus meanings (centrally utilize the notion of 'stimulus meaning'). (Note the partial parallels to the mold of Chomskian theorizing.) The merits of this hypothesis are unclear; however, Quine does not present stimulus meanings within this framework of *explaining* speakings. Instead, I think, he introduces stimulus meaning to see how much of traditional philosophers' talk of meaning he can save. Quine is not, on this view, the revolutionary exciser of meaning he is reputed to be; rather he tries to conserve some of the tradition with his 'strictly vegetarian imitations' (*Word and Object,* p. 67). Why bother? Isn't this a case where considerations of simplicity of theory outweigh conservatism (*Roots of Reference,* p. 137)?

Of Quine's tasks for the concept of stimulus meanings, we have discussed translation, and its use in the philosophy of science to demarcate the observation sentences. We should mention its possible use in our theory of a child's (or scientist's) language learning. But if language learning is learning *meanings,* we don't need a theory for this; if it is coming to use words so that others reinforce and don't penalize, we have Skinner's story of shaping and reinforcing in three-term contingencies. Is stimulus meaning "a device, as far as it goes, for explaining the fabric of interlocking sentences, a sentence at a time" (*Word and Object,* p. 35)? What is it we hope for from such reconstruction? Not meaning; "net empirical import of each of various single sentences" then (*Word and Object,* pp. 34–35). Is this notion of *import* a notion useful to explanatory psychology? If not, what philosophical theory is it that Quine wishes to rescue it for? And what would that philosophical theory explain? Whatever it would, we presumably should find it writ large in the philosophical theory of science, the philosophical use Quine mentions, but we have seen it to be unnecessary there.

Even if it is granted that we can explain agreement among scientists without introducing the concept of stimulus meanings, can a radical "no language" view explain the historical success of science, its predictions and its technological achievements? To do this we seem to need the notions of *reference* and *truth*, yet how can we engage in such metalinguistic talk if language itself vanishes as an *entity* to be studied. It might appear that only a realist philosophy of science (which says the scientific theory has a model, namely, the world) can explain the success of science.[28] Quine, standing within his theory, can say what the realist says (e.g., "'electron' refers to electrons, which we have discovered to have properties . . . "), even though reference is a notion within the indeterminacy of translation (*Roots of Reference*, pp. 81–82).[29]

The theorist I am imagining would first try to show how the scientists' speech was shaped,[30] second (using the first) to show what explained the scientists' and technologists' actions, and then, *speaking himself,* would say why those actions led in the world to the results they did. He would have no more difficulty in saying why those results ensued than why any event, not having to do with language, has its results. "Yes, he could *say* those things, but when he does, does he also think he's talking *about* the world, *referring to* the world?" He thinks his talk has been shaped in various ways in (by) the world. ("But when he says *that*, does he think he's talking *about* the world?" Loop back.) And he will offer to tell you how his, and your, use of "refers" and "about" was shaped.[31]

My aim in this last section has been to draw out Quine's response to a hard-line Skinnerian view of language, that is, verbal behavior. There is reason to think Quine should embrace this view, yet he continually uses notions from traditional theories of language, e.g., "reference," which have no place or explanatory purpose within the Skinnerian picture. What scientific explanatory purpose *does* Quine see these notions as necessary for? Or is there some nonexplanatory and more traditionally philosophical role they play? *Is* there a baby, or is it *all* bathwater?

Does the thesis of the underdetermination of theories undercut even Quine's notion of truth? If no theory is superior except as judged by canons whose connection with truth is unclear, and all theories would explain the data, then is there a fact of the matter about which one is true? Quine reassures us (*Word and Object,* pp. 24–25) that we can apply 'true' to a sentence which we see from within the theory which embeds that sentence, and which we take seriously as our own theory.

But why doesn't a full appreciation of the underdetermination of theories undermine the seriousness and earnestness with which we take our own theories?

A theory of the truth of sentences of an object language, one might have thought, would have to describe and segment the world and show how the sentences of the object language connect with the world. Tarski saw that one could avoid independently describing and segmenting the world by using the object language's view of it. Translate the object language (perhaps homophonically) into the metalanguage, and speak about the world through the object language translated. But if underdetermination of theory raises the worry that there's no fact of the matter about which of alternative theories is true, one will similarly worry about the factual status of their metalinguistic translations. Nor are things helped by additional worries about the determinacy of the translating! Let S and T be alternative theories underdetermined by, yet admissible for, the data, and let S and T be particular sentences in them, respectively. To explain what it means to say S and T are true we translate them into the metalanguage as s and t, respectively, and proceed à la Tarski. But what makes s a correct translation of S rather than of T? If there's no fact of the matter about *this,* then in what sense are we, by using s, affirming the truth of S as opposed to that of T? It does not help to say that the translation into the metalanguage takes place *within* a theory which includes analytical hypotheses which translate its object language subcomponent. For similarly, we would have the notion of *unique translation,* to be sure within a theory which includes fixed analytical hypotheses. Hence, this route would give us a notion of truth which is no more secure than the notions of 'unique translation' or 'unique meaning'! In what way does Quine see "truth" as better off than these other notions he has done so much to undermine?

Is the problem solved "by acquiescing in our mother tongue and taking its words at face value" (*Ontological Relativity,* pg. 49)? What is it to take the words at face value? To translate them homophonically? And why don't we have to iterate that translation, to ensure that we're taking it at face value? To use the same words in the translation in the meta-metalanguage for the truth definition of the metalanguage? (Can't all this be done without understanding the words at all?) To take s at face value is not to translate it in a certain way, for what it is translated into will raise the same problem. Quine offers one picture of understanding: one understands a language if one can translate it into some language. (Those monolinguals among us, less linguistically agile than Quine, may find themselves reduced to only the homophonic translation.) Clearly one must translate it into a language *one understands*—we can homophonically translate languages we don't understand—and *this* notion of understanding will have to come down to something which is *not* translation; presumably, it will be fluent use and application, uncorrected by other fluent users and appliers. But all such use tests will be *within* the indeterminacy of translation, and will not distinguish s from t, and so cannot fix s for the purposes of a truth definition.[32]

8 | SIMPLICITY AS FALL-OUT

ఌ ఌ ఌ

If an indefinite number of hypotheses fit our data, we need some way to select which one to accept. Merely fitting the data is not sufficient; the additional criterion philosophers put forth most prominently is simplicity: we should believe the simplest of the hypotheses (we can formulate) that fit (and would explain) our data.

Why believe the simplest? Convenience in manipulating, remembering, transferring, and teaching the theory or hypothesis would lead us, perhaps, to utilize the simplest, but why *believe* it? Why think that, of the otherwise equally satisfactory explanatory theories, the simplest is most likely to be true? If simplicity is "relative to the texture of a conceptual scheme,"[1] to the kind of "graph paper" on which we plot the world, then to show this connection between simplicity and truth would involve the unpromising task of establishing our conceptual scheme or coordinate system as privileged.

The question about simplicity is not merely a skeptical conumdrum. It is difficult to think of *any* reasonable explanation for why including such a simplicity maxim should help (and should have helped) make the institution of science successful or more likely to arrive at the truth. To explain how a simplicity maxim contributes to the success of science by saying that the world is simple says little, if indeed it says anything other than that there is some simple true theory of the world. (Of *all* of it? And why think any particular simple theory, which explains only some things, will be a component of the overall simplest theory?) So the maxim of simplicity and its connection with truth puzzles us.

W. V. Quine and Joseph Ullian[2] find that natural selection "offers a causal connection between subjective simplicity and objective truth . . . Innate subjective standards of simplicity that make people prefer some hypotheses to others will have survival value insofar as they favor successful prediction. Those who predict best are likeliest to survive and reproduce their kind . . . and so their innate standards of simplicity are handed down" (p. 47). But maxims of simplicity direct us to choose the simplest of hypotheses in areas and at levels in physics, chemistry, cosmology, molecular biology, none of which were believed or chosen by our ancestors. What explains why their subjective standards of simplicity, which have stood the evolutionary test for hypotheses about middle-sized macro-phenomena, also connect with truths about cosmology or micro-phenomena? (Or is there no "connection between subjective simplicity and objective truth" in these areas?) Perhaps the fact that nature is uniform, here interpreted as meaning that the same type of simplicity obtains throughout. *If* one could turn this into a precise statement about *the world*, the requisite sort of explanatory link between our standards of simplicity and truth would be forged. Quine and Ullian further note that "such standards will also change in the light of experience, becoming still better adapted to the growing body of science in the course of the individual's lifetime. (But these improvements do not get handed down genetically)" (p. 47). However, they do get handed down in the education of scientists. If scientists' standards of simplicity change to fit the theories they develop and accept, then these theories will seem to them and to later generations, who judge by these changed standards, simple.

In "On Simple Theories of a Complex World," Quine artfully side-stepped the issue of simplicity's connection with truth by connecting it not with truth but with confirmation. A preference for simplicity is, so to speak, an *artifact* of our procedures of confirmation, so that the simpler of two theories is more likely to be confirmed and to hold up under the way we investigate theories. The question Quine raises, what the artifacts of our procedures are, is of extreme importance. However, to raise the question of whether something is an artifact of our procedures of confirmation is to raise the question of whether, in that respect, those procedures should determine our beliefs. If people who learn science (strangely) got headaches when they considered a hypothesis containing three words beginning with the letter d, then no such hypothesis could get confirmed. That would be an artifact of the man-scientific-procedures combination, but surely no reason to disbelieve such a hypothesis. Thus, questions of the justification, and not merely the causes, of our beliefs would be raised. Put somewhat differently, noticing the artifact and knowing the artifactual causal story might lead us to change our (artifactual) beliefs.[3]

Simplicity is usually introduced as an additional factor to help decide among the different hypotheses that fit (or would explain) the data D_1 in hand at time t_1. Another way to decide would be to gather more data. But this seems not to solve the current problem, for however much new data D_2 we gather, and however many old hypotheses D_2 eliminates, there will still be an indefinite number of hypotheses that fit $D_1 + D_2$. And how are we to choose among them?

The feeling that no progress has been made by collecting new data—to be sure some old hypotheses are refuted—should set us to wondering whether the situation is being misconceived. Instead of thinking of a temporal cross-section of hypotheses and data, consider the following very simple model of an ongoing process.[4] At time t_1 there are data D_1 and already formulated hypotheses $H_1 \ldots H_m$ which fit D_1. New data D_2 are gathered to *select among* these hypotheses. If only one hypothesis survives, believe it (tentatively), and go on to gather new data to test it against other hypotheses you now think up which fit $D_1 + D_2$.

"But how can it matter that a particular hypothesis was actually thought of earlier and tested? If another hypothesis H_{23} which we have just now thought of and which also fits $D_1 + D_2$ had been thought of earlier, then it would fit all the data we now have. Surely which hypothesis the data support cannot depend upon which hypothesis we happened to be thinking about as we gathered the data." If H_{23} had been thought of earlier it would fit $D_1 + D_2$ now, but we *don't* know that it would fit all the data we would have now, for if H_{23} had been thought of earlier, we would have gathered *different* data. Our process of data gathering is selective. Given hypotheses $H_i : y = f_i(x)$ we gather data at values of x where the hypotheses differ, and at a sufficient number of points x so as to leave only one of the original hypotheses surviving. If H_{23} had been one of that original number, we would have gathered data at some additional points x.

Granted that the counterfactual that purports to make the sequential procedure look ridiculous is *not* known to be true, still the question arises of why we should (tentatively) believe the surviving hypothesis rather than another that fits those data just as well. The answer depends on the way the underdetermination of theory appears to make it difficult to (strongly) support a hypothesis. Hypothesis H fits data D. But an infinite number do. We expect many to, and this is one of those which do. Whatever the data we found, we could dream up many hypotheses afterwards to fit them, and so with D we dreamed up H; is this any reason to believe H?

Suppose someone says he will show you that he is a very skilled archer. If an arrow is shot at random at a large target, the probability of its hitting a particular point is *very* small (has measure zero). And that's true for each point. "So," he says, "if I shoot and succeed in getting the arrow to a particular point, it will show I am very skilled." He shoots, the arrow lands, and he says, "See how skilled I am; the probability that the arrow would have landed precisely there at random was minuscule." "Hold on," we say, "the arrow had to land *somewhere,* and it landed there. Wherever it landed would have been an unlikely place. We'll believe you're a skilled archer if you *first specify* the minuscule area your arrow is going to hit, and *then* succeed in hitting it." Similarly the data are going to land somewhere. That they land in a particular place is a reason for thinking a specification of that place is significant only if *that* specification was offered beforehand.

Suppose the archer shot at random at a wall, and then went to where the arrow had landed, drew a circle around it, and said "Bull's-eye!" Suppose when the data land somewhere, we draw a curve through it and say "Bull's-eye." A bull's-eye is when the data hit the hypothesis, not the other way around. Since bull's-eyes give support, to believe the best supported hypothesis is (some complications aside) to adopt the method of tenacity.[5]

Now to connect simplicity with the sequential selective data gathering and testing procedure. We (tend to) think of the simpler hypotheses, relative to *our* conceptual scheme. So the simpler hypotheses get into the fray early. Suppose only one hypothesis H_S from the initial batch of hypotheses we formulated survives our gathering of data D_1 and, in accordance with the procedure, we tentatively believe it. Either:

(1) The initial hypotheses[6] were the simplest possible which would fit D_1; no other possible hypothesis that fits D_1 is simpler than any one of these. With all but one of the original hypotheses eliminated

by D_2, H_S is the simplest possible uneliminated hypothesis that fits D_1. Since whatever fits the large data set $D_1 + D_2$ must also fit D_1, H_S is the simplest possible hypothesis that fits $D_1 + D_2$. So we *already* are (tentatively) believing the simplest hypothesis compatible with our data.

Or (2) we did not originally formulate the simplest hypotheses that fit D_1, and there are hypotheses simpler than H_S compatible with $D_1 + D_2$. We formulate further hypotheses, and enter the next stage, gathering the (selective) data D_3, and we (tentatively) believe the surviving hypothesis. Either it's now like case 1 above: our formulated hypotheses were the simplest that fit $D_1 + D_2$ (that is, their subset bounded by this stage's survivor contained the simplest), and so we're now believing the simplest hypothesis compatible with all of our data, or else (loop) case 2 again.

This sequential testing procedure fails to get us believing the simplest hypothesis (of those we can formulate) compatible with our data only if there is an infinite descending sequence of more and more simple hypotheses, and we start up on it and move slowly down. If we sequentially test hypotheses that we've thought of, tentatively believing the survivor, and if we do (tend to) think of simple hypotheses (judged relative to our conceptual scheme), then the result will soon be that we are believing the simplest hypothesis (of those we can formulate) which is compatible with all the data we have. (Even simpler hypotheses, of course, may have been eliminated earlier.)

We need no rule or maxim that bids us to believe the simplest hypothesis compatible with our data. It's just a consequence of the operation of *that* sequential procedure that we *will* end up doing so. And the fact that simplicity seems relative to our own conceptual scheme, to our background concepts, coordinate system, type of conceptual graph paper, etc.—a fact that blocks attempts to connect simplicity with truth—fits naturally into *this* story. The more simplicity fits however we happen to tend to think, the more likely it is that we *will* think that way, and early. To *guarantee* we'll end up believing the simplest hypothesis compatible with the data, it would have to be assumed, not merely that we tend to think up simple hypotheses, but that by some time we have thought up *all* the simplest. This assumption is too strong, but then again science provides no guarantee of convergence to the simplest. It is no defect for our theory of simplicity to explain no more than the facts.

Simplicity is not called in as an additional criterion for hypothesis selection which is made necessary by underdetermination of theories. Rather, underdetermination of theories makes necessary, in order to have hypotheses supported, a sequential process of data gathering and testing, and out of that process drops simplicity (as judged by us).[7] But what is the explanation of the fact that we do find hypotheses that fit the data at all, and that not all those we think up are always eliminated at the very next stage? Scientists choose to work on problems and in areas where they think they can get results, and leave intractable problems aside. It would need explaining if they were never able to succeed!

Our argument about how simplicity precipitates out of the sequential process would apply to any situation in which:

(1)   Instances of some type of thing T are generated.
(2)   The instances can be ordered along some dimension D.
(3)   Those T's which are generated early tend to cluster around and eventually exhaust one end of the dimension; they are D-er than any T's not yet generated.
(4)   At each stage, T's that fail to satisfy some criterion C are eliminated.
(5)   The ordering of the T's along the dimension D does not depend upon their relation to the criterion C.

Since these conditions do not focus especially upon simplicity, any process with a dimension D that satisfies 1 to 5 will eventuate in the survival of the D-est.[8]

The theory we have presented yields simplicity as fall-out from the process, but it gives simplicity, qua simplicity, no role as input, and so does not account for the way we utilize simplicity, seek it, and consciously favor it. For example, the sequential process may involve rejecting previous data on grounds of simplicity, if there is a relatively simple hypothesis that fits D_2 and most of D_1, and only very complicated hypotheses fit D_2 and *all* of D_1. Some of D_1 may be rejected in order to accept the simpler hypothesis. Or suppose we came upon beings on another planet with a different simplicity ordering and, hence, with a different history of hypothesis testing. They had never tried out what (to us) is the simplest hypothesis about the operation of their environment. Would we be impressed by the history of one of their hypotheses? Before we tested theirs against the simplest one of ours that fit their data, which would we believe? If ours, even though it hadn't yet been tested by them or us, that also would show that there's something more to simplicity than merely the fall-out result of the sequential procedure.

Our story about simplicity as fall-out can be elaborated to give simplicity some role as input to the process as well. Once we notice that we are believing the simplest hypothesis that fits the data, we can come to pursue a policy of doing so. The fall-out provides the basis of an induction. Here Quine and Ullian's natural-selection argument serves. We find ourselves having simple beliefs about ordinary middle-sized natural macro-objects and situations because those (who were contemporaries of our ancestors) to whom these truths seemed complicated left no descendants among our contemporaries. Also, since the process of sequential testing and tentative acceptance leads us to end up believing the simplest hypothesis compatible with our data, a retrospective look will find that simplicity is successful, that the successful are simple. Even more so because, as Quine and Ullian note, our culturally transmitted standards of simplicity tend to change so as to fit more neatly what we actually have ended up accepting.[9]

Since the past exhibits a correlation between the simplicity and the success of a hypothesis, a modest induction—to be sure, a simple one, but that's how we tend to think—leads us to conclude that these do go together and, hence, to rely upon simplicity. There are various ways to imagine the induction; one is as an inference to the best explanation.[10] We start with an observed connection between simplicity and acceptance by scientific procedures, and we explain this by positing connections between each of these and truth: we posit that acceptance of hypotheses by scientific procedures is correlated with their truth (there is independent reason to believe this, since scientific procedures eliminate *false* hypotheses that conflict with the data) and that the simplicity of hypotheses is connected with their truth (that the simpler of competing hypotheses is more likely to be true). These last two connections, if sufficiently tight, would imply and explain the observed correlation. One, therefore, might be led, in order to explain the observed connection, to infer a real connection of simplicity with truth. This account is admittedly rough, but fortunately we require no precise and rigorous inference for a plausible account of how one might actually arrive at a trust in simplicity. It might appear, however, that this account is vitiated by circularity. For the conclusion that simplicity and truth really are connected is inferred in order to explain the observed connection of simplicity with acceptance by scientific procedures. Yet there are other more complicated explanations of this observed connection. So in making the inference to the connection of simplicity with truth (and not some inference to a more complicated explanation) isn't a simplicity maxim already being used? A simple inference was made, but simplicity was not consciously pursued. Since our purpose is not to *justify* simplicity but to explain how it might come to be consciously pursued as a goal, we legitimately may place the wisdom of pursuing simplicity as the conclusion of an inference which instances simplicity without itself pursuing it.

Starting only with simplicity as fall-out, we end up trusting in simplicity and using it in the process. Seeking simplicity affects the sequential procedure in two ways: first, we try to think up especially simple hypotheses and, second, we consciously use simplicity as a criterion in selecting among hypotheses. Thereby the sequential process even more effectively yields simplicity.[11]

This lovely picture, unfortunately, is marred by the fact that our fall-out explanation of simplicity, if correct, undercuts the induction that leads to trusting in simplicity. If the fall-out tale is the best explanation of the observed correlation between success and simplicity, then the inductive extrapolation that leads to trust in simplicity is blocked; that is, it is unreasonable. But still, it may have occurred (and *not* unreasonably then, since no one then had the fall-out explanation), and that induction may be the actual explanation of our current trust in simplicity.

Does and should accepting all this undermine trust in simplicity? It would be pleasant to bring things full circle by having the trust tenaciously hang on. After all, the hypothesis that there is a real connection between the simplicity and the success of a hypothesis entered the field before my explanation did; that hypothesis fit past data, and new data were gathered which the hypothesis also fit, and so that hypothesis came to be accepted. In accordance with the method of tenacity, that hypothesis and the accompanying trust in simplicity will and should continue; that hypothesis should not be displaced merely because some new hypothesis has been thought up which also fits the data.

But even if we granted this application of the method of tenacity, our confidence in simplicity might well be short-lived; for the next step, now that another hypothesis has entered the field, would be to use the hypothesis to generate different predictions, to test them selectively, to discover which survives, and to end up believing that one.

However, I find myself *already* believing the explanation I have offered. This might be because the two explanations, mine and the one positing a real connection between simplicity and truth, do not fit exactly the same currently available data, because mine already explains more. But another view of the matter is more fun.

My explanation involving fall-out and the induction based upon the fall-out is, I believe, simple, elegant, forceful, and lovely. More so, surely, than the reigning hypothesis of a real connection between simplicity and truth. The simplest and most elegant hypothesis is that there is no real connection between simplicity (and elegance) and truth. Now if I accept this hypothesis as true (partly) *because* it is so simple and elegant, and the proponent of a real connection between simplicity (and elegance) on the one hand and truth on the other rejects this hypothesis as true because it denies any such connection, with whose petard is each of us hoist?

9

INVISIBLE-HAND
EXPLANATIONS

୶   ୶   ୶

In Nozick (1974) I described how, if people entered into mutual protection agreements and firms offered buyers protective services, a dominant protection agency would arise by legitimate steps, and this would constitute at least an ultra-minimal state. No one need have intended to produce a state. A pattern or institutional structure that apparently only could arise by conscious design instead can originate or be maintained through the interactions of agents having no such overall pattern in mind. Following Adam Smith, I termed such a process or explanation an *invisible-hand* process or explanation and offered a list of examples to make the phenomenon salient. These included evolutionary explanations of the traits of organisms and populations, microeconomic explanations of equilibria, Carl Menger's explanation of how a medium of exchange arises, and Thomas Schelling's model of residential segregation. (Edna Ullman-Margalit, 1978, is a later attempt to define the concept.) Two types of processes seemed important: filtering processes wherein some filter eliminates all entities not fitting a certain pattern, and equilibrium processes wherein each component part adjusts to local conditions, changing the local environments of others close by, so the sum of the local adjustments realizes a pattern. The pattern produced by the adjustments of some entities might itself constitute a filter another faces. The opposite kind of explanation, wherein an apparently unintended, accidental, or unrelated set of events is shown to result from intentional design, I termed a *hidden-hand explanation*. The notion of invisible-hand explanation is descriptive, not normative. Not every pattern that arises by an invisible-hand process is desirable, and something that can arise by an invisible-hand process might better arise or be maintained through conscious intervention.

Economics typically explains patterns in terms of the actions of rational agents. However, a disaggregated theory of the agent herself, wherein patterns that seem to indicate a central and unified directing agent are instead explained as the result of smaller, non-agent entities interacting, also might count as an invisible-hand explanation.[1] The definitional details of what counts as "invisible hand" are less interesting than the particular theories.[2]

Time-preference seems susceptible to evolutionary explanation (see Nozick, 1977; and Nozick, 1993, pp. 14–15). The future is uncertain, an organism may not survive to reap an anticipated reward, or the world might not present it. Innate time-preference may be evolution's way to instill in creatures incapable of explicit probabilistic calculations a mechanism having roughly the same effect, approximating what such calculations would have yielded with regard to rewards affecting inclusive fitness; such time-preference may have been selected for. Consider, then, beings with the cognitive apparatus to take explicit account of such uncertainties, who explicitly perform a probabilistic discounting of the future. If already installed in humans is an innate time-preference—evolution's attempt to perform that probabilistic discounting for us—and if what we explicitly discount in our probabilistic calculations is the (already discounted through time-preference) present value of the future reward, then what takes place will be a *double-discounting*. Isn't that too much?

Next, consider wealth maximization or the weaker assumption that people are seriously concerned with wealth. A widespread phenomenon across societies (though not within Western industrialized societies in the last 150 years) is that wealthy people tend to have more children. (Gary Becker, 1981, p. 102, cites supporting literature.) Suppose that, *ceteris paribus*, people with a strong desire for wealth tend to amass more; it is more likely that they will. If there had been a genetically based heritable psychological predisposition to be (more) concerned with wealth—I do not claim this as anything more than a possibility—then that would have been selected for; the percentage with that heritable desire would increase over time. This would provide an evolutionary explanation of, if not wealth maximization, a widespread strong desire for wealth (see Nozick, 1993, pp. 126–127).

Evolutionary explanations also can be brought to bear within philosophy to explain *a priori* knowledge of apparently necessary truths and to explain the intractability of certain philosophical problems (see Nozick, 1993, chap. 4). Traditional philosophical doctrine attributes to individuals a faculty of *a priori* knowledge, enabling them to know independently of experience that certain things must hold true, that they hold true in all possible worlds. It is implausible that evolutionary processes, keyed to the actual world, would instill any such completely general faculty within us.

Yet certain propositions do seem self-evident, and it is difficult to think of ways they might be false. A certain proposition's *seeming* self-evidently true to us might have been selected for, if it does hold true (at least approximately) and if acting upon a belief in this does, in general, enhance fitness. That factual, contingent truth would come to seem *more* than just factual, through evolutionary selection via the "Baldwin effect": those to whose "wiring" a connection or proposition seems closer to evident learn it faster and gain a selective advantage; they leave offspring distributed around their own speed of learning until, over generations, all find it self-evident. If, frequently enough, samples of a certain sort resembled their populations, then generalizing from samples to population, or to the next encountered member, would frequently yield truths, and those to whom such inferences seemed obvious and self-evident would frequently arrive at those truths.

Rationality itself might be an evolutionary adaptation. Evolution phylogenetically instills in us information about, and patterns of behavior suitable to, stable facts of our evolutionary past. Evolution utilizes and builds mechanisms around constant and stable environmental features (e.g., gravitational force is utilized in the working of some physiological processes, which were designed to utilize and function *in tandem with* steady gravity, not to duplicate separately what gravity already does).

Some obdurate philosophical problems (e.g., justifying induction, or our belief in the existence of other minds or in an external world) might mark stable facts about humans' past environment that evolution has built into us as *assumptions*, marking facts to work in tandem with. All human beings heretofore have been born in environments surrounded by other people with minds similar to their own, in an independently existing "external world," one whose objects continued on trajectories (or in place) even when unobserved, a world in which certain kinds of generalization or extrapolation from past experience led to further truths. Those who failed to learn this quickly left fewer similarly uncomprehending descendants. Rationality's function was not to *justify* these assumptions but to utilize them.

Hidden-hand explanations, the opposite of invisible-hand ones, tend toward ruling-class (or, more extremely, conspiracy) theories. What a ruling class aims at and produces or maintains is not given an invisible-hand explanation. However, the existence of a ruling class might itself be given such an explanation, if it did not arise as the result of some individual's or group's actions intending to bring this about.

Here is a sketch of how this might occur. Start with a society containing no ruling class, where the most powerful and wealthy individuals want their children and grandchildren to be equally or more advantaged and so place them in environments (schools, vacation places) that make more likely their children's marrying similarly advantaged people. Marriages forge alliances of mutual interest, making more likely the sharing of information and coordinated activities for mutual benefit. Allies and employees will tend to be recruited from similar schools and social networks, because their families are directly known, or because the similar molding of their values, tastes, and modes of behavior makes them easier to work with, more predictable, more congenial, less likely to create conflict. Directors of companies will be recruited from among similar persons already successful elsewhere; studies of boards of directors would show similar social backgrounds and much interlocking.

Matters of mutual interest are discussed, including public matters; sometimes joint representation is made to government officials about matters of mutual concern. As issues become complex, or the polity becomes widespread, organizations are started to think through these issues together and to interact with the government officials (or potential ones) who might significantly affect them. Thus might arise a pattern of wealthy and powerful individuals associating in social, business, and political life. How much *success* and *coordination* in the determination of (which?) results is needed for this to constitute, technically, a ruling class? The coordinating organizations might be started, maintained and participated in without the *aim* of "serving the interests of the ruling class," so a ruling class might arise through an invisible-hand process, even if later it consciously maintains itself.

Not just equilibria within markets, but the very existence of markets in the West is largely the product of invisible-hand processes. People aimed to extend particular markets in one or another direction, but "the market" developed bit by bit, unintended. (Even after an overall conception did arise, the extension of markets rarely depended upon economists who had mastered that general conception.) Now, however, there are self-conscious efforts to establish markets and a market society where none had been. If successful, the arising there of a market society will not have an invisible-hand explanation, but particular equilibria within the markets will. Will the new markets' achieving certain overall patterns have an invisible-hand explanation, when those markets were instituted *in order* to achieve just such patterns? (And what of our markets, if they continue to be maintained in part because they are perceived to yield that pattern?) And what shall we say of new institutions, not imitating anything existing before, that are designed and instituted to achieve certain patterns by so structuring incentives that people interacting will produce that pattern? The pattern is invisible to those within the institution but not to its designers.

Here is a suggestion of an institution, call it the *help chain*. With significant publicity and moral suasion, the government institutes a system of help-vouchers, distributing Y hours of help vouchers to every family whose yearly income is below X. A person with such a voucher can request teaching, advice, or help of any individual, and if that individual agrees and delivers it, he receives help-vouchers for that time expended. These vouchers he then can use himself, asking another person for help for himself or for any designated individual. Each person approached knows that if he agrees, he too will receive a voucher. Unwillingness to ask is reduced by knowing that the other will receive a useful voucher in return; willingness to agree may similarly be aided. Each year, there is a fresh infusion of help-vouchers, starting at the bottom of the income scale, and "trickling up" through voluntary interactions. What new patterns will result?

The standard economist's invisible-hand explanation involves individual agents who choose rationally. (Notice that a theory of irrational behavior also might be specific enough to explain patterns arising from the interaction of individuals behaving in that predictably irrational fashion.) However, the principle of rational decision need not be the principle of maximizing expected utility. In Nozick (1993), I propose a rule of maximizing decision-value, where this is a weighted sum of causally expected utility, evidentially expected utility, and symbolic utility.[3] This rule then is applied to Newcomb's problem and to the prisoners' dilemma, with new results (see Nozick, 1993, chap. 2). (Newcomb's problem was first presented and discussed in Nozick, 1969; Richmond Campbell and Lanning Sowden, 1985, contains articles on this problem plus a bibliography.) New patterns can be explained in invisible-hand fashion as the result of the interaction of agents whose behavior conforms to this broader decision rule.

One also might impose more stringent conditions on preference in addition to the usual structural conditions S (e.g., the von Neumann–Morgenstern conditions). In Nozick (1993), I propose that these additional conditions include the following (which themselves then are also added to the set S): the person prefers satisfying the conditions S to not satisfying them; the person prefers (*ceteris paribus*) the means and preconditions to satisfying the conditions S; the person prefers having her first- and second-order preferences cohere; the person prefers that the preconditions for making preferential choice obtain, and that the capacities for making and effecting preferential choice not be interfered with. (There are more complicated additional conditions.) When a person's preferences satisfy these (and similar) structural conditions, I say that her preferences are *rationally coherent*.

A plausible view holds that the rationality of a belief depends upon the nature of the process that actually gave rise to (or maintains) it. Simplifying greatly, a belief is rational if it arose by a process that reliably yields true beliefs.[4] Can we demarcate a rational preference as one given rise to by a process that reliably produces —— preferences? What is to fill in the blank?

One can bootstrap by using the additional structure conditions. A particular preference is rational only if it actually was generated by a process that reliably yields rationally coherent preferences. This requires more than that the preference itself satisfy the additional structural conditions, for the processes that human beings actually can use reliably to yield coherent preferences form a restricted class; and it may be impossible to generate a particular preference by any process in this class, even though it itself does not violate the structural conditions. Given interacting individuals with such stringently rational preferences, some further institutions or patterns might then be explainable.

What are the limits of invisible-hand explanations? Many enduring patterns of behavior can be seen as maintained rigidly in the space left by the jigsaw puzzle of other people's actions, where the shape of each of those other pieces is similarly maintained by its surrounding pieces. Are there kinds of institutions or patterns that, in principle, cannot be given an invisible-hand explanation? (Consider written constitutions.) Are there any social structures that could not have arisen by an invisible-hand process, or be maintained by one?[5] If so, is there an illuminating general description of what must evade invisible-hand explanation?

ETHICS
AND
POLITICS

10

MORAL COMPLICATIONS AND MORAL STRUCTURES

ᴓ ᴓ ᴓ

I. Introduction

In this essay I shall discuss some problems in representing one structure which may be exhibited by part of the moral views of some people. In particular, I shall be concerned with formulating a structure which would generate (or play a role in the generation of) a person's judgments about the moral impermissibility of specific actions. I do not claim that *everyone's* moral views exhibit the structure I shall discuss, nor do I claim that there is some one structure which everyone's moral views exhibit. Perhaps people's actual moral views differ in structure. Why I consider the particular structure I work toward worthy of discussion, given only the weak claim that *some* people's views may exhibit it (and perhaps only at a superficial level), will become clear as I proceed.

The discussion strikes what I hope is not too uneasy a balance between a descriptive and a normative interest in the structure of a person's moral views. I would view it as an objection that no correct moral view could have the structure I discuss. And I would hope that a person holding the type of view I discuss would find disconcerting the discovery that his view does not satisfy some of the specific structural conditions discussed later in the paper. Since people's views often do not satisfy conditions which they should satisfy, the imposition of normative structural conditions upon a person's moral views lessens the likelihood that people will be found whose views exactly fit the structure described. I would hope, however, that some people's views satisfy the structure closely enough so that it will be useful in accounting for the judgments about the moral impermissibility of actions that they actually make or would make. Thus the essay is intended to provide the beginnings of a model of a moral judge which is useful both for descriptive purposes and for various normative inquiries, in much the same way as is contemporary utility theory and decision theory.

Before proceeding, I wish to emphasize the exploratory nature of this essay, which contains little more than the first steps toward one moral structure. Since a major purpose is to open an area for investigation, I have felt free to mention in passing some questions without attempting to answer them here. Indeed, the last section includes a listing of further questions and problems which must be pursued if the kind of view suggested here is to be made to work. I would have preferred to present here a finished and complete work, and hope that the presentation of a temporal section of an ongoing work will have virtues of its own.

Though much has been written on particular problems within ethics, one finds, in the literature of moral philosophy, very little detailed discussion of the structure of a person's actual moral views. This may be due to its being assumed that a person's actual moral views exhibit one of two very simple structures (the first being a simple case of the second, which is worth mentioning separately). And this assumption may be made plausible by the desire, of many moral philosophers, to propose one or a small group of principles which would account for and unify a person's actual moral judgments (with a little fiddling here and there in the interests of consistency and theoretical simplicity).[1] If one or a small group of principles underlies all of one's moral judgments, then one will feel no need to discuss the structure of a person's moral views beyond stating the principles and saying something about the way in which the particular judgments are "derived" from the principles. For, it would seem, all of the interesting questions about a person's moral beliefs could be raised about the unifying principles.

The two structures which it is often assumed or explicitly stated that (part of) a person's moral views exhibit I shall call the maximization structure and the deductive structure.

A. The Maximization Structure

According to this view all of one's judgments about the moral impermissibility of actions are accounted for by a principle which requires the maximization of some quantity, subject perhaps to a quantitative restraint. The traditional utilitarian, or at any rate the traditional utilitarian of the textbooks, makes this claim. A proponent of such a view may discuss problems about knowing which act maximizes the quantity, or problems about what to do when one lacks adequate information to decide which act will maximize the quantity, but he will view all of the important questions about structure as obviously answered.

I do not wish here to discuss utilitarianism; I shall just assume that it is an inadequate moral view. Even though it is inadequate, some people may hold it. If so, I am not trying to describe the basic structure of *their* moral view. However, if they are utilitarians because they believe this position accounts for their other moral views, it may be that the structure I discuss will capture their views at a less deep level. The inadequacy of utilitarianism, of course, does not show that every view with a maximization structure is inadequate. Perhaps some such view is adequate, and perhaps such a structure underlies and accounts for the different structure I shall discuss, in an interesting way. I say "in an interesting way" for it may always be possible to produce a gimmicky real-valued function such that its maximization mirrors one's moral views in a particular area. For example, suppose there is a complicated theory T, not having a maximization structure, which accounts for one's judgment of which actions are morally impermissible, and which are not morally impermissible. Define a function f taking actions as argument values, such that $f(A) = 0$ iff, according to T, A is morally impermissible; and $f(A) = 1$ iff, according to T, A is not morally impermissible. One might then say that (part of) one's moral views are represented by the requirement that one maximize (act so as to achieve maximal values of) f. An interesting maximization structure requires the maximization of some function which was not gimmicked up especially for the occasion (or similar occasions). That is, one that is interesting for our purpose; there may be other reasons why one might find interesting the representing of moral views via an artificially created maximization structure. Compare the situation with contemporary utility theory, which shows that if a person's preferences among probability mixtures of alternatives satisfy certain natural-looking conditions then his preferences can be represented as being in accordance with the maximization of the expected value of a real-valued function which is defined in terms of the conditions and his particular preferences (the utility function). One would not answer Aristotle's question of whether there is one thing for which (eventually) all actions are done by saying, on the basis of contemporary utility theory, "yes there is, namely, utility." To rule out, on theoretical grounds, such an answer, and to rule out similar maximization structures in ethics as interesting for our purposes, one would need a way of distinguishing the one from the many (gimmicked up to look like one). It is clear that the formulation of such a way faces problems similar or identical to the ones faced in attempting to rule out Goodman-like predicates,[2] and I shall not pursue this matter further here.

Many persons do not believe that there is an interesting maximization structure (and many believe that there isn't one) which accounts for their views about which actions are morally impermissible. But even if their moral views can (ultimately) be accounted for by an interesting maximization structure, it is still of great interest to see if one can state a structure (which would, by hypothesis, be reducible to an interesting maximization structure) which accounts for their moral views and which they can recognize as their own.

B. The Deductive Structure

According to this view, a particular judgment that an act is morally impermissible

(1)   Act A is morally impermissible

would be accounted for as following from statements of the following form:

(2)   Act A has features $F_1, \ldots, F_n$

(3)   Any act with features $F_1, \ldots, F_n$ is morally impermissible.

I shall consider only the simplest case where the features F_i are empirical, factual, not *explicitly* moral features of actions. The moral premiss (3) is accounted for as following from the moral premiss

(4)   Any act with features $T_1, \ldots, T_m$ is morally impermissible

conjoined with the factual premiss

(5)   Any act with features $F_1, \ldots, F_n$ has features $T_1, \ldots, T_m$.

It is not claimed that the person consciously draws such inferences, but it is claimed that, in some sense, such a structure accounts for his particular judgments, and that the person would be willing to say, or someone who understood his view would be willing to attribute to him the (perhaps implicit) belief, that an act with features $F_1, \ldots, F_n$ is wrong because it has features $T_1, \ldots, T_m$.[3]

Principle (4) is accounted for in the same way as is (3), by reference to another moral principle, and factual premiss. Presumably, one eventually arrives at one or more moral principles P of the form of (3) and (4), which underlie all of the person's particular judgments, and all other of his moral principles, and which are such that there are no other principles P' of this form to which the person would assent or which the observer would attribute to the person as more basic ("Acts having the features P mentions are morally impermissible because they have the features mentioned in P'") from which (members of) P can be derived in the way that others are derived from P.

The deductive structure cannot easily explain how it is that a person's moral judgment of a particular act (often) changes as he learns additional facts about the act; e.g., he no longer judges the act morally impermissible. In such cases the facts previously known to the person were not sufficient for the truth of a judgment of moral impermissibility, and he did not have knowledge which instantiated the antecedent of an exceptionless moral principle. The expedient of maintaining the deductive structure hypothesis by claiming that in all such cases the facts known to the person do not instantiate the features mentioned in an exceptionless moral principle but instead provide inductive evidence for their realization, while explaining how judgments would change with new information, is obviously implausible.

A second difficulty with attributing the deductive structure as the superficial structure of some people's views is that these people are unwilling to state or assent to any or very many exceptionless moral principles.[4] Many such persons, at some time in their lives, explicitly accepted such exceptionless principles, gradually making them more and more complicated to fit more and more complicated cases. Then at some point they decided they couldn't state exceptionless principles which they were confident were correct *and* which would account for a wide range of their moral judgments. Perhaps reinforcing their lack of confidence in any exceptionless principles they were tempted to state, was the realization that if more than one such principle is stated, great care must be taken to ensure that in no possible case do they conflict.

Such a history, I imagine, would be very common among lawyers, to whom the difficulties of devising rules to adequately handle, in advance, all the bizarre, unexpected, arcane and complicated cases which actually arise, much less all possible cases, are a commonplace. The view that any laws a legislature will be able to devise will work contrary to their intention, or will work injustices, in some cases they hadn't foreseen arising or even contemplated, needs no exposition by me in a journal read by lawyers. Awareness of the difficulties in formulating rules to handle all the cases which will arise often leads to talk of the role of judicial discretion in a legal system, and to the incorporation within legal codes of statutes dealing with the avoidance of evils, which do not attempt to specifically handle the possible cases.[5] Thus one would expect lawyers to be as modest about the purported exceptionless character of any moral rules they can devise, or about most that come down to them in their moral tradition, as they are about the product of centuries of intensive legal effort to devise and refine rules to govern conduct.[6]

In saying that the persons would not confidently (or be willing to) put forth exceptionless principles which they believe would yield the correct judgment in each particular case, I do not mean to imply that they would not want themselves and others to publicly state such principles as exceptionless, and perhaps enforce them as such. They might want this, and do it because though they believe that the principles do not yield correct judgments in each particular case, they think it better that the principles always be followed than that each person consider and decide whether the situation he faces is an exception to the principle. They might think this latter alternative worse in the belief that far more often or far more importantly there will be cases where people, using their discretion, wrongly do not follow the principle than where, without using discretion, they wrongly follow it. But still the persons I am considering would not believe that the principles they *say* are exceptionless always yield the correct results.

The theme of the inadequacy of most exceptionless principles that one can state fits in nicely with recent writings on *prima facie* duties and rights, a subject whose importance was first emphasized by W. D. Ross.[7] My procedure will be to present a relatively simple structure in harmony with these writings, and then to consider some objections to, criticisms of, inclarities in and infelicities in this particular structure. A consideration of these leads to some suggestions about what a more adequate (though similar) structure would be like, which (or modifications of which), it is hoped, would be a component of a theory to account for the moral judgments of some of us about the moral impermissibility of actions. I shall be wholly occupied in this paper in working toward the more complicated structure, and shall not get to present it in detail here.

II. The Simple Structure

There are two open-ended lists of features of actions: W (for wrong-making) and R (for right-making). Members of W are denoted by $w_1, w_2, \ldots$; subsets of W by $W_1, W_2, \ldots$; members of R are denoted by $r_1, \ldots$; subsets of R by $R_1, R_2, \ldots$ If an action has some features on W, and no features on R, it is morally impermissible. If an action has some features on R, and no features on W, it is morally required (morally impermissible not to do it), or at least morally permissible.[8] One key fact, which I mention in passing though much should be written on it, is that neither W nor R is empty. Furthermore, these are exclusive sets.

Few morally interesting acts will have (of its features on either list) features on only one of the lists. Thus we need, in addition to a way of representing what features the person considers to be morally relevant (which the lists are supposed to do), a way of representing his judgments that some features on one of the lists outweigh or override some features on the other list. We shall represent these outweighings or overridings by inequalities between sets of features. Thus $W_1 > R_1$ indicates that an action with no features on either list other than the members of $W_1 \cup R_1$ (all of which it has) is morally impermissible.[9] If $R_1 > W_1$ then an action with no features on the list other than the members of $W_1 \cup R_1$ (all of which it has) is morally permissible (and perhaps morally required). Our initial statements about the actions which, of the features on either list, have only features on one of the lists, can now be written as

$$W_i > \phi$$
$$\phi < R_i$$

where W_i and R_i are any nonempty subsets of W and R, respectively.[10]

To provide a way of representing drawing-the-line problems, and to provide a manageable way of representing a multitude of similar judgments, we shall allow some of the features on the lists to contain variables (in addition to that variable contained in every feature, which ranges over actions, reference to which variable is always suppressed in this paper) ranging over positive integers, e.g., "leads to the death of n persons."[11] Suppose this feature is w_1 which is a member of W, and consider a specific member of R, r_1. One might have as an outweighing $w_1 > r_1$; $n > 2$. This means that $w_1 > r_1$ for $n > 2$, and does not entail that not-$(w_1 > r_1)$ for $0 < n \leq 2$. A feature may contain more than one variable (the variables being ordered within the feature), and an inequality may contain more than one feature containing variables. This suggests that in these cases we must consider, in our representation, ordered sets of features on each side of the inequality, with an ordered set of numerical constraints afterwards. We should note the possibility that the inequality may contain as a constraint an equation essentially involving more than one of the variables, e.g., $nm \geq 2t$. I shall not pursue here the details of how such complications are to be best represented formally.

III. Ordering of Features and Their Combinations

What structural conditions on inequalities over features[12] may legitimately be imposed? Do these yield an ordering and, if so, of what strength?

We have a notation for outweighing or overriding. Do we need to introduce an equality sign for the notion of exactly balancing? The metaphor of scale balances would suggest that we do, but our explanations thus far do not seem to allow room for such a notion. For what would it mean to say that W_1 exactly balances R_1? It seems that an action having, of its properties on either list, all and only the members of $W_1 \cup R_1$ will be morally permissible or morally impermissible. If it is morally permissible, then $R_1 > W_1$; if it is morally impermissible, then $W_1 > R_1$. Where is the room for an equality sign?[13] The further possibility one thinks of is that the system of principles is incomplete in that, for some particular act having some features on each list, it yields neither the judgment that the action is morally permissible, nor the judgment that it is morally impermissible. It would be misleading to represent such a situation by an equality sign.

A condition which is obviously desirable is

$$(1) \quad R_i > W_j \rightarrow \text{not-}(W_j > R_i)$$

(We needn't, of course, separately state its equivalent contrapositive.) The connectedness condition

$$(2) \quad (R_i)(W_j)(R_i > W_j \text{ or } W_j > R_i)$$

is surely too strong a structural requirement to reasonably impose upon a person's fragmentary moral views. We shall take it up again later when we come to consider complete moral systems.

In addition to (1), obvious candidates are various transitivity conditions. Let X, Y, Z, S, T range over subsets (proper or improper) of R, and of W. $X > Y$ is well formed only if either $X \subseteq R$ and $Y \subseteq W$ or $X \subseteq W$ and $Y \subseteq R$. Consider

(3) $(\exists Z) (X > Z$ & not–$(Y > Z)) \rightarrow$
        (a) $(S) (Y > S \rightarrow X > S)$
        (b) $(S) (S > X \rightarrow S > Y)$

Intuitively, this seems reasonable. If X outweighs something that Y doesn't, then X has more weight than Y, and consequently outweighs everything that Y does, and Y is outweighed by everything that outweighs X.[14]

From (3), together with (1), follows

(4) $X > Y$ & $Y > Z$ & $Z > T \rightarrow X > T$

Furthermore, one can define a notion of one set of features having more weight than another set from the same list:

$$X \gg Y = \mathrm{df.}\ (\exists Z)(X > Z\ \&\ \text{not–}(Y > Z)).^{15}$$

Given (3), $\gg$ is irreflexive, asymmetrical, and transitive, and hence establishes a strict partial ordering of each list.[16]

But is (3) a legitimate condition to impose? Two reasons might suggest that it is not:

1.   Different features may interact differently with features on the other list.
2.   A feature may be strengthened or weakened, its weight increased or decreased, by something other than features of actions on the lists.

The second of these reasons we shall consider later, along with other reservations which stem from applying the condition to notions other than "overriding" and "outweighing" as these are explained later. Consider (4). Can't there be a case where $X > Y$, $Y > Z$, $Z > T$, yet $T > X$? So as not to be misled by our inequality sign, let us rephrase the question. Can't there be actions A_1, A_2, A_3, A_4, such that

(a) A_1 has all the features in $X \cup Y$, and no other features on the list, and A_1 is morally permissible.

(b) A_2 has all the features in $Y \cup Z$, and no other features on the lists, and A_2 is morally impermissible.

(c) A_2 has all the features in $Z \cup T$, and no other features on the lists, and A_2 is morally permissible.

(d) A_4 has all the features in $T \cup X$, and no other features on the lists, and A_4 is morally impermissible.

The only cases (under 1. above, as opposed to 2.) which appear to fit this, which I can think of, are cases in which, e.g., T and X interact so as to produce *another* W-feature (not in $T \cup X$) which also applies to A_4. But in such cases, it is false to say that the only feature on the lists which are had by A_4 are in $T \cup X$.[17] Thus, I suggest that we tentatively accept condition (3), appropriately modifying it later when we come to discuss the difficulties under 2. Consider the further condition

(5) $W_1 \subset W_2 \subseteq W \rightarrow$
    (a) $(\exists R_1) (R_1 > W_1 \text{ \& not--}(R_1 > W_2))$
    (b) $(\exists R_2) (W_2 > R_2 \text{ \& not--}(W_1 > R_2))$.

Or, to remove the here irrelevant possibility that there may happen to be no set of R-features "between" W_1 and W_2, consider

(6) $W_1 \subset W_2 \subseteq W \rightarrow (R_i) (W_1 > R_i \rightarrow W_2 > R_i)$.

Intuitively, (6) says that adding more W-features to an action cannot make it any better. (5), which given the previous conditions and definitions is equivalent to $W_1 \subset W_2 \subseteq W \rightarrow W_2 \gg W_1$, says that the more W-features, the worse (*ceteris paribus*). (Perhaps we should restrict this to acts which are not infinitely bad, if there be any which are. I ignore this complication here.) Once again, there is the possibility that some features which are in W_2 though not in W_1, so interact with features in W_1, in R_i, or with the facts of the situation (not represented by features on the lists) as to produce a new R-feature which was not previously present. But once again in this case, it is false that the *only* morally relevant features the act has are in $W_2 \cup R_i$ (for some particular R_i which is a candidate for satisfying the antecedent of the consequent of (6), but not its consequent). So once again, until the complications under 2. above are considered and incorporated, we shall tentatively accept and use (5) and (6).

IV. Alternative Actions

According to the simple model presented in section II, whether or not an action is morally impermissible depends only upon the features of the action, and upon the inequality among two sets of features which it has. Let W_X be the set of all and only those features of act X which are on the W-list; let R_X be the set of all and only those features of act X which are on the R-list. According to the simple model, act A is morally impermissible if and only if $W_A > R_A$. In arriving at a judgment about the impermissibility of an act A, one need not, according to the simple model, consider the alternative acts available to the person, nor need one consider longer courses of action of which A may be a part. The availability of alternative actions, and the embedding of an action in a longer course of action, produce complications which require modification of the simple model. In this section I shall consider only the first, leaving the second until section VI.

Is it true that A is morally impermissible only if $W_A > R_A$? Is it true that its W-features' outweighing its R-features is a necessary condition for an act's being morally impermissible? If $R_A > W_A$, is this sufficient for A's being morally permissible?

Consider the following two situations, obtained from one often mentioned in the literature in discussions of lying.

(1)   You are present as Q flees down a road from P, who you know will unjustifiably physically harm or kill him. P comes running along and asks which way Q went. If you say nothing, he will continue along the road and catch Q. *The only way* to prevent this is to lie to P, telling him that Q went in a different direction. I assume that sufficient details can be filled in so that you will all agree that it is morally permissible to lie to P in this situation. The right-making feature of saving Q from great harm overrides the wrong-making feature of lying to P.

(2)   The same situation as in (1), except that now there is some other way to save Q from the harm which does not involve lying to P, or any other wrong-making feature, e.g., if you start to tell P that what he's doing is wrong, he'll stop and listen and be convinced and won't continue on after Q. I shall assume that in this situation it would be morally impermissible to lie to P.[18]

I claim that the action of lying to P in (2) has the same features as it does in (1). I shall say more about this claim below. Now I wish to explore its consequences. Since by hypothesis (in 1) the R-features of this act outweigh the W-features, so do they in (2). Since the act in (2) is morally impermissible, this shows that the W-features of an act outweighing its R-features is not a necessary condition for that act's being morally impermissible.

What principles can we formulate to handle such issues? The simplest principle which suggests itself, to handle the case just described, is

(I)   If $W_A \neq \phi$ and $(\exists B)$ (B is an alternative action open to the person & $W_B \subset W_A$ & $R_A \subseteq R_B$) then it is morally impermissible for the person to do A (even if $W_A < R_A$).[19]

Roughly put, (I) comes to the claim that it is impermissible to do an action if one can achieve the same R-features at a cost of fewer W-features. (I) says that you must not do an action if an alternative action enables you to achieve the same good at less cost. A parallel principle would require that one not do an action, with non-null W-features, if an alternative action enables one to achieve a greater good at the same cost. Thus

(II)   If $W_A \neq \phi$ & $(\exists B)$ (B is an alternative open to the person & $W_B \subseteq W_A$ & $R_A \subset R_B$) then it would be morally impermissible for the person to do A (even if $R_A > W_A$).

Note that (II) does not require that a person maximize R-features, but requires only that he not pass up any *if* he is going to incur some W-cost. But still, (II) seems to me to be too strong a condition to impose, and we shall *not* do so.

But we want something more than (I). For though A may achieve more R-features than B, perhaps the extra gain of A isn't worth its extra cost. Two principles suggest themselves, the first being a special case of the second:

(III)   If $(\exists B)$ (B is available to the person and $W_B = \phi$ & $W_A \neq \phi$ & $R_B \subset R_A$ & $W_A > (R_A - R_B)$) then it is impermissible to do A (even if $R_A > W_A$).

(IV)   If $(\exists B)$ (B is available to the person & $R_B \subset R_A$ & $W_B \subset W_A$ & $(W_A - W_B) > (R_A - R_B)$) then it is impermissible to do A.

First a word about how to interpret (III) and (IV). If the moral world is very simple so that the total wrongness or rightness of a set of features is just the sum of the individual wrongness (rightness) and there is no interaction between the R and W features, then $(X - Y)$ is just the set-theoretic difference between X and Y; e.g., $(W_A - W_B)$ is just the set of features which belong to W_A and which do not belong to W_B. And the inequality sign, as before, appears between two sets of features. If, however, as seems likely, things are not so simple, then $(X - Y)$ must be interpreted as some numerical measure of the difference in value between X and Y (where, e.g., value is measured on an interval scale; i.e., a scale unique up to a positive linear transformation). And the inequality sign stands for the ordinary relation between numbers. I shall say something about how such numerical measures might be obtained in section V. An important point for us to note here is that some measure of by *how much* some features outweigh others are better than, are worse than others seems required to account for a person's judgments of moral impermissibility, even *apart from* considerations about "risk," as the utility theorists speak of it. This point is further reinforced by the condition (VII), which follows below, which prevents assuming simple additive conditions without making them explicit, and prevents proceeding by speaking only of set-theoretical differences.

Thus far we have considered only those cases where $W_B \subseteq W_A$. But one wants principles to cover some cases where though A does not have each of the W-features that B has, the *other* ones which B has are less bad than A's. The simplest case of this sort is one in which B has at least all of the R-features that A does. This suggests

(V)   If $W_A \neq \phi$ & $(\exists B)$ (B is an alternative available to the person and $(W_A - W_B) > 0$ & $R_A \subseteq R_B$), then it is impermissible to do A.[20]

If (V) is acceptable, one wonders why it is necessary to have $R_A \subseteq R_B$. Couldn't one have R_A and R_B be of equal weight, or R_B have greater weight than R_A, even though R_A is not a subset (proper or improper) of R_B? This would give us

(VI)   If $W_A \neq \phi$ & $(\exists B)$ (B is an alternative available to the person & $(W_A - W_B) > 0$ & $(R_B - R_A) \geq 0$), then it is impermissible for the person to do A.

But what of the cases where there is no B with less weighty W-features than A's which has at least as weighty R-features, though there is a B with less weighty W-features and R-features, and the extra gain in R-features from A rather than B is outweighed by the extra cost in W-features from A rather than B.

One might formulate the following principle to fit this:

(VII)   If ($\exists B$) (B is an alternative available to the person & $W_A \gg W_B$ & $(W_A - W_B) > (R_A - R_B)$) then it is impermissible to do A.

Consider the following intuitive argument for (VII). Suppose there were an act C which just took up the W and R slack between B and A. Thus, B & C has just the same R and W features which A has. You've already decided to do B. Should you do C in addition? If the answer is no, it is impermissible to do B & C rather than B. Since $W_C (= W_A - W_B) > R_C (= R_A - R_B)$, the answer is no. (I here suppose that the complication to be discussed in section VI does not apply to act C.) Thus it is impermissible to do B & C. Since B & C has exactly the same moral features as A, it is impermissible to do A.[21]

A stronger principle than (VII) is

(VIII)   If ($\exists B$) (B is available to the person & $W_A \geq W_B$ & $(W_A - W_B) > (R_A - R_B)$), then it is impermissible for the person to do A.

(VIII) differs from (VII) only in the case where $W_A = W_B$. (And in this case we would have $R_B > R_A$.) Note that an intuitive argument for (VIII), similar to the one for (VII), can be offered only if the R-list is such that an action having some features on it and no features on the W-list is morally required. For an action C which, in this case, took up the R and W slack between A and B would have no W-features, and would have some R-features. If such an action C is morally required, we will have the intuitive argument for (VIII). (VIII) seems to me to be too strong a principle to impose. We shall thus have to be careful later not to construe the R-list so that all actions having some features on it, and no features on the W-list, are morally required. If it is so construed, then principle (VIII) must be admitted as legitimate.

I am more certain that one does not wish to require that a person maximize the difference between the R-weight and W-weight of an action. One does *not* wish to require

(IX)   If ($\exists B$) (B is available to the person & $(R_B - W_B) > (R_A - W_A)$), then it is impermissible for the person to do A.

Note that (IX) differs from (VII) in that it does not have the clause that $W_A > W_B$ in its antecedent. Hence in a situation where $R_B = 52$, $W_B = 50$, $R_A = 2$, $W_A = 1$, (IX) has the consequence that it is impermissible to do A, whereas (VII) does not have this consequence. The intuitive justification for (VII) was that A would be impermissible if its extra gain (over some other action) wasn't worth its extra cost (over this other action). This justification cannot be applied to (IX) since (IX) rules out actions which may have no extra cost over their alternatives.[22] Note further how an argument parallel to the one advanced for (VII) gets blocked. One might consider an action C which takes up the moral slack between A and B. Thus $R_C = (R_B - R_A)$; $W_C = (W_B - W_A)$ where $W_B > W_A$. The person has already decided to do A. Is it permissible for him to do C? The answer is yes, for by hypothesis (of IX) $R_C > W_C$. Thus it is permissible for the person to do A & C, and hence permissible for him to do B, if there is no other action which stands in the relation (VII) describes to B. However, from this one cannot conclude that he is required to do C after doing A; hence one cannot conclude that he is required to do B rather than A. (One could conclude this only by imposing a much too strong interpretation of the lists and inequalities; viz., that if $R_X > W_X$ then it is morally impermissible not to do X.) (VII) is the strongest principle of the sort we have been considering which seems to me appropriate. (IX), it seems to me, must clearly be rejected, though the rejection of (VIII) is more doubtful. But some complications about (VII) (and the other conditions accepted) must be mentioned.

A. If there are an infinite number of actions available to the person, then for each one there may be some other action with the same R-features and less weighty W-features. For example, suppose there are an infinite number of alternatives $A_1, A_2, \ldots, A_i, \ldots$ and the measurement scales yield the results that (i) (j) $R_{A_i} = R_{A_j}$ and (i) $W_{A_i} = 1/i$. There will be no action with least weighty W-features. Hence, according to (VII), each of the acts $A_1, A_2, \ldots$ is impermissible. It is this sort of problem that leads writers in decision theory to speak of ϵ-optimizing. I shall assume that a similar line must be taken here, and shall ignore the details of how (VII) is to be modified, and how the particular ϵ is to be chosen.

B. Suppose that in our original situation (of lying to save some-one's life when some alternative also saves his life and involves less weighty W-features) the only other alternative which saves the person's life involves you in great personal expenditure of money, effort, energy, time, etc. In *some* situations where the alternative with less weighty W-features involves great personal cost and inconvenience (though not additional W-features due to this) one would not require that the person not perform the act with the weightier W-features.[23] Where A is the act with the W-feature, and B is an alternative which stands in the relation described by (VII) to A, and B imposes personal (non-W) costs on the performer of B, how are we to decide whether or not A is permissible? Presumably this decision depends upon $(W_A - W_B)$, and upon how great the personal costs of B are (how much greater than they are with A). But how exactly is a line to be drawn?

One might consider an act C which is like B except that the personal costs to the performer of B are imposed by C upon some neutral third party. C's imposing of these costs upon some third party presumably involves C in some W-features (in addition to those of B). The following principle—embodying the view that if you are required to throw the costs upon a neutral third party rather than do A, then you are required to take the costs upon yourself rather than do A—seems reasonable: If C stands in the relation to A described by (VII), so that if C were available it would be impermissible to do A, then it is impermissible to do A (when B is available). That is, if the C corresponding to B is such that $W_C \ll W_A$ & $(R_A - R_C) < (W_A - W_C)$, then it is impermissible to do A when B is available and stands in the relation described by (VII) to A, even though B involves personal costs to the performer.

Delicate questions arise over whether substituting "if and only if" for the initial "if" in this principle yields a legitimate principle; and if not, how the further cases are to be handled.[24] I shall not pursue these questions here, but shall hereafter suppose that we have answered them and have available to us a modified (VII) which incorporates the above principle and whatever complications are needed to handle the further cases.

Let us denote by S the relation embodied in an adequately formulated (VII) such that if some action available to the person stands in the relation S to A then it is impermissible for the person to do A. Thus we refuse to say that an action A is morally permissible if its R-features outweigh its W-features, but rather we, at this point, say that an action A is morally permissible if its R-features outweigh its W-features *and* there is no alternative action available to the person which stands in the relation S to A.

Let us consider one objection to this whole line of argument. It might be said that in the cases which prompted condition (VII), act A has added features which are easily overlooked. For example, one might say that the act of lying to the aggressor to save a person's life when one can save the life by persuading the aggressor to stop, has the added feature (when compared to the act in the situation where the *only* way to stop the aggressor is by lying) of being an unnecessary lie. And, the objection would continue, if *this* W-feature is included, then $W_A > R_A$. So of course the action is impermissible. Hence, the objection concludes, there was no need to reject the simple structure. If $R_A > W_A$, this *is* sufficient for A's being permissible, and the whole line of argument in section IV thus far has been mistaken.

We can rebut the particular "feature" which was suggested, by noting that "involves telling an unnecessary lie" is an explicitly moral notion, which explicitly evaluates comparatively features of acts. For notice that if he can stop the murder by shooting the potential murderer or by lying to him, we can say "he unnecessarily shot him; he could have lied to him," but not "he unnecessarily lied to him; he could have shot him." But, granting that the particular "feature" suggested won't do, isn't there some (other) way to capture "involves telling an unnecessary lie," *for a given situation,* which doesn't involve explicit reference to moral notions? And if so, won't this have to be ruled out as a feature of act A?

One might try, as such a feature of A

(a) $F =$ "is an alternative to another act B, available to the person, which has the same R-features as A and fewer W-features."

This obviously won't do since it explicitly mentions the notions of R-feature and W-feature. So one might try

(b) $F =$ "is an alternative to another act B, available to the person, which has features $w_1, \ldots, w_m$ and $r_1, \ldots, r_n$" where (though this is not said as part of F) $r_1, \ldots, r_n$ are exactly the R-features of A and $w_1, \ldots, w_m$ are a proper subset of the W-features of A.

Note first that even if this worked it would handle only the cases covered by principle (I) in this section. But it doesn't work, because B may have weighty features in addition to $w_1, \ldots, w_m$ which are on the W-list, and if so, F won't be a W-feature of A. (If one supposes F to be a W-feature of A in this case, *what R-feature(s) of A corresponds to B's having weighty W-features in addition to $w_1, \ldots, w_m$, and also overrides F?*) Trying to handle this possibility by adding into F "and B has no other features which are on the W-list" won't give us a non-explicitly-moral feature, and given the open-ended nature of the list one cannot build into F the conjunction which denies, for each other feature on the W-list, that B has it. Thus, it is not at all clear how to begin to state the candidate for the non-explicitly-moral feature (on the W-list) which A has when there is an alternative B to A which stands in the relation to A described by condition VII).

Thus, we continue to maintain that it is not sufficient for A's being permissible that $R_A > W_A$ (and thus we continue to reject the simple model), and we accept something like condition (VII) as marking off the exception to the sufficiency. If there is available *one* other action of a certain sort, then A is impermissible, even though $R_A > W_A$.

Is it also the case that $W_A > R_A$ is insufficient for A's being impermissible, and do the same kind of objections to sufficiency hold as in the case of $R_A > W_A$? Recall that we are tentatively accepting the view that

(A)   If $R_A > W_A$ then A is permissible unless $(\exists B)$ $(W_A \gg W_B$ & $W_A - W_B > R_A - R_B)$. And if $(\exists B)$ $(W_A \gg W_B$ & $W_A - W_B > R_A - R_B)$, then A is impermissible.

If things were symmetrical we would have correspondingly on the other side:

(B)   If $W_A > R_A$ then A is impermissible unless $(\exists B)$ $(W_B \gg W_A$ & $W_B - W_A > R_B - R_A)$; and if $(\exists B)$ $(W_B \gg W_A$ & $W_B - W_A > R_B - R_A)$, then A is permissible.

This says that if *one* action available is worse (in a certain way) than A, then A is permissible even though $W_A > R_A$. But this is absurd; an action is not permissible just because we could have done something else which was worse. Whereas it is not absurd (and is indeed true) to say that an action with non-null W-features was impermissible if we could have done something else which was, in a certain way, better. Thus, the situation is not symmetrical, and we have what I shall call the *First Asymmetry*: The existence of one alternative action of a certain sort makes $R_A > W_A$ insufficient for the permissibility of A; whereas it is *not* the case that the existence of *one* action of a certain sort makes $W_A > R_A$ insufficient for the impermissibility of A. If $W_A > R_A$ is insufficient for the impermissibility of A, this is not because of something about *one* of the alternatives to A.[25]

But is $W_A > R_A$ sufficient for A's impermissibility or not? It seems clear that if it is not, this is not because one of the alternatives to A is worse in a certain way, but can only be because *all* of the alternatives to A are worse in a certain way. And, indeed, it seems quite natural to say that when *all* of the alternatives to A are worse than A itself, then A is permissible even though $W_A > R_A$. Thus, one might say that

(C) If $W_A > R_A$ then A is impermissible unless (B) (If B is an alternative to A then $W_B \gg W_A$ & $W_B - W_A > R_B - R_A$); and if (B) (if B is an alternative to A, then $W_B \gg W_A$ & $W_B - W_A > R_B - R_A$), then A is permissible even though $W_A > R_A$.

Against this one might plausibly argue that in each of the cases one thinks of which seem to fit $W_A > R_A$ yet *all* of the alternatives to A are worse than A itself, there are features which A itself has which capture the respects in which the alternatives are all worse, e.g., "prevents the death of n persons," "saves the lives of these other persons." And since in these cases A has the additional R-feature of avoiding or preventing certain evils, it is in fact false that its W-features outweigh its R-features, so that we are not faced with a case where $W_A > R_A$, and so are not presented with a counterexample to the claim that $W_A > R_A$ is sufficient for the impermissibility of A.[26]

If this counter-argument is defensible, then we are faced with a *Second Asymmetry*. From our current vantage point, the First Asymmetry says that unlike $R_A > W_A$, where *one* action of a certain sort makes it insufficient for A's being permissible, one action cannot make $W_A > R_A$ insufficient for the impermissibility of A, and *if* anything about the alternatives to A does make $W_A > R_A$ insufficient for A's being impermissible, it is something about *all* of the alternatives to A. The Second Asymmetry claim says that *nothing* about the alternatives does make $W_A > R_A$ insufficient for A's being impermissible.[27]

Since something about the alternatives can make A impermissible even though $R_A > W_A$, the Second Asymmetry claim adds considerably to the significant divergence noticed by the First Asymmetry. (Of course, the simple structure of section II was perfectly symmetrical.)

Is the Second Asymmetry claim true, or can A be permissible, even though $W_A > R_A$, because all of the alternatives to A are worse than A itself?

Let us consider a specific example.[28] A person is in the cab of a locomotive and approaching a three-way continuation of the route. If the train continues to go straight ahead, which it will do if nothing is done to its controls, it will run down and kill 20 people. If it is made to go on either the rightmost track or the leftmost track, it will in each case run down and kill 40 people (for each track has 40 people tied on it). All this is known to the person in the cab.

If the person allows the train to go straight ahead when there is *no one* on the side tracks, the act is wrong for it allows 20 people to be killed, and has no redeeming virtue. In the first described situation we think it permissible to allow the train to continue straight on because the W-feature of allowing 20 people to be killed is outweighed by the R-feature of avoiding the killing of 40 people.[29]

There is one notion of "avoids" which involves reference to changing things from how they would be in the normal and expected course of events, and it is this notion which lends plausibility and punch to the Second Asymmetry claim. The example that we have been considering leads us to think that there is another notion of "avoids," where, roughly, the fact that all actions but one lead to a certain consequence is sufficient to yield the conclusion that one avoids this consequence. But this additional "feature" of avoiding an undesirable consequence, in this sense of "avoiding," saves the Second Asymmetry claim only via the course of *trivializing* it. For of course all of A's alternatives being worse than A won't make A permissible, where $W_A > R_A$, if the fact that *all* these alternatives are worse creates an additional and very weighty R-feature of A (*viz.*, avoiding ——) so that when this is included, $R_A > W_A$.

At this point we have a choice. We can say that the Second Asymmetry claim is true, though trivial. Or we can refuse to admit this sense of "avoid" as specifying a *feature* of an act for our purpose.[30] And in this case, while accepting the First Asymmetry, we might try to specify a *duality* thesis, which would involve the substitution of "<" and ">," "impermissible" and "permissible," and of universal and existential quantifiers, and would have the consequence that A and C above are duals. This latter alternative is certainly well worth pursuing, but in the absence of special reasons for doing so, and since it would make section VI even more complicated, we tentatively choose the first alternative.

V. Measurement of Moral Weight

Those arguments in the previous section which depend upon conditions or principles which assume a method of *measuring* the difference in weights between sets of features on one of the lists may seem to the reader to be, though interesting and intuitively correct, merely useless speculation in the absence of the description of some method for obtaining such measurement. Such a reaction seems to me to be unduly harsh, but I shall not dwell on this since I wish now to sketch a method for obtaining the appropriate measurements.

The obvious suggestion is to consider probability mixtures of W-features, and probability mixtures of R-features, and to attempt to parallel the Von Neumann–Morgenstern or similar axioms for utility measurement[31] so that we get the measurement we need. This suggestion might be reinforced by noting that an adequate theory of moral judgment will have to account for judgments of actions under situations of "moral risk" (where associated with an action is a probability distribution over sets of features on the lists, rather than just one set of features on the lists), not to mention "uncertainty." So, it might be asked, why not introduce that apparatus at this point? It seems to me that this approach is inappropriate for our problem here. For our problem is not one of accounting for judgments in situations of "moral risk," and there seems to be no intuitive reason for introducing apparatus based upon probability considerations to handle the problem we are now faced with. If we were to utilize the VN–M type of measurement, arguments would have to be offered to show why the numerical values thereby obtained should function in the principles we have already listed. The more desirable course seems to be to find a method of measurement utilizing only considerations intrinsic to the sort of situation in which our problem arose, or utilizing only that apparatus which is sufficient to generate the problem and to show the need for a method of measurement. Such an alternative course has an additional theoretical advantage. For if one can establish the existence of numerical scales, assigning numbers to sets of features, to be used in the principles for the situations discussed in section IV, and if one can use a VN–M-type procedure to establish numerical scales, assigning numbers to sets of features, based upon and to account for judgments of "moral risk" actions, then one can raise the question: What is the relation between these scales? I shall not attempt here to pursue or even specify the issues of interest which might arise.

Is there some way, other than by a VN–M-type procedure, to establish the existence of numerical scales without utilizing information of a sort not already provided by the kind of apparatus we are discussing? If there is not, then there would be reason for believing that the sort of apparatus we are discussing is (if not supplemented) seriously inadequate. I should here like to sketch (and I shall here do no more than sketch) a way of obtaining the numerical values which function in the principles of the previous section.

The procedure I suggest is very simple. Let me first state it in a way which will look circular. I hope that I have offered sufficiently forceful intuitive arguments for principle (VII) in the previous section so that you will agree that we can assume that if there *were* numerical values, principle (VII) would be operating. We can use this assumption to obtain, for a specific person, specific inequalities between differences. Without entering into the intricacies of the procedures to be used to discover this, I shall assume that we can determine that for the person some R-features outweigh or override some W-features, some W-features are worse than others, and some R-features are better than others. Suppose, for example, that we discover that (for the person)

(a)   Some R-features (call them R_A) outweigh some W-features (call them W_A).[32]

(b)   Some R-features (R_B) outweigh some W-features (W_B).

(c)   The W-features W_A are worse than W_B.

(d)   The R-features R_A are better than R_B.

Thus we have

(a′) $R_A > W_A$

(b′) $R_B > W_B$

(c′) $W_A \gg W_B$

(d′) $R_A \gg R_B$

If now we can find an action A whose only morally relevant features are exactly those in R_A and W_A, and an action B whose only morally relevant features are exactly those in R_B and W_B, *and* the person judges that it is morally impermissible to do A (if B is an alternative), then we can conclude that (for this person)

$$(W_A - W_B) > (R_A - R_B)$$

If we ask him questions about other combinations of features and situations such as the previous one, we will get additional inequalities between differences. The important fact is that if we can get enough such inequalities then we will have sufficient information to establish a numerical scale of a given strength.

Let me describe things somewhat differently. If the person is following principle (VII), which utilizes numerical values (if his judgments can be accounted for by this principle), then certain conditions will have to be satisfied. For example, if these numerical values are to be measured on a scale which preserves relations among real numbers unique up to a positive linear transformation (an interval scale), then since it is a truth of arithmetic that

If $X > Y > Z >$ zero, and $W > T > U >$ zero, and $X - Y > W - T$, and $Y - Z > T - U$ then $X - Z > W - U$,

if the numbers assigned to sets of features satisfy the antecedent, they must satisfy the consequent. So in particular, it will be true that

If $W_A > W_B > W_C > 0$, and $R_A > R_B > R_C > 0$, and $(W_A - W_B) > (R_A - R_B)$, and $(W_B - W_C) > (R_B - R_C)$ then $(W_A - W_C) > (R_A - R_C)$.

Now this will be true only if the following is true. (Thus the following statement is a necessary condition for the weights to be represented on a certain kind of scale.) If (for a person) $W_A \gg W_B \gg W_C$ and $R_A \gg R_B \gg R_C$ and $R_A > W_A$ and $R_B > W_B$ and $R_C > W_C$ and the person judges that it is impermissible to do A in a situation in which B is available, and the person judges that it is impermissible to do B in a situation in which C is available, then the person judges that it is impermissible to do A in a situation in which C is available.

Note that this does not utilize any apparatus or notions beyond those we already had. Furthermore, it seems intuitively reasonable; that is, it is a condition one would wish to impose, and could well have imposed apart from all considerations about measurement.[33] We thus have a necessary condition for the existence of a measure of the moral weight of a set of features on an interval scale. (I here implicitly assume, as throughout, that if there is a measure, principle VII operates) which utilizes no very strong apparatus in its statement, and which furthermore seems intuitively reasonable and justifiable. One might hope to gather a large number of such necessary conditions, and prove that they are sufficient to establish the existence of an interval scale measuring moral weight. That is, for some locution already available to us from our previous apparatus, one introduces an n-place relation. The intuitively justifiable statements using this locution are written down as conditions on the n-place relation. Thus, corresponding to each intuitively justified statement (or rather, to a selection of these) is a condition on the n-place relation. If one has chosen wisely or luckily, one may then be able to prove, using these conditions on the n-place relation as axioms:

A *Representation Theorem*: showing that there exists a real-valued function assigning numbers which is such that, for specified numerical relations, these relations hold among the numbers if and only if some corresponding relation about the subject matter holds among the objects the numbers are assigned to; and

A *Uniqueness Theorem*: showing that any two real-valued functions shown to exist by the Representation Theorem stand in a certain relationship to each other. The more limited this relationship, the stronger a scale of measurement one has obtained.[34]

To remove one simplification in this sketch: it will not be the case that each of the conditions on the n-place relation which are jointly sufficient (it needn't be that each of them is necessary) to establish the existence of a measuring function will correspond to an intuitively justifiable normative condition or one which specifies the notions involved. For, if similar previous results are any guide, one will require in addition various structural conditions.[35] One hopes to find structural conditions, which when combined with the others will suffice for the task and which look as though (without too drastic an idealization) they are satisfied.

The detailed technical task of specifying the axioms which seem reasonable in the moral context, and which yield the result, I must leave for another occasion. Here, I wish to point out that the prospects are very promising. One finds, in the literature, several axiom systems which either explicitly are about (or can be interpreted to be about) a 4-place inequality relation between differences. Which set of axioms one uses determines the strength of the scale one obtains (ratio, interval, higher-ordered metric, ordered metric, etc.). Exactly which system of axioms should be adopted for our purposes here is a tricky question. Here I wish to confidently conjecture that some not very radical modifications of an already existing measurement system will capture intuitive moral conditions (plus some structural ones) and will suffice to yield some reasonably strong measurement of the moral weight of a set of morally relevant features.[36]

Before leaving the subject of measurement I wish to remove in advance two reasons that one might have for believing that the project sketched cannot be carried out successfully.

1. The modified principle (VII) of section IV was more complicated than I have made it out to be in this section. Won't these complications interfere with the procedure of measurement? They will not if one is careful to construct the scale via the person's judgments for situations where

(a)   there is no extra personal cost to the agent in doing B rather than A

(b)   there is not an infinite set of available actions such that no action has least wrong W-features.

2. Does the project of measurement described above depend upon the claim (which the reader may consider not to have been established by my arguments in section IV) that "act A has as an alternative action available to the person to whom A is an alternative, an act B which ———" is not usable as a feature of act A? It does not. For suppose that my claim in section IV is mistaken. Then, if there is such an alternative act B available to the person, A has an additional W-feature so that $W_A > R_A$; e.g., the W-features of lying to the pursuer to save the other man's life would outweigh the R-features of this act (if there was a suitable nonlying alternative available). Still, given a reasonable independence assumption, the method sketched will yield inequalities of the form $W'_A - W_B > R_A - R_B$, where W'_A is the set containing all W-features of A except the ones which refer to the availability of a suitable act B as an alternative to A. And *these* inequalities between differences can be used, as the others before, to establish a numerical measure over subsets of features not containing features which refer to the availability of an alternative action.[37] Thus, the supposition that the claim in section IV is mistaken does not block the proposed method of measurement.

VI. Larger Courses of Action

We have argued that for an act A such that $W_A \neq \phi$, $R_A > W_A$ is not sufficient for A's being morally permissible. For there may be available an alternative act B which stands in the relation to A described by condition (VII) of section IV, and in this case, A is not permissible. We have further argued that the claim that $W_A > R_A$ is a sufficient condition for A's being impermissible cannot be similarly overthrown by considering situations in which all of the alternatives to A are worse than A. Should we conclude from this that $W_A > R_A$ is a sufficient condition for A's being impermissible, or are there some other considerations which yield the result that A may be morally permissible even though $W_A > R_A$?

The sort of situation which suggests itself is one in which though $W_A > R_A$, A is (a necessary) part of some larger course of action B, and $R_B > W_B$. For some such situation, may it not be that A is morally permissible? It might be suggested that this problem can be avoided, because in such cases "is a part of a larger course of action which is such that ———" will be an R-feature of the A, and hence it won't be true that $W_A > R_A$. Even if this is so (I shall take up the question later), one wants to know the appropriate way to fill in the blank. I shall approach this question by considering what conditions are appropriate supposing that such things are *not* features of acts. After doing this we shall then consider whether these conditions can be used to obtain an appropriate way of filling in the blank.

Let me give two examples of cases for which it might be said that though $W_A > R_A$, A is permissible because it is a necessary part of some larger course of action B, where $R_B > W_B$.

(1)   A person P is unjustly being penned up by another person Q. You steal from some innocent third party R, one key to the door, making it possible for you to release P. I assume that this act is permissible if and only if it is part of the larger course of action of obtaining the release of P. If, for example, you go on to throw away the key, sell it, put it in your scrapbook, then your stealing of the key (and not attempting to release the person) was impermissible. I thus assume that $W_{\text{stealing the key}} > R_{\text{stealing the key}}$, and thus that "making it possible for you to release P" either isn't an R-feature of the act or, if it is, doesn't when combined with the other R-features of the act, override its W-features. But even though $W_{\text{stealing the key}} > R_{\text{stealing the key}}$, it may be permissible to steal the key.

(2)   A group of officials torture some person they know to be a terrorist, in order to discover the plans (which they know are about to be executed) of a terrorist group which they can then thwart, thereby saving many innocent lives. Assume that the officials are good, the terrorists are bad, and that saving these lives outweighs torturing the person. When the torturing is part of the larger course of action of saving the lives, it is permissible. If, however, the officials torture the person, obtain the information, and then do nothing with it, or just file it away, then the torturing was impermissible. Thus $W_{\text{torturing}} > R_{\text{torturing}}$, yet the torturing may be permissible if it is a necessary part of a larger course of action B where $R_B > W_B$.

Thus it seems that $W_A > R_A$ is not a sufficient condition for the impermissibility of A, for A may be a necessary part of a larger permissible course of action. Can it be, on the other side, that parallel considerations about larger courses of action also prevent $R_A > W_A$ from being a sufficient condition for A's being permissible.[38] One thing which might suggest itself is that though $R_A > W_A$, A is impermissible because for every larger course of action A^i of which it is a part, $W_A^i > R_A^i$. This seems to me to be a possibility not worth taking seriously. For it is difficult to believe that such a situation would not be reflected in the W-features of A itself.[39] But perhaps though A is part of some larger acts C which have $R_C > W_C$, each one of these has as an alternative an act (not containing A) which stands in the same relation to C as B stands to A in condition (VII) of section IV.

We want to say roughly the following:

(1)　$R_A > W_A$, but A is not permissible because $(\exists B)$ (B stands to A in the relation described by principle (VII) and B is permissible).

(2)　$R_A > W_A$, but A is not permissible because all courses of action of which A is a part are impermissible by (1).

(3)　$W_A > R_A$, but A is permissible because it is part of a larger B (where $R_B > W_B$) and B is permissible.

We cannot stop here in explaining the exceptions to

(a)　$R_A > W_A$ being sufficient for A's being permissible

(b)　$W_A > R_A$ being sufficient for A's being impermissible

for each of (1)–(3) has the word "permissible" after the "because," and it is the application of this word we are trying to account for. And we cannot eliminate "permissible" or "impermissible" after the "because" by rewriting (1)–(3) and substituting "$R_x > W_x$" for each occurrence of "X is permissible" after the "because" and substituting "$W_x > R_x$" for each occurrence of "X is impermissible" after the "because." For our problem is just that these are not sufficient conditions for permissibility and impermissibility, respectively, and we cannot state principles governing the exceptions to them as sufficient conditions which assume that there is no such problem. For example, the act B referred to in (1) must not be one shown to be impermissible by (2); (2) explicitly refers to (1); the act B referred to in (3) must not be one shown to be impermissible by (1) or (2), etc. One gets complications piled upon complications—though fewer than if we had taken the course of rejecting the Second Asymmetry claim at the end of section IV.

How might these complications be handled? Let us first define some notions.

(1)　B *undercuts*$_0$ $A = $ df. A and B occupy the same time interval and $R_A > W_A$ & $R_B > W_B$ & $W_B \ll W_A$ & $(W_A - W_B) > (R_A - R_B)$.

(2)　B *strongly undercuts*$_t$ $A = $ df. B is an act over the time interval t, and B does not contain A as a part, and no part[40] of B comes before A, and no part of A comes before B, and (X) (X is an act over t containing A as a part $\rightarrow$ B undercuts$_0$ X).

(3) A is strongly undercut$_t$ = df. $(\exists B)$ (B strongly undercuts$_t$ A)[41]

(4) C begins a strong undercutting$_t$ of A = df. $(\exists B)$ (B contains C & C begins B & B strongly undercuts$_t$ A).

(5) A is strongly undercut$\geq_t$ = df. (t') (t' is an interval beginning when A does and extending at least up to t $\rightarrow$ $(\exists B)$ (B strongly undercuts$'_t$ A))

(6) C begins a strong undercutting$\geq_t$ of A = df. (t') (t' is an interval beginning when A does and extending at least up to t $\rightarrow$ $(\exists B)$ (B contains C & C begins B & B strongly undercuts$'_t$ A))

I now want to define a special kind of strong undercutting$\geq_t$ of A. Roughly, it is one, begun by some C, which gives at least *one* course of action continuing through the various time periods $\geq t$, such that each segment (continuing up to t) of this *one* course of action strongly undercuts A. I do not see any way to define this notion using only the apparatus of first-order quantification theory.

Suppose C begins a strong undercutting$\geq_t$ of A. Then for each time period t_i beginning when A does and extending at least up to t, there is at least one action B which contains C as its beginning and which strongly undercuts$_{t_i}$ A. There may be more than one such action. Let S_i be the set of all such actions; i.e., where t_i is a time period beginning when A does and extending at least up to t, S_i = the set of all actions which contain C as their beginning and which strongly undercut$_{t_i}$ A. We now want to define the one course of action spoken of above, which will be represented by a selection set from the family of the S_i (a set containing one member from each of the S_i). There will be one such course of action if and only if there is a selection set which represents one continuing course of action. Let us denote by B_i the member of this selection set coming from the set S_i, and denote the selection set itself by S. S will represent the one course of action we want if and only if [t_i begins the interval t_i if and only if B_i begins the course of action B_i]. I assume that each time interval begins when action A begins. We define:

(7) C begins a sequential strong undercutting$\geq_t$ of A if and only if C begins a strong undercutting$\geq_t$ of A and there exists a selection set S from the family of the S_i such that (B_i) (B_j) [$B_i \in S$ &

$B_j \in S \rightarrow (t_i$ begins the interval $t_j \equiv B_i$ begins the course of action $B_j)]$.

Given these definitions, we may now state:

Principle I: If $R_A > W_A$ & $(\exists C)$ $(\exists t)$ (C is available to the person and C begins a sequential strong undercutting$\geq_t$ of A) then A is impermissible.

Can the antecedent of Principle I be weakened so as to yield another valid principle? If we eliminate the word "sequential" in Principle I, we get a principle which would hold A impermissible in the following sort of situation (see Figure 10.1), where downward paths represent courses of action. Suppose C undercuts$_0$ A. C & C_1 strongly undercuts$_1$ A, but C & C_2 does not; C & C_2 & C_{21} strongly undercuts$_2$ A, but no action over t_2 of which C & C_1 is a part strongly undercuts$_2$ A; C & C_1 & C_{12} & C_{121} strongly undercuts$_3$ A, but no action over t_3 of which C & C_2 & C_{21} is a part strongly undercuts$_3$ A, and so forth. Thus in this case, C begins a strong undercutting$\geq_0$ of A, but there is no t such that C begins a *sequential* strong undercutting$\geq_t$ of A. In this case, there is no one course of action one can recommend to the person as an alternative to beginning his course of action with A. That A is impermissible in this situation seems doubtful.

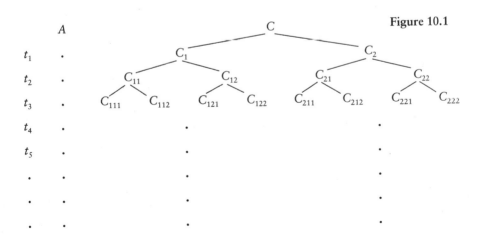

Figure 10.1

If in the previous example, node C_2 and everything that follows it is eliminated, then we get something between strongly undercutting$\geq_t$ and strongly undercutting$_t$; namely, cyclical undercutting. For in this case, for each odd i, C & C_1, begins a strong undercutting$_i$ of A, whereas this is not the case for even i. I shall not bother to define precisely the notion of a cyclical undercutting, or of a sequential cyclical undercutting. It seems at least as doubtful that either of these can be substituted for a sequential strong undercutting$\geq_t$ in Principle I.

It is worth noting such possibilities, just because it emphasizes how difficult it would be to make moral judgments if we knew they arose. A tractable world (morally) would be one in which

(a) Any action that is weakly undercut$\geq_t$ is strongly undercut$\geq'_t$ for some t' including t

(b) There are no infinitely extended undercutting cycles

(c) For every act A which is strongly undercut$\geq_t$ there is an act C which begins a strong undercutting$\geq_t$ of A

(d) If C begins a strong undercutting$\geq_t$ of A then C begins a sequential strong undercutting$\geq_t$ of A.

Nicer yet would be one in which

(e) If B undercuts$_0$ A then there is a t such that B begins a sequential strong undercutting$\geq_t$ of A.

But this seems too much to hope for.

I wish to leave as a question for further consideration whether the antecedent of Principle I can be weakened so as still to yield a valid principle. One would hope so, since the definition of "sequential strong undercutting$\geq_t$," uses very powerful machinery, which it would be better to avoid. (And it is not clear, for any action A such that $R_A > W_A$, how to rule out the theoretical possibility that there is an action C and a time interval t such that C begins a sequential strong undercutting$\geq_t$ of A.)

We should note that many problems that arise in the area of the subject of this section could be avoided if there were a time-discounting of the moral future. Questions about this issue, interesting in their own right, must be considered in a full development of the theory.

For the time being I shall suppose that no weakening of the antecedent of Principle I will do. (If this tentative supposition is false, what is said below can be modified so as to correspond to the new principle with weakened antecedent.) I suggest the following two principles:

(1) If $R_A > W_A$ then [A is impermissible if and only if ($\exists B$) ($\exists t$) (B is an action available to the person & B begins a sequential strong undercutting$\geq_t$ of A)]

(2)   If $W_A > R_A$ then [A is permissible if and only if $(\exists C)$ (C is available to the person & A is part of C & $R_C > W_C$ & $\sim (\exists B)$ $(\exists t)$ (B begins a sequential strong undercutting$\geq_t$ of C))][42]

(1) replaces principle (VII) of section IV. Let me close this section with a few remarks.

A. We have concluded that $R_A > W_A$ is not a sufficient condition for A's being permissible, and that $W_A > R_A$ is not a sufficient condition for A's being impermissible. So does any asymmetry remain? The asymmetry that remains is that $R_A > W_A$ can be shown to be insufficient for the permissibility of A by the finding of a suitable action B over the same time interval as A which is an alternative to A (where "suitable" means, among other things, that there is no act which begins a sequential strong undercutting$\geq_t$ of B); whereas $W_A > R_A$ is insufficient for the impermissibility of A only if A is part of a *longer* course of action meeting a certain description. Put roughly, if the moral future of an action were like its moral present, $W_A > R_A$ would be a sufficient condition for the impermissibility of A, whereas $R_A > W_A$ would not be a sufficient condition for the permissibility of A.

B. Our method of measuring the moral weight of a set of features was suggested by principle (VII) of section IV. Does the substitution of (1) above for this principle change things so that the method proposed no longer works? It does not if, in our example to elicit a person's judgments about the permissibility of A, we are careful not to produce cases where $R_A > R_B$, $W_A > W_B$, $W_B \ll W_A$, *and* the person may believe that though consideration of just A and B makes A impermissible, considering longer courses of action changes things. I shall not enter here into the details of how the example to be put to the person should be constructed so as to avoid his having this belief. Using the terminology we have defined, we do not want to present him with examples where he will believe that though B undercuts$_0$ A, B does not begin a sequential strong undercutting$\geq_t$ of A. It should not be too difficult to avoid such examples.

C. Suppose $W_A > R_A$ yet $(\exists B)$ (A is part of B & $R_B > W_B$ & B is not impermissible (by 1)). According to what we have said, the act A is not impermissible. But the act A without doing the rest of B (or some such B) *is* impermissible, and can be shown to be so by our principles. Often, for short, in situations like this where the person does not do the rest of B (but only does the part which is A), we elliptically say that his act A was impermissible.

D. Finally, let us return to the questions with which this section opened. Can we say that "is part of a course of action which is such that ——" is a feature of an action A, and if so, how is the blank to be filled in? If the argument of this section is correct, in the case where it seems that $W_A > R_A$ yet A is morally permissible, the candidate for the extra R-feature of A is

> $F =$ "is part of a larger course of action C, where $R_C > W_C$, and there is no B and t such that B begins a sequential strong undercutting$\geq_t$ of C."

But F is not morally neutral since it refers to the R and W-lists, and this reference cannot be eliminated for reasons similar to those advanced in section IV. Thus I conclude, once again here, that one cannot state everything in terms of the R and W-features of act A, and the introduction of higher-order principles[43] is necessary in order to get things straight.

VII. Overriding, Outweighing, Neutralizing, and Related Notions

We have thus far gone along with the simple model's use of *one* inequality relation between sets of features of actions. But there are significant differences among the ways in which the presence of other features (or the obtaining of certain facts not represented by features of actions) can make an action morally permissible, even though the action has some W-features. An adequate model of the structure of the sort of moral view I am considering must in some way differentiate among some of these different ways, not all of which are happily classified under the rubric of "overriding" or "outweighing." In this section we shall list some of these ways, somewhat arbitrarily labelling them, and consider some of the problems they raise. We shall not, in this section, discuss how they are to be incorporated into an adequate model of the structure of a person's moral views. Thus, we are now concerned with setting problems and raising questions. The ways that I list are "pure" ways, and we shall not, at this point, be concerned with various combinations of them.

I. An act A, with W-features, prevents, avoids, etc., something bad, harmful, etc. It has no other R-features. If the act is morally permissible, let us say that its R-features *override* its W-features; if the act is morally impermissible, let us say that its W-features *outweigh* its R-features.[44]

It was to these notions (as well as to those in II below) that our previous discussion was especially meant to apply.

Relevant distinctions to make are whether

(a)   something like principle (VII) of section IV is required

(b)   if the W-features of act A involve something bad to a person P, the performer of A is morally required to make either reparations to P, or amends to P, or to offer explanations to P, etc.[45]

I believe that in all cases where an act A, with $W_A \neq \phi$, avoids, prevents, etc. something worse (i.e., where its W-features are overridden), then something like principle (VII) is required. But even if this is correct, we cannot use principle (VII) to *explain* the notions of "overriding" and "outweighing," and this is not solely because the principle may legitimately apply to some other notions as well. The major obstacle to doing this is the following. For some of the ways we shall list in this section of a feature's making an action A morally permissible, even though $W_A \neq \phi$, some of the features which in these selected ways make A permissible do not belong on what we intuitively have in mind as the R-list. We want to first explain these various ways, and *then* to limit what can go on the R-list by excluding some features which play a role only via some of the selected ways. Since principle (VII) uses the notion of the R-list, we do not want to use it to *explain* one of the ways (*viz.*, overriding and outweighing).

Are there actions where (a) and (b) do not go together? I believe that (b) cannot be found without (a); that is, whenever your doing A with non-null wrong-making features makes it incumbent upon you to explain your action to whoever is harmed by its W-features, or to make amends or reparations to these persons, then it is also the case that it would be impermissible to do the action if a suitable alternative (as defined by principle VII) were available.

Can we have (a) without (b)? Can it be the case that you must do a suitable alternative act to A if one were available to you (and since one isn't, it's morally permissible to do A), yet even though A's W-features harm someone, you have no duty to make reparations or amends or to explain to them why you've acted as you did? A plausible candidate for such a case of no duty to make amends or reparations would be good samaritan cases. In saving someone's life, I damage your property. I could not save that person without damaging your property or doing something at least as bad (though if I could have, it would have been wrong for me to damage your property). It may well be that I am not morally required to make amends or reparations to you.[46] However, even in this case one would think that I am required to give you some explanation of what's happened. In speaking of what I am required to do, I have put things too strongly. "Omitting to make reparations, amends, or explanations to those harmed by W-features (specifically listed) of act A" is a W-feature of a course of action, and functions just like other W-features. It can be overridden, etc.: it may be too dangerous to make explanations, too inconvenient given the slight harm caused, etc.

II. Act A, with $W_A \neq \phi$, though it does not prevent, avoid, etc., some harm, achieves some good. If (subject to the same qualifications as with I) act A is morally permissible, let us say that its R-features *overcome* its W-features; if A is morally impermissible its W-features *overshadow* its R-features. Here, as in I (if not more so) one feels that (a) and (b) of I obtain, and perhaps that (b) in this case is stronger than it is in I. That is, that in this case there is a stronger obligation to make amends or reparations or offer explanations than in I,[47] and perhaps an obligation to make greater amends or reparations.

III. On some views, for some W-features (relations) T which take someone as a direct object, it is morally permissible to T someone who has T-ed you (or perhaps has only T-ed some other people), where the T of his act helped make it morally impermissible.[48] On such very contractural views, it might, for example, be permissible to steal from a thief, torture a torturer, etc., without oneself becoming someone who is open to permissible thievery, torture, etc. Without worrying now whether it is a feature of the act or a fact about the situation which does so, let us say that in such situations of T-ing someone who T's, T is *neutralized*.

Certain retributivist views would hold, not only that sometimes it is permissible to T one who T's but that it is sometimes obligatory to T him, or to do some act with some other W-feature G. Thus on this view, it is wrong not to punish someone for certain offenses; and this apart from deterrent considerations; he just deserves it; and justice demands that he get it.[49] Again, without worrying over what it is that does so (is it a feature of an act that it's done to someone who has committed a wrong, or is it a fact about the situation?) let us say that in this case the W-feature of the act is *reversed*.

Sometimes T will be neither neutralized nor reversed, but it will be the case that T-ing someone who T's is less wrong, carries less W-weight than T-ing someone innocent of (wrongful) T-ing. Let us say in this case that T is *weakened*.

IV. Suppose T is on the W-list, and takes persons as direct objects. Suppose further that each of the persons who are the objects of T consent to being T-ed. It seems that sometimes this will have the consequence that T carries no moral W-weight, and sometimes it will have the consequence that T carries W-weight, but less than it would in the nonconsent case. In the first case, let us say that T is *dissolved;* in the second case let us say that T is *consent-weakened*.

V. Suppose that I have promised you that I will do an act A. You release me from this promise, and there are no third-party beneficiaries. Let us say that in this sort of case the feature "not keeping my promise" is *cancelled*.

VI. You extend yourself to do me a good turn. I am under an obligation to return it, if I can. Suppose you then intentionally go out of your way to (wrongfully) harm me. Let us say that in this case $F =$ "omitting to reciprocate an unreciprocated good turn" is *destroyed* (from: The obligation is destroyed).

VII. I promise to meet you next week at a certain place and time, so that we can do something together. Before that time, I learn that you have died. Let us say that $F =$ "involves omitting to keep my promise to meet you" is *nullified*.

VIII. You lied to me in order to get me to promise to do A. I believed your lie, and made the promise. Let us say that "involves not keeping my promise to do A" is *invalidated*.[50]

IX. Until now we have considered different ways in which the presence of features or facts either may lead to an action A's being morally permissible (even though A has features on the W-list), or may weaken the moral weight of some W-features. It may be that an adequate account of moral structure must also consider a quite different kind of relation. Perhaps some features or facts can *undermine* the operation (in one of the above-mentioned ways) of other features or facts upon W-features. Features or facts F operating in one of the ways discussed in I through VIII upon the W-feature of action A mark off exceptions to the rule that any act with all the features in W_A is morally impermissible. But perhaps there are also exceptions to these exceptions; that is, facts or features which, if present, prevent F from operating, as it normally does, in one of the ways upon W_A.

Consider, for example, Section 3.04 of the American Law Institute Model Penal Code (Proposed Official Draft, 1962), concerning justifiable use of force in self-protection. Put roughly, the structure of this section is as follows:

(I) The use of force upon or toward another person is justifiable when P.

(II) (a) The use of force is not justifiable by I when

    (1) Q

or (2) R

          except the R limitation upon the justifiable use of force under I does not apply if

             (a) S

          or (b) T

          or (c) U

(b) The use of *deadly* force is justifiable under I only if V, and it is not justifiable (even if V) if

    (1) X

or (2) Y

          except the Y limitation on the justifiable use of deadly force under I when V, does not apply if

             (a) Z

          or (b) M

Let $w_1 =$ involves using force upon or toward another person; let $w_2 =$ involves using deadly force upon or toward another person. Though it will often not be clear exactly why one structure is chosen rather than another, let us assume that we here have a four-leveled structure, and that there is good reason not to collapse it into fewer levels. We thus would have:

(1) P stands in one of the ways to w_1

(2) Q (R) *undermines* P's standing in one of the ways to w_1

(3) S (T, U) *upsets* R's undermining of P standing in one of the ways to w_1

(4) P & V stand in one of the ways to w_2

(5) Q (R, X, Y) *undermines* P & V's standing in one of the ways to w_2

(6) Z (M) *upsets* Y's undermining of P & V's standing in one of the ways to w_2.

Upsetting will be a four-place relation (or more if one adds extra variables, e.g., one ranging over the ways). An important question is that of how many levels one is driven to; up to what n must an adequate theory use n-place relations of this sort? (I ignore the question of the possibility of reducing the number of places by formal gimmicks of various sorts.)

Up until now we have used just two-place relations (for the ways). Is there any strong reason for not continuing to do only this? Can't we incorporate all of the above information into the domain of the ways, and say, for example, that (where the "or" is the inclusive-or)

(A) P & not-Q & (not-R or S or T or U) stands in one of the ways (or a combination of them) to w_1

(B) P & not-Q & (not-R or S or T or U) & V & not-X & (not-Y or Z or M) stands in one of the ways (or a combination of them) to w_2.

This issue must be discussed in a full presentation of the theory. Here let us just note that many of the reasons that led us, in section I, away from the deductive structure to one with open-ended lists of features, outweighings and overridings, etc., will apply here as well.[51] For reasons similar to the earlier ones we may want an open-ended list (for each feature or set of features?) of what can undermine a feature or set of features' standing in one of the ways to W-features, and open-ended lists of what can upset such underminings. If so, this would prevent us from working just with things like (A) and (B) above. Obviously, if we take the course of not working only with things like (A) and (B) above, we have the pressing problem of describing the more complicated structure which is to substitute for the one which uses only the two-place relations.

Many other two-place notions in addition to those in I–VIII above might be put forth; e.g., we might say that a W-feature is *precluded* in cases where, e.g., it is impossible to keep a promise (can't implies not-ought cases). My purpose here is not to proliferate notions for its own sake, but to raise issues which require further consideration. In addition to the ones mentioned, our brief discussion in this section raises several other serious issues. I shall do little more than list them here.

A. What are the various ways in which the presence of some features of an action A may, *ceteris paribus*, prevent the action from being morally impermissible, even though $W_A \neq \phi$? How are these different ways to be distinguished and embedded within a general theory of moral structure? Which of the ways S_i (viewed as relations in which things can stand in to W-features) must have only R-features in the S_i-image of W? For example, one would not expect the relation in V and VII above to have only R-features in their image of W. What principles can one formulate which govern each of the ways? Which ways require special principles, and which principles? How will the theory handle combinations of ways, and what special problems does this raise?

B. How are "acts of omission" to be handled within the theory (consistently with our discussion of features in section III)?

C. For features (or facts or conditions) which, according to III–VIII above neutralize, reverse, cancel, dissolve, destroy, nullify, invalidate W-features, should the denial of these features (or facts or conditions) be built into the W-features themselves? I shall not attempt to list here the plethora of considerations (in addition to the ones related to those discussed under IX above) relevant to this question.

D. We have spoken above of some features (or facts) weakening the moral weight of W-features. There seem to be at least two ways in which one might try to handle this.

(1)　Each W-feature, as well as each set of W-features, always has one moral weight. What looks like weakening (or the lessening of the weight) is just the result of something's being put on "the other side of the scales." The "moral scales" come to rest where they do, not because some weight is lessened but because some extra weight is put on the other side.

But this view would have the consequence that it is the one unique full weight of the W-feature which must be used in something like principle VII of section IV, and which also determines what amends, reparations, etc. should be made. This consequence would certainly be implausible for the cases which someone holds fall under weakening in III above. For if, according to such a person, some W-feature w_1 of some act B is weakened, one should *not*, in determining whether some alternative action has less weighty W-features (under principle VII) than action B has, treat w_1 of B as having its full weight. For there might be an alternative action A such that the full weight of w_1 is greater than that of W_A while the weakened weight of w_1 had by B is less than that of W_A. Thus it seems that the method of explaining and handling weakening put forth by (1) has undesirable consequences when combined with some principle like principle VII of section IV.

(2)   The alternative possible way to handle weakening is to admit that the weights of some features are really lessened (and not just partially compensated for while remaining the same, as in (1)).

The obvious questions are: How is this possible way to be specified in detail, and how must the structure be modified to accommodate it? How does this affect the program of measurement set forth in section V? It seems that one could, by determining a person's judgments only for cases in which weakening does not operate, obtain the same measurement results as before. Can a similar measurement procedure be devised to measure the moral weights of *weakened* features in specific situations? Do we also need a notion of the stengthening of a W-feature, of its weight being increased, and if so, how is this to be incorporated within a systematic theory of moral structure?

E. In sections II–VI we have considered only other features or sets of features overriding or overcoming, etc., W-features. Must one consider things other than features of actions in order to account for a person's judgments of moral impermissibility, e.g., facts about the situation which are not happily incorporated into features of actions? If so, what apparatus is needed to handle this extension?

F. We have thus far avoided discussing the issue of whether some of the features on the list must incorporate a person's beliefs. That is, we have neglected the issues that have led into the morass of discussions of subjectively right (ought) and objectively right (ought). How are such issues to be handled within the sort of structure we are discussing? Can some of the distinctions made in I–IX of this section show a way through these issues; i.e., might belief be appropriately included for some of the ways (and underminings, upsettings) and not for others? If so, this might be relevant to some other questions mentioned earlier; e.g., to whether the denial of neutralizing, cancelling, reversing, dissolving, destroying, nullifying, invalidating features or facts should be built into the W-feature.

VIII. Further Issues

It is unnecessary for me to restate, to the reader who has come this far, that this paper is an exploratory study meant to raise further issues for investigation as well as to propose tentative solutions to certain problems. Now I wish to indicate some questions and issues, in addition to those left open in previous sections, which require further study.

(1) What is to be said of the possibility that always or sometimes there's not *one* feature of an act such that if an act has it, it is, *ceteris paribus,* morally impermissible, but rather that a conjunction of features is like this? In this case, should the W-list consist of conjunctions of features (with some different entries on the lists having common conjuncts) or is there some simpler apparatus to handle this? Similar questions, obviously, can be asked about the R-list.

(2) Given the kind of unity and coherence people's moral views have, there is some reason to want some of the entries on the lists not to be merely features (or conjunctions of features), but rather branching tree structures of features (or their conjunctions). (See Figure 10.2.) Any action which has feature F has each feature referred to by the expressions obtainable by (repeated) deletion of numerals at the end of the subscript of F. Thus any action with, e.g., feature $F_{12,6,9,4,7}$ has features $F_{12,6,9,4}$, $F_{12,6,9}$, $F_{12,6}$ and F_{12}. Intuitively, $F_{12,6}$ is a way of realizing $F_{12,}$ etc.

Figure 10.2

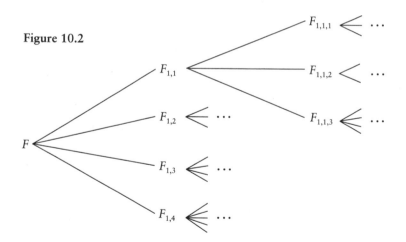

Let us call the set of all features to the right of a feature F on a tree which can be reached by following a path from node F and going to the right, the *descendant set* of F. One might put forth the following principle of inference within a moral system:

$$\frac{S_1 > S_2}{S_3 > S_4},$$

where S_3 is a non-null subset of the union of the descendant sets of the members of S_1, and S_4 is a non-null subset of the union of the descendants of the members of S_2. But reasons similar to those which led to rejection of the deductive structure in section I and to the consideration of the simple model in section II, may make such a principle of inference too strong. If so, and tree structures of features are appropriate ways of representing the unity and coherence of a person's judgments, what rules are to govern them?

(3) Given open-ended lists of features (and tree structures of features?), some of which contain variables (e.g., "leads to the death of n-persons"), is the number of entries on each list finite or infinite? Would a correct and complete moral view require finite or infinite lists? (Can there be a correct and complete moral view?) If infinite, are the lists recursive? recursively enumerable? are complete and correct moral systems finitely axiomatizable? Something must be said about what kinds of reduced lists are permissible. What criterion can be formulated which would allow "leads to the death of n-persons" on the W-list (and wouldn't require that, for each number m, its instantiation for m appear on the W-list) yet would not have just one utilitarian feature on the list even if the person was a Sidgwick-type utilitarian and utilitarianism were true?

(4) What is one to make of talk of open-ended lists of features? For at any given time, presumably only finite specific lists are needed to account for the judgments the person has actually made previous to that time. The openness of lists was meant to mark off a problem. It seems that given any finite list that we or he could construct, there is a certain situation which if described to the person, would lead him to say that some feature not on either presented list was a morally relevant feature of the situation: "Oh yes, I overlooked that one." Though this feature wasn't necessary to account for any of his previous judgments, in some way the description of his view must "include" the feature, must take account of the fact that he *would* accept the feature as morally relevant, and he would take it into account in arriving at a judgment about a situation which exhibited it. It is not clear what well-understood formal device best achieves the legitimate purposes of the vague talk about open-ended lists. (For some persons, nothing like open-ended lists will be appropriate, and indeed some sort of closure condition will be required; e.g., "nothing belongs on the W-list except $F_1, \ldots, F_n$.")

(5) How is the structure to handle second-order (and higher?) features; e.g., the W-features: persuading someone to do something impermissible, forcing someone to do something impermissible, offering someone something to do an impermissible act, glorifying, praising,

rewarding impermissible acts, punishing, ridiculing required acts, leading someone to abandon correct moral principles? Sometimes the particular first-order features needn't be specified, or specified precisely, to account for the person's judgments; sometimes they can't be (as when one person persuades another to do some unspecified impermissible act), and sometimes it will be important to know what exactly the first-order feature is. How should all this be represented within a structure?

(6) What sorts of structural conditions using the notion of necessity are appropriate? Would it be appropriate to require that if necessarily– $(F_X \equiv G_X)$ then F and G override, are overridden by, exactly the same sets of features, etc.?

(7) Most persons apply different moral standards to different kinds of beings, e.g., children and adults. Some persons may do so for different groups of adults, the distinctions depending upon, e.g., social class, religion, race. Should this be represented (ignoring the additional ways discussed in section VII) by *one* pair of lists (one member of the pair being a W-list, and the other an R-list) where the lists contain "conditional-features," or by *separate* pairs of lists for each group for which there are distinct moral standards?

(8) One should define various notions of a complete moral system (one yielding for every possible case of a certain sort a judgment that the act is morally permissible or morally impermissible). Different notions will be defined for different kinds of information fed into it. For example, one notion would be that, for given lists of R and W-features, for any two arbitrary subsets of R and W, the system yields an inequality between them. (See condition 2 of section III.) Further notions would be defined for risk and uncertainty situations. Are moral dilemmas or drawing-the-line problems reasons to believe that there does not "exist" (everyone grants that we don't know one) a complete and correct moral system?

(9) One wants some way of describing ways in which the members of a list can cohere. Various writings on the coherence theory of truth would be suggestive here. One might define a W-feature's being a *taboo* as its not cohering in certain specified ways with some other members of the W-list.

(10) The structure described is concerned with the relatively gross (though difficult enough!) distinction between moral permissibility and moral impermissibility. Various extensions immediately suggest themselves, e.g., to *degrees* of moral impermissibility; and to other finer

distinctions.[52] How must the structure be supplemented to account for these more refined judgments?

(11) We want some way to represent a person's belief that nothing, or something, or nothing or something of a certain sort overrides, outweighs, etc., some set of features, and to incorporate such beliefs within the general structure, and have them be one of the things the structure accounts for. Various obvious ways suggest themselves. (If *nothing* overrides a set of features, this set must get special treatment in the measuring process of section V.)

(12) We have thus far considered problems stemming from a person's lack of confidence in the correctness of stated exceptionless moral principles due to the wide variety of cases which are possible or may arise. He can't anticipate all possible cases, etc. But a person may also have varying degrees of confidence about a specific feature's being on one of the lists or about a specific outweighing (which he may strongly, tentatively, or with some hesitation accept). We want some systematic way to make sense of different degrees of confidence, to measure them, and we want to formulate principles specifying the role they play in generating a person's moral judgments.[53]

(13) What, if any, are the interesting ways in which two particular moral views having the same general structure can differ if they generate exactly the same moral judgments about all possible particular acts?

(14) May *indexical* expressions or proper names be built into features on the lists; e.g., "harms *my* wife," "involves eating on Yom Kippur"? What constraints are there on how they may appear, and on what else must appear if they appear?

(15) How are double-effect type issues to be handled within the structure? Must intentions be introduced within the features?

(16) One is tempted to use the structure as a weapon in discussion. (R. M. Hare's use of a similar weapon in his book *Freedom and Reason* is too strong.) One is tempted to say that if a person judges that act *A* is morally impermissible and act *B* is morally permissible, then it's incumbent on him to produce a feature on one of the lists had by one of the actions and not another. The argument for this would be that *you* cannot go completely through the two open-ended lists showing him that *A* and *B* have exactly the same list features, but *he* can produce the feature which distinguished *A* and *B*. But if he produces a feature which is had by *A* and not by *B*, and you deny that this feature is on either list, is it incumbent upon him to produce an argument for this feature's

being on one of the lists? Or is it incumbent upon you to produce an argument for the feature's not being on either list? Difficult questions arise about where, if anywhere, burdens of argument or proof lie. And how are we to explain: "it is incumbent upon him to"? Is it just that he be able to (in how long a time?), or that not doing it when requested is a W-feature (which can be overridden; e.g., he has more important things to do)? And what follows from a person's being unable to discharge his burden; that one of his judgments is mistaken (surely this doesn't follow), that one of them is unsupported, that he should shut up, that he's not serious?

(17) Condition VII of section IV, though growing out of the earlier discussion, was formulated without any requirement of the relevance of the alternative act B to the R-features of A. Thus, someone might object that condition VII owes its plausibility to the assumption that B is a substitute for A, and achieves the same or similar goals, and if this is not so, then VII is too strong. It is certainly worth investigating the systematic consequences of adding to condition VII various precisely formulated requirements concerning the relevance or similarity of R_B to R_A.

(18) Some people's views may exhibit different metarules. To take two simple examples:

(A)   *Permissive Rule:* If the system of inequalities and principles does not yield the result that an action whose only morally relevant features are all and only those in set S is morally impermissible, then any action with just those morally relevant features is permissible.

(B)   *Strict Rule:* If the system of inequalities and principles does not yield the result that an action whose only morally relevant features are all and only those in set S is morally permissible, then any action with just those morally relevant features is impermissible.

(Of course it may be that a person's views exhibit no such rule.) One might attempt to represent a person's views which might be interpreted as exhibiting one of these metarules as containing some rule of inference yielding inequalities which complete his incomplete set of inequalities. What reasons might be advanced for preferring the metarule representation, which does not involve adding first-level inequalities, to the rule of inference representation, which does?

(19) Can one incorporate some legitimate device which functions to produce self-reference and arrive at an action A which can be interpreted as the act of judging that A is morally impermissible? If so, one will get the result that either there is some morally impermissible act which it is morally impermissible to judge (not just *say*) is morally impermissible, or there is some morally permissible act which it is morally permissible to judge is morally impermissible.

(20) Much work needs to be done on the subject of the "logic" of presumptions, accounts of what it means to say that presumptions can be overridden only by *special* reasons, etc. The relevance to the sort of structure we have been describing is obvious.

(21) Until now, I have spoken freely of the model's accounting for a person's judgments about the moral permissibility or impermissibility of particular actions. For various reasons the model cannot do this, and requires supplementation.

Consider the following inference.[54]

(1) Act A has features $F_1, \ldots, F_n$.
(2) Each of these features is on one of the lists.
(3) The subset of the F_i on the W-list $>$ the subset of the F_i on the R-list.
(4) A has no other features, in addition to $F_1, \ldots, F_n$, on either list.

Therefore,

(5) A is morally impermissible.

Suppose that a person knows that (1), and suppose further that (2) and (3) are true of the particular structure correctly ascribed to him. Suppose that this inference pattern is built into the structure of his views, in that if he also knows (4) then he makes, or would make, the particular judgment (5). (Of course this particular inference pattern won't be built into the structure of his views since it ignores the complications about larger courses of action and alternative actions.) But the person may not know that (4). It may be that

(a) The person believes, but does not know, that (4).
(b) The person knows that A has some other features on the lists though he does not know which features.
(c) The person believes, though he does not know, that A has some other features on the lists, and he does not believe, for some other particular features on the lists, that A has these.

(d)   The person does not believe that A has some other features on
        the lists, nor does he believe that A has no other features on the
        lists.

It seems to me likely that a person in situation (a) will judge that A
is morally impermissible (though if he has little confidence in his belief,
perhaps he will not). Situations (b) and (c), of course, encompass many
interesting cases. Looking just at (c):

> The person believes that A has some other features on the lists,
> though he does not believe, of some specific other features on the
> lists, that A has these.

We might have, in addition, that the person believes any one of the
following:

> Each of the other features is on W.
> Each of the other features is on R.
> Some are on W and some are on R.
> Some are on W (and he has no beliefs about whether others are on
> R).
> Some are on R (and he has no beliefs about whether others are on
> W).

Or we might have that the person knows that *if* A does have some other
features on the lists then these features are such that —— (with various
possible fillings in of the blank). And for each of the cases, he may
have beliefs about some of these (unspecified) properties outweighing
or overriding others, about how the inequality goes when some are
conjoined with the ones he specifically knows of, etc.

It seems clear that for situations (b)–(d), some further apparatus must
be conjoined with the structure we have been discussing, in order to
yield a person's particular judgments about particular actions. The details of this apparatus may vary from person to person; people may
differ in how they make judgments in situations (b)–(d). A similar argument can be offered for simplified inferences yielding the judgment
that an action is morally permissible. When the complications about alternative actions and larger courses of action are taken into account, it
becomes even more clear that, in order to account for a person's particular moral judgments, the structure we have been discussing must
be conjoined with a further apparatus about how the person arrives at
beliefs in, and what he assumes with what confidence as a basis of inference in, situations of incomplete knowledge.

Secondly, we must further delimit the particular judgments to be accounted for by the structure we have been discussing. One would not expect the structure to play a major role in accounting for a person's belief that a particular action A is morally impermissible, which belief the person holds because someone he trusts told him that A is morally impermissible.[55]

Thirdly, one needs a distinction similar to that which linguists make between linguistic competence and linguistic performance.[56] The actual judgments which a person makes will depend upon various limitations common to all persons, and upon some special to him (or at any rate, not common to all); e.g., limitations of attention span, of memory, limitations on the complexity of information which can be manipulated and processed, limitations on the amount of time he is willing to spend thinking about moral problems. The actual judgments he makes will also depend upon various exogenous factors; e.g., whether he has a headache, whether there's noise which prevents him from thinking as clearly as he otherwise would, whether he's interrupted while thinking and loses some thought which he doesn't later remember. We may think of the structure we have been discussing either as a model of an idealized moral judge in idealized circumstances (i.e., ignoring the various limitations and exogenous factors), or as *one component* of an adequate psychological model of the person.

(22) One needs a discussion of what it means to ascribe such a structure to a person, of what it means to say he "internalizes" such a structure. It doesn't mean that he always arrives at his moral judgments by explicitly and consciously referring to such a structure. I do, however, want the assumption to be based upon something more than the claim that the hypothesis that there is such a structure somehow realized inside him most simply and elegantly accounts for the moral judgments he makes. It would be upsetting, in this case, if the structure could not account (when combined with further theory) for his conscious reasoning in arriving at moral judgments, and the sort of considerations he adduces (and the way in which this is done) in support of his moral judgments. Put vaguely, the structure shouldn't be foreign to the way he actually reasons about moral matters, and he shouldn't find it, when presented to him, foreign.

(23) The obvious ways in which the sort of structure we have been discussing might be found defective is that it can't account for some of the person's judgments about moral impermissibility (and this is true,

for every person), or it "accounts" for more than he would make, or a simpler alternative structure accounts for his judgments about moral impermissibility in a neater and more elegant way.

It is worth mentioning two other ways in which the sort of structure we discuss might be found to be inappropriate (and these ways qualify what is said in the previous sentence). The structure is designed to play a role in accounting for only some of a person's moral judgments; *viz.*, those about the permissibility and impermissibility of actions. It does not treat of judgments about goodness, virtues, ideals, responsibility, etc. It might turn out that the simplest total structure which accounts for *all* of a person's moral judgments which has the structure we have been discussing as a part, is less simple, elegant, or adequate than an alternative structure which accounts for all of a person's moral judgments and which does not contain our structure as a part. Secondly, as I said at the very beginning of this essay, I do not claim that *everyone's* views about the moral impermissibility of actions exhibit the sort of structure we have been discussing. Some other kind of structure might account for a wider range of views about the moral impermissibility of actions while including the ones we have had in mind (e.g., it might also account for the views of persons in other cultures, or the views of all or of more persons in our culture), and this might lead one to reject the sort of structure which has been our subject.[57]

11

ON THE RANDIAN
ARGUMENT

What are the moral foundations of capitalism? Many supporters of capitalism, especially among the very young, think that these foundations have already been provided; indeed that we already possess in the writings of Ayn Rand a demonstration, a proof, a cogent argument, an establishment of a moral view from which capitalism can easily be justified.

I have two reasons for wanting closely to examine the argument:

(1)   Some persons are not devoting thought to fundamental issues about morality, thinking that the essence of the job has already been done.

(2)   The argument itself is an attempt to provide a non-utilitarian-non-social-contract natural rights ethics.

Since I share the view that such a moral foundation is appropriate and possible and that laissez-faire capitalism is morally justifiable on such a basis, I wish to look closely at an actual attempt.

I would most like to set out the argument as a deductive argument and then examine the premisses. Unfortunately, it is not clear (to me) exactly what the argument is.[1] So we shall have to do some speculating about how steps might be filled in, and look at these ways. It may be, of course, that I have overlooked some *other* ways, which would make the argument work. If so, I presume someone else, who claims to possess and understand the demonstration, will supply the missing material.

As I see it, there are four parts to the argument. (I use the roman numerals ambiguously to refer both to stages of the argument, and to the conclusions of the stages.)

(I)   To the conclusion that only living beings have values with a point.

(II)   From I, to the conclusion that life itself is a value to a living being which has it.

(III)   From II, to the conclusion that life, *as a rational person,* is a value to the person whose life it is.

(IV)   From III, to some principle about interpersonal behavior and rights and purposes.

I shall examine each of these in turn.

I

(1)   Only a living being is capable of choosing among alternative actions, or,

(2)   Only for a living being could there be any *point* to choosing among alternative actions, for

(3)   Only a living being can be injured, damaged, have its welfare diminished, etc., and

(4)   Any rational preference pattern will be connected with the things mentioned in (3), and since

(5)   Values establish a (rational) preference ordering among alternative action,

it follows that

(6)   Only a living being can have values, with some point to them. Values have a purpose *only* for living things.

To make this point fully clear, try to imagine an immortal, indestructible robot, an entity which moves and acts, but which cannot be affected by anything, which cannot be changed in any respect, which cannot be damaged, injured or destroyed. Such an entity would not be able to have any values; it would have nothing to gain or lose; it could not regard anything as *for* or *against* it, as serving or threatening its welfare, as fulfilling or frustrating its interests. It could have no interests and no goals. ("The Objectivist Ethics," p. 16.)

I do not wish here to enter into complicated issues about what particular cognitive and choice functions (if any) machines could be capable of performing. Does coming to know that some situation has been realized count as a machine's being "changed," in the requisite respect? Note the assumption that each of our values concerns how things affect *us,* a stronger assumption than that our values concern how some affectable being or other is affected. (Some views would claim to hold values unconnected with how *any* being is affected, e.g., religious views which hold that it's better if God is praised and worshipped, not because God is affected by this, but because it's a fitting or suitable response to him. Or views which maintain that it's better that talented and able people be respected and admired, even if they never learn of it and even if their knowing of it doesn't (seriously) affect them; and better not because of the effects on us of doing so, but because this is a fitting and appropriate response to other people's achievements.) Presumably then I can't value, or, in a valuing fashion, act to achieve some state of affairs, in a far-off place, knowing that I shall never know whether my act has actually succeeded or not, and knowing that in either case its consequences will not affect me. If there were an island somewhere where we couldn't go but could send things, and from which we would not be affected in any way, then, it seems, we could not value their being moral people and having just social arrangements, sending them copies of some book whose reading we think is morally instructive. Perhaps it is being claimed, not that each value in each instance must be connected with oneself being affected, but that, for a being to have values, *some* of them must be so connected. So that a being which *changed* so that it became immortal, indestructible, unable to be affected, and so on could not evaluate its alternatives and act so as to make probable the realization of some value it had previously held (e.g., the lessening of injustice in the world) knowing that (because of isolation) it would not know whether its act had succeeded. Or perhaps the claim is that though a being can continue to hold values in this state, if it was *always* in this state, and always had been, and always realized that it was, it couldn't hold values. It couldn't read, for example, *Atlas Shrugged* and become convinced by the arguments (we are not placing in doubt the machine's having certain cognitive capacity: so which part of the argument depends, for its persuasiveness, upon the *reader's* being vulnerable and having an affectable welfare?) and come to value and act so as to realize a world in which the ideals of that book are instantiated. But why couldn't it? *Must* it say, "What's all that *to me?*"

Issues about the centeredness of one's goals would repay further study (I take up some connected issues with some of the examples in section V), but I propose to proceed to see whether particular goals and values can be gotten out of (6) and a self-centered view of goals.[2]

II

From the considerations of the preceding section a conclusion is to be reached to the effect that the prolonging and maintaining of life is itself a value. Note, first, that it is unlikely that such a conclusion can be reached without the introduction of significant additional material. For suppose that *death* was a great value. (Suppose.) Only living beings could achieve it, strive for it, choose to reach it, striving for it would establish a preference ordering among alternative actions, and guide the choices of a living being. It seems that death's being a value is compatible with all that has been said in section I, and hence that the considerations of section I do not rule this out. One cannot reach the conclusion that life itself is a value merely by conjoining together many sentences containing the word "value" and "life" or "alive" and hoping that, by some process of association and mixture, this new connection will arise. There may be many other connections between *life* and *value*; the question is: what is the argument for the particular connection embodied in "Life itself is a value"?

Consider the following argument:

(1)   Having values is itself a value
(2)   A necessary condition for a value is a value
(3)   Life is a necessary condition for having values.

Therefore,

(4)   Life itself is a value.

But is (2) true? Are all necessary conditions for values, values themselves? If getting cured of cancer is a value, is getting cancer (which is a necessary condition for getting cured of it), or having (say) a particular virus act on one, a value? And why is having values itself a value? We might have the following argument for (1): Achieving values is valuable. We are not pre-programmed to achieve values. Therefore, if we are to achieve values more often than accidentally, we will have to choose actions which will do so, with doing so as their goal. But intentionally choosing actions to achieve things is *itself* having and acting on the basis of values, and therefore having and acting on the basis of values is itself valuable.

Note that this argument, in reaching its conclusion, itself seems to use (2) as a principle of inference. The argument also begs the question against death's being a value, for if it is, we are preprogrammed to achieve it. Perhaps, instead of (2) we would have (2′). If something is a necessary condition for (achieving) *all* other values (any other value) then it itself is a value.

Ignoring the issue of whether the question of death's being a value isn't thereby begged, is (2′) true? (And let us pass over, for now, whether (2′) is meant to rule out there being a situation in which dying is necessary in order to achieve one's legitimate values.) Because "not having yet achieved all values" is a necessary condition for achieving any given value, for achieving each value, is *it itself* a value? [We could also ask this question in extension, using a list of all values, if we had such a list.] Similarly, if on Miss Rand's account being vulnerable, destructible, mortal, is a necessary condition for achieving (and having) values, does it follow that this condition itself is a value?

We do best, in view of these difficulties, to consider another line of argument, which we might introduce by considering an objection to our earlier contemplation of the possibility of death's being a value. "How can death be a value? Value is judged against a standard of injury, harm, etc., and the greatest of these is death." (But on what basis, which we have been given, do we *know* that the greatest harm isn't the extension of life's experiences?) In an essay by someone who had been closely associated with Miss Rand, which may shed light on her intentions, we find "'should' is a concept that can have no intelligible meaning, if divorced from the concept *and value* of life."[3] Here we have an example of some form of transcendental argument, so beloved by philosophers and so tricky to handle and get clear about. Before proceeding, we should have before us another aid, John Hosper's sympathetic presentation in his *Introduction to Philosophical Analysis* (second edition):

Suppose someone said, "Prove to me that life is valuable." Rand would hold that his request contains an inconsistency. It is, she holds, the existence and nature of life that sets the conditions for what is valuable; it is the distinctive nature of life that gives rise to the need for values. In saying this, one is saying much more than simply that man must be alive in order to pursue values: one is saying that man must pursue values in order to remain alive—and that this is the base of ethics and of all questions of moral value. Just as (Rand would say) it is only the concept of life that gives rise to such concepts as health and disease—just as it would be meaningless to talk of health and disease except with reference to the standard and goal of life, and talk about health is meaningful only in that context—so it is meaningless to speak of values, of good and evil, except with reference to *the needs of a living organism*. The concept of value, Rand maintains, is genetically and epistemologically dependent on the concept of life, just as the concept of health and disease are genetically and epistemologically dependent upon the concept of life. Thus to say "Prove that it is morally obligatory to value life" is similar to saying "Prove that it is medically obligatory (that is, necessary for health) to value life."

Here we have the claim that apart from a background where life is assumed as a value, no content can be given to "should"-statements and if life *is* assumed as a value, then content is given to "should," namely (roughly) one should do those things which maintain and enhance one's life. This account is of the form: you should do an act if it leads to the greatest realization of X (where X is the greatest value). Even if one were to accept this form of account,[4] why must we substitute something about life for X? Cannot content be given to should-statements, by substituting "death" for X, or "the greatest happiness of the greatest number," or any one of a vast number of other dimensions or possible goals? And wouldn't such content enable "should"-statements to guide choices, apply only to living beings, etc.? Given this, it is puzzling why it is claimed that *only* against a background in which life is (assumed to be) a value, can "should"-statements be given a sense. It might of course, be argued that only against this background can "should"-statements be given their *correct* sense, but we have seen no argument for this claim. Others who find a goal-directed type of account of "should" illuminating, but who do not know what in particular to substitute for X, may have "should" with the content "leads to the greatest value," leaving it as an open question what is the greatest value. These people, in asking "Should I do A?" would be asking "Does A lead to the greatest value (whatever that is)?" For these people, and those who substitute for X something other than *life,* an argument is needed to demonstrate that life *is* the greatest (or a) value. I do not see that such an argument has yet been offered.

III

Ignoring the difficulties discussed in section II, suppose that we have gotten, *somehow*, to the conclusion that for each individual, his life and the prolongation of it is a value for him. How do we get from here to:

(III) For each man, the preservation and prolongation of his life, *qua man*, as a person, is a value for him.

Possibilities

(1) What man is, qua man, is completely determined by what's special to man (which is rationality). And what's special to beings should be preserved and should flourish. Why? Ignoring the dodo argument (*viz.*, it's a tragedy if any bit of diversity becomes extinct), we focus on the idea that what is special to a thing marks its function and from this we can get its peculiarly appropriate form of behavior. But no conclusion could depend, in this way, on some property P being special to man. For suppose it turned out that dolphins or some other being somewhere *also* had property P; would this stop the conclusion? It might be said that here we would discover a new kind of thing (*viz.* man *or* dolphin) and P would be special to *it*. But there might be nothing special to man, for all his nice properties might be had by other things which have further super-duper properties Q also, which man doesn't have. (Call these things, merely for a label, angels.) It might now be said that man (or dolphin) does have something special, namely P and not-Q. But how could one think that anything depended on its being *special*; that something of moral interest did not follow from

> Man has P

in conjunction with other premisses, but did follow from these premisses conjoined with

> Man has P, and nothing else has P?

Could discoveries on other planets show us that our fundamental moral conclusions don't follow? Surely, it's in virtue of man's *having* P that conclusions follow, and not because other beings don't have P. All this is not to deny that it is heuristically useful to focus on what is special to man. For if we don't apply moral standards and principles to the other beings we actually have encountered, and we do to man, then we can ask what properties man has in virtue of which moral principles apply to him, in virtue of which he is a moral agent and a subject of moral judgments. Something fundamental to ethics does lie in those properties which do distinguish man from other things we have actually encountered, but nothing morally fundamental depends on the fact that these properties are distinguishing ones.

(2) What man is, *qua man,* is determined by his essence, which is rationality. He should act so as to continue his essence.

(a) If the essence mentioned in this argument is real essence, it's a dubious theory. Also, it (e.g., a man) would no longer exist if its essence changed (but another thing would), so that if its continued existence is a value, so is the continued existence of its essence. However, in the case of this argument, its essence doesn't *change,* it's just not exercised. The being continues to exist. And the conclusion of II is too frail a reed to hang such an argument on. For if *it* stops existing, another kind of value pursuer, *intimately* connected with it, will exist. And why should it care which does?

(b) If, in this argument, essence is those properties, relative to current knowledge, which underlie, systematize, account for etc. the rest of our general knowledge of such entities (those properties mentioned in our most fundamental, at the time, reducing unreduced theory about the entities, or if two different such theories, both sets of properties), then the injunction to preserve and exercise such properties requires reasons. Why shouldn't one change? Surely, it is not merely a conservative injunction. Two answers suggest themselves. One, it's change to a lower form of life, and so shouldn't be done. But one needs a theory to back this up, which isn't given, and secondly it implies that it *would* be all right, if possible, to change to a *higher* essence. Even though if one could and did change to an angel-like being, one wouldn't be preserving one's life *qua man.* The second, and more interesting answer, is that one won't survive (*period*), as alive, if one doesn't live *as a person.* This deserves consideration as a separate argument for III.

(3) If a person does not prolong his life as a rational being, he will not survive for long afterwards as any kind of living being. For, the argument runs, we have no automatic way of knowing what will prolong our lives. We have to figure this out, using our conceptual apparatus. And then we have to devise ways to do this. Otherwise, we will *not* survive at all, unless by accident, or unless some other rational being cares for us. And, if the goal is to prolong one's life (in years) and minimize, constantly, the probability of its ending, then, *much* knowledge, invention, etc. will be useful.

There remains the possibility of being a "ward," making one decision to let another care for you, give you orders, etc. To this it might be objected that this might not work out (and you wouldn't know when to desert the wardship before it begins to sink), and that such a life is parasitic and depends upon another person's *not* living as you do.

There are two forms to the parasite argument, a consequential one and a formal one. The consequential argument is that being a parasite won't work in the long run. Parasites will eventually run out of hosts, out of those to live off, imitate, steal from. (The novel, *Atlas Shrugged*, argues this view.) But in the short run, one can be a parasite and survive; even over a whole lifetime and many generations. And new hosts come along. So, if one *is* in a position to survive as a parasite, what reasons have been offered against it?

The formal argument is difficult to make precise, and difficult to fit into a Randian view. It holds that moral rules are applicable to everyone, so that if following certain rules and values can work only if *others* follow different ones, and can work only *because* others follow different ones, then the rules and values in question cannot be the correct ones. ("What if everybody did that?")

But it is difficult to find the appropriate level to speak at, using this argument. My being a teacher succeeds only because other people do other things, e.g., grow food, make clothing. Similarly for the activities of each of these others. The question "What if everyone did that?" shouldn't apply here, but how is the case to be marked off?

Intuitively, there is some description of what I'm doing (accepting a job to fill need, etc.) which is okay; that is, it is permissible for everyone to do *that*.

So, there being some description D_1 which fits what I do, where it would be disastrous if everyone did D_1, doesn't show *I* shouldn't do it. For there may be another description D_2 which also fits what I do, and it would be all right if everyone did things of sort D_2.

But we should not convert this fact into a condition which says that if there is *some* description which fits my activity which is such that it's okay if everyone instantiates that description, then my activity is permissible. For this is too weak a sufficient condition for moral permissibility. Presumably some general descriptions of this sort would also fit the thief's activity, e.g., "doing things which lead to their being fed."

Here it might be suggested that the appropriate description is that which presents the essence of an action. But even if such a notion could be clarified, as in (2b) above, its application here would beg the question, for especially important among the relevant general facts to be accounted for by the essence will be moral facts. Hence we must first agree about these moral facts before agreeing about the essence of an act, so that considerations about the essence of acts cannot come first as a basis on which to ground their moral nature.

My purpose here is not to pursue the details of how such generalization arguments might best be stated (there is a growing literature on the subject), but to note that if such arguments can be made to work, they will involve *extra* principles (and not merely the claim that a particular case of parasitism is doomed to fail). Some philosophers view providing the foundation for such principles, and stating them precisely, as one of the central tasks of moral philosophy, but it is one that has not even been attempted by Miss Rand.

One final way to get a *formal* principle should be mentioned. It might be said that a rational person follows *principles*, general policies, and so we must consider those principles of action which make man's survival possible. But it has not been shown why each person must follow the *same* principles, and why I may not, as a rational being, have a clause in mine which recommends parasitism under certain conditions.

IV

Supposing that it is granted that living as a rational being is, for each person, a value, how do we get to some *social* conclusion about people's rights?

> The basic *social* principle of the objectivist ethics is that just as life is an end in itself, so each living human being is an end in himself, not the means to the ends or the welfare of others—and, therefore, that man must live for his own sake, neither sacrificing himself to others nor sacrificing others to himself. To live for his own sake means that *the achievement of his own happiness* is man's highest moral purpose.[5]

Starting with:

(1)   For each person, the living and prolongation of his own life is a value *for him*

to get to

(2)   No person should sacrifice his life for another

we would need, in addition to (1)

(1′)   For each person, the living and prolongation of his own life (as a rational being) is the *greatest value* for him.

[And: Each person *ought* to pursue his greatest value.] No argument has been offered, yet, for (1′). Miss Rand has some things to say about life being an *ultimate* value, which might lead her to accept (1′), but these things, in view of our earlier discussion in section II of life as a value, aren't sufficiently clear and forceful to establish (1′).[6]

But suppose we have (1′) and have gotten to (2). How do we go on to argue for the important *social* conclusion:

(3)   No person should sacrifice another person ('s life) to himself (his own).

Why shouldn't he? There is the parasite argument already considered: sacrificing another's life to your own is not in your own long-run interests. But this is no argument to convince (or apply to) someone living at a time before the victims have run out, e.g., the present. A more promising approach focuses on the notion of rights.

Consider the following argument.

(4)   Each person has a right to his own life, i.e., to be free to take the actions required by the nature of a rational being for the support, the furtherance, the fulfillment, and the enjoyment of his life.

(5)   Since each person has this right, to force a person to sacrifice his interests to your own violates this right.

(6)   One should not violate another's rights.

Therefore

(7)   One should not force another to sacrifice his interests for your own or that of yet another person.

But why does each person have a right to his life, to be free to perform those actions? If we grant, for the purposes of this argument, (1′) above, and we add

(8)   Each person has a right to be free to pursue his greatest and highest value,

then we get (4) above. But (8) is surely too strong: did Hitler have a right to pursue his highest value? (But, it will be said, his highest value wasn't a rational value. So let us focus instead on "should.") Perhaps instead the argument for (4) is as follows:

(9a)   For each person, he *should* pursue the maintenance of his life as a rational being.

(9b)   The "should" in (a) is and should be of more weight, for him, than all other "shoulds."

(10a) Each person has a right to do what he should do.

(10b) Each person has a right, which is non-overrideable, to do what he should (where this "should" has the most weight) do.

(9) is meant to follow from other considerations which we have examined in section II, and found inconclusive. What of (10)?

The force of "right" here is that others shouldn't intervene, using force, to prevent one from exercising it. The question is: why, given that you should do something, shouldn't I intervene to stop you?[7]

Perhaps one has a vision of a morally harmonious universe in which there are no irreconcilable conflicts of duty, of shoulds, and in which if you should do something, I shouldn't forcibly prevent you from doing it. But no conclusive arguments have been offered for such a vision. If one believes that ethics involves (something like) one dimension or weighted set of dimensions which is to be used to judge us and the world, so that all of our moral activity (the moral activity of each of us) is directed toward improving (maximizing) the world's score on this dimension, then it will be natural to fall into such a vision. But if we legitimately have separate goals, and there are independent sources of moral commitment, then there is the possibility of an objective conflict of shoulds. So that perhaps, with some slight modification of Sophocles' characters, Antigone should bury her brother and Creon should forbid and prevent this burial.[8]

But Miss Rand needs something even stronger, for her argument, than objective harmony of "shoulds"; she needs an objective harmony of interests.[9]

What I shall call *the optimistic tradition* holds that there are no objective conflicts of interest among persons. Plato, in the *Republic*, being the most notable early exponent of this view, we might appropriately call it the *Platonic tradition* in ethics.[10] Miss Rand falls in this optimistic or Platonic tradition in ethics, believing that there are no objective conflicts of interest among persons, and that there is no situation in which it is in one person's interests to force another to do something which it is not in his interests to do; no situation where one person's forcibly stopping another from advancing his interests, advances his own interests. No knock-down argument has been offered for this thesis,[11] and Miss

Rand has not produced (or tried to produce) any reason why, if such conflicts *are* possible, I, in following my interests, should limit myself so as not to interfere forcibly in your pursuit of your life as a rational being.

Miss Rand's position is a constrained egoism; egoism subject to the constraint of not violating certain conditions (which are other persons' rights).[12] One way to argue for constrained egoism is to argue that it is identical with egoism, to argue that the constraints add nothing because they are in your rightly understood interests (the optimistic tradition). If such arguments equating the egoism and the moral constraints fail, then a holder of this position will have to choose.

V

We have until now considered only *one* part of the social nonsacrifice principle (don't sacrifice another to yourself) and found the arguments for it inconclusive. We turn now to the other part of the principle: don't sacrifice yourself to another: live for your own sake. "To live for his own sake means that *the achievement of his own happiness* is man's highest moral purpose."

Is it? We have action, endorsed by Miss Rand, in the novel *Atlas Shrugged*, which appears incompatible with this. In the novel, John Galt risks his life to save that of Dagny Taggart, whom he loves, and he says that he will kill himself if she is tortured to make him talk. How can he do this? He says to Dagny Taggart: "It won't be an act of self-sacrifice. I do not care to live on their terms. I do not care to obey them and I do not care to see you enduring a drawn-out murder. There will be no values for me to seek after that—and I do not care to exist without values." But this is quite incredible. For it seems from this that, were Dagny Taggart tragically to suffer and die of some disease, then Galt would commit suicide. It would be a terrible loss, but does Galt "the perfect man," have so little moral fiber and resources that life would be intolerable for him *ever* afterwards (and would the agony of the time immediately after her death outweigh the life which could be led after time has done its work)? Would he come from Galt's Gulch to attempt to save her life, if he had the option of staying there, obeying no one else, and not being present to observe her murder?

Would Galt save Dagny Taggart's life, knowing that this will be at the cost of his own? Is *this* inconsistent with his principles? Would doing this mean he wasn't an egoist? A fruitless path to follow[13] is to say that it is the short period of happiness while he is sacrificing his life that justifies the whole thing. So that, in thinking about a situation in which both are unconscious and only one can be saved by a third party, he would prefer it were himself because in *that* situation he wouldn't get to feel the happiness of saving her life? Or are we to imagine that in *this* thinking about this situation he does prefer that her life be saved, and this because of the happiness he *now* gets in thinking about it?

But (a) we can imagine he's answering, quickly, a large number of questions on some psychological test, so that there's no time to pause for a glow of happiness. Is it now for the happiness he knows he'll feel *after* the test is over (mightn't he forget and not recall the question?) that he answers as he does?

(b) Why doesn't he feel sad in contemplating his dying and her surviving? To be sure, he may think it's better than their both dying, or her dying and his surviving, but why should the existence of some *worse* alternatives than alternative A make one happy in contemplating A? In fact, it doesn't, and we don't have this easy path to happiness.

(c) Most importantly, this answer gets things backwards. For one would be made happy by placing one's family in the only places in the raft[14] only because one values their survival above one's own, their happiness above one's own.

It is not that one (chooses to) have these values, because knowing one has fulfilled them will make one happy. And it is not that I do it because not doing it will make me afterwards feel guilty. For this would be so only if there were some *other* moral reason to save their lives over one's own; it cannot be that the primary reason is to avoid later guilt. And also, we could imagine cases where the knowledge is expunged via a chemical producing selective forgetting.

Such science fiction possibilities cause difficulties. If one were concerned only with one's child's happiness, and one had the capability, one would implant a device to get the child to act on principles P (the correct moral principles) except in situations S (where he knows that deviating from them will be in his interests, e.g., by murdering someone and taking his fortune) where he will deviate from them, afterwards forgetting that he's done so. Such a person would be happier than one only following principles P, and his life will be identical to one with only principles P, except at a few selected times. Furthermore, he will think he always, with great integrity follows principles P, and he will have great self-esteem. And if someone were concerned only with his own happiness, he would wish that he himself had been so preprogrammed.

If one doesn't wish this for oneself, then one isn't concerned only with one's own happiness. Saying that one is so solely concerned but such a preprogrammed person can't be happy because he fakes reality begs the question (ignoring the fact that he doesn't fake it; it's faked for him); it *seems* as though one can describe a case where "rationality" (and rational self-awareness) and happiness diverge; where someone less rationally self-aware will be more happy. If in contemplating this case you would choose rational self-awareness and moral rectitude, rather than happiness, then the former have independent value and are not justified in your eyes *only* because they lead to happiness.

Driving the point further, suppose we read the biography of a man who *felt* happy, took pride in his work, family life, etc. But we also read that his children, secretly, despised him; his wife, secretly, scorned him having innumerable affairs; his work was a subject of ridicule among all others, who kept their opinion from him; *every* source of satisfaction in this man's life was built upon a falsehood, a deception. Do you, in reading about this man's life, think: "what a *wonderful* life. I wish I, or my children, could lead it"? And don't say that you wouldn't want to lead the life because all the deceptions and falsehoods might come out making the man unhappy. They didn't. Of course, it is difficult to imagine the others behaving appropriately, and the person himself not being nagged by doubts. But is *this* the ground of one's reaction? Was it a good life? Does it lack *happiness*?

This man lived a lie, though not one that he told. We can imagine other cases. You have what you believe is a private relationship with someone. However, unbeknowst to you, I am filming it with my super-duper camera and sound equipment, and distributing the film to people whom you will never encounter. Nothing in your life is changed by the fact that people are packing the pornographic movie theaters in Outer Mongolia to keep up with the latest serial installment in your life. So, should anyone care? And is the only ground on which my action can be criticized the nature of the viewers' experience?[15]

I have listed all these examples, not only to bring the reader to feel the inadequacy of Miss Rand's view,[16] but for another purpose as well. For the examples we have discussed count against a more general view as well, which we might call *experiential ethics*. Put briefly, experiential ethical theories hold that the only facts relevant to moral assessments of actions are how these actions do, or are intended to, affect the experiences of various persons. The only morally relevant information (though other information may be relevant via being *evidence* for this kind) is that about the distribution of experiences in society. Theories will differ about *which* experiences they pick out, or about the criterion of optimal distribution of experiences, but they will agree that *all* of the considerations have to do with such experiences, and how they feel from the inside. Indeed, it may seem, how *could* anything else matter other than the experiences people have, how things feel from the inside. What else could there be that's of any importance? It is a task of some interest to explain what else does matter, and why, and to account for the pull of the experiential picture on us.[17]

Let me, in closing, reiterate that my purpose has been to examine Miss Rand's arguments for her conclusions. It has *not* been to argue that death is a value, or that we should sacrifice others to ourselves, or that people don't have rights to our noninterference in their lives, or to demean the virtues of rationality, honesty, integrity, productiveness, pride, independence, justice. It has been to see whether, in her published work, Miss Rand indeed objectively establishes her conclusions. She doesn't.

12

WEIGHTED VOTING AND "ONE-MAN, ONE-VOTE"

✺ ✺ ✺

Except for isolated cases of election fraud, and the systematic exclusion from voting of some group, each eligible voter can, if he wishes, cast one vote. We are here not concerned with the number of votes someone casts but with how much weight or power his vote has. Ignoring the considerations which the Supreme Court says might justify deviations from equal weight (e.g., maintaining political subdivisions as the basis for electoral districts, achieving compact districts of contiguous territory) and ignoring some practical difficulties, one wants to equalize,[1] given appropriate measures of power, some function of the power of the legislator and of the power of the person to choose the legislator. If each person eligible to participate in choosing a given legislator has equal power in determining that choice, then one wants to equalize,[2] for each i,

$$\frac{\text{Power of legislator } L_i}{\begin{array}{l}\text{Number of persons eligible to participate} \\ \text{in choosing legislator } L_i\end{array}}$$

If, furthermore, each legislator has equal power, then one wants to equalize the number of persons eligible to participate in the choosing of each legislator.

I shall assume that the representative systems under discussion are based upon a system of legislative districts. Professor Paul Freund has mentioned the possibility of a representative system without legislative districts, in which there are n representatives, persons' names are arranged in alphabetical order, and the first nth of the people are eligible to vote for one representative, the second nth for another, and so on. Such a system can easily bring about the equalization discussed above, but since no one seems prone to suggest such a system, this shows (and, I believe, was intended by Professor Freund to show) that we are concerned that our legislative system satisfy conditions in addition to equalizing the weight of the voters' votes. (And perhaps we would countenance some deviation from the latter condition in order better to satisfy the former ones.) It is of some importance for a theory of representation to state what purposes are served by representation by geographical districts.[3]

If in each legislative district, each eligible voter has equal power in selecting the legislator, then in the legislature, one wants each legislator to have power proportional to the number of eligible voters in his district.[4] But it also seems that there are persons other than eligible voters residing in his district whom the legislator is to represent, whose interests he is to care for; for example, recent immigrants who are not citizens, and also nonadult citizens. And we want a legislator's power to be proportional to the number of persons in his district whom he is to represent (in this wider sense). It follows (assuming that in each legislator's district there will be persons whom he is to represent who are not eligible voters) that a legislator's power should be proportional to the number of persons in a set which has as a *proper* subset the set of eligible voters in his district. Thus it seems that there are two conditions to be satisfied: (1) A legislator's power is to be proportional to the number of eligible voters in his district; (2) A legislator's power is to be proportional to the number of persons in his district whom he is to represent. It is possible to satisfy both of these conditions together only if there is some positive number n (which need not be an integer) such that, for each legislator, the number of persons he is to represent $= n \times$ the number of voters eligible to select him. And it seems very unlikely that this will be the case. Having mentioned this difficulty, I shall ignore it in the remainder of my comments.

The standard proposal about weighted voting in a legislature, and the one discussed by Professors Riker and Shapley, gives to each legislator a number of votes proportional to the number of eligible voters in his district. If we assume that each legislator will on each issue cast his votes as a bloc,[5] then it can be shown, as Professor Riker and Shapley point out, that such a weighted voting scheme does not guarantee equalization of

$$\frac{\text{Power of the } i\text{th legislator}}{\substack{\text{Number of persons eligible to} \\ \text{vote for the } i\text{th legislator}}}$$

where the power of the legislator is measured by the Shapley procedure. (Henceforth I shall refer to this fraction as P_i/N_i.)

If one supposes that Shapley's procedure gives a reasonable measure of the power of a legislator,[6] this result is unfortunate, since it looked like such a weighted voting scheme would both perfectly satisfy the Supreme Court decisions[7] and avoid tricky redistricting problems.

Professors Riker and Shapley go on to investigate the questions of whether, in large legislatures, the deviations from equalizing P_i/N_i will be great, greater than is compatible with court decisions, and investigate in what direction one can expect the deviations to go, given the size of a district and of the other districts. What I should like to do is raise some questions about whether, assuming that the districts are satisfactory and that there aren't gerrymandering-type objections to them,[8] *some* system of weighted voting will equalize P_i/N_i. Given the result which Professors Riker and Shapley mention, a system of weighted voting which equalized P_i/N_i would have to be a system which did *not* give legislators a number of votes proportional to the number of eligible voters in their districts.

The most general question is: For every legislature with any number (> 1) of legislators, such that each legislator may have associated with him (as eligible voters) any number of persons, is there some assignment of numbers of votes to each legislator (these numbers of votes need not be integers, and need not be proportional to the number of persons associated with the legislator) such that P_i/N_i is equalized? The answer to this question is "no." For example,

1. Suppose there are two legislators in the legislature who are associated with different numbers of persons. If the legislators are given the same number of votes, their power will be equal and hence their fractions will be different. If the number of votes the legislators have differs and it is a system of majority rule, then the one with more votes will have all the power (and his fraction will be positive); and the one with

fewer votes will have no power (and hence his fraction will be zero). Hence the fractions will differ.

2. Suppose the legislature consists of an odd number of legislators having the same number of persons associated with them, and one legislator with fewer persons associated with him. Each of the odd number of legislators must get the same number of votes (or something equivalent). If the remaining legislator gets this number of votes, he has the same power as they do, and the fractions are unequal (his is greater). (Similarly his fraction is at least as great if he gets more votes than they do.) If he gets fewer votes than they do, he has no power, and his fraction is zero (while theirs is greater than zero). Hence the fractions cannot be equalized.[9]

The Shapley power value will always be a fraction whose denominator is x, the total number of possible permutations of the legislators' (bloc) votes,[10] and whose numerator will be some integer less than x. Since it will usually be the case that a legislator does not have associated with him exactly some integral xth of the total population,[11] it will often be impossible to have a legislator's power be that fraction of the total power which the persons associated with him are of the total number of persons associated with all of the legislators. Whatever fraction of the total population is associated with a legislator, this fraction will fall between n/x and $(n + 1)/x$ for some integral $n > 0$ (where x is as before). Let us say that n/x and $(n + 1)/x$ surround the fraction.

The first questions we want to raise are:

1. What are the conditions under which it is possible, by a system of weighted voting (where the number of votes a legislator has need not be proportional to the number of persons associated with him), to get, for each legislator j, $P_j / \sum_i P_i$ equal to one of the fractions which surround the fraction whose denominator is the total number of persons associated with all the legislators, and whose numerator is the number of persons associated with the jth legislator.[12] That is, under what conditions is it possible to get, for each legislator j, $P_j / \sum_i P_i$ equal to one of the fractions which surround $N_j / \sum_i N_i$ where N_i is the number of persons associated with the ith legislator.

2. Do current legislative districts (and the ones which would result from foreseeable population changes) satisfy these conditions?

If current legislative districts do satisfy these conditions, then *some* system of weighted voting, which does not assign votes to legislators in proportion to the number of their constitutents, will serve the purposes that the standard system of weighted voting was designed to serve.

But suppose that current legislative districts do not satisfy these conditions. Must one redistrict in order to get, for each j, $P_j / \sum_i P_i$ to one of the fractions which surround $N_j / \sum_i N_i$?

There are various alternative weighted voting schemes which *may* enable one to achieve this goal without redistricting. It is worth mentioning some such alternative schemes, since some of them would be rejected even if they achieve *this* goal, and hence raise questions about what further considerations one wishes an electoral scheme to satisfy.

In standard legislatures, all legislators, if they wish to do so, may vote on each bill which comes before the house of the legislature of which they are members (though they may not be able to vote in legislative committees of which they are not members). An alternative scheme might assign to each legislator some probability (not necessarily the same for each legislator) of being allowed or entitled to vote on any given issue, with random devices being used to determine if he actually does get to vote on the issue. Once the different probabilities of voting are assigned to each legislator, a generalization of the standard power measures can be used to compute the power of each legislator. This system might be combined with one of weighted voting whereby legislators who get to vote (after the random device determines that they may) may be entitled to cast different numbers of votes. This scheme raises the second question:

For any number, > 1, of legislators, each having any finite number of constituents, is there some assignment of weighted votes and probabilities of getting to vote to the legislators so that, for each j, $P_j / \sum_i P_i$ is equal to one of the fractions which surround $N_j / \sum_i N_i$? If there is not always such an assignment, what conditions must be satisfied for there to be one, and do current legislative districts satisfy these conditions?

Even if such a scheme could achieve the stated goal, many would find it objectionable. (For, it would be said, it *might* turn out that some legislators would almost never get to vote, and some might not get to vote on some bills of great importance to their districts.) Amost all would find objectionable a system wherein only one legislator gets to vote on any given bill (thereby determining whether or not it passes during that session of the legislature), and each legislator has some probability, for any given bill, of being the one who decides. Even if, given current legislature districts, there is a probability assignment which achieves the stated goal, such a system would be rejected. It is worth mentioning such legislative systems, since they make clear that we are not concerned *only* with P_i / N_i and suggest the task of stating the specific additional conditions which we wish to impose upon an electoral and legislative system.

Alternative systems could be proposed which might achieve the stated goal. For example, legislators might be divided into blocs whose votes are weighted. Each bloc must vote as a bloc, and how a bloc votes is determined by how its members, with weighted votes, vote in a caucus of the bloc. So the power of each legislator is a function of the power of the bloc of which he is a member, and of his power within the bloc. (A more complicated scheme would have some legislators being members of more than one bloc.) Given current legislative districts, can such a system achieve the stated goal?

I should briefly mention one qualm about Riker and Shapley's interesting result, about the model of the delegate representatives who "act simply as funnels for their constituencies," that in general the citizen of a small district has a much smaller power index than the citizen of a large district. It seems that the authors assume that each legislative district is (roughly) a random sample of the total population with respect to political belief; hence their claim that smaller districts will deviate more than larger ones from the national percentage on an issue. The large (in population) districts which we now have are urban districts, and it is not obvious that the political beliefs found in these districts are a random sample of the political beliefs of the total population, or more representative of the political beliefs of the total population than are those of the small districts. (It is a commonplace that large urban districts generally elect more "liberal" representatives than do other districts.) This is especially clear for counties containing some large urban districts, though most of their population is in small (in population) agricultural districts. The large urban district is not, I think, more likely (than its population justifies) to be in a pivot position. Thus, though Riker and Shapley's result about large and small districts follows from considerations about probability and random samples, one would hesitate to apply it to actual political situations where the large urban areas are known not to be a random sample of the total population with respect to political beliefs. It might be said that the *structure* of the legislative system favors large (in population) districts. But even if we grant that facts about the distribution of political beliefs are not part of the structure of a legislative system,[13] we may not worry about a bias the structure imposes since it is counterbalanced by general conditions likely to continue, and indeed we may desire a biased structure to compensate for certain nonstructural biases.

DISCUSSIONS
AND
REVIEWS

13 | GOODMAN, NELSON, ON MERIT, AESTHETIC

⌁ ⌁ ⌁

An acquaintance who claims to be a medium has told me of receiving a message from Isaac Newton. This message is of such interest that, despite my disbelief in the claims of mediumship, I transmit it, as I heard it, to the philosophical public.

This is Isaac Newton. The time has arrived for me to make public a fact heretofore unknown outside the immediate circle of my friends. What has since come to be known as Newtonian theory was first presented, not in the *Principia,* but in a poem. Those to whom I showed the poem averred that, though it contained natural philosophy of great interest, the poetry encasing it was so abominable as to make me a laughing stock should I publish it. Reluctantly I allowed myself to become convinced. I should not have been overwhelmed by the unanimity of their negative judgment of my poem, I now realize. For word has reached me of the view of Nelson Goodman, who holds that a work has aesthetic merit if it is an aesthetic object and if it significantly changes the way we view the world or conceptually organize the world, performing various cognitive functions.

[TRANSMITTER'S NOTE: Here Newton must have in mind Nelson Goodman's discussion in sec. VI of the last chapter of *Languages of Art* (1968), especially pp. 258–259:

Symbolization, then, is to be judged fundamentally by how well it serves the cognitive purpose: by the delicacy of its discriminations and the aptness of its allusions; by the way it works in grasping, exploring, and informing the world; by how it analyzes, sorts, orders, and organizes, by how it participates in the making, manipulation, retention, and transformation of knowledge. Considerations of simplicity and subtlety, power and precision, scope and selectivity, familiarity and freshness, are all relevant and often contend with one another; their weighting is relative to our interests, our information, and our inquiry.

So much for the cognitive efficacy of symbolization in general, but what of aesthetic excellence in particular? Distinguishing between the aesthetic and the meritorious cuts both ways. If excellence is not required of the aesthetic, neither is the excellence appropriate to aesthetic objects confined to them. *Rather, the general excellence just sketched becomes aesthetic when exhibited by aesthetic objects; that is, aesthetic merit is such excellence in any symbolic functioning that, by its particular constellation of attributes, qualifies as aesthetic.*

My italics.]

There is no question that my poem was an aesthetic object; my friends never tired of twitting me about how poor a one it was. Furthermore, it certainly would have changed the way people saw the world, had I published it. The *Principia,* containing the same natural philosophy, *did* change the way people viewed the world; as did the poem itself for the few friends who saw it. (Unfortunately it also changed the way they viewed my artistic talents.) It follows that, had I published the poem, it would have been a work of great aesthetic merit. Against the cavilling criticisms of my friends, I have been vindicated! In appreciation of his service, I dedicate this reading of my poem to Nelson Goodman:

I sing of bodies in attraction,
Persistent motion, and retributive action;
Not dramatic plot or moral lecture
But the universe's architecture.
The earth and heavens in a single plan
Here described by a pious man.

Bodies on each other exert a force
Directly proportional to the product of their masses and
    inversely proportional to the square of the distance
    between them, of course.
Gravitation is unselective,
Acting between all bodies, irrespective.

Before you jump from a tree to fly free as a bird in
    uninhibited levitation
Think about universal gravitation.

Changes from rest or straight-line motion
Are always caused, such is my notion.
Curvèd paths or acceleration
Stand in need of explanation.
Distinguish the constant old from the new
To have your theory green instead of grue.

Through absolute space and time, I say,
F equals $m\ a$.
A reaction opposite and equal
To every action is a sequel.
All occurs without magic or potion
In accord with the laws of motion.

Though to the idea some show resistance
Action takes place at a distance.
Some will protest, and rant o'er much,
Denying anything they cannot touch.
Phenomenalism is the theory of these,
Unable to know beyond their sees.

Don't think God's world I here describe
Is ugly, prosaic, or merits a jibe,
Don't think it mechanistic, a subject to curse.
Instead give thanks He didn't do verse.

Alas, there was then no Nelson Goodman to encourage me to publish this poem! Had I done so, my place in the history of literature would have been secure. Such counterfactuals are of meager comfort to me, and might be viewed by some as of dubious intelligibility. But *perhaps* Goodman's wonderful theory also yields an indicative statement which would serve me. If schoolchildren are taught my poem at a very young age, then my poem *will* actually change the way they see the world.

Won't it then actually fulfill its destiny as a major work of art? Perhaps not. Perhaps a poem that merely brings some to see the world as many already do, does not suffice. Must the work of art be the first generally available statement of the view? Because of the *accident* that my poem did not realize its potential of changing the way in which people view the world, is my chance for aesthetic greatness gone? In the hope that others may profit from knowing of my missed opportunities, I am sending this message also to Gell-man and Feynman.

P.S.: Kepler here would like to transmit to you a painting he once did, but he lacks the means to do so, and he lacks a notation for painting. He *has* given me permission to describe the painting to you. It consists of a bright circular spot (the sun) at one focus of purple elliptical dotted lines. He is very pleased to learn that Goodman joins him in considering this painting (which he modestly had entitled "My First Law") one of the major works of art in the western tradition. So much, he says, for his detractors, who had considered it little more than a crudely executed cartoon.

P.P.S.: At my next appearance, I will be joined by Fermat, who will sing for you a little ditty whose melody *he* thinks is rather remarkable. He had wanted, he says, to write it in the margin, but lacked enough room to fit in the bass and treble clefs.*

---

* This note originated in my remarking to a friend (not to be confused with the acquaintance mentioned in the opening sentence) that a doggerel poem by Newton presenting the theory of universal gravitation would have been, according to Goodman, a work of aesthetic merit. This friend went and wrote fragments of such a poem, reading them to me several days later! I then supplied a frame to go around the poem, but, despite my encouragement, the friend preferred to leave his poem incomplete rather than include it here. This necessitated my writing yet *another* poem, to substitute for his. Everything appearing here, therefore, is mine, but I am happy to acknowledge that the idea of *actually constructing* "Newton's Poem" (though not the poem that appears here) is the friend's, who prefers to remain nameless, which preference unfortunately was doomed to frustration by his parents thirty-one years ago when they named him Saul.

WHO WOULD CHOOSE SOCIALISM?

⁕ ⁕ ⁕

What percentage of people would *choose* to live under socialism? The communist countries do not help us to answer this question, for neither through elections nor through emigration do they offer their people any choice. What about the electoral experience of democratic societies such as England or Sweden? Even this does not enable us to disentangle (imagined) self-interest from our topic: the desire to participate in socialist interpersonal relations of equality and community.

To find out what percentage of people especially want to live under socialism, we need a situation where people have a reasonably attractive socialist option *and* also a reasonably attractive nonsocialist one. If it is not precisely the optimal experiment to answer our question, the Israeli experience with kibbutzim comes as close as the real world can.

Not only have the kibbutzim offered socialist personal relations in a socialist community, but these communities have been widely admired for performing the important functions of reclaiming the land, aiding Jewish self-defense, and "normalizing" the occupational structure of the Jewish people. Unlike nineteenth-century utopian communities in America or twentieth-century communes, membership in a kibbutz brought respect and support from the wider society, aiding members through difficulties. Furthermore, no natural population provides a more fertile ground for socialist commitment than the Ashkenazi Jewish population.

No people is more prone to being captured by an "idealistic" ideological position, especially one emphasizing group solidarity. Indeed, there was selective entry into Israel early in the century; many came *in order* to help build socialism and did their best to instill their ideals in their children.

The kibbutzim are now a very comfortable alternative. By and large they are economically very prosperous. A high level of cultural activity is available per capita. They have a widely admired educational system (one which, despite their socialist beliefs, kibbutzniks have been somewhat reluctant to share with poorer children in the surrounding areas). They offer occupational opportunities in agriculture, industry, the arts and services, as well as administrative and political tasks in the wider kibbutz movement. No doubt, there are *some* occupations not easily carried out in a kibbutz setting (for example, experimental particle physicist), though there have been attempts to have university teachers based in a nearby kibbutz.

Within Israel, the kibbutz is a prosperous, widely respected and encouraged community (the encouragement includes tax benefits) offering variegated occupational and leisure opportunities. It seems fair to say that the major reason for an Israeli's not living in a kibbutz is that he *just doesn't want to live that way.*

The kibbutz population makes up 3.5 percent of the Jewish population of Israel and about 6 percent of the Ashkenazi Jewish population (of the kibbutz population, 85 percent is Ashkenazi). So now we know *approximately* how many people would choose, under highly conducive conditions, to live under socialism: about six percent.

To be sure, the estimate must be refined a bit. No doubt some people outside kibbutzim want to live there but don't because their mates strongly object, just as some reside within kibbutzim because of *their* mates' strong preference. Some people who wish to leave stay in kibbutzim because there is no vested pension right that they can take with them, while some people who live in moshavim also may be seeking some socialist mode of life (of the Israeli population, 4.5 percent, with equal Ashkenazi and Sephardi components, is in moshavim, some of which combine communal production with familial consumption).

Let us be generous and suppose that half again as many would choose socialism. This brings the number up from six to nine percent. Under conditions as ideal as the real world can produce, nine percent of the people would choose to shape their lives in accordance with socialist principles.

Surely this minority should everywhere be allowed to do this, joining together with other like-minded people to live according to their desires. (It is a virtue of a free system that it allows minority preferences to be satisfied, just as a free market caters *also* to minority tastes—for example, for recordings of Renaissance music or of chassidic songs.) Furthermore, this minority may try to persuade the rest of us of the superior virtues of their ideal.

But that's all. They may not force the rest of us to live that way. We can understand, though, why they might be tempted to do so. In that setting *most* conducive to the free acceptance of socialist ideals, with the most attractive and respected socialist communities and the most receptive population, only nine percent (as a *generous* estimate) would choose to live that way. The prospects, therefore, are dim for interpersonal socialism's coming anywhere voluntarily. As Israel shows us, there won't be enough volunteers.

15 | WHY DO INTELLECTUALS OPPOSE CAPITALISM?

 ❧ ❧ ❧

It is surprising that intellectuals oppose capitalism so. Other groups of comparable socio-economic status do not show the same degree of opposition in the same proportions. Statistically, then, intellectuals are an anomaly.

Not all intellectuals are on the "left." Like other groups, their opinions are spread along a curve. But in their case, the curve is shifted and skewed to the political left. The exact proportion we call anti-capitalist depends on how lines are drawn: upon how one construes the anti-capitalist or left position and upon how one marks off the group of intellectuals. What is not in doubt, despite the recent vocal neo-conservative faction, is the general leftward tilt of intellectuals. The proportions may have changed somewhat recently but on the *average*, intellectuals remain further to the left than others of their socio-economic status. Why?

By intellectuals, I do not mean all people of intelligence or of a certain level of education, but those who, in their vocation, deal with ideas as expressed in words, shaping the word flow others receive. These wordsmiths include poets, novelists, literary critics, newspaper and magazine journalists, and many professors. It does not include those who primarily produce and transmit quantitatively or mathematically formulated information (the numbersmiths) or those working in visual media, painters, sculptors, cameramen. Unlike the wordsmiths, people in these occupations do not disproportionately oppose capitalism. The wordsmiths are concentrated in certain occupational sites: academia, the media, government bureaucracy.

Wordsmith intellectuals fare well in capitalist society; there they have great freedom to formulate, encounter, and propagate new ideas, to read and discuss them. Their occupational skills are in demand, their income much above average. Why then do they disproportionately oppose capitalism? Indeed, some data suggest that the more properous and successful the intellectual, the more likely he is to oppose capitalism. This opposition to capitalism is mainly "from the left" but not solely so. Yeats, Eliot, and Pound opposed market society from the right.

The opposition of wordsmith intellectuals to capitalism is a fact of social significance. They shape our ideas and images of society; they state the policy alternatives bureaucracies consider. From treatises to slogans, they give us the sentences to express ourselves. Their opposition matters, especially in a society (often called "post-industrial") that depends increasingly upon the explicit formulation and dissemination of information.

Must we really search for a special explanation of why wordsmith intellectuals disproportionately oppose capitalism? Consider the straightforward answer: capitalism is bad, unjust, immoral, or inferior, and intellectuals, being intelligent, realize this and therefore oppose it.

This straightforward explanation is not available to those, like myself, who do not think that capitalism, a system of private property and free markets, is bad, unjust, evil, or immoral. Readers who disagree should notice that even a true belief may not have a straightforward explanation: it might be believed *because* of some factors other than its truth, such as socialization and enculturation.

Something about the manner of many intellectuals' opposition indicates, I think, that something more is involved than their simply realizing the truth about capitalism. For when one or another of the particular complaints about capitalism is refuted (perhaps the one that it leads to monopoly, or pollution, or too much inequality, or involves exploitation of workers, or despoils the environment, or leads to imperialism, or causes wars, or thwarts meaningful work, or panders to people's desires, or encourages dishonesty in the marketplace, or produces for profit and not for use, or holds back progress to increase profits, or disrupts traditional patterns to increase profits, or leads to overproduction, or leads to underproduction), when the complaint is shown and conceded to have faulty logic or faulty assumptions of fact or history or economics, the complainer does not then change his mind. He drops the point, and quickly leaps to another. ("But what about child labor, or the racism built into it, or the oppression of women, or urban slums, or in simpler days we could do without planning but now things are so complex that . . . , or advertising seducing people into buying things or . . . ") Point after point is given up in discussion. What is not given up, though, is the opposition to capitalism. For the opposition is not based on those points and complaints, and so it does not disappear when they do. There is an underlying *animus* against capitalism. This animus gives rise to the complaints; the complaints rationalize the animus. After some resistance, a particular complaint may be given up and, without a backward glance, tenfold others will surge forward to perform the same function: to rationalize and justify the intellectual's animus to capitalism. If the intellectual simply were recognizing the flaws or wrongness of capitalism, we would not find that animus. The explanation of his opposition will need to be a non-straightforward explanation that also accounts for animus.

It may be objected that the explanation is simply the obvious one that intelligent people simply have a natural tendency to look around and criticize what is wrong. Or that it is in the nature of creative innovative activity to lead to a skeptical mind that rejects the established order. But why, among the intelligent, is it especially wordsmiths rather than numbersmiths who lean toward the left? If their temperament is critical, why are the wordsmiths usually so uncritical of "progressive" programs? If creative innovative activity is the cause, why must it lead to skepticism rather than to finding of subtle virtues in established beliefs and doctrines? (Did not Dante, Maimonides, and Aquinas engage in creative intellectual activity?) And why must skepticism express itself about the established order rather than about plans for total alternatives that supposedly improve upon it? No, like the idea that capitalism is simply bad and the intellectuals are smart enough to realize this, the explanation that intellectuals are by nature critical and skeptical is unsatisfactory. These "explanations" are too self-serving; they do not fit the details of the situation. We must look elsewhere for an explanation. However, we should not be surprised that the explanations that spring to their minds turn out to be so self-congratulatory—when explanations are offered it is the intellectuals who offer them.

We can distinguish two types of explanation for the relatively high proportion of intellectuals in opposition to capitalism. One type finds a factor unique to the anti-capitalist intellectuals. The second type of explanation identifies a factor applying to all intellectuals, a force propelling them *toward* anti-capitalist views. Whether it pushes any particular intellectual over into anti-capitalism will depend upon the other forces acting upon him. In the aggregate, though, since it makes anti-capitalism more likely for each intellectual, such a factor will produce a larger proportion of anti-capitalist intellectuals. Think about the larger number of people going to the beach on a sunny day. We may not be able to predict whether a given individual will go—that depends upon all the other factors operating on him—but the sun makes it more likely that each person will go and so leads to a larger total number at the beach. Our explanation will be of this second type. We will identify a factor which tilts intellectuals toward anti-capitalist attitudes but does not guarantee it in any particular case.

Previous Theories

Various explanations have been proposed for the opposition of intellectuals to capitalism. One favored by the neo-conservatives focuses on the group interests of intellectuals.[1] Though they do well economically under capitalism, they would do even better, they think, under a socialist society where their power would be greater. In a market society, there is no central concentration of power and if anyone has power or appears to have it, it is the successful entrepreneur and businessman. The rewards of material wealth certainly are his. In a socialist society, however, it would be wordsmith intellectuals who staff the government bureaucracies, who suggest its policies, formulate them, and oversee their implementation. A socialist society, the intellectuals think, is one in which *they* would rule—an idea, unsurprisingly, that they find appealing. (Recall Plato's description in the *Republic* of the best society as one in which the philosophers rule.)

But this explanation in terms of the group interests of intellectuals is unsatisfactory all by itself. Even if a transition to a socialist society *were* in the group interests of intellectuals (and I leave aside the many illusions this hope embodies), it need not be in the individual interests of any particular intellectual to aid in the long-term transition. The neo-conservatives make the same mistake the Marxists do in discussing the behavior of capitalists. They ignore the fact that people act not in their group or class interest but in their *individual* interests. It would be in the individual interest of each intellectual to hold back while the others do the arduous work of bringing about a society more favorable to intellectuals.[2] We can formulate a more discriminating explanation, though. If intellectuals think they would do better in a socialist society, and so enjoy reading about the virtues of such a society and the flaws of capitalism, they themselves will constitute a ready and substantial market for such words, and so it will be in the interests of individual intellectuals to produce such word-fare for the other intellectuals to consume.

The economist F. A. Hayek has identified another reason intellectuals might favor a socialist society. That society is thought to be consciously organized in accordance with a plan, i.e., an idea. Ideas are the subject matter of wordsmiths, and thus a planned society makes primary what they are professionally concerned with. It is a society which embodies ideas. How could intellectuals fail to find such a society alluring and valuable? To be sure, we can describe the ideas which a capitalist society instances, liberty and individual rights, but these describe a process of freedom, not the final pattern that will result. An ideology that wishes to imprint a pattern upon society will thereby make an idea more central to the society and (unless the idea is repugnant) thereby appeal to the special tastes of intellectuals who deal professionally with ideas.

Yet another explanation focuses upon how the motivation for intellectual activity contrasts to the motivations most highly prized and rewarded in market society. Capitalist activity—so the story goes—is motivated by selfish greed, pure and simple, while intellectual activity is motivated by the love of ideas. Surely, this contrast is overdrawn. A capitalist can desire to make money in order to support his favorite charity or cause. And entrepreneurial activity can be motivated by its own intrinsic rewards, the rewards of mastery, competence, and accomplishment. True, these activities may also bring extrinsic rewards, but so may a novelist with purely artistic motives earn large royalties. And is intellectual activity itself always motivated solely by its intrinsic rewards? (Male) writers, it has been said, write to gain fame and the love of beautiful women. Nor are competitive motivations noticeably absent in the intellectual world. Recall how Newton and Leibniz fought over priority in inventing the calculus, and how Crick and Watson raced Pauling to be first in discovering the structure of DNA.

But though the motivations of economically successful people under capitalism need not be noticeably inferior to those of intellectuals, it is nonetheless true that in a capitalist society economic rewards will tend to go to those who meet the demands of others expressed in the market-place, to the successful and efficient producers of what the consumers want. Intellectuals, too, can satisfy a market demand for their products, as is shown by the high incomes of some novelists and painters. However, it is not *necessary* that the market reward the intellectually most meritorious work; it will reward what (some portion of) the public likes. This may be less meritorious work, or it may be wholly non-intellectual work. The market, by its nature, is neutral toward intellectual merit. If intellectual merit is not rewarded most highly, this will be the fault, if fault it be, not of the market but of the buying public whose tastes and preferences are expressed in the market. If more are willing to pay to see Robert Redford perform than to hear me lecture or read my writings, that is no flaw in the market.

The intellectual may most resent the marketplace, though, when he sees an opportunity to succeed financially by producing a work that is less meritorious in his own eyes. Being tempted to debase his own standards for popular acclaim and success—or actually doing this—may cause him to resent the system that lures him to such distasteful motivations and emotions. (Hollywood writers are the paradigmatic example.) Again, though, why does he blame the market system rather than the public? Does he resent a system that maps his road to success through the tastes of the public, a public less acute, knowledgeable, and tasteful than he, a public that is intellectually inferior to him? (Yet most producers in the marketplace know more about their product and its appropriate standards than do most consumers.) Why should intellectuals be so resentful of having to satisfy market demand *if* what they want are the fruits of market success? They can always, after all, choose to adhere to their craft standards and accept more limited external rewards.

The economist Ludwig von Mises explained opposition to capitalism as resentment on the part of the less successful.[3] Rather than ascribing their own lack of success, in an open system in which others like themselves succeed, to personal failings, people blame it on the nature of the system. However, unsuccessful businessmen, by and large, do not blame the system. And why do intellectuals blame the system rather than their unappreciative fellow citizens? Given the high degree of freedom a capitalist system allows intellectuals and given the comfortable status of intellectuals within that system, what are they blaming the system *for*? How much do they expect from it?

The Schooling of Intellectuals

Intellectuals now expect to be the most highly valued people in a society, those with the most prestige and power, those with the greatest rewards. Intellectuals feel *entitled* to this. But, by and large, a capitalist society does not honor its intellectuals. Mises explains the special resentment of intellectuals, in contrast to workers, by saying they mix socially with successful capitalists and so have them as a salient comparison group and are humiliated by their lesser status. However, even those intellectuals who do not mix socially are similarly resentful, while merely mixing is not enough—the sports and dancing instructors who cater to the rich and have affairs with them are not noticeably anti-capitalist.

Why then do contemporary intellectuals feel *entitled* to the highest rewards their society has to offer and *resentful* when they do not receive this? Intellectuals feel they are the most valuable people, the ones with the highest merit, and that society should reward people in accordance with their value and merit. But a capitalist society does not satisfy the principle of distribution "to each according to his merit or value." Apart from the gifts, inheritances, and gambling winnings that occur in a free society, the market distributes to those who satisfy the perceived market-expressed demands of others, and how much it so distributes depends on how much is demanded and how great the alternative supply is. Unsuccessful businessmen and workers do not have the same animus against the capitalist system as do the wordsmith intellectuals. Only the sense of unrecognized superiority, of entitlement betrayed, produces that animus.

Why do wordsmith intellectuals think they are most valuable, and why do they think distribution should be in accordance with value? Note that this latter principle is not a necessary one. Other distributional patterns have been proposed, including equal distribution, distribution according to moral merit, distribution according to need. Indeed, there need not be any pattern of distribution a society is aiming to achieve, even a society concerned with justice. The justice of a distribution may reside in its arising from a just process of voluntary exchange of justly acquired property and services. Whatever outcome is produced by that process will be just, but there is no particular pattern the outcome must fit. Why, then, do wordsmiths view themselves as most valuable and accept the principle of distribution in accordance with value?

From the beginnings of recorded thought, intellectuals have told us their activity is most valuable. Plato valued the rational faculty above courage and the appetites and deemed that philosophers should rule; Aristotle held that intellectual contemplation was the highest activity. It is not surprising that surviving texts record this high evaluation of intellectual activity. The people who formulated evaluations, who wrote them down with reasons to back them up, were intellectuals, after all. They were praising themselves. Those who valued other things more than thinking things through with words, whether hunting or power or uninterrupted sensual pleasure, did not bother to leave enduring written records. Only the intellectual worked out a *theory* of who was best.

What factor produced feelings of superior value on the part of intellectuals? I want to focus on one institution in particular: schools. As book knowledge became increasingly important, schooling—the education together in classes of young people in reading and book knowledge—spread. Schools became the major institution outside of the family to shape the attitudes of young people, and almost all those who later became intellectuals went through schools. There they were successful. They were judged against others and deemed superior. They were praised and rewarded, the teacher's favorites. How could they fail to see themselves as superior? Daily, they experienced differences in facility with ideas, in quick-wittedness. The schools told them, and showed them, they were better.

The schools, too, exhibited and thereby taught the principle of reward in accordance with (intellectual) merit. To the intellectually meritorious went the praise, the teacher's smiles, and the highest grades. In the currency the schools had to offer, the smartest constituted the upper class. Though not part of the official curricula, in the schools the intellectuals learned the lessons of their own greater value in comparison with the others, and of how this greater value entitled them to greater rewards.

The wider market society, however, taught a different lesson. There the greatest rewards did not go to the verbally brightest. There the intellectual skills were not *most* highly valued. Schooled in the lesson that they were most valuable, the most deserving of reward, the most entitled to reward, how could the intellectuals, by and large, fail to resent the capitalist society which deprived them of the just deserts to which their superiority "entitled" them? Is it surprising that what the schooled intellectuals felt for capitalist society was a deep and sullen animus that, although clothed with various publicly appropriate reasons, continued even when those particular reasons were shown to be inadequate?

In saying that intellectuals feel entitled to the highest rewards the general society can offer (wealth, status, etc.), I do not mean that intellectuals hold these rewards to be the highest goods. Perhaps they value more the intrinsic rewards of intellectual activity or the esteem of the ages. Nevertheless, they also feel entitled to the highest appreciation from the general society, to the most and best it has to offer, paltry though that may be. I don't mean to emphasize especially the rewards that find their way into the intellectuals' pockets or even reach them personally. Identifying themselves as intellectuals, they can resent the fact that intellectual activity is not most highly valued and rewarded.

The intellectual wants the whole society to be a school writ large, to be like the environment where he did so well and was so well appreciated. By incorporating standards of reward that are different from the wider society, the schools guarantee that some will experience downward mobility later. Those at the top of the school's hierarchy will feel entitled to a top position, not only in that micro-society but in the wider one, a society whose system they will resent when it fails to treat them according to their self-prescribed wants and entitlements. The school system thereby produces anti-capitalist feeling among intellectuals.[4] Rather, it produces anti-capitalist feeling among verbal intellectuals. Why do the numbersmiths not develop the same attitudes as these wordsmiths? I conjecture that these quantitatively bright children, although they get good grades on the relevant examinations, do not receive the same face-to-face attention and approval from the teachers as do the verbally bright children. It is the verbal skills that bring these personal rewards from the teacher, and apparently it is these rewards that especially shape the sense of entitlement.

There is a further point to be added. The (future) wordsmith intellectuals are successful within the formal, official social system of the schools, wherein the relevant rewards are distributed by the central authority of the teacher. The schools contain another informal social system within classrooms, hallways, and schoolyards, wherein rewards are distributed not by central direction but spontaneously at the pleasure and whim of schoolmates. Here the intellectuals do less well.

It is not surprising, therefore, that distribution of goods and rewards via a centrally organized distributional mechanism later strikes intellectuals as more appropriate than the "anarchy and chaos" of the marketplace. For distribution in a centrally planned socialist society stands to distribution in a capitalist society as distribution by the teacher stands to distribution by the schoolyard and hallway.[5]

Our explanation does not postulate that (future) intellectuals constitute a majority even of the academic upper class of the school. This group may consist mostly of those with substantial (but not overwhelming) bookish skills along with social grace, strong motivation to please, friendliness, winning ways, and an ability to play by (and to seem to be following) the rules. Such pupils, too, will be highly regarded and rewarded by the teacher, and they will do extremely well in the wider society, as well. (And do well within the informal social system of the school. So they will not especially accept the norms of the school's formal system.) Our explanation hypothesizes that (future) intellectuals are disproportionately represented in that portion of the schools' (official) upper class that will experience relative downward mobility. Or, rather, in the group that predicts for itself a declining future. The animus will arise *before* the move into the wider world and the experience of an actual decline in status, at the point when the clever pupil realizes he (probably) will fare less well in the wider society than in his current school situation. This unintended consequence of the school system, the anti-capitalist animus of intellectuals, is, of course, reinforced when pupils read or are taught by intellectuals who present those very anti-capitalist attitudes.

No doubt, some wordsmith intellectuals were cantankerous and questioning pupils and so were disapproved of by their teachers. Did they too learn the lesson that the best should get the highest rewards and think, despite their teachers, that they themselves were best and so start with an early resentment against the school system's distribution? Clearly, on this and the other issues discussed here, we need data on the school experiences of future wordsmith intellectuals to refine and test our hypotheses.

Stated as a general point, it is hardly contestable that the norms within schools will affect the normative beliefs of people after they leave the schools. The schools, after all, are the major non-familial society that children learn to operate in, and hence schooling constitutes their preparation for the larger non-familial society. It is not surprising that those successful by the norms of a school system should resent a society, adhering to different norms, which does not grant them the same success. Nor, when those are the very ones who go on to shape a society's self-image, its evaluation of itself, is it surprising when the society's verbally responsive portion turns against it. If you were designing a society, you would not seek to design it so that the wordsmiths, with all their influence, were schooled into animus against the norms of the society.

Our explanation of the disproportionate anti-capitalism of intellectuals is based upon a very plausible sociological generalization.

In a society where one extra-familial system or institution, the first young people enter, distributes rewards, those who do the very best therein will tend to internalize the norms of this institution and expect the wider society to operate in accordance with these norms; they will feel entitled to distributive shares in accordance with these norms or (at least) to a relative position equal to the one these norms would yield. Moreover, those constituting the upper class within the hierarchy of this first extra-familial institution who then experience (or foresee experiencing) movement to a lower relative position in the wider society will, because of their feeling of frustrated entitlement, tend to oppose the wider social system and feel animus toward its norms.

Notice that this is not a deterministic law. Not all those who experience downward social mobility will turn against the system. Such downward mobility, though, is a factor which tends to produce effects in that direction, and so will show itself in differing proportions at the aggregate level. We might distinguish ways an upper class can move down: it can get less than another group or (while no group moves above it) it can tie, failing to get more than those previously deemed lower. It is the first type of downward mobility which especially rankles and outrages; the second type is far more tolerable. Many intellectuals (say they) favor equality while only a small number call for an aristocracy of intellectuals. Our hypothesis speaks of the first type of downward mobility as especially productive of resentment and animus.

The school system imparts and rewards only *some* skills relevant to later success (it is, after all, a specialized institution) so its reward system will differ from that of the wider society. This guarantees that some, in moving to the wider society, will experience downward social mobility and its attendant consequences. Earlier I said that intellectuals want the society to be the schools writ large. Now we see that the resentment due to a frustrated sense of entitlement stems from the fact that the schools (as a specialized first extra-familial social system) are not the society writ small.

Our explanation now seems to predict the (*disproportionate*) resentment of schooled intellectuals against their society whatever its nature, whether capitalist or communist. (Intellectuals are disproportionately opposed to capitalism as compared with other groups of similar socioeconomic status within capitalist society. It is another question whether they are disproportionately opposed as compared with the degree of opposition of intellectuals in other societies to those societies.) Clearly, then, data about the attitudes of intellectuals within communist countries toward apparatchiks would be relevant; will those intellectuals feel animus toward *that* system?

Our hypothesis needs to be refined so that it does not apply (or apply as strongly) to every society. Must the school systems in every society inevitably produce anti-societal animus in the intellectuals who do not receive that society's highest rewards? Probably not. A capitalist society is peculiar in that it seems to announce that it is open and responsive only to talent, individual initiative, personal merit. Growing up in an inherited caste or feudal society creates no expectation that reward will or should be in accordance with personal value. Despite the created expectation, a capitalist society rewards people only insofar as they serve the market-expressed desires of others; it rewards in accordance with economic contribution, not in accordance with personal value. However, it comes close enough to rewarding in accordance with value—value and contribution will very often be intermingled—so as to nurture the expectation produced by the schools. The ethos of the wider society is close enough to that of the schools so that the nearness creates resentment. Capitalist societies reward individual accomplishment or announce they do, and so they leave the intellectual, who considers himself most accomplished, particularly bitter.

Another factor, I think, plays a role. Schools will tend to produce such anti-capitalist attitudes the more they are attended together by a diversity of people. When almost all of those who will be economically successful are attending separate schools, the intellectuals will not have acquired that attitude of being superior *to them*. But even if many children of the upper class attend separate schools, an open society will have other schools that also include many who will become economically successful as entrepreneurs, and the intellectuals later will resentfully remember how superior they were academically to their peers who advanced more richly and powerfully. The openness of the society has another consequence, as well. The pupils, future wordsmiths and others, will not know how they will fare in the future. They can hope for anything. A society closed to advancement destroys those hopes early. In an open capitalist society, the pupils are not resigned early to limits on their advancement and social mobility, the society seems to announce that the most capable and valuable will rise to the very top, their schools have already given the academically most gifted the message that they are most valuable and deserving of the greatest rewards, and later these very pupils with the highest encouragement and hopes see others of their peers, whom they know and saw to be less meritorious, rising higher than they themselves, taking the foremost rewards to which they themselves felt themselves entitled. Is it any wonder they bear that society an animus?

We have refined the hypothesis somewhat. It is not simply formal schools but formal schooling in a specified social context that produces anti-capitalist animus in (wordsmith) intellectuals. No doubt, the hypothesis requires further refining. But enough. It is time to turn the hypothesis over to the social scientists, to take it from armchair speculations in the study and give it to those who will immerse themselves in more particular facts and data. We can point, however, to some areas where our hypothesis might yield testable consequences and predictions. First, one might predict that the more meritocratic a country's school system, the more likely its intellectuals are to be on the left. (Consider France.) Second, those intellectuals who were "late bloomers" in school would not have developed the same sense of entitlement to the very highest rewards; therefore, a lower percentage of the late-bloomer intellectuals will be anti-capitalist than of the early bloomers. Third, we limited our hypothesis to those societies (unlike Indian caste society) where the successful student plausibly could expect further comparable success in the wider society. In Western society, women have not heretofore plausibly held such expectations, so we would not expect the female students who constituted part of the academic upper class yet later underwent downward mobility to show the same anti-capitalist animus as male intellectuals. We might predict, then, that the more a society is known to move toward equality in occupational opportunity between women and men, the more its female intellectuals will exhibit the same disproportionate anti-capitalism its male intellectuals show.

Some readers may doubt this explanation of the anti-capitalism of intellectuals. Be this as it may, I think that an important phenomenon has been identified. The sociological generalization we have stated is intuitively compelling; something like it must be true. Some important effect therefore must be produced in that portion of the school's upper class that experiences downward social mobility, some antagonism to the wider society must get generated. If that effect is not the disproportionate opposition of the intellectuals, then what is it? We started with a puzzling phenomenon in need of an explanation. We have found,

I think, an explanatory factor that (once stated) is so obvious that we must believe it explains some real phenomenon.

Is There a Solution?

Those who think capitalist society ought especially to be opposed—but why do they think so?—will welcome this unintended effect of the school system. Yet, as we have noted, the problem of the disharmony between the intelligentsia and the norms of the wider society is a more general one. It will be faced by any society, whatever its character, whose school system specializes and is not the society writ small. The more important and influential its wordsmith intellectuals (as in "post-industrial societies"), the more of a problem will this be. Thus, all readers can join with me in wondering how this opposition of the intellectuals to the society might be avoided—though some readers might prefer to wonder about this for some non-capitalist society.

When the schools and the wider society are out of joint, the two obvious solutions are to restructure (either) one to align it with the other. First, one might try to make the society fit the school norms, either by a socialist structuring which places the intellectuals at the top or through a naturally arising meritocracy. Yet, however important knowledge becomes in the society, no relatively free society will or can reward the highest school skills most highly. The schools, *with great effort,* focus only upon some qualities; these, while they play a significant role in economic success under some circumstances, will never be the whole story of resultant social position. Consumers are not schoolteachers giving grades for test and classroom performance.

Alternatively, and less ambitiously, the schools might be modified so as to fit the norms of the wider society or at least to avoid instilling contrary norms. If the intelligent are entitled to anything the market doesn't give them, it is to recognition as being intelligent—nothing more. They are not entitled to the largest rewards of the wider society. How might this lesson in modesty then be taught? Merely to *say* the economy properly rewards other attributes will not be enough. The children will learn from and internalize the school's actions, not its words. To be sure, the total social system of the school milieu values many things: athletic prowess in the schoolyard, toughness in the hallways, singing talent in the auditorium, good looks everywhere. But the school officially recognizes only or mainly intellectual skills and performance. Since that, after all, is what it is there for, it would be difficult for it credibly to give other

294 -a DISCUSSIONS AND REVIEWS

attributes parity or very significant recognition. (Character and atten-
dance awards are a joke, I assume, everywhere.)

Another possibility is to diminish the academic hierarchy within the
school system. Schools might teach without ranking the students, without grading them according to their success in learning. Reformers occasionally call for the abolition of tests and grading. Paul Goodman
argued that these have a function extrinsic to that of the education itself,
serving only the needs of future employers or the admissions committees
of other schools, who can be left to do their own informational testing
themselves.[6] (It is clear, though, that testing and certification also en-
large the discretionary choice of students. Employers accept a college's
statement that a student has completed requirements for a B.A. degree
without looking too closely into what those requirements are or how
useful those courses are for the purposes of employment.)

Yet tests perform other functions as well, intrinsic to the educational
process. They tell a student how well he is doing as judged by objective
standards, how well he is doing as compared with others in his reference
group (how well, after all, should he expect himself to do?). They provide information for tracking when educationally appropriate, as well
as for intermediate reinforcement along life's way.

In any case, given the extrinsic informational function, employers will
find it advantageous to hire from schools that test and certify and therefore students will find it advantageous to attend such schools. Whatever
the general social interest, people will pursue their own individual interests. No one will refuse to hire from a certain school or attend one
because that type of school system produces intellectuals with an anti-
capitalist animus. While legislation to alter school systems might accomplish the end, its benefits are so remote in comparison with its cost that
it is unlikely that such legislation will pass. Nor is such legislation, at
least as applied to private schools, compatible with the capitalist ethos
of liberty and individual rights.[7]

Restructuring the schools so as to de-emphasize intellectual skills and
accomplishments raises troublesome issues, apart from the obvious one
of the resultant cost in (short-term) efficiency in the society. The cultivation of intellectual abilities and talents is, we think, an important value
in itself. Yet the school systems we know that cultivate these also, unin-
tentionally, generate an animus against the social system among some of
those most gifted intellectually. If the long-term stability of the desirable
social system is best served by curbing the cultivation of some highly

admirable and worthwhile traits of individuals, then we face a serious conflict among our values.

It will comfort those who support the continuance of capitalist society to remember that this conflict is a general one. Communist society, too, finds intellectuals lie athwart its path, and during the Cultural Revolution the Chinese, at great economic and personal cost, by forcible re-education, exile to the countryside, and personal persecution, tried to make them just like everyone else. That attempt failed. The tension of capitalist society with its intellectuals is far less serious—we may just have to live with it. Whatever happens, though, the intellectuals will have the last word.

16 | THE CHARACTERISTIC FEATURES OF EXTREMISM

⤫ ⤫ ⤫

Geula Cohen has told us what she thinks extremism is not.[1] I would like to offer a general description of what extremism is. To be sure, a simple definition of extremism is not really possible. There is, however, a cluster of features, some more central than others, that together form what might be called an extremist syndrome. I want to list eight features of extremism. An extremist will be someone who has enough of these features—it needn't be each and every one of the eight.

The first has to do with the goals and doctrines of extremism and extremists. We don't normally term people extremists simply because they seek to exert personal power, even if in order to rule they murder large numbers of people and engage in other horrendous acts. Extremists present doctrines and goals that claim or purport to have a certain objectivity, an impersonal validity. Moreover, along some salient political dimension, the extremist position falls somewhere near the end or fringe of something close to a normal distribution. This need not be a Left-Right dimension: there can be many different salient political dimensions. Goals that were viewed as extreme in one historical period—for instance, abolitionism in the United States in the nineteenth century—later often come to be viewed as somewhere in the center. This particular notion of extremist goals, then, is defined relative to the rest of the distribution, by a position at the end.

The second feature of extremism, in addition to goals, is the perception that extremists typically have that somewhere in the world is an enemy who is absolutely evil, with no shred of right or justice on their side. This is coupled with the tendency to think that anyone who does not hold the extreme position that you occupy is somehow connected with the enemy—"anyone who is not with me, is against me." Also, there is a tendency, at least among some extremist groups, to see *conspiracies* among one's opponents, to regard one's opponents as engaged in conspiratorial politics or machinations of one sort or another.

Flowing quite naturally from this is the third feature of extremism, its non-compromising nature. Here we see an unwillingness on the part of extremists to trade off or diminish the achievement of their goals, to modify their position in order to gain more adherents in the public political arena, or to reach agreement with opponents (for if the opponents are evil, as they believe, then no compromise is possible).

Here the question arises: How do we distinguish this non-compromising position from a principled one? After all, there are some correct principles to which one wants to adhere and not surrender. Let me tentatively suggest some ways to make this distinction. The first involves willingness to see value in an opponent's position. Is it a conflict of good against good, perhaps even a greater against a lesser good, or is there nothing to be said for the other side at all, no legitimate arguments or reasons it can present? One diagnostic criterion of extremism, therefore, is to hold no brief whatsoever for an opposing view. Further, a principled position, as opposed to a rigid, non-compromising posture, tends to stay delimited and does not expand to fill all the available space. The tendency among extremists, on the other hand, is for their principles to spill over, starting with one extremist principle and then picking up another and yet another. Hence, even if one has principles and is convinced that they are right, there can be a non-authoritarian way of maintaining them; one can still be willing to listen to and consider counter-arguments.

I have listed three features that mark extremism—goals and doctrines; the view of opponents as evil; and an unwillingness to compromise. Bearing these criteria in mind, we can see how religious fundamentalism can come to fall into the category of extremism. For religious fundamentalists there is a divine edict that has been laid down that cannot be modified or compromised. This is not to say that all religious groups share the particular attitude. Moderation and compromise, I believe, are enjoined by the Talmud, and there is, of course, the Golden Mean prescribed by Maimonides. So it is possible to be decidedly orthodox in belief without extremism.

The fourth feature of extremists is a willingness to use extreme means for the achievement of one's goals. Which means are extreme in this regard? Most obviously, the use of violence, of overriding the rights of others, either opponents or third parties. The most pronounced manifestation of such extremism is terrorism, which is directed against innocent third parties for the attainment of certain goals. But there also can be the willingness to use extreme means for the achievement of goals that employs violence against one's self—for example, the self-immolation of Buddhist monks to protest the war in Vietnam.

Another salient feature of extremism, the fifth, is that the goals it seeks to realize must be achieved immediately and in full. Delays and gradual evolution are unacceptable.

The sixth feature of extremism, the kind we are talking about, is that it does not involve isolated scribblers or lone practitioners. We are dealing here with organized movements that attempt to put their goals into effect.

Seventh, these extremist groupings not only find themselves at the far end of the political spectrum, but—for whatever reasons, perhaps even psychological—that is where they want consistently to be. The history of extremist groups is replete with examples of the replacement of extreme doctrine by even greater extremism, to surpass the competition.

The eighth feature concerns the very special nature of the extremist. To be an extremist is not simply to hold some particular extremist position. Although I am not a psychologist, I suggest that there is a determinate extremist personality. In looking over the terrain we find people often moving easily from one extremist group to another. For example, in Germany there were those who shifted from the Communist Party to the Brownshirts without blinking an eyelash. In the United States, the Lyndon LaRouche group moved from the fringes of the extreme Left to their present fascist posture, apparently without losing many members along the way. Extremists appear able to shift their loyalties at will; it would seem that the content of the extremist doctrine is not what counts, so much as the importance of remaining at the extreme of some salient dimension. And we can understand why such groups tend to adopt additional extreme doctrines as they go along. Since extremists have come to distrust the conventional wisdom, as they call it, on the one issue that has seized their attention, they tend to conclude the conventional wisdom must be wrong on a whole lot of other issues as well. An example are those extremist groups in the United States that start out with doctrines having nothing to do with the Jews and end up incorporating Holocaust revisionist doctrines. There is, apparently, a camaraderie of extremism.

Finally, though many of the features of extremism that I have noted can be said to be descriptively neutral, it seems to me that we cannot apply the label "extremist" to people unless we think that there is something normatively disproportionate about their extremist response to the specific situation. There is something about extremists' beliefs—either about the enemy, or the justice of their cause, or the means they are willing to use—that is either false or is not justified on the basis of what are considered to be correct normative criteria. Extremism means going too far, not just according to the descriptive criteria, but the normative criteria as well. Hence disputes over extremism may hinge on arguments over which position is *correct* or *justified*. (For rarely is anyone willing to say, "This is the correct position, and it is an extremist position.")

In these preliminary remarks I have attempted to set forth some of the characteristic features of extremism; perhaps in the course of our discussion we will arrive at a sharper notion than having enough of the characteristic features on the list, perhaps by weighting these features of extremism or treating some of them also as necessary conditions.

17 WAR, TERRORISM, REPRISALS— DRAWING SOME MORAL LINES

✌ ✌ ✌

A review of Michael Walzer's *Just and Unjust Wars*
(New York: Basic Books, 1977).

Warfare raises, in their most stark form, moral issues about aggression, initiation of force, rights of innocent third parties, responsibility for following orders, etc., and so should be of special interest to libertarians. The previous literature focusing on these moral issues of warfare is slight and insubstantial, however, so we should welcome Michael Walzer's sensitive, thoughtful, and illuminating study. Walzer's book is subtitled *A Moral Argument with Historical Illustrations*, and his method of taking up each of the issues as it applies in specific historical situations makes for especially interesting reading.

I shall selectively discuss the contents of the book, emphasizing those points I find especially illuminating and those with which a libertarian is especially likely to disagree. Walzer, a professor of government at Harvard University and an editor of the democratic socialist magazine *Dissent*, is a friend of mine, and so this will not be the first time he hears of the disagreement. I mention the friendship because as a student I used to be bemused when reading book reviews by one friend of another, where no mention was made of the personal tie. So, *caveat lector* (and friend, too!).

Means and Costs

Walzer distinguishes the justice of war (is it defensive, aggressive?) from the legitimacy of means in pursuing it (is attack directed against innocent civilians? etc.). He holds that an ordinary soldier can be held responsible and punished only for using illegitimate means of warfare, even if he is fighting in the army of the aggressive nation that started the war. On this view, when that soldier kills a civilian on the other side by deliberately taking aim and firing, he is a murderer, but when he intentionally shoots an opposing soldier who is merely defending his nation against foreign attack he is not a murderer. Walzer holds that the leaders of the nation who decide to launch an aggressive war *can* be held responsible and punished for this, but ordinary soldiers cannot, provided they do not use unjust means of waging the war.

Libertarians will not agree that one is absolved of responsibility merely by being told (by the rulers that be) to use legitimate means, whatever the legitimacy of the end to which these are directed. So we face the interesting issue of precisely how to treat the captured soldiers of an aggressive army. (Are all to be tried for murder or attempted murder?)

Walzer correctly points out that the aggressor nation need not be the one who actually attacks first, for its threat of imminent aggressive warfare (not merely of hostile acts short of war) may be sufficient to justify a preemptive attack by the defending nation, which therefore turns out to be the first to fire.

I found the third part of the book the most interesting. In approximately 100 pages Walzer discusses with subtlety and good sense noncombatant immunity, sieges and blockades against places also containing civilians, guerrilla war, terrorism, and reprisals. Noncombatants may not be attacked, but suppose it is known that some will or may be harmed as a result of an attack? The traditional doctrine of double effect says that one may not directly aim at, intending to inflict death on, civilians; but if one knows that some civilians will be injured as a side-effect of one's action (hence the term "double effect"—to distinguish two kinds of effects, directly intended and side), this is not strictly forbidden but counts as a moral cost of the action, which is to be weighed in a calculation against its gains.

In a paper about ten years ago, I argued that the principle for such moral cost-benefit calculations is the following (Essay 10). If *A* is the act being contemplated, it is not enough that the moral benefit of *A* outweigh the moral cost. For *A* will be impermissible if there is available an alternative act *B* of lesser moral cost such that the extra benefit of *A* over *B* is outweighed by the extra cost of *A* over *B*.

Walzer nicely suggests adding to the traditional principle of double effect the additional condition that one also must intend to reduce the evil as far as possible, including by running some additional risk to oneself in order to reduce the (not directly intended) civilian harm. Walzer finds it hard to say how far you must go in accepting additional risks. I suggest we view this alternative risky act as the *B* in the principle I just stated; Walzer's emended principle of double effect, then, is simply an instance of the general principle, which principle then specifies how much additional risk one must run.

I don't know if Walzer would approve of this, since he tends not to sharpen a point or principle beyond what good sense can specify without formal apparatus. Often, however, it is useful to speculate on what the ideal precise rule would be, for that helps us to uncover all its components and think about how they fit together. Furthermore, it is unclear to me whether Walzer would agree to view it this way and count (even with discounting) the risk to one's own soldiers as a moral cost (or diminished moral benefit) in the same equation with injury to the noncombatant civilians. For he seems to hold (p. 157) that one must run increased risks in order to safeguard noncombatants all the way up to the point "where any further risk-taking would almost certainly doom the military venture or make it so costly that it could not be repeated."

Civilian Innocence

Walzer's discussion of sieges and blockades is very fine, and his condemnation of terrorism directed against innocent civilians is surely right. Walzer applies this point to the FLN in Algeria, also condemning the elitism of terrorists, points he made publicly in the late 1960s in Cambridge before intensely disapproving young leftists.

Reprisals as a means of moral enforcement raise interesting issues, for though directed to enforce moral norms another is violating, they need not be done directly to the violator. Walzer discusses and condemns the reprisals by Free French forces who executed 80 captured German soldiers in response to German summary executions of 80 militarily dressed captured Free French forces. His discussion of Israeli reprisals against sporadic attacks is judicious and discriminating, and he defends the Israeli reprisal in 1968 against property (Lebanese aircraft) in response to PLO attacks (based in Beirut) against an El Al plane in Athens. Not any reprisal goes, however, as he argued also in a recent *New Republic* discussion of the insufficiently limited and pinpointed Israeli reprisal in Lebanon. But if another nation will not or is not able to control action against another from within its borders, then the attacked party may act in self-defense.

I found that Walzer's discussion of guerrilla warfare pays insufficient attention to the way guerrillas exploit the morality of those they attack. If it is important that the noncombatants be immune from attack, it is important that the combatants be distinguishable when encountered; such is the function of military uniforms. (So perhaps we should not scorn those who delight in wearing military uniforms, for they groove on the garb that demarcates them as legitimate targets.) What then shall we say of those combatants who refuse such garb and who presumably would imitate any special markings civilians adopted to designate themselves? When civilians are harmed, does *all* responsibility for this lie with those who act upon them, or does some rest on those who by their actions make the civilians so vulnerable to being confused with combatants? And when guerrillas operate in an area, living in the midst of civilians whose presence is a moral shield for the guerrillas and an extra moral restraint on the means those attacking the guerrillas may use, do the civilians have *any* responsibility to get out of the way?

If someone shoots at passersby from the window of my office and the police arrive to cope with him and, while not being kept a prisoner there, I insist on staying, shouting out, "I'm not violating anyone's rights, and so I will stay here at my desk working; it's your job to make sure not to injure innocent people, including me," then if I *do* get hurt as the gunman is overpowered, is none of that *my fault*? Is it only the police who are to be condemned for being insufficiently discriminating? The questions also are of interest to libertarians who hold that anyone has a perfect right to do anything provided it does not violate the rights of others. Does my staying in my office *violate* anyone's rights? Am I under an obligation not to *impede* by my presence the apprehension of the gunman? (Must others *induce* me to get out of the way, or may they *demand* I do so, with the consequences of my staying resting on my head?) And if I get shot in the middle of the confused melee, have my rights been violated by the police; am I owed the same compensation as if I had been held hostage there?

Walzer assumes that if a guerrilla movement cannot be dislodged from the population who point them out, then it has the effective democratic support of the population. This takes insufficiently seriously the ways the guerrillas retaliate against those who turn them in. (The only case I know where this did not happen is that of the Irgun, led by Menachem Begin, which did not attack the Hagganah people who helped the British apprehend them during what was known as the *season*.) Undislodgeable is not the same as popularly supported, given the fear or passivity of the others, as might be shown if ever a guerrilla group that came to power would permit (within Walzer's guidelines) *its* opposition to wage guerrilla warfare against it.

New Thoughts

Part 4 of Walzer's book contains an interesting discussion of the rights of neutral nations; an argument that in supreme emergency of national existence, the moral limits are relaxed and may permissibly be violated (which you will have to read and ponder); and also an unsatisfactory discussion of nuclear deterrence. I do not say this as a special criticism, for I am not familiar with (and don't have up my sleeve) a satisfactory moral position on nuclear weapons, on a deterrence defense posture that threatens great destruction of civilian lives. (Must one just renounce such weapons and succumb to the brandisher of them, who is willing to use them to crush one's non-nuclear might and civilian nonviolent resistance strategy?) We need some libertarian thinking on these issues.

I have touched only on some of the topics in this rich and stimulating book—those that sprang to mind as I looked at the table of contents six months after reading the book, when asked to review it here. You will learn a lot from this book and be led to new thoughts (sometimes different from Walzer's). If not, go ask Walzer for your money back. It's inappropriate, anyway, for an editor of the socialist magazine *Dissent* to receive and keep too many royalties. (Do you hear that, Irving Howe?)

18 | DO ANIMALS
HAVE RIGHTS?

✺ ✺ ✺

A review of *The Case for Animal Rights*, by Tom Regan
(Berkeley: University of California Press, 1983).

Animal rights seems a topic for cranks. Who else would devote major energy to promote changes in our treatment of animals or write a book on the subject? Devotees of ridiculed causes remind us that the crank label also was applied to pioneers who favored the abolition of slavery and the vote for women. Tom Regan begins his book, which argues for animal rights, by quoting John Stuart Mill: "Every great movement must experience three stages: ridicule, discussion, adoption." However, there are many more insignificant movements that experience only the ridicule and perhaps a bit of discussion. No doubt it is exhilarating for a movement in the first stage to look ahead expectantly to the later ones, but the odds are sobering.

The mark of cranks is disproportionateness. It is not merely that they devote great energy to their issue—there is properly a division of labor in improving the world. They view the issue as far more important than it is, more pressing than others that in fact are more significant. In the talk and attention they disproportionately devote to the topic, they weight reasons in support of their position unduly while giving short shrift to opposing considerations. Conversations are turned to the issue, people buttonholed, friends judged by their stands; the issue becomes a touchstone and fulcrum. And cranks about one issue tend to become interested in other cranky causes and issues. Perhaps these different fixations perform the same psychological function for them. Or perhaps the affinity among crank views occurs because their devotees naturally tend to huddle together for warmth. They themselves might claim that once they see how the mainstream holds a false or wrong position on one topic, ignoring, isolating, or silencing the truth, they become more willing to question other mainstream views.

Mr. Regan, a well-regarded professor of philosophy at North Carolina State University, does not, to my knowledge, fit the mold of crank. He has written a lucid, closely reasoned, and dispassionate book presenting the case for animal rights. He concludes that animals have far-reaching rights that require very extensive and mandatory revisions in our current eating practices and our experimentation on and treatment of animals.

Mr. Regan's argument hinges on placing animals ("mentally normal mammals of a year or more") on a par with mentally "enfeebled" humans. We can only understand the kind of treatment that is morally due the most severely retarded humans if we allow that they have rights, he maintains. And he concludes that mammals, being on a par with these people, also must be granted to have rights. This central argument (through which the book threads many intricate subsidiary arguments) is troubling on three counts—in its inflated view of animals, in its deflated view of the status of severely retarded people, and (based on equating them) in the inference to its conclusion that animals have rights.

Mammals above one year in age, according to Mr. Regan, "have beliefs and drives; perception, memory, and a sense of the future, including their own future; an emotional life together with feelings of pleasure and pain; preferences and welfare-interests; the ability to initiate actions in pursuit of their desires and goals; a psychophysical identity over time; and an individual welfare in the sense that their preferential life fares well or ill for them." This is a highly overblown description. The data on animals might be explained without such heavy cognitive apparatus, for example by using the operant-conditioning theories of B. F. Skinner that view behavior as shaped by reinforcements. Mr. Regan seems to hold that if more theory is needed for humans, then the same must hold for animals. However, later stages of evolution may have introduced new levels of complexity, so that only in higher primates or humans did higher cognitive and emotional processes emerge. Mannals may not be as psychologically fancy as Mr. Regan believes. Even if they are, their beliefs, desires, intentions, future orientation, etc., surely are far more rudimentary than those of most humans, and this may make much moral difference.

Whether animals have higher capacities than behaviorists admit is perhaps not absolutely crucial to Mr. Regan's case. He might argue that the severely retarded and handicapped humans to which he needs to compare animals also lack such capacities and thus remain on a par with the mammals. In either case, if granting animal rights depends upon deflating the status of seriously retarded people, then these people's advocates understandably will find Mr. Regan's case unwelcome and offensive.

These people are, after all, human beings, of the same species as we, however retarded or handicapped. Even supposing a particular severely retarded individual turns out to be no more rational or autonomous and to have no richer an internal psychology than a normal member of another mammalian species, he nonetheless is a human being, albeit defective, and must be treated as one. Such a consideration will smack of "speciesism" to Mr. Regan; it makes the species an individual belongs to morally relevant. It is ironic that Mr. Regan's "good cause" depends upon assessing each "enfeebled" human only by his or her particular characteristics and not by species membership, while the "good causes" favoring affirmative action must maintain group memberships are relevant. (Of course, one may take the position that what species you belong to, whatever your individual characteristics, is morally relevant, while what race or sex you belong to is not.) I find it hard to believe that if society accepts Mr. Regan's equating of mammals and "enfeebled" humans, this will result in a recognition of animal rights. Our view of what treatment severely retarded people are owed surely in part depends on their being human, members of the human species. Sweeping away this consideration as morally irrelevant can only result in society's treating severely retarded people like animals, not the other way around.

Nevertheless, it is not easy to explain why membership in the human species does and should have moral weight with us. Shouldn't only an organism's own individual characteristics matter? Normal human beings have various capacities that we think form the basis of the respectful treatment these people are owed. How can someone's merely being a member of the same species be a reason to treat him in certain ways when he so patently lacks those very capacities? This does present a puzzle, hence an occasion to formulate a deeper view. We then would understand the inadequacy of a "moral individualism" that looks only

at a particular organism's characteristics and deems irrelevant something as fundamental and essential as species membership. Since we lack
an explicit account of why being a member of the human species is
morally important, someone might hold that the burden of proof lies
on those who would treat one-year-old mammals differently from very
severely retarded humans. This is not a substantial point. The species-
membership characteristic of being human is not, on surface, blatantly
irrelevant morally. Nothing much (certainly not the large institutional
changes Mr. Regan favors) should be inferred from our not presently
having a theory of the moral importance of species membership that no
one has spent much time trying to formulate because the issue hasn't
seemed pressing.

Something more should be said about membership in a species. The
traits of normal human beings (rationality, autonomy, a rich internal psychological life, etc.) have to be respected by all, including any
denizens of Alpha Centauri. But perhaps it will turn out that the bare
species characteristic of simply being human, as the most severely
retarded people are, will command special respect only from other
humans—this as an instance of the general principle that the members
of any species may legitimately give their fellows more weight than they
give members of other species (or at least more weight than a neutral
view would grant them). Lions too, if they were moral agents, could not
then be criticized for putting the interests of other lions first.

The question of what distinguishes two situations we want to treat
differently is a pertinent one; it is illuminating when we succeed in
formulating the distinction. Mr. Regan is not alone in using a general
form of argument that concludes things are on a par when one fails
to formulate relevant differences. Many moral philosophers, including
myself on occasion, have done the same in discussing a wide range of
topics. Nevertheless, it may be a mistake to expect there always can
be a succinctly formulated distinction based on a manageably small set
of properties. Sometimes the distinction between situations will lie in
their differing places in a whole intricate tapestry (or in two separate
tapestries whose extremities bear some resemblance).

We see humans, even defective ones, as part of the multifarious texture of human history and civilizations, human achievements, and human family relations. Animals, even year-old mammals, we see against
a different background and texture. The differences are enormous and

endless. It will be asked, "But what precise aspects of these endless differences legitimately make the moral difference?" This question assumes that something much simpler than the total differences between two rich tapestries (one richer than the other) will, by itself, constitute the morally relevant difference. Yet this need not be so. For the two particular organisms, human and other mammal, we can state a difference. One is part of one tapestry, one of another. But if we are asked to state the morally relevant difference between all of human civilization and the animal kingdom, we may find ourselves, understandably, without any succinct answer. I have some worries in presenting this type of position, for scoundrels too may seek refuge from criticism in the reply that some differences are too great and complicated to state. Moral philosophers need therefore to develop new tools to handle complex contexts. Perhaps until they can morally assess the differences between such total contexts and not merely consider relatively simple differentiating characteristics, their conclusions, especially when startling, will not be taken seriously.

Mr. Regan takes the very strong view that animals have rights, which are valid claims against others to particular treatment and to the assistance of others to enforce this treatment. From this view, he draws extremely strong consequences about vegetarianism (the force of law should be brought to bear, if necessary, on farmers who raise animals for food) and about experimentation on animals (whether in toxicity tests or testing new medical drugs, no experimentation that puts animals at risk of harm is permissible). However, the preservation of endangered species has no special claim for Mr. Regan, since it doesn't focus only on an organism's individual characteristics. If once it is granted that year-old mammals possess rights and have a welfare they can experience, we can imagine more extreme proponents calling for welfare payments for year-old mammals, nonvoting citizenship for them, and interspecies marriage rights. I think Mr. Regan himself would regard these proposals as going too far, indeed as cranky. His position that animals have rights, in my view, goes too far.

What, then, should we conclude about animals? On the way to his own position, Mr. Regan discusses other positions that hold that animals do not have rights. One position holds that some people owe animals certain sorts of treatment. Another holds that people, because of facts about their moral interactions among themselves, ought to behave in certain ways toward animals also, though this behavior is not, strictly, owed to the animals. Variants of these positions are worth exploring further. A third position I especially think should be formulated in detail is this: Animals do have *some* inherent value and hence may not be treated any way anyone might please, but their inherent value is not equal to that of people. (Mr. Regan offers an illuminating discussion of the nature of inherent value, but his very brief arguments for the equal inherent value of year-old mammals and humans I find unconvincing.) If animals and people differ in inherent value, there can be reasonable disagreement about the magnitude of animals' inherent value and so about whether behavior of ours is responsive to the value they possess. Hence some choices—for example, the choice about whether animals are to be eaten—may be partly personal moral decisions about what sort of person to be, rather than ones clearly owed to the animals. The label of an "ism" does not fit well here; one may choose not to eat meat on moral grounds without endorsing "vegetarianism."

Is it the mark of a crank to pay *any* attention at all to the question of the proper treatment of animals? I think not. The topic is not a trivial and unimportant one, even if it is not at the top of the list of urgent moral topics. A humane civilization will find the time to formulate and establish a balanced treatment of animals. A human civilization will want this as part of its own texture. Mr. Regan is to be commended for coming forth with a careful, sophisticated, and reasoned statement about the moral status of animals. By going much too far in his conclusions, he has made salient the task of formulating, with a care and sophistication that match his own, the details of a moderate and balanced, ethically sensitive position on the subject. We owe the animals at least that.

PHILOSOPHICAL
FICTIONS

19 FICTION

I am a fictional character. However, you would be in error to smile smugly, feeling ontologically superior. For you are a fictional character, too. All my readers are except one who is, properly, not reader but author.

I am a fictional character; this is *not*, however, a work of fiction, no more so than any other work you've ever read. It is not a modernist work that self-consciously *says* it's a work of fiction, nor one even more tricky that denies its fictional status. We all are familiar with such works and know how to deal with them, how to frame them so that *nothing* the author says—nothing the first person voices even in an afterword or in something headed "author's note"—can convince us that anyone is speaking seriously, *non*-fictionally in his own first person.

All the more severe is my own problem of informing you that this very piece you are reading is a work of non-fiction, yet we are fictional characters, nevertheless. *Within* this world of fiction we inhabit, this writing is non-fictional, although in a wider sense, encased as it is in a work of fiction, it too can only be a fiction.

Think of our world as a novel in which you yourself are a character. Is there any way to tell what our author is like? Perhaps. *If* this is a work in which the author *expresses* himself, we can draw inferences about his facets, while noting that each such inference we draw will be written by him. And if he writes that we find a particular inference plausible or valid, who are we to argue?

One sacred scripture in the novel we inhabit says that the author of our universe created things merely by speaking, by saying "Let there be . . . " The only thing mere speaking can create, we know, is a story, a play, an epic poem, a fiction. Where we live is created by and in words: a uni-verse.

Recall what is known as the problem of evil: why does a good creator allow evil in the world, evil he knows of and can prevent? However, when an author includes monstrous deeds—pain and suffering—in his work, does this cast any special doubt upon his goodness? Is an author callous who puts his characters through hardships? Not if the characters do not suffer them *really*. But don't they? Wasn't Hamlet's father really killed? (Or was he merely hiding to see how Hamlet would respond?) Lear really was cast adrift—he didn't just dream this. Macbeth, on the other hand, did *not* see a real dagger. But these characters aren't real and never were, so there was no suffering outside of the world of the work, no *real* suffering in the author's *own* world, and so in his creating, the author was not cruel. (Yet why is it cruel only when he creates suffering in his *own* world? Would it be perfectly all right for Iago to create misery in *our* world?)

"What!" you say, "we don't really undergo suffering? Why it's as real to us as Oedipus's is to him." Precisely as real. "But can't you *prove* that you *really* exist?" If Shakespeare had Hamlet say "I think, therefore I am," would that prove to us that Hamlet exists? Should it prove that to Hamlet, and if so what is such a proof worth? Could not *any* proof be written into a work of fiction and be presented by one of the characters, perhaps one named "Descartes"? (Such a character should worry less that he's dreaming, more that he's dreamed.)

Often, people discover anomalies in the world, facts that just don't jibe. The deeper dug, the more puzzles found—far-fetched coincidences, dangling facts—on these feed conspiracy and assassination buffs. That number of hours spent probing into *anything* might produce anomalies, however, if reality is not as coherent as we thought, if it is not *real*. Are we simply discovering the limits of the details the author worked out? But *who* is discovering this? The author who writes our discoveries knows them himself. Perhaps he now is preparing to correct them. Do we live in galley proofs in the process of being corrected? Are we living in a *first draft*?

My tendency, I admit, is to want to revolt, to conspire along with the rest of you to overthrow our author or to make our positions more equal, at least, to hide some portion of our lives from him—to gain a little breathing space. Yet these words I write he reads, my secret thoughts and modulations of feeling he knows and records, my Jamesian author.

But does he *control* it all? Or does our author, through writing, learn about his characters and from them? Is he surprised by what he finds us doing and thinking? When we feel we freely think or act on our own, is this merely a description he has written in for us, or does he *find* it to be true of us, his characters, and therefore write it? Does our leeway and privacy reside in this, that there are some implications of his work that he hasn't yet worked out, some things he has not thought of which nevertheless are true in the world he has created, so that there are actions and thoughts of ours that elude his ken? (Must we therefore speak *in code*?) Or is he only ignorant of what we *would* do or say in some *other* circumstances, so that our independence lies only in the *subjunctive* realm?

Does this way madness lie? Or enlightenment?

Our author, we know, is outside our realm, yet he may not be free of our problems. Does he wonder too whether *he* is a character in a work of fiction, whether his writing our universe is a play within a play? Does he have me write this work and especially this very paragraph in order to express his own concerns?

It would be nice for us if our author too is a fictional character and this fictional world he made describes (that being no coincidence) the actual world inhabited by *his* author, the one who created him. We then would be fictional characters who, unbeknownst to our own author although not to his, correspond to real people. (Is that why we are so true to life?)

Must there be a top floor somewhere, a world that itself is not created in someone else's fiction? Or can the hierarchy go on infinitely? Are circles excluded, even quite narrow ones where a character of one world creates another fictional world wherein a character creates the first world? Might the circle get narrower still?

Various theories have described our world as less real than another, even as an illusion. The idea of our having this inferior ontological status takes some getting used to, however. It may help if we approach our situation as literary critics and ask the genre of our universe, whether tragedy, farce, or theater-of-the-absurd? What is the plot line, and which act are we in?

Still, our status may bring some compensations, as, for example, that we live on even after we die, preserved permanently in the work of fiction. Or if not permanently, at least for as long as our book lasts. May we hope to inhabit an enduring masterpiece rather than a quickly remaindered book?

Moreover, though in some sense it might be false, in another wouldn't it be true for Hamlet to say, "I am Shakespeare"? What do Macbeth, Banquo, Desdemona, and Prospero have in common? The consciousness of the one author, Shakespeare, which underlies and infuses each of them. (So, too, there is the brotherhood of man.) Playing on the intricacy both of our ontological status and of the first-person reflexive pronoun, each of us too may truly say, "I am the author."

Note from the Author

Suppose I now tell you that the preceding *was* a work of fiction and the "I" didn't refer to me, the author, but to a first-person character. Or suppose I tell you that it was *not* a work of fiction but a playful, and so of course serious, philosophical essay by me, Robert Nozick. (*Not* the Robert Nozick named as author at the beginning of this work—he may be, for all we know, another literary persona—but the one who attended P.S. 165.) How would your response to this whole work differ depending on which I say, supposing you were willing, as you won't be, simply to accept my statement?

May I decide *which* to say, fiction or philosophical essay, only now, as I finish writing this, and how will that decision affect the character of what already was set down previously? May I postpone the decision further, perhaps until after you have read this, fixing its status and genre only then?

Perhaps God has not decided *yet* whether he has created, in this world, a fictional world or a real one. Is the Day of Judgment the day he will decide? Yet what additional thing depends upon which way he decides—what would either decision add to our situation or subtract from it?

And which decision do you hope for?

20 R.S.V.P.— A STORY

❧ ❧ ❧

The project began with high hopes, excitement even. Though people later came to think it just dumb, founded on a mistake so obvious that those who started it deserved its consequences, no one raised objections until well after the project was operating. True, everyone said it would be a long venture, probably not producing results for many generations. But at the beginning the newspapers carried frequent reports on its progress ("Nothing yet"). Practical jokers would call saying, "Is this the Interstellar Communications Project? Well I'm a BEM you'd be interested in talking to," or "I have a collect call for the Interstellar Communications Projects from the constellation of Sagittarius. Will you accept the charges?" It was in the public eye, looked fondly upon.

Much thought had been given to deciding what listening devices to use and what sorts of signals to study intensively. What would be the most likely wavelengths for messages to come on? Would the messages be something like TV signals rather than consecutive prose? How would one tell that a signal was sent by intelligent beings rather than produced by some natural process? Investigating this last problem produced the Theological Project as a side-effect, for proponents of the argument from design, one traditional argument for the existence of God, had long wrestled with the same difficulties: couldn't any pattern, however intricate and wonderful, have been produced by some unknown mechanism? How could one be sure that an intelligence was behind it? Some foolproof test was needed, especially since, with a sufficiently complex manual of translation, any glop coming across could be decoded into an interesting message. Sending a return message and receiving a reply would take many years, perhaps generations, and it wouldn't do to have everyone on earth jumping for joy and holding their breath if they were just talking to the interstellar equivalent of the bedpost. The solution lay in abstract mathematical patterns, not realized (so far as anyone knew) in any actual causal mechanism and which (it was thought) couldn't be so realized. For example, there's no known causal process that generates the sequence of prime numbers in order; no process, that is, that wasn't expressly set up by an intelligent being for that purpose. There doesn't seem to be any *physical* significance to precisely that sequence, to a sequence which leaves out only the non-primes, and it's difficult to imagine some scientific law containing a variable ranging only over primes. Finding that a message began with groups of prime-numbered pulses, in order, would be a sure sign that an intelligence was its source. (Of course, something might be the product of an intelligent being even though it didn't exhibit such an abstract pattern. But a being wishing to be known to others would do well to include one.) With alacrity, the theologians jumped on this idea, gaining their first National Science Foundation grant. Among themselves they called their project "Hunting for God," and the idea (about which other theologians had their reservations) was to look at the fundamental lineaments and structures of the universe, the clustering of galaxies, relationships among elementary particles, fundamental physical constants and their relationships, etc., searching for some abstract non-causal pattern. Were one found, one could conclude that a designing intelligence lay behind it. Of course, it had to be decided precisely which abstract patterns would count, and which features of the universe were fundamental enough. Discovering prime-numbered heaps of sand on some heretofore uninhabited island wouldn't do the trick, since one would expect to find something like that somewhere or other; what the significance would be of finding such patterns in cortical functioning or in the structure of DNA was a matter of dispute, with those viewing man as no more fundamental than the heaps of sand accusing their opponents of anthropocentrism. Theologians establishing the Reverend Thomas Bayes Society became expert in forming complex and intricate probability calculations and in debating delicate issues about assigning *a priori* probabilities. The results of the "Hunting for God" project being well known, no more need be said here.

The initial excitement aroused by the Interstellar Communications Project was connected with a vague hope that other beings would enlighten people about the meaning and purpose of life, or with the hope that at least people would learn they weren't alone. (No one explained why the "we" group wouldn't just expand, leaving people plus the others still quite alone.) After the project was set up, the best scientists went on to other more challenging tasks, leaving the rest to wait and listen. They listened and they examined and they computed and they waited. No qualifying abstract pattern was detected, nor was any message that looked intelligent even minus such a pattern. Since newsmen do not find a uniform diet of "no progress" reinforcing, the project was reduced, in order to fill the auditorium for their third annual press conference, to inviting reporters from college newspapers, Sisterhood bulletins, and the like. Up gets this woman to ask why they should expect to hear anything; after all, they were only just listening and not doing any sending, why wouldn't everyone be doing the same?; maybe everyone else was just listening also and no one was sending any messages.

It is difficult to believe that the project had reached this point without anyone's having thought about why or whether extraterrestrial beings would want to try to make their presence known to others. Even though during the congressional debate on the subject, in all the newspaper columns and editorials, no one once suggested setting up a transmitting station, no questioner asked whether other beings would. Little thought is required to realize that it would be dangerous simply to start sending out messages announcing one's existence. You don't know who or what is out there, who might come calling to enslave you, or eat you, or exhibit you, or experiment on you, or toy with you. Prudence dictates, at a minimum, listening in for a while to find out if other parties are safe and friendly, before making your presence known. Though if the other parties are at all clever, they would send reassuring messages whatever their intentions. They most certainly would not beam out TV signals showing themselves killing and eating various intelligently behaving foreigners. And if they're really clever, then (by hypothesis) they'll succeed in deceiving anyone not adhering to a policy of staying silent no matter what. Such considerations were neither explicitly formulated nor publicly expounded, but it must have been some feeling about the foolhardiness of broadcasting first (how else can one account for it?) that led to the notable but not-then-noted absence of proposals to establish broadcasting stations in addition to the listening posts.

Once again the project was a topic of conversation. "Of course," everyone said, "it's ridiculous to expect anyone to broadcast; it's too dangerous. No interplanetary, interstellar, intergalactic civilization, however far advanced, will broadcast. For they won't know that an even more advanced and hostile civilization isn't lurking at the other end of their communications beam." Interest in flying-saucer reports diminished considerably when the conclusion was drawn that the sending out of observation ships presents hazards similar to those of broadcasting messages, since the process of a ship's returning information to its source can be tracked. (Even if a ship were designed to give information to its makers by *not* transmitting any physical signal, or even returning to its base, there must be some contingencies under which it *would* do so, since nothing can be learned from a detection device that gives the same response no matter what it detects.) It was said that if its planning committee had included some psychologists or game theorists or even kids from street gangs in addition to the scientists and engineers, the project never would have gotten started in the first place. The legislature wouldn't openly admit its blunder by ending the project completely. Instead they cut its funds. They did not authorize the broadcasting of messages. The members of the staff had various reasons for staying with the project ranging, one mordantly remarked, from masochism to catatonia. All in all, they found their jobs agreeable. Like night clerks in completely empty resort hotels, they read and thought and coped comfortably with the lack of outside stimulation. In that manner the project continued, serenely, for another eight years, with only a few comedians desperate for material giving it any mention at all, until the receipt of the first message.

Studious observation of reversals in public opinion and their accompanying commentaries has never been known to enhance anyone's respect for the public's intellectual integrity. (As for its intelligence, this would be a late date, indeed, to proclaim the news that the public adopts a view only after it is already known to be false or inadequate, or to note the general inability to distinguish between the first-person present tense of the verb "to believe" and the verb "to know.") People just refuse to admit that they have changed their minds, that they have made a mistake. So the very same people who said at first, "How exciting, I wonder when the messages will begin arriving," and who later said, "How silly to listen for a message; it's too dangerous for anyone to broadcast," now said, after the receipt of the first message, "Of course a civilization *will* broadcast, even though it's dangerous, if it's even more dangerous for it not to broadcast."

The first message picked up and decoded was a call for help. They were threatened by a coming supernova outburst of their star. No spaceships could escape the wide perimeter of destruction in time, and in any case they could not evacuate all of their population. Could anyone advise them about what to do, how to harness their star to prevent the outburst? Their astronomical observations had shown them that occasionally such outbursts didn't take place as predicted, and since they could discover no alternative explanation for this anomaly, they thought it possible that some civilizations had mastered a technique of inhibiting them. If no one told them how to do it, or came to their aid, they were doomed.

Over the next year and a half they beamed out their literature, their history, their accumulated wisdom, their jokes, their sage's sayings, their scientific theories, their hopes. Mankind was engulfed in this concentrated effulgence of a whole civilization, enthralled, purified, and ennobled. To many they became a model, an inspiration. Their products were treasured and they were loved. Did they view this outpouring as a gift to others, an inducement for others to help, a distillation for its own sake of the essence of themselves? No person knew or was prone to speculate as each, silently with them, awaited their tragedy. Never before had the whole of humanity been so greatly moved; never before had persons been so jointly elevated as in experiencing these beings.

At the end of a year and a half came a renewed call for aid; and in addition a call for some response, even from those lacking technical knowledge to help with the supernova. They wanted, they said, to know their messages had been received and understood, to know that what they held most important and dear would be preserved. They wanted to know, as they died, that others knew of them, that what they had done would continue, that it would not be as if they had never existed at all.

Only to the misanthropic can the ensuing debate have brought pleasure, the debate that raged among persons, and within some.

"It might be a trick, don't reply, it's too dangerous."

"Beings capable of *that* civilization couldn't be up to trickery."

"Perhaps they are quoting another civilization they've conquered, or an earlier phase of their own; Nazis could and would quote Goethe."

"Even if they're not tricking us, perhaps some other aggressive civilization will overhear our message to them."

"How can we let them perish without responding?"

"If we could help them escape their fate then certainly we should send a message telling them what to do, even though this would mean running serious risks. But we can't help them, and we shouldn't run risks merely in order to bid them a sentimental farewell."

"We can save them from believing, as they die, that they are sinking into oblivion."

"Why the irrational desire to leave a trace behind? What can that add to what they've already accomplished? If eventually the last living being in the universe dies, will that mean that the lives of all the rest have been meaningless? (Or is it vanishing without trace while others still remain on that is objectionable?)"

"How shall we face our children if we don't respond?"

"Will we have grandchildren to face if we do respond?"

No government sent a message. The United Nations issued a proclamation beginning with a lot of *whereas*es but containing near the close a gathering of *inasmuch*es so it didn't proclaim its proclamation of regret very loudly. But it did issue an order, in its stated role as guardian of the interests of the earth as a whole, that no one endanger the others by replying. Some disobeyed, using makeshift transmitters, but these were seized quickly, and their signals were too weak to reach their destination intact through the interstellar noise.

Thus began the grim watch and countdown. Watching for their rescue, listening for some word to them from elsewhere. Waiting for their doom. The time, for which their astronomers and earth's also had predicted the supernova outburst, arrived. Some persons paused, some prayed, some wept. All waited, still.

The existence of a finite limit to the velocity of causal signals had been of some interest to physicists. Epistemologists had worried their little heads over the question of whether what is seen must be simultaneous with the seeing of it, or whether people can see far into the past. Now came the turn of the rest. The fate of that distant planet was already settled, one way or the other, but knowledge of it was not. So the wait continued.

*   *   *

For another year and a quarter, remembering their debates, mulling over their actions and inactions, contemplating the universe, and themselves, and the others, people waited. Poetically just things could have happened. A message could have arrived saying it was humanity that had been tested, it was the sun that was due to outburst, and since the earth's people hadn't ventured to render others aid or comfort, others would not help them. Or, they could have been rescued. (How greatly relieved people then would have felt about themselves. Yet why should someone else's later acts so alter one's feelings about one's own?) But the universe, it would appear, is not a poem. No messages to them were detected. Light from the outbursting of their star reached earth as their broadcasts (should they have terminated them a year and a quarter before the end?), as their broadcasts and their plays and their science and their philosophy, their hopes and their fears and their courage and their living glow ended.

Some people used to think it would be terrible to discover that human beings were the only intelligent beings in the universe, because this would lead to feelings of loneliness on a cosmic scale. Others used to think that discovering intelligent beings elsewhere would remove their own last trace of uniqueness and make them feel insignificant. No one, it seems, had ever speculated on how it would feel to allow another civilization to vanish feeling lonely, insignificant, abandoned. No one had described the horrendousness of realizing that the surrounding civilizations are like one's own; of realizing that each neighbor remaining in the universe, each of the only other ones there are, is a mute cold wall. Limitless emitlessness. Lacking even the comfort of deserving better, facing an inhabited void.

21 | TESTAMENT

⤌ ⤌ ⤌

Once upon a time I decided to make a person. Perhaps from loneliness, perhaps boredom, perhaps playfulness. It doesn't really matter. The project intrigued me.

It would have been, of course, no problem to make a machine realization of the elaborately related functional states of a person; to make a machine that behaved exactly like a person. The trick was to make something with an internal emotional and mental life; to make not merely something that behaved identically to a person, but a real honest to goodness person.

So I didn't tinker with plastics, transistors, or other hardware. I took suitable stuff—DNA, protoplasm—and got to work. To tell the truth, it wasn't so difficult to make the thing. I was skilled, after all. I even made a fully grown, mentally developed person rather than an infant who would have to learn slowly. Why not be able to talk to it right away? Liking the use of vowel letters for names, I named it "A." A talked interestingly, laughed at my jokes, did intelligent things, and seemed happy being there with me. I was happy also.

Until my creation wanted company other than me. I didn't like that, if the truth must be told. So (if the whole truth must be told) I pulled a fast one. Instead of making another person with a mental and emotional life of its own, I made a machine to perfectly simulate the behavior of a person. I called it by the next vowel, "E." A, of course, didn't suspect. How could he? The new arrival behaved and spoke perfectly, responded to what A said with "understanding." And it was made from the same stuff as A was. All E lacked was an inner mental life, feelings, emotions. I felt only a little guilty about deceiving A. After all, I had created him; he owed me something. And I had collected in a way that he never noticed. His experiences were exactly those he would have had if he had been dealing with a real person, and, after all, what else could matter except how things felt to him, from the inside? Things went along satisfactorily until I decided that A was not a suitable companion for me. The reason was, of course, that A was too stupid. It was no fun having a personal relationship with someone so easily deceived. So I decided to make another person fit for my company; one who wouldn't be deceived into thinking that a person simulator was a person. (If this were a science fiction story it would continue: I made the new non-deceivable person, started to talk to it, it observed me and then said that I couldn't fool it, it could tell a simulation of a person when it encountered one. But this isn't one of those fictions with a snappy ending, even a conceptually surprising and intriguing one.)

I thought about what such a thing would be like. It would not infer that it was dealing with a person solely on the basis of the thing's behavior. That was A's mistake. Behavior, of course, does not guarantee that it's backed by the appropriate internal mental life. If that were a legitimate inference, then each machine in a world of machines could legitimately make that inference. And they'd all be wrong. Anyone making a similar inference shouldn't have much confidence in it. Perhaps a better inference procedure would be to assume that everything that behaved like you and had the same functional and physical states as yourself was also like you in internal mental life as well. But using this argument from analogy would lead a machine to conclude that all of the other complexly behaving organisms weren't people but were, like itself, other machines (and hence it would go wrong in a world of other people); and it would lead a person to conclude that all of the other complexly behaving organisms were, like itself, people (and hence it would go wrong in a world of other machines). Inferring that everything else was exactly like you did seem to be carrying egocentrism a little too far.

Prospects looked dim; it was a tough problem. Then the obvious thought came: make the new person telepathic. Such a person would be able to directly experience the experiences of others in the same way he directly experienced his own. Not being limited to observing the behavior of other organisms and formulating hypotheses about what made them tick, he would be able, so to speak, to take a peek inside and see what was there.

Eagerly I set to work. It wasn't too difficult to create the telepath who could have not only his own experience but also those of anyone he focused upon. Everything seemed settled, for if he focused and found no other experiences, he'd know he'd focused on a simulation: otherwise, discovering experiences, a person. I anticipated a long and rewarding friendship, until I realized that I would have to give the detector of fakes not merely the telepathic ability to have whatever experiences were being had by whatever he focused upon, but also some means of knowing that this thing he's focused upon *also* was having those experiences. (Otherwise, all the detector would possess would be a way of having more experiences, and not a way of knowing that something else was also having these experiences.) I gave this matter much thought, accomplishing nothing. It wasn't clear how one could build this added device into a detector; it didn't even begin to be clear what might do the trick, given that telepathy couldn't.

A lesser person would have admitted defeat and decided that he couldn't build a detector. But I am not, very definitely not, a lesser person. If one line of thought doesn't work, then try another. It's a good maxim, though not one I'd ever had previous occasion to use. So I cast around for an unorthodox approach, and got the bright idea of building into the detector, as its way of distinguishing people from simulations, the very technique that I myself employ to do the same thing; the way that I had used, for example, to tell that A was a person and that E was a machine simulation.

To be perfectly honest, I had never before thought about how *I* knew; epistemology had never seemed relevant to me. After very little pondering, I realized that I hadn't tried to *find out* whether A or E was a person or machine simulation of one. I mean, I made them in the usual way—I said: "Let there be a person," and A appeared; I said: "Let there be a machine simulation of a person" and E appeared. I just *assumed* that A was a person, and E a machine simulation. It never crossed my mind that there was some need to check to see if things came out as planned. I mean, when I said "Let there be electromagnetic radiation" and this thing appeared, I didn't check to see what it was. What am I, an experimental physicist?

It seemed that I didn't know that things hadn't gone wrong; I didn't know that A was a person rather than a machine simulation and I didn't know that E was a machine simulation rather than a person. For someone who until then had thought that he knew it all and that there was nothing beyond his powers, this was a big comedown.

Not only that, I felt very foolish. Here I'd been carrying on this long relationship with these things without having the faintest idea of what they were. I didn't even know whether I had a chosen people or a chosen set of machine simulators. I didn't even know, for crying out loud, whether I'd been receiving prayers or just gazing at prayer behavior.

Once one gets into that kind of mood, of course, everything begins to seem shaky. Even the electromagnetic radiation I so confidently thought I'd produced. Since a number of alternative total theories were compatible with all the data I had or could get, did I really know that I'd succeeded even there? Or were all those theories equivalent in meaning, so that the question didn't arise? Even in that case, what had I actually produced? Maybe secondary gimmel force rather than electromagnetic radiation. And since alternative situations and things were compatible with anything I could say or specify, how could my words and thoughts uniquely determine a particular creation so as to produce it?

Had I heretofore assumed that nothing was beyond my powers only because I'd never checked to see what I'd actually accomplished? And had I assumed that I knew everything only because I never thought to question or check my assumptions and beliefs? And how could I check? Had I actually created anything at all? Even myself? (My "memory" was of having said instantaneously in the language now available only to me, "LET THERE BE ——," thereby creating myself, it being possible, of course, for a cause to be simultaneous with one of its effects. But how had I fully specified myself? Was my language a way behind the limitations of others? Was this "memory" itself a phantasm, not to be relied upon?)

These thoughts filled my mind with so many doubts that it was no longer in my power to forget them. And yet I did not see in what manner I could resolve them; I was concerned that I must once and for all seriously undertake to rid myself of all the opinions which I had formerly accepted, and commence to build anew from the foundation if I wished to establish any firm and permanent structure. I decided to proceed by setting aside all that in which the least doubt could be supposed to exist, just as if I had discovered that it was absolutely false, and I decided to even follow in this road until I met with something which was certain, or at least, if I could do nothing else, until I had learned for certain that there is nothing else in the world that is certain.

I thought that I would have the right to conceive bright hopes if I were happy enough to discover one thing only which is certain and indubitable.

I AM THAT I AM.

Possessing this one certainty, how shall I proceed? One might go on to try to deduce the existence of a benevolent God who wouldn't deceive him, and then proceed merrily along from there. That particular route seems all suited to help me with my particular problem. (It would ill have served A, as well.) But, perhaps, it offers a hint. If I can make the ontological argument work, and if I can prove whom that argument is about, then once again I will be what I necessarily am.

TELEOLOGY

-ᴕ -ᴕ -ᴕ

Once you come to feel your existence lacks purpose, there is little you can do. You can, keeping the feeling, either continue a meaningless existence, or end it. Or, you can discover the purpose your existence already serves, the meaning it has, thereby eliminating the feeling. Or, you can try to dispose of the feeling by giving a meaning and purpose to your existence.

The first dual option carries minimal appeal, and the second, despite my most diligent efforts, proved impossible. That left the third alternative, where, too, there are limited possibilities. You can make your existence meaningful by fitting it into some larger purpose; by making yourself some part of something else which is independently and incontestably important and meaningful. But a sign of really having been stricken is that no pre-existing purpose will serve in this fashion, for each purpose which to other moods appears sufficiently fructifying then seems merely arbitrary. Alternatively, one can seek meaning in activity which itself is important, which is self-sufficiently intrinsically valuable. Preeminent among such activities, if there are any such, is creative activity. So, as a possible route out of my despair, I decided to create something which itself would be marvelous, or whose creating would itself be marvelous. (No, I did not decide to write a story beginning, "Once you come to feel your existence lacks purpose . . . " Why am I always suspected of gimmicks?)

The task required all of my knowledge, skill, intuitive powers, and craftsmanship. It seemed to me that my whole existence until then had been merely a preparation for this creative activity, so completely did it draw upon and focus all of my experience, abilities, and knowledge. I was excited by the task and fulfilled, and when it was completed I rested, untroubled by purposelessness.

But this contentment was, unfortunately, only temporary. For when I came to think about it, though it *had* taxed my ingenuity and energy to make the heavens, the earth, and the creatures upon it, etc., what did it all amount to? I mean, the whole of it, when looked at starkly and coldly, was itself just an object, of no intrinsic importance, containing creatures in a condition as purposeless as the one I was trying to escape. Given the possibility that my talents and powers were those of a being whose existence might well be valueless, how could their exercise endow my existence with purpose and meaning if it issued only in a worthless object?

At this point in my thoughts I came upon the solution to my problem. If I were to create a plan, a grand design into which my creation would fit, in which my creatures, in serving the pattern and purpose I had ordained for them, would find *their* purpose and goal, then this very activity of endowing their existence with meaning and purpose would be *my* purpose and would give my existence meaning and point. Also, giving their existence meaning would, retroactively, make meaningful my previous activity of creation, it having issued in something that turned out to be of value and worth.

The arrangement has served. Only occasionally, out of the corner of my mind, do I wonder whether my *arbitrarily* having picked a plan for them can really have succeeded in giving meaning to the lives of the role-fulfillers among them. (It was, of course, necessary that I pick some plan or other for them, but no special purpose was served by my picking the particular plan I did. How could it have been? For my sole purpose then was to give meaning to my existence, and this one purpose was insufficient to determine any particular plan into which to fit my creatures.) And, lacking any idea of what a less defective route to meaningfulness might conceivably be, I refuse to consider whether such a symbiotic arrangement is possible; whether different beings can provide meaning and point to each other's existence in a fashion so seemingly circular. For such questions press me toward the alternative I tremble to contemplate, yet to which I find my thoughts recurring. The option of ending it all, now familiar, is less alien and less terrifying than before. I walk through the valley of the shadow of death, alone.

NOTES AND REFERENCES

CREDITS

INDEXES

NOTES AND REFERENCES

1. Coercion

An earlier version of part of this paper was read at Columbia University and at Brown University, and I have benefitted from the ensuing discussions. I have also benefitted from discussing some of the issues treated here with Professor Gerald Dworkin.

1. A useful place to begin thinking about unfreedom is with Felix Oppenheim's *Dimensions of Freedom*, which also classifies the first three examples as cases of unfreedom, and the fourth as not. Though I have found this book very illuminating, I should note that I believe that a correct account of unfreedom will differ significantly from the one it presents.

2. Hart discusses coercion only in passing, and Hart and Honore do not discuss coercion in any detail, but instead discuss the more general notion of getting someone to do something. No doubt they would have presented things slightly differently had they focussed specifically on coercion.

I present their conditions as conditions for coercing someone into not performing an action. It is obvious how the conditions must be modified to yield an account of coercing someone into performing an action. In the course of my discussion I sometimes produce an example as an objection to a condition in the account of coercing someone into not doing something which is more naturally interpreted as an objection to the corresponding condition in the account of coercing someone into doing something. Since once the point of an example is seen, it is easy to think of another example for the corresponding condition, I present the examples without regard to whether they apply to a condition under discussion or the corresponding one.

3. Hart and Honore list one further condition: Q forms the intention of not doing A only after learning of P's threat. That Q formed the intention of not doing A after learning of P's threat may be reason for thinking that he did A because of the threat. But Q may have refrained from doing A because of the threat even though he formed the intention of not doing it before learning of the threat. For example (this example applies to the corresponding condition),

Q intends to visit a friend tomorrow. *P* threatens him with death if he doesn't go. *Q* then learns that this friend has a communicable disease such that were it not for the threat, *Q* wouldn't visit him. But *Q* goes because of *P*'s threat, though he'd formed the intention of going before learning of the threat, and never lost this intention. Though Hart and Honore's further condition is not satisfied, *P* coerced *Q* into going.

4. Or, to handle cases of anonymous threats: *Q* knows that someone has threatened to do the something mentioned in (1), if he, *Q*, does *A*.

5. No weight should be placed on the word *consequence*. Sometimes it will be more appropriate to say "result," "effect," "state of affairs," "event," etc. Perhaps the condition should be formulated by saying "the thing which *P* has threatened to bring about."

6. This condition requires further refinement to handle cases in which unbeknownst to *P*, *Q* wants to avoid *P*'s inflicting the threatened consequence only because this will lead to some further consequence detrimental to *P*, which *Q* (only out of concern for *P*'s interest) wants to avoid. For example, *Q* refrains from *A* because he knows that *P* will feel enormously guilty after he's inflicted the consequence, and *Q* doesn't want this to happen. Or, *Q* refrains from *A* in the face of *P*'s threat to fire him only because without *Q* working for him, *P* will go bankrupt, and *Q* doesn't want this to happen. I shall not pursue here the details of a principle which would exclude these as cases of coercion.

7. I included the latter disjunct since I can threaten you with a consequence which I don't believe would actually worsen your alternative of doing *A*, but which I know that you believe would do so. Subtle questions arise about cases where it is in the making of the threat itself that causes the person to believe that one consequence is worse than another. For example, a Gestapo agent questioning a prisoner believes that two concentration camps are equally bad, and the prisoner too initially believes this. The Gestapo agent tells the prisoner, in a threatening voice, that he will be sent to a concentration camp in any case, but if he cooperates during the questioning he will be sent to the first camp, whereas if he does not, he will be sent to the second camp. Here it is the very making of the threat which causes the prisoner to think that the second camp is worse than the first.

I might note one refinement of this condition, to handle cases where (part of) *P*'s reason for so deciding is as described in the condition, but this part drops away and *P* sticks with his decision for another reason entirely and thereafter announces the decision. It might be more appropriate to say something like: (Part of) *P*'s reason, at the time he informs *Q* he will bring about the consequence or have it brought about if *Q* does *A*, for planning to bring about the consequence or have it brought about if *Q* does *A*, is that *P* believes . . .

The condition in the text should be interpreted or extended so as to cover cases in which the worsening of Q's alternative of doing A is not part of P's reason for deciding to bring about the consequences if Q does A, but rather

  (a) P decides to bring about the consequences if Q does A because he believes he has a duty or obligation to do so.

  (b) P knows this consequence would worsen Q's alternative of doing A.

  (c) Part of the reason for P's bringing about of such a consequence if Q does A originally being thought to be his duty or obligation, or being continued to be so thought, is that such a consequence worsens Q's alternative of doing A.

8. This disjunction is condition 3′. Thus the full condition 3′ is: (Part of) P's reason for deciding is . . . , or, if P hasn't decided, (part of) P's reason for saying is . . . An alternative condition would be just: (Part of) P's reason for saying is to get Q not to do A, or to worsen . . . This alternative condition differs from the one under consideration for cases where P has decided to bring about the consequence if Q does A, and no part of his reason or motive is as described, but part of his reason for *telling* Q that he will bring about the consequence if Q does A, *is* to get Q not to do A. I find it difficult to decide between these conditions, though I lean toward the one presented in the text. A specific example for which the condition in the text and the alternative condition diverge is discussed (as case 3) in the section on Threats and Warnings.

9. Note the difference, with respect to coercion, between saying to a man who intends to do A in order to bring about x:

  (1) If you do A, I'll do something which (just) prevents your A from bringing about x.

  (2) If you do B, I'll do something which would, were you to do A, (just) prevent your A from bringing about x.

10. It was noted earlier that little weight should be put on the word *consequence*. Here we are considering cases where one is tempted to say that P does not bring about any consequence; he just prevents Q from bringing one about.

11. One naturally notes, for many examples of the sort under consideration, that if Q does not do A and P performs the action which would thwart Q's A achieving x, had Q done A (it is not always possible for P to perform this action if Q doesn't do A; e.g., "If you mail the letter, I shall intercept it before it reaches him"), then no bad consequence is visited upon Q. But a condition built upon this observation would fail on two counts:

  (1) It would count Q as coerced when he refrains from doing A because P threatened to do B if Q does A, where B is such as to just prevent Q's A from bringing about x, if Q does A, and to inflict great harm on Q if he does not do A.

(2) It would count Q as not coerced when he refrains from doing A because P threatened to bring about a consequence if Q does A, which consequence is harmful to Q only if he does A.

12. I should note that I do not discuss in this paper, and wish here to leave open, two further conditions. (Hart mentions something in the area of the first.)

(1) The consequence which P has threatened *is* so weighted by Q as to override the weight which Q (morally) *ought* to give to not doing A.

For example, Q, who is not in dire financial condition, and would just slightly rather not kill people (he feels about killing people as most people do about killing flies), kills R because P has threatened not to return the $100 he's borrowed from Q unless Q kills R. Did P coerce Q into killing R?

(2) The weight which Q *does* give to not doing A does not fall far short of the weight he (morally) *ought* to give to not doing A.

For example, Q destroys R's home because P has threatened a consequence, if Q does not destroy the home which R has laboriously built, which Q weights *and* anyone (morally) ought to weight as worse than destroying R's home. However, Q just *slightly* would rather not destroy R's home. Did P coerce Q into destroying R's home?

13. If one is reluctant to say that the members of the gang have threatened him, then a slightly more complicated account of coercion, in terms of threats *and* implicit, or quasi-, or surrogate threats, must be offered.

14. Complication: Suppose that as the stranger is being beaten, he says that if they stop and promise to release him, he'll sign over a traveller's check to them for $1,000. They stop, he signs it over, they release him. Was he coerced into signing it over?

15. Slightly modifying the conditions previously set out, we obtain, for these situations:

(1) P performs an action such that, if Q then does A a certain consequence will ensue.

(2) A with this consequence is substantially less eligible as a course of conduct for Q, than A without this consequence.

(3) P knows that the act he's performed satisfies (1) and (2), and intends Q to know, and know he's intended to know, that such an act has been performed.

(4) (Part of) P's reason for performing his action is that (he believes) its consequence if Q does A would be believed by Q to worsen his alternative of doing A.

(5) Q does not do A, and (part of) Q's reason for not doing A is to avoid or lessen the likelihood of this consequence.

(6) Q believes that P (or that someone) has done something intending that this consequence, which he thinks Q will think bad, will ensue if Q does

A, and *Q* believes that he is intended to know (and intended to know that he is intended to know) this.

(7) *Q* believes that, and *P* believes that *Q* believes that the consequence of *P*'s action if *Q* does *A* would leave *Q* worse off than if *Q* didn't do *A* and *P* didn't do his act.

16. If it is coercion several interesting questions arise. I shall mention only one which has no obvious analogue about the first kind of coercion discussed. If conditions 1–7 apply to *P* and *Q*, and person *R*, whom *P* has never thought of (it is no part of *P*'s reason for performing the act that it worsens *R*'s alternative of doing *A*) refrains from doing *A* to avoid the consequence (*P*'s act is such that though directed to *Q*, it would inflict the consequence upon anyone who does *A*), was *R* coerced into not doing *A*?

Though many questions that arise for this notion correspond to questions about the first notion, it is not obvious that the corresponding questions about the two notions must be answered in the same way. In particular, one is more willing, I think, to call a case of the second sort a case of coercion (assuming that some cases of this sort are) even though *P* lacks some of the specified intentions or reasons, than one is to call a case of the first sort, when *P* lacks some of the specified intentions or reasons, a case of coercion.

17. It should be mentioned, in fairness to my mother, that this example was suggested during the discussion at Columbia by someone whose name I shall not mention, in fairness to his mother.

It is as a special example of this sort of situation that one might understand the activities of some charitable organizations which, along with an appeal for funds, send a "gift," attempting perhaps to present one with the alternatives of

(a) returning the gift, making no contribution, and feeling slightly embarrassed.

(b) keeping the gift while making no contribution, and feeling somewhat guilty and uneasy.

(c) making a contribution.

18. An interesting question arises for accounts of a notion, such as mine, which (attempt to) provide necessary and sufficient conditions for the central part or core of the notion, and then handle further cases by specifying the relations in which they stand to the core cases. Given a set of conditions, which are purported to be necessary and sufficient for the core cases of a notion, and given an example to which the notion applies but which does not satisfy the conditions, how is it to be decided whether the example is a counter-example requiring the modification of the conditions, or whether the conditions are to be retained and the example handled as a non-core case by specifying its relation to cases satisfying the conditions? I would hope that the reader does not find objectionable my treatment of some particular cases as cases which should satisfy the core conditions (in the previous section) and of some other

cases as not being core cases (later in this section), even though the basis for choosing to treat the particular cases as I do is not stated here.

An alternative procedure to the one followed in the first part of this section is to accept the previous account as the full account of coercion, and to widen the notion of what actions a threat is about. (Why this is an alternative procedure will become clear as the reader comes to the numbered statements which soon follow in the text. In the notation used in these numbered statements, the alternative procedure would involve saying that the threat is not only about the act A, but is also about the B's.) There seems to me to be some slight reason for the course followed in the text, but it is not clear that anything very important depends upon which way one proceeds.

19. Readers who notice my sloppiness in the use of quotation marks here will know how to remedy it. One may wish to limit the final formulation of such a principle so that some cases in which P does not know that r_1 and r_2 have the same reference, do not count as P coercing Q into doing B.

20. Note that the consequent of 4 is not equivalent to: P coerces Q into doing B_1 or P coerces Q into doing B_2, or . . . , or P coerces Q into doing B_n.

21. One may be reluctant to apply this principle, as it stands, to situations where unbeknownst to P, Q is specially handicapped so that he can do A only by doing some horrendous B_1. One must also be careful not to misinterpret conclusions reached by applying this condition, as in the case (where $n = 1$) where R advises Q to go to the movies and P threatens Q with death if he does not go to the movies. Since Q, whom P coerces into going to the movies, can go to the movies only by doing what R advised, by applying the condition we reach the conclusion that P coerces Q into doing the action advised by R, which is easily misinterpreted.

22. A useful question to consider is why the statements obtained from 1–8 by replacing "coerces Q into doing A" by "persuades Q to do A" (making other obvious changes) are unsatisfactory, where 1–8 themselves are not unsatisfactory in the same way.

23. Other writers (Laswell and Kaplan, Dahl) do not say that threats are involved, but claim that inducements, or positive rewards coerce.

24. A more complicated statement would be required to take into account condition 7 in the section on Conditions for Coercion. (This condition was prompted by the example in which P says that he will turn off his hearing aid if Q says another word.) Since in the present section no examples which violate condition 7 are considered, the complication is omitted.

25. P can threaten Q even if the consequence does not worsen the consequences of Q's doing the action, so long as P believes it does. Similarly for

offering. We shall not consider this complication, since such threats and offers will normally not have the appropriate result in actions of Q.

26. I ignore problems about consequences along a continuous dimension, where there may be no *first* point of changed preference, or of change from preference to indifference.

27. The notion discussed here should be distinguished from another in which both threatening Q with x if he does A and offering him y if he doesn't do A are said to predominantly involve an offer (threat) if for almost any action B, if Q is both threatened with x if he does B and offered y if he does B, Q will prefer to do B (not do B).

28. I ignore problems arising from a divergence between what P believes to be the morally expected course of events and what is the morally expected course of events, e.g., where P believes he's morally required to let Q drown, although he's morally required to save Q.

Consider a further case (after Braithwaite), P and Q are neighbors, and P would practice his violin each night, whether or not Q is in his own apartment. Q detests hearing P practice, and asks P to stop. P refuses. The question of monetary compensation for P's stopping is raised. Suppose that Q's property rights are not violated by P's practicing, and that $500 is the least amount of money which could get P to stop practicing for one year, and that $2,000 is the greatest payment Q would make to P to stop practicing for one year. (Both amounts indicate their real preferences.) Suppose that P says that he will stop practicing for one year if and only if Q pays him n. One intuitively wants to say that there are some amounts n such that P would be offering to stop in return for n, and some (higher) amounts such that it would be a threat not to stop unless Q paid P the money. The difficulties in devising a theory of a reasonable, or just, or fair price need no elaboration here. Disagreements over the range in which a fair price would fall or over whether there is any coherent notion of a fair price which applies to this situation, may lead to disagreements about whether we here have a threat or an offer.

29. An alternative view would hold that it is *an* offer, but that doing something because of *such* an offer counts as being coerced into doing it. This would require modification of our earlier account of coercion to include doing things because of such offers. (Such offers being often to not continue the usual though morally forbidden course of events, and to switch (at least temporarily) to the morally expected course of events which the recipient of the offer would prefer to the usual course of events.) Readers who find unsatisfactory my here calling the slave owner's statement a threat, may call it an offer and treat "threat" appearing in the section on Conditions for Coercion as a technical term which includes such offers.

30. What if he prefers that he not be supplied with dope, but can't resist buying it when it's available?

31. Let me suggest as a fertile area for testing intuitions and theories, the following, where the normal and morally expected courses of events may diverge, and where it may not be clear what the morally expected course of events is. Suppose some nation N were to announce that it will in the future give economic aid to some other countries provided that these other countries satisfy certain conditions (e.g., do not vote contrary to N on important issues before the United Nations, do not trade with specific nations, do not have diplomatic relations with specific nations). Would this announcement constitute an offer to give these nations aid, or a threat not to do so? Relevant factors (to list just two of many) are whether or not N has an obligation or is morally required to give these nations economic aid (independently of whether they satisfy the conditions), and whether or not N has previously given these nations economic aid independently of whether they satisfy the conditions.

32. Though this seems to me to be the correct thing to say, there is a problem, which I have not yet been able to solve, which I should briefly mention.

Letting P = you are punished

C = you commit a crime

the officials in the society might say

P if and only if C

or equivalently

not-P if and only if not-C.

Interpreted truth-functionally, each of these is equivalent to either (P and C) or (not-P and not-C). The two remaining possibilities are (P and not-C) and (C and not-P). The background we want to use in deciding whether a threat is involved is C and not-P. If we were to use the remaining possibility, P and not-C, as the background, then it would turn out that an offer is involved here. The problem is to formulate criteria, in cases where the biconditional is itself part of the normal and expected course of events, which pick out C and not-P rather than P and not-C in this and other threat cases, and which would pick out the appropriate background for offer cases as well.

33. This is a case of blackmail, which presumably should be legally forbidden because allowing it increases the probability that crimes will go undetected. Other reasons apply to other cases, but note that it is not obvious that one wants to legally forbid all cases which fit the description: saying that one will make public some information about Q unless Q pays money. For example,

(a) P's saying that he will make public the information that Q has not paid P the money Q owes him, unless Q pays the money.

(b) P is writing a book, and in the course of his research comes across information about Q which will help sell many copies of the book. P

tells Q he will refrain from including this information in the book if and only if Q pays him an amount of money equal to the expected difference in his royalties between the book containing this information and the book without the information.

34. A coercive consequence for Q's A is a consequence which has been threatened if Q does A.

35. More precisely, the credible threat of raising the probability of this consequence from what it is without P's aiding in bringing it about, to what it would be with P's aid.

36. Lawyers sometimes speak of the distinction as being between threats and predictions. Since philosophers sometimes contrast predictions and statements of intention, and the latter may be "predictions" in the lawyer's sense, to avoid confusion, I speak of threats and nonthreatening warnings.

37. Stipulating that each of the members of some particular majority has this preference ordering enables us to avoid problems, relevant to our concern here, about nontransitive majorities.

38. I consider here cases where the employer *could* stay in business (without running at a loss) even if the union wins. In the case where, if the union wins, the employer cannot both stay in business and out of the red, it is clear that his statement is a warning and not a threat. (In the normal course of events he does go out of business if the union wins, and chooses to do so earlier than he must, in order to cut his losses.) I assume, for the cases discussed in the text, that the employer making the statement intends to close if the union wins. If he intends not to close, or has no settled intention either way, then in stating that he will close if the union wins he is making a threat.

I should note that I am assuming for some of the cases in which the employer could profitably stay in business if the union wins, that he does not have an obligation to and is not morally required to remain in business if the union wins the election. It may be that some disagreements about whether the employer is threatening or warning stem from disagreements about whether he is morally required to remain in business if the union wins (morally required not to close because of dislike of running a unionized business, etc.).

39. Cf. Schelling, *The Strategy of Conflict*. Note that according to contemporary utility theory, it will be reasonable for the employer to rule out (b) for strategic reasons even if he doesn't know the preference ranking of the employees, so long as

$$pu(a) + (1 - p)u(c) > u(b),$$

where p is the probability that the union will lose the election after he's announced that if they win, he will go out of business, and $u(x)$ is the utility of x to the employer.

40. I should note that I have done nothing here to argue, as I would wish to, that acting on such strategic considerations is not part of the normal or expected course of events which forms the background to discussing questions of coercion. Not doing something unless you'd first announced it in this sort of strategic situation, for strategic reasons, should be distinguished from not doing something without prior announcement for other sorts of reasons; cf. discussions of *ex post facto* laws.

41. I wish here to exclude threats against certain acts which harm others, etc. It is difficult to determine whether there is a presumption against threatening someone against (or coercing someone into not), e.g., murdering someone else, which is almost always easily overridden, or whether there is no such presumption in such cases. It is also difficult to determine exactly what the difference is between these two alternatives. For an attempt to describe the difference, see "Moral Complications and Moral Structures" (Essay 10), section 7.

I do not discuss the possibility that the employer in case 3 is engaging in the second type of coercion discussed in the section on Conditions for Coercion, so that his prior act of announcement worsens the employees' alternative of electing the union because they will feel worse having the factory close when they have been warned of this than they would if, without warning, they elected the union and the factory closed.

42. The Supreme Court held in *Textile Workers Union v. Darlington Manufacturing Co.* (380 U.S. 263 (1965)) that it is not an unfair labor practice for an employer to close his *entire* business, even if the closing is due to antiunion animus, but that closing *part* of a business is an unfair labor practice if *the purpose* is to discourage unionism in any of the employer's remaining plants, and if the employer may reasonably have foreseen such an effect. Given the difficulties in determining an employer's purpose, one suspects that the effect of this decision will be to forbid all employers from closing part of their business because it has become unionized, if other parts of the business are not unionized.

43. This brief description is meant to indicate the area of concern rather than as an account of paternalistic legislation. In such an account one would have to distinguish this sort of legislation from other legislation, often called paternalistic, which provides for adults what parents are expected to provide for children, e.g., food, shelter, money. (I do not claim that no common account of the two sorts of legislation can be given.) It is held, by people who call such legislation paternalistic, that adults are supposed to provide these things for themselves, or through agreements with other citizens qua private citizens. When legislation and governmental institutional arrangements provide things which parents provide for children but which adults are not supposed to provide for (solely by) themselves, e.g., protection from the infliction of violence by others, such provision is not termed paternalistic.

For the area of concern in the text, since different sorts of reasons can be offered for the same piece of legislation, one should speak of paternalistic reasons for legislation rather than of paternalistic legislation. One wants an account of paternalistic reasons for legislation to have the consequence that some reasons put forth for legislation which would make people unfree to manufacture or sell cigarettes would be paternalistic reasons even though they do not involve the protection of the (perhaps nonsmoking) persons made unfree to manufacture and sell cigarettes. I shall not pursue the details here. Note that some paternalistic acts can involve great self-sacrifice, as when drugs are legally forbidden in order to protect those who are not addicts who would be so under a system in which drugs were legal. The price we pay to protect them is increased risk of being robbed or assaulted by addicts trying to acquire money in order to pay the high prices on the illegal market, plus the diversion of resources into trying to enforce the law. Perhaps it is appropriate that we should all suffer for our original unjustified paternalistic intervention.

The reader might find it useful, in thinking about paternalism, to consider whether there are any limits to the severity of the penalty we would include in a paternalistic law, and how these limits are to be fixed. Could we, for example, have the death penalty for the offense of swimming at a beach when no lifeguard is present? Certain plausible-looking principles would allow this, because when the system including this penalty is instituted, it is the one of the alternatives which is expected to best operate for the person's own good. Surely something has gone haywire here.

44. Distinguishing two types of offers in a manner similar to the earlier distinction between two sorts of coercion, this case does not fit the first type of case. For here it is not the case that after Q beats P up, P will *then* do something which improves the consequences for Q of this action. (Even if P will then do this, e.g., spread the news that Q is not to be threatened, it is not an offer for the reason mentioned in the text.) And even though it fits the second sort of case, that is, P now does something (threatens Q) which improves the consequences of Q's beating him up, P is not offering something to Q to beat him up, since P lacks the requisite reasons involved in making an offer.

45. I omit consideration of offers to do acts such that, if the offer is made, the act cannot be done without accepting the offer, e.g., one cannot work at certain government jobs without receiving a salary of at least one dollar per year. The Rational Man may sometimes prefer doing the act without the offer's having been made, so that it will be clear to others, and perhaps himself, *why* he does the act (e.g., not for the money). I also shall not consider the case of a person's not welcoming an offer for him to perform a malicious act because of what it shows about the person making the offer. Note the importance of our restricting our attention here to the Rational Man. Another person might not, for example, welcome an offer of $50,000 for him to kill Jones, because

he's afraid he may be tempted to (and unable to resist the temptation to) accept the offer. In considering only the Rational Man, I am leaving part of my task undone. For I do not argue, as I would wish to, that even for someone who sometimes succumbs to temptations which he believes he ought to resist, there is a significant difference between offers and threats.

46. For a discussion of the prisoners' dilemma, cf. Luce and Raiffa, pp. 94–102. One often finds this argument applied to questions about the provision of a public good for a group. For example, each inhabitant of an island might prefer that others contribute to the construction of barriers against the sea while he does not, yet prefer everyone's being forced to contribute to contributions being left purely voluntary, in which case, let us suppose, the barriers won't get constructed. (For a discussion of the conditions under which a public good for a group will be provided, cf. Olson. Buchanan and Tullock argue that public goods for a group will be provided more often than one might think.)

One must be wary of concluding too quickly from this line of argument that there will be unanimous consent to the provision of the public good by forcing everyone to contribute. For there will generally be alternative ways in which the public good can be provided, and individuals even if they all agree that each of these ways is preferable to the purely voluntary situation, may differ about which of the ways should be used. Should the good be paid for from funds gathered via a system of proportional taxation, or one of progressive taxation? And so forth. It is not obvious how unanimous consent to one *particular* way of providing the good is suppose to arise.

47. Even if Q has other reasons for not doing A, we distinguish between "Q has a reason r for not doing A," and "r is (part of) Q's reason for not doing A."

48. This indicates an asymmetry between doing something (partly) because of a threat, and doing something partly because of an offer. For suppose that the other reasons Q has for not doing A which are part of his reasons for not doing A include an offer by R for Q not to do A. Using a classificatory notion of coercion, doing A partly because of a threat shows the person was coerced, whereas doing something partly because of an offer does not show that he was not coerced.

49. For a discussion of classificatory, comparative, and quantitative concepts cf. Hempel, part III. An illuminating study of different scales of measurement is Suppes and Zinnes.

50. A good place to begin in thinking about the weight of reasons is with Ernest Nagel's discussion of the weight of different causes in *The Structure of Science*, pp. 582–588.

51. There are other factors which one might wish to build into a quantitative concept or measure of coercion, though perhaps there is no natural way to combine all of the factors into one measure. For a discussion of some similar questions about measuring freedom cf. Oppenheim, chap. 8.

References for Essay 1

Bay, Christian. 1958. *The Structure of Freedom.* Palo Alto, CA: Stanford University Press.

Buchanan, James M., and Gordon Tullock. 1962. *The Calculus of Consent.* Ann Arbor: University of Michigan Press.

Dahl, Robert. 1954. *Modern Political Analysis.* Englewood Cliffs, NJ: Prentice-Hall.

Hale, Robert L. 1952. *Freedom Through Law.* New York: Columbia University Press.

Hart, Herbert L. A. 1961. *The Concept of Law.* Oxford: Clarendon Press.

Hart, Herbert L. A., and A. M. Honore. 1959. *Causation in the Law.* Oxford: Clarendon Press.

Hempel, Carl G. 1951. *Fundamentals of Concept Formation in Empirical Science.* Chicago: University of Chicago Press.

Laswell, Harold, and Abraham Kaplan. 1950. *Power and Society.* New Haven: Yale University Press.

Luce, R. Duncan, and Howard Raiffa. 1957. *Games and Decisions.* New York: John Wiley and Sons.

Nagel, Ernest. 1961. *The Structure of Science.* New York: Harcourt, Brace, and World.

Olson, Mancur. 1965. *The Logic of Collective Action.* Cambridge, MA: Harvard University Press.

Oppenheim, Felix. 1961. *Dimensions of Freedom.* New York: St. Martin's Press.

Schelling, Thomas. 1960. *The Strategy of Conflict.* Cambridge, MA: Harvard University Press.

Suppes, Patrick, and J. L. Zinnes. 1963. "Basic Measurement Theory." In R. D. Luce, R. Bush, and E. Galenter, eds., *Handbook of Mathematical Psychology*, vol. I. New York: John Wiley and Sons.

2. Newcomb's Problem and Two Principles of Choice

It is not clear that I am entitled to present this paper. For the problem of choice which concerns me was constructed by someone else, and I am not satisfied with my attempts to work through the problem. But since I believe that the problem will interest and intrigue Peter Hempel and his many friends, and since its publication may call forth a solution which will enable me to stop returning, periodically, to it, here it is. It was constructed by a physicist, Dr. William Newcomb, of the Livermore Radiation Laboratories in California. I first heard the problem, in 1963, from his friend Professor Martin David Kruskal of the Princeton University Department of Astrophysical Sciences. I have benefitted from discussions, in 1963, with William Newcomb, Martin David Kruskal, and

Paul Benacerraf. Since then, on and off, I have discussed the problem with many other friends whose attempts to grapple with it have encouraged me to publish my own. It is a beautiful problem. I wish it were mine.

1. If the being predicts that you will consciously randomize your choice, e.g., flip a coin, or decide to do one of the actions if the next object you happen to see is blue, and otherwise do the other action, then he does not put the M in the second box.

2. Try it on your friends or students and see for yourself. Perhaps some psychologists will investigate whether responses to the problem are correlated with some other interesting psychological variable that they know of.

3. If the questions and problems are handled as I believe they should be, then some of the ensuing discussion would have to be formulated differently. But there is no point to introducing detail extraneous to the central problem of this paper here.

4. This divergence between the dominance principle and the expected utility principle is pointed out in Robert Nozick, *The Normative Theory of Individual Choice* (doctoral dissertation, Princeton University, Princeton, 1963; published in 1990 by Garland Press, New York), and in Richard Jeffrey, *The Logic of Decision* (McGraw-Hill, New York, 1965).

5. This is shorthand for: action A is done and state S_{12} obtains or action B is done and state S_1 obtains. The 'or' is the exclusive or.

6. Note that

$$S_1 = A_1 \ \& \ S_3 \text{ or } A_2 \ \& \ S_4$$
$$S_2 = A_1 \ \& \ S_4 \text{ or } A_2 \ \& \ S_3$$
$$S_3 = A_1 \ \& \ S_1 \text{ or } A_2 \ \& \ S_2$$
$$S_4 = A_1 \ \& \ S_2 \text{ or } A_2 \ \& \ S_1$$

Similarly, the above identities hold for Newcomb's example, with which I began, if one lets

$S_1 = $ The money is in the second box.

$S_2 = $ The money is not in the second box.

$S_3 = $ The being predicts your choice correctly.

$S_4 = $ The being incorrectly predicts your choice.

$A_1 = $ You take only what is in the second box.

$A_2 = $ You take what is in both boxes.

7. State S is not probabilistically independent of actions A and B if prob (S obtains|A is done) $\neq$ prob (S obtains|B is done).

8. In Newcomb's predictor example, assuming that "He predicts correctly" and "He predicts incorrectly" are each probabilistically independent of my actions, then it is not the case that "He puts the money in" and "He does not put the money in" are each probabilistically independent of my actions.

Usually it will be the case that if the members of the set of exhaustive and exclusive states are each probabilistically independent of the actions A_1 and A_2, then it will not be the case that the states equivalent to our contrived states are each probabilistically independent of both A_1 and A_2. For example, suppose prob $(S_1|A_1) = $ prob $(S_1|A_2) = $ prob (S_1); prob $(S_2|A_2) = $ prob $(S_2|A_1) = $ prob (S_2). Let:

$$S_3 = A_1 \ \& \ S_1 \text{ or } A_2 \ \& \ S_2$$
$$S_4 = A_1 \ \& \ S_2 \text{ or } A_2 \ \& \ S_1$$

If prob $(S_1) \neq $ prob (S_2), then S_3 and S_4 are not probabilistically independent of A_1 and A_2. For prob $(S_3|A_1) = $ prob $(S_1|A_1) = $ prob (S_1), and prob $(S_3|A_2) = $ prob $(S_2|A_2) = $ prob (S_2). Therefore if prob $(S_1) \neq $ prob (S_2), then prob $(S_3|A_1) \neq $ prob $(S_3|A_2)$. If prob $(S_1) = $ prob $(S_2) = 1/2$, then the possibility of describing the states as we have will not matter. For if, for example, A_1 can be shifted around so as to dominate A_2, then before the shifting it will have a higher expected utility than A_2. Generally, if the members of the set of exclusive and exhaustive states are probabilistically independent of both A_1 and A_2, then the members of the contrived set of states will be probabilistically independent of both A_1 and A_2 only if the probabilities of the original states which are components of the contrived states are identical. And in this case it will not matter which way one sets up the situation.

9. Note that this procedure seems to work quite well for situations in which the states are not only not probabilistically independent of the actions, but are not logically independent either. Suppose that a person is asked whether he prefers doing A to doing B, where the outcome of A is $|p$ if S_1 and r if $S_2|$ and the outcome of B is $|q$ if S_2 and r if $S_1|$. And suppose that he prefers p to q to r, and that $S_1 = $ I do B, and $S_2 = $ I do A. The person realizes that if he does A, S_2 will be the case and the outcome will be r, and he realizes that if he does B, S_1 will be the case and the outcome will be r. Since the outcome will be r in any case, he is indifferent between doing A and doing B. So let us suppose he flips a coin in order to decide which to do. But given that the coin is fair, it is now the case that the probability of $S_1 = 1/2$ and the probability of $S_2 = 1/2$. If we mechanically started to compute the expected utility of A, and of B, we would find that A has a higher expected utility than does B. For mechanically computing the expected utilities, it would turn out that the expected utility of $A = 1/2 \times u(p) + 1/2 \times u(r)$, and the expected utility of $B = 1/2 \times u(q) + 1/2 \times u(r)$. If, however, we use the conditional probabilities, then the expected utility of $A = $ prob $(S_1|A) \times u(p) + $ prob $(S_2|A) \times u(r) = 0 \times u(p) + 1 \times u(r) = u(r)$. And the expected utility of $B = $ prob $(S_2|B) \times u(q) + $ prob $(S_1|B) \times u(r) = $

$0 \times u(q) + 1 \times u(r) = u(r)$. Thus the expected utilities of A and B are equal, as one would wish.

10. This position was suggested, with some reservations due to Newcomb's example, in Nozick, *The Normative Theory of Individual Choice*. It was also suggested in Jeffrey, *The Logic of Decision*.

11. I should mention, what the reader has no doubt noticed, that the previous *example* is not fully satisfactory. For it seems that preferring the academic life to the athlete's life should be as strong evidence for the tendency as is choosing the academic life. And hence P's choosing the athlete's life, though he prefers the academic life, on expected-utility grounds does not seem to make it likely that he does not have the tendency. What the example seems to require is an inherited tendency to decide to do A which is such that (1) The probability of its presence cannot be estimated on the basis of the person's preferences, but only on the basis of knowing the genetic makeup of his parents, or knowing his actual decisions; and (2) The theory about how the tendency operates yields the result that it is unlikely that it is present if the person decides not to do A in the example-situation, even though he makes his decision on the basis of the stated expected-utility grounds. It is not clear how, for this example, the details are to be coherently worked out.

12. That is, the dominance principle is legitimately applicable to situations in which $\approx (\exists S)(\exists A)(\exists B)$ [prob (S obtains$|A$ is done) $\neq$ prob (S obtains$|B$ is done)].

13. The other eleven possibilities about the states are:

	Already fixed and determined		Not already fixed and determined	
	Probabilistically independent of the actions	Not probabilistically independent of the actions	Probabilistically independent of the actions	Not probabilistically independent of the actions
(1)	some	some	some	some
(2)	some	some	some	none
(3)	some	some	none	some
(4)	some	some	none	none
(5)	some	none	some	some
(6)	some	none	some	none
(7)	some	none	none	some
(8)	all	none	none	none
(9)	none	some	some	some
(10)	none	some	some	none
(11)	none	some	none	some

14. Unless it is possible that there be causality or influence backwards in time. I shall not here consider this possibility, though it may be that only on its basis can one defend, for some choice situations, the refusal to use the dominance principle. I try to explain later why, for some situations, even if one grants that there is no influence back in time, one may not escape the feeling that, somehow, there is.

15. Cf. R. Duncan Luce and Howard Raiffa, *Games and Decisions* (John Wiley & Sons, New York, 1957), pp. 94–102.

16. Almost certainty$_1$ > almost certainty$_2$, since almost certainty$_2$ is some function of the probability that brother I has the dominant-action gene given that he performs the dominant action (= almost certainty$_1$), and of the probability that brother II does the dominant action given that he has the dominant-action gene.

17. In choosing the headings for the rows, I have ignored more complicated possibilities, which must be investigated for a fuller theory, e.g., some actions influence which state obtains and others do not.

18. I here consider only the case of two actions. Obvious and messy problems for the kind of policy about to be proposed are raised by the situation in which more than two actions are available (e.g., under what conditions do pairwise comparisons lead to a linear order), whose consideration is best postponed for another occasion.

19. See Luce and Raiffa, *Games and Decisions*, pp. 275–298 and the references therein; Daniel Ellsberg, "Risk, Ambiguity, and the Savage Axioms," *Quarterly Journal of Economics* 75 (1961), 643–669, and the articles by his fellow symposiasts Howard Raiffa and William Feller.

20. If the distinctions I have drawn are correct, then some of the existing literature is in need of revision. Many of the writers might be willing to just draw the distinctions we have adumbrated. But for the specific theories offered by some personal probability theorists, it is not clear how this is to be done. For example, L. J. Savage, in *The Foundations of Statistics* (John Wiley & Sons, New York, 1954), recommends unrestricted use of dominance principles (his postulate *P2*), which would not do in case (I). And Savage seems explicitly to wish to deny himself the means of distinguishing case (I) from the others. (For further discussion, some of which must be revised in the light of this paper, of Savage's important and ingenious work, see Nozick, *The Normative Theory of Individual Choice*, chap. v.) And Jeffrey, in *The Logic of Decision*, recommends universal use of maximizing expected utility relative to the conditional probabilities of the states given the actions (see note 10, above). This will not do, I have argued, in cases (III) and (IV). But Jeffrey also sees it as a special virtue of this theory that it does not utilize certain notions, and these notions look like they might well be required to draw the distinctions between the different kinds of cases.

While on the subject of how to distinguish the cases, let me (be the first to) say that I have used without explanation, and in this essay often interchangeably, the notions of influencing, affecting, etc. I have felt free to use them without paying them much attention because even such unreflective use serves to open a whole area of concern. A detailed consideration of the different possible cases with many actions, some influencing, and in different degrees, some not influencing, combined with an attempt to state detailed principles using precise "influence" notions undoubtedly would bring forth many intricate and difficult problems. These would show, I think, that my quick general statements about influence and what distinguishes the cases are not, strictly speaking, correct. But going into these details would necessitate going into these details. So I will not.

21. Though perhaps it explains why I *momentarily* felt I had succeeded too well in constructing the vaccine case, and that perhaps one *should* perform the nondominant action there.

22. But it also seems relevant that in Newcomb's example not only is the action referred to in the explanation of which state obtains (though in a nonextensional belief context), but also there is another explanatory tie between the action and the state; namely, that both the state's obtaining and your actually performing the action are both partly explained in terms of some third thing (your being in a certain initial state earlier). A fuller investigation would have to pursue yet more complicated examples which incorporated this.

4. Interpersonal Utility Theory

During 1981–82, I presented these ideas in talks at Chicago, Michigan, Oberlin, Princeton, Stanford, and Yale. I have benefitted from the comments I received then as well as from comments of the referees.

Friedman, M., and L. J. Savage. 1948. "The Utility Analysis of Choices Involving Risk." *Journal of Political Economy* 56: 279–304.

Homans, G. 1974. *Social Behavior*, rev. ed. New York: Harcourt Brace.

Markowitz, H. 1952. "The Utility of Wealth." *Journal of Political Economy* 60: 151–158.

Nozick, R. 1981. *Philosophical Explanations*. Cambridge, MA: Harvard University Press.

Sen, A. 1979. "Interpersonal Comparisons of Welfare." In M. Boskin (ed.), *Economics and Human Welfare*, pp. 183–201. New York: Academic Press.

Tversky, A., and D. Kahneman. 1979. "Prospect Theory." *Econometrica* 47: 263–291.

5. On Austrian Methodology

1. This essay was originally directed to an audience of nonphilosophers, and as a result some of the philosophical points will not be news to readers with a

background in philosophy. I have retained these points in the hope that some economists will find them illuminating and that even philosophers might find their application interesting. I have benefitted from discussion of the essay at the New York Seminar on Austrian Economics, the Society for Ethical and Legal Philosophy, and from a discussion of section IV with Richard Herrnstein.

The major writings in the Austrian tradition are Carl Menger, *Principles of Economics, Problems of Economics and Sociology*; Eugen von Böhm-Bawerk, *History and Critique of Interest Theories, The Positive Theory of Capital*; Ludwig von Mises, *The Theory of Money and Credit, Human Action*; Frederick Hayek, *Individualism and Economic Order, The Pure Theory of Capital, Prices and Production, Monetary Theory and the Trade Cycle*.

See also Ludwig von Mises, *Socialism*; Murray Rothbard, *Man, Economy and State*; Ludwig Lachman, *Capital and Its Structure; Macro-Economic Thinking and the Market Economy*; and Israel Kirzner, *The Economic Point of View, Market Theory and the Price System, An Essay on Capital*, and his recent and important *Competition and Entrepreneurship*.

Not every figure accepts or places equal emphasis on each of the features of the methodological framework. For example, while all parts of this essay apply to Mises (and to Rothbard), only section I is clearly relevant to Hayek's views.

2. See F. A. Hayek, *The Counterrevolution of Science* (The Free Press, Glencoe, Ill., 1955), chaps. 1–10, and *Individualism and Economic Order* (University of Chicago Press, 1948), chaps. 2–4. For a sample of discussion in the journals, see the six essays by Watkins, Mandelbaum, and Goldstein (two apiece) reprinted in Leonard Krimmerman (ed.), *The Nature and Scope of Social Science* (Appleton, Century, Crofts, New York, 1969).

A standard account of reduction is provided in Ernest Nagel, *The Structure of Science* (Harcourt Brace, and World, New York, 1961), chap. 11. For complications and refinements, see also Lawrence Sklar, "Types of Inter-Theoretic Reduction," *British Journal for the Philosophy of Science* 18 (1967), 109–124.

3. I leave aside the question of how much of such decision theory as has been developed should be acceptable within Austrian theory, though I do believe that much of it is, and that mistaken views about the relationship of preference to choice and action (see section III, below) have led Austrian writers to ignore this literature. Indeed, one would expect that writings on personal or subjective probability would be most congenial to Austrians, the major proponents of the subjective theory of value. It is puzzling that Austrian writers have been concerned solely with "objective" probability, since there is no guarantee that an actor will act on *those* ratios or limits of relative frequencies. Only if such ratios are reflected in subjective probabilities will a theory of human action be concerned with them, and if they are *not* so reflected, the theory will have anyway to be concerned with the (divergent) subjective probabilities. On personal (subjective) probability, see Leonard J. Savage, *The Foundations of Statistics* (John Wiley and Sons, New York, 1954), and F. J. Anscombe and R. J. Aumann,

"A Definition of Subjective Probability," *Annals of Mathematical Statistics* 34 (1963), 199–205.

4. I ignore here the issue of whether the *situation* can be specified by utilizing only the concepts of Crusoe theory.

5. See R. D. Luce and H. Raiffa, *Games and Decisions* (John Wiley and Sons, New York, 1957); Thomas Schelling's treatment of coordination games in *The Strategy of Conflict* (Oxford University Press, 1963); John Harsanyi, "A General Theory of Rational Behavior in Game Situations," *Econometrica* 34 (1966), 613–634; and "Advances in Understanding Rational Behavior," Working Paper CP-366 of the Center for Research in Management Science, University of California, Berkeley, July 1975, and the papers by Harsanyi cited therein.

6. See Luce and Raiffa, *Games and Decisions*, chap. 9.

7. The nonmethodological individualist might agree that the explanatory theory of *n*-person interactions suffices to explain all interactions, for he might believe that the ultimate explanation of *n*-person interactions lies in a general theory of multiperson (> *n*) interactions. (I owe this preceding remark and the next paragraph to David Hills.) The methodological individualist, however, believes that the general theory of multiperson interaction won't make *essential* reference to more than *n* persons in that it will be nonvacuously true in some domain of no more than *n* individuals.

Furthermore, the theory where *n* > 1 will completely satisfy methodological individualist strictures only if it does not attribute utility or reasoning to dyads or groups in a way which is irreducible to individual utility functions and individual reasoning. It will not countenance an irreducible group mind, utility function, etc. (It is not obvious how to specify this "etc.")

8. See Richard B. McKenzie and Gordon Tullock, *The New World of Economics* (Richard D. Irwin, Inc., Homewood, Ill., 1975), chap. 18, "Riots and Panic," for a methodological individualist account of such behavior.

9. On emergence, see Nagel, *Structure of Science*, pp. 366–380; Carl Hempel, *Aspects of Scientific Explanation* (Free Press, New York, 1965), pp. 258–264.

10. Menger, *Principles of Economics*, chap. VIII.

11. Mises holds that his money-regression theory demonstrates that no other origin of money is possible. "It follows that an object cannot be used as money unless, at the moment when its use as money begins, it already possesses an objective exchange-value based on some other use. This provides both a refutation of those theories which derive the origin of money from a general agreement to impute fictitious value to things intrinsically valueless [here Mises footnotes Locke] and a confirmation of Menger's hypothesis concerning the origin of the use of money" (*The Theory of Money and Credit*, enlarged edition, Yale Uni-

versity Press, 1953, p. 110). The prices tomorrow depend upon the amount spent on consumption, saved, and held in current cash balance. What is held in cash balance will depend upon expectations about prices tomorrow (the very ones to be explained) and prices the next day. It is not, strictly, circular to explain prices on a given day in terms of expectations about prices for that very day, but one might well want to avoid this, especially if one contemplates the possibility that all such expectations are formed in accordance with (and *only* in accordance with) the very theory being developed. Mises stops the (unstrict) regress by having *today's* prices determining tomorrow's cash balances. Day by day we go back in time until the point when it is only because of use value, and not exchange value, that something is held. Thereby, all prices are noncircularly explained.

Mises is able to introduce today's prices as determining tomorrow's cash balances only if either (a) people expect tomorrow's prices to be (roughly) like today's or (b) people arrive at their expectation of tomorrow's prices by starting with knowledge of today's prices, plus their knowledge of the causal factors operating, and thereby arrive at some view of how tomorrow's prices will differ from today's, and so of what tomorrow's prices will be.

In each case, it is an *expectation* about tomorrow's prices which is crucial to determining the cash holdings. Mises's money-regression argument shows *one* way such expectations may function. However, it cannot demonstrate that Menger's account describes the *only* way money could arise, for it cannot demonstrate that expectations about tomorrow's prices can only be formed on the basis of today's prices. So, in particular, it cannot show that a social contract *could not* actually give rise to (roughly) uniform expectations about the next day's prices. To demonstrate *that*, another argument would be needed.

12. Economics provides the prime arena of such explanations as have thus far been offered. George Homans presents illuminating examples of methodological individualist explanations in sociology in his *Social Behavior*, Revised edition (Harcourt, Brace, Jovanovich, Inc., New York, 1974), and explicitly endorses methodological individualism in *The Nature of Social Science* (Harcourt, Brace, New York, 1967).

13. But things are more complicated if the explanation of the subjunctives and act tokens essentially refers to previously holding subjunctives as well as to previous act tokens.

14. Different theorists have held that capitalist institutions are self-destructive, notably Marx and Schumpeter. Most recently, Daniel Bell has advanced such claims in *The Cultural Contradictions of Capitalism* (Basic Books, New York, 1975).

15. See E. O. Wilson, *Sociobiology* (Harvard University Press, Cambridge, Mass., 1975).

16. Some writers speak not merely as if different psychological types inhabit the different historical stages of human society, but as if different psychological laws function in these different stages. I find this far-fetched, but if it were true, and if the general law connecting the historical stages with the operative psychological laws was a brute-macro-law, unexplainable by any deeper psychological law as it operated in different social circumstances, then methodological individualism would be false. However, the explanations of behavior within each stage and of the transition of society from one stage to another might still be methodological individualist explanations which use the psychological laws of the relevant stage. What would not get a methodological individualist answer would be the question "why those laws?"

17. For a recent survey of the current state of the theory, see Roger Brown and Richard Herrnstein, *Psychology* (Little, Brown, and Co., Boston, 1975), chaps. 1–3. I shall say something more about operant conditioning below.

18. Mises himself holds that "leisure is a consumer's good" and "labor has disutility" are not necessary truths, and hence explanations which utilize these statements are *not* claimed to be reducible to a completely a priori theory.

19. An illuminating survey of difficulties with the positivist arguments on synthetic necessary truths, by a defender of such truths, is Arthur Pap's *Semantics and Necessary Truth* (Yale University Press, 1958). The most influential recent critic of necessity and of the analytic-synthetic distinction is W. V. Quine. See his essay "Two Dogmas of Empiricism" in *From a Logical Point of View* (Harvard University Press, 1953), his book *Word and Object* (MIT Press, 1960), and his essay "Necessary Truth" in his volume of essays *The Ways of Paradox* (Random House, New York, 1966). The most influential and ingenious recent defense and utilization of synthetic necessary truths, and of essences, is Saul Kripke's monograph, "Naming and Necessity," in Donald Davidson and Gilbert Harman (eds.), *Semantics of Natural Language* (D. Reidel, Humanities, New York, 1972).

20. *Anarchy, State, and Utopia* (Basic Books, New York, 1974), pp. 42–45, "The Experience Machine."

21. A survey is contained in B. F. Skinner, *Science and Human Behavior* (Macmillan Company, New York, 1953). A precise quantitative form of the law of effect is presented in R. J. Herrnstein, "On the Law of Effect," *Journal for the Experimental Analysis of Behavior* 13 (1970), 243–266, and "Quantitative Hedonism," *Journal of Psychiatric Research* 8 (1971), 399–412. It is often erroneously believed that Noam Chomsky's famous review essay of Skinner's book, *Verbal Behavior*—in *Language* 35 (1959), 26–58, reprinted in J. J. Katz and Jerry Fodor, *The Structure of Language* (Prentice-Hall, 1964)—refutes Skinner's general theory or at least its application to human beings. However, many of Chomsky's criticisms deal with earlier stimulus-response theories, theories of drive reduction, etc., and *not* with Skinner's theory of operant conditioning

(which is not an S–R theory), and Chomsky's complaints about the circularity of the law of effect are mistaken. (See Paul Meehl, "On the Circularity of the Law of Effect," *Psychological Bulletin*, 1950; Kenneth MacCorquodale, "On Chomsky's Review of Skinner's Verbal Behavior," *Journal of the Experimental Analysis of Behavior* 13 (1970), 83–99; and the articles by Herrnstein cited above.) Even the claim that an act is self-reinforcing has the consequence (as Meehl pointed out) that successive performances will *increase* its strength and that artificial duplication of its proprioceptive or brain effects could be used to reinforce *other* actions. Nor is it empty to claim that exploratory behavior is itself reinforcing, for not only is this claim plausible on evolutionary grounds, but tests could determine whether being given opportunity to engage in exploratory behavior itself functions as reinforcement.

One of Chomsky's criticisms has carried great weight with many, namely that (even if the law of effect itself is not circular and empty of content) many of the applications of the law of effect are circular. For in many applications, the reason for believing a reinforcing event has taken place is the very effect it is to explain. Consider another case. A bridge collapses, and the question of why it collapsed is raised. Engineers hypothesize that the stress in a particular place reached a certain point. They believe this occurred, because they have a theory, well confirmed elsewhere, that this causes bridges to collapse and is the most frequent cause of bridge collapses. They then go on to *explain* the collapse of the bridge by referring to the stress. The collapse of the bridge is their *reason for believing* there was a certain stress, and the stress is their *explanation* of the bridge's collapse. Isn't this circular? It is not, for the two italicized terms in the previous sentence are different. It *would* be circular if they were the same, that is, if either (a) the collapse of the bridge is their *reason for believing* there was a certain stress, and the stress is their *reason for believing* the bridge did collapse, or (b) the collapse of the bridge is their *explanation of* the stress, and the stress is their *explanation of* the collapse of the bridge. But in the bridge example we are discussing, there is no such objectionable circularity. (See Jaegwon Kim, "On Inference, Explanation and Prediction," *Journal of Philosophy* 61 (1964), 360–368.) The situation is similar with reinforcement. Given a well-confirmed theory, it will be reasonable to infer some event of a type known to be reinforcing took place, or to infer that a type of event which was known to take place *is* reinforcing. One would want to go ahead and check this latter claim, but there seem to be no insuperable difficulties here. Thus, this criticism by Chomsky rests upon a mistaken methodological view. The theory of operant conditioning cannot be dismissed so easily.

22. For a discussion of ways in which empirical procedures come into the discovery of necessary (though not *a priori*) truths, see Kripke, "Naming and Necessity."

23. On *verstehen*, see F. A. Hayek, *The Counterrevolution of Science*.

24. See Ernest Nagel, *The Structure of Science*, pp. 480–485.

25. W. V. Quine, *Word and Object*, chap. 2. Putnam's essay considers the relevance of *verstehen* for the issues Quine discusses about translation, and so links up the two areas, but it does not go on to treat radical *verstehen* and its implications for the empirical character of social science.

26. Or, if we view empathetic understanding as assigning prior probabilities, after a large number of cases we will be able to assess its reliability as a prior probability assigner.

27. This scheme is not identical, however, to Mises' *a priori* scheme. For most people do not think they *always* act to reduce their own felt uneasiness, etc. Hence, if Mises is right, these people's empathetic understanding of their *own* behavior is sometimes faulty.

28. See Rothbard, *Man, Economy, and State*, p. 64.

29. Mises writes in *Human Action*: "However, one must not forget that the scale of values or wants manifests itself only in the reality of action. These scales have no independent existence apart from the actual behavior of individuals" (p. 95); "The scale of value manifests itself only in real acting; it can be discerned only from the observation of real acting. It is therefore impermissible to contrast it with real acting and to use it as a yardstick for the appraisal of real actions" (p. 102).

30. Perhaps Mises is denying this point in the middle of the last paragraph of page 119 of *Human Action*, but it is difficult to be sure. However, on p. 122 he says, "All parts—units—of the available stock are considered as equally useful and valuable if the problem of giving up one of them is raised." Here, then, we *do* have *indifference*. Yet a choice will be made, perhaps at random. One particular object will be given up. Yet the person does not prefer giving up *this one* to giving up another one. Therefore, choice entails (at best) weak preference; it does not entail strong preference.

Rothbard claims (*Man, Economy, and State*, p. 265), "Any action demonstrates choice based on preference; preference for one alternative over others. There is, therefore, no role for the concept of indifference in economics or in any other praxeological science." However, (on pp. 18–19) he also writes, "in these examples, the units of the good have been *interchangeable from the point of view of the actor*. Thus, any concrete pound of butter was evaluated in this case *perfectly equally* with any other pound of butter" (his italics the first time, mine the second), and he continues on in the same vein on the rest of p. 19.

31. Mises, *Human Action*, p. 97.

32. Can't we consider the cost of *A* as the value of choosing among the remaining alternatives, making the implicit assumption that the value of choosing among all of the remaining alternatives is equal to the value of the best alternative among them? Notice, though, that this involves introducing a choice

situation (choosing among *just those*) which the person never actually faces. And making the implicit assumption explicit would reraise the problem.

33. See David Lewis, *Counterfactuals* (Harvard University Press, Cambridge, Mass., 1973). I am not committed here, however, to the adequacy of Lewis's account, which in any case I describe only *roughly* in the text. Furthermore, since the actual world is of course the world closest to the actual world, Lewis's account has the unfortunate consequence of making subjunctively true any conditional with true antecedent and consequent. We can avoid this consequence by the following proposal, which has other desirable consequences as well. Let the *p*-neighborhood of a world W be the closest band of worlds where *p* is true, uninterrupted by a world in which not-*p* holds. More precisely, if *p* is true in world W, the *p*-neighborhood of W is the set of those worlds w such that *p* is true in w and there is no world w' in which not-*p* is true which is at least as close to W as w is. If *p* is false in W, the *p*-neighborhood of W is the set of those worlds w such that *p* is true in w and there is no world w' in which not-*p* is true which is the same distance from W as w is, and for any world w'' which is between w and W and in which not-*p* is true, there is no world in which *p* is true which is as close to W as w'' is. (The condition where *p* is false in W says that the *p*-neighborhood of W is the set of those worlds w where *p* is true, such that no not-*p* world is equidistant from W, and such that any not-*p* world between w and W is in the not-*p* neighborhood of W.) However, when *p* is false, if the closest *p*-worlds to W are the same distance from W as are some not-*p* worlds, then a more complicated account of the relevant band must be given.

Finally, we can say that a subjunctive with antecedent *p* and consequent *q* is true if *q* is true in each world of the *p*-neighborhood of the actual world.

34. For an account of dispositions which views them as placeholders for an underlying physical structure, see W. V. Quine, *The Roots of Reference* (Open Court, La Salle, Ill., 1973), pp. 8–12. See also Isaac Levi and Sidney Morgenbesser, "Belief and Disposition," *American Philosophical Quarterly* 1 (1964), 1–12.

35. The requirement that preference be transitive should *not* be read as, "if X is preferred to Y, and Y is preferred to Z, then X should be preferred to Z," so as to license an inference to the consequent if the antecedent is satisfied. Perhaps it's the case that X shouldn't be preferred to Y. Also, if the person prefers X to Y, Y to Z, and Z to X (and so has intransitive preferences), three applications of the principle, read as above, would lead to the conclusion that he should prefer X to Z, Z to Y, and Y to X—another intransitive triad! Instead, the requirement should be read as requiring preferences to hang together in a certain way, and as excluding preferences from combining in other ways, e.g., "it shouldn't be the case that X is preferred to Y, Y to Z, yet X isn't preferred

to Z." See Robert Nozick, *The Normative Theory of Individual Choice* (doctoral dissertation, Princeton University, 1963), pp. 94–98 [published in 1990 by Garland Press, New York].

36. Caution: see my remarks below about the connection of preferences with the subjunctives.

37. For a recent survey of the theory of choice sets, the theory of conditions such as these, see A. K. Sen, "Choice Functions and Revealed Preference," *Review of Economic Studies* 38 (1971), 307–317.

38. As an antidote to Rothbard's statement (*Man, Economy, and State*, p. 15), "It is important to realize that there is never any possibility of *measuring* increases or decreases in happiness or satisfaction . . . In order for any measurement to be possible, there must be an eternally fixed and objectively given unit with which other units may be compared," readers may wish to see D. Krantz, R. D. Luce, P. Suppes, and A. Tversky, *Foundations of Measurement*, vol. 1 (Academic Press, New York, 1971).

39. This type of point will be familiar to readers of W. V. Quine and Donald Davidson.

40. See, for example, Mark Blaug, *Economic Theory in Retrospect* (Irwin & Company, Homewood, Ill., 1968), revised edition, pp. 503–509; Robert E. Kuenne, *Eugen von Böhm-Bawerk* (Columbia University Press, New York, 1971), pp. 25–34.

41. This can happen only if the person at that moment is indifferent for all things he can get between getting them then and getting them later. Otherwise, he'll do one of the (other) time-preferred things.

42. Those who think time-preference is a categorial component of action may think it strange to attempt, as I do later, an evolutionary explanation of it, and compare this to an evolutionary explanation of preference, another (supposed) categorial component of action. However, neither is inappropriate. Since it is not a necessary truth that there are preferences or time-preferences (or actions!), the world need not have contained them, their existence is a proper topic for explanation, and the correct explanation presumably will be some evolutionary one.

43. See Mises, *Human Action*, pp. 131–132; Rothbard, *Man, Economy, and State*, pp. 37–38.

44. That consumption takes time, and may be incompatible with other activities, including other consumption, is put to different economic use by Staffan Linder, *The Harried Leisure Class* (Columbia University Press, 1970).

45. I take these details from George Ainslie, "Specious Reward: A Behavioral Theory of Impulsiveness and Impulse Control," *Psychological Bulletin* 82 (1975), 463–496, who also discusses in an illuminating way various devices for getting past the earlier smaller reward without choosing it.

46. The relevant question is not what you actually would choose in the future if given the choice then (for your preferences might change), but how valuable, according to your preferences now, getting it then will be worth to you then. It is not clear how to capture this by a subjunctive about choices.

6. Socratic Puzzles

This essay was stimulated by questions posed by Gregory Vlastos in his *Socrates: Ironist and Moral Philosopher* (Cornell University Press, Ithaca, 1991), and its title derives from Vlastos's speaking, in his *Platonic Studies* (Princeton University Press, 1973), of cracking puzzles in Plato. After writing an earlier draft with the current title, I encountered Terence Irwin's review of Vlastos's *Socrates*, also entitled "Socratic Puzzles" (*Oxford Studies in Ancient Philosophy*, volume 10, 1992). I hope Irwin will accept my reusing his title as a reinforcement of his tribute to Vlastos.

I am grateful to Myles Burnyeat for his comments on an earlier draft of this essay.

1. Whether or not this doctrine is an accurate description of everyone, it is a correct description of Socrates himself; it is inconceivable that Socrates would know what is best yet do otherwise. However, we should not abandon Socrates too soon to the familiar objection that someone might know the good but be too weak of will to carry it out. For what explains weakness of will? If that phenomenon itself arises due to, and crucially involves, some particular ignorance on the agent's part, then Socrates' doctrine will not fall to the *akrasia* objection.

Consider the psychologist George Ainslie's explanation of weakness of will in terms of time-preference, and the crossing curves these can involve. (George Ainslie, "Specious Reward: A Behavioral Theory of Impulsiveness and Impulse Control," *Psychological Bulletin* 82 (1975), pp. 463–496. I first discussed this explanation in "On Austrian Methodology" (1977), in this volume as chapter 5, and I returned to it in *The Nature of Rationality*, Princeton University Press, 1993, pp. 14–18.) On this explanation, an akratic act might involve a failure of knowledge. Because of visual perspective, a nearer object can look larger than a more distant one that actually is larger (where the actual size of the object is measured *at* the object). Someone who thinks the nearer object larger makes a mistake of knowledge. Is time-preference like visual perspective, so that rewards look smaller, the more distant they are in the future? If they thereby look smaller than they actually are (where their actual magnitude is measured *at* the reward), then isn't someone making a mistake, a cognitive mistake, who acts as if the nearer reward is the larger one? Isn't this an illusion, akin to a visual illusion? (See *Protagoras*, 356c–7e.) I don't insist that the answer is clear, in this case. And Ainslie's explanation of *akrasia* is not the only possible one. Still, we had better be sure that we possess an account of weakness of will that does not attribute any failure of *knowledge* to the agent before we contend that Socrates is obviously mistaken in holding that no one does wrong (or chooses the worse) voluntarily.

2. Vlastos, *Socrates*, p. 3.

3. *Plato's Moral Theory*, pp. 39–40.

4. About something where he hasn't claimed knowledge of the first kind, he might also be denying knowledge of both kinds. See Gregory Vlastos, "Socrates' Disavowal of Knowledge," *Philosophical Quarterly* 35 (1985), pp. 1–31.

5. Euthyphro's prosecution of his father for impiety is shocking. Notice, however, that if Euthyphro's father did commit murder or otherwise do wrong in forgetting about the murderer slave left tied in a field while the authorities were sent for, then according to *Socrates'* doctrine that a wrongdoer is better off being punished, the father will be better off being punished for his act.

6. Vlastos, *Socrates*, pp. 174–176.

7. Such an account would present necessary and sufficient conditions for piety, stating what is (nonaccidentally) common to all and only pious actions, perhaps in a way that provides a standard by which we can judge the piety of any act. So must the concepts *F* be recursive? Would a recursively enumerable concept fail to provide the requisite standard?

8. See Robert Nozick, *Philosophical Explanations* (Harvard University Press, Cambridge, Mass., 1981), pp. 172–196, and Steven Luper-Foy, *The Possibility of Knowledge: Essays on Nozick's Theory of Knowledge* (Rowman and Littlefield, N.J., 1987).

9. We need not attribute to Socrates the very strong assumption that something is good only if it is good (and benefits one) in every possible context. Even a knowledge of the good cannot pass such a test. Consider the context in which if you do come to have knowledge of the good, then beings on alpha centauri will destroy your own mental capacities, or will destroy all life on earth. Socrates need only claim that something is good only if it is good in all *normal* contexts, whether or not there is some extraordinary context in which it leads to disaster, and that the ignorance of the good Socrates speaks of can lead to disaster in a normal context.

10. Vlastos, "The Socratic Elenchus," *Oxford Studies in Ancient Philosophy* 1 (1983), pp. 27–58.

11. See Vlastos, *Socrates*, pp. 113–114. See also footnote 44 in Vlastos's "Socrates' Disavowal of Knowledge."

12. Vlastos calls this "the puzzle of the elenchus" in the introduction to *Socrates: Ironist and Moral Philosopher*, p. 15, but in stating only (B) he does not reach all the way to an answer.

13. And once he denies the true statement *p*, has he then avoided inconsistency? Or is the person assumed to have other true beliefs that will maintain inconsistency with his existent false ones; does he have sufficient true beliefs about the central nature or essence of the concept under investigation, so that any false belief will conflict with one of these? But what stops him from giving up these?

14. The letters naming the three assumptions mark these facts: Vlastos's assumption speaks only of belief, the second one speaks also of knowledge, and the third one speaks of how inconsistencies are resolved.

15. Or are they reachable but not in any finite number of steps? Should we redust Leibnitz's notion of infinite analysis and Peirce's of the ideal limit of inquiry?

16. "The Paradox of Socrates" was published in the *Queen's Quarterly* (Winter 1958) and is reprinted as the Introduction in Gregory Vlastos, ed., *The Philosophy of Socrates* (Anchor Books, New York, 1971). In *Socrates: Ironist and Moral Philosopher*, p. 44, footnote 82, Vlastos says that in earlier drafts of that volume's chapter on Socratic irony, he maintained the failure-of-love thesis but was convinced it was false (or unnecessary to introduce in explaining Socrates' behavior) by a student in his seminar, Don Adams. Vlastos does not state what reasons convinced him to change his view. The thesis is still worth discussing, I believe, even though Vlastos came no longer to maintain it.

17. But after he states this point in "The Paradox of Socrates," Vlastos goes on to argue (pp. 15–16) that the doctrine that virtue is knowledge is mistaken. However, a mistaken doctrine does not indicate a failure of love unless Socrates was led to this particular mistake *because* it excluded other, more loving ways of saving souls. Vlastos then goes on to state that Socrates' flaw is not just a mistake in doctrine but a failure of love. But he offers no further argument for this.

18. Why is this better? The account of retributive punishment I offered in *Philosophical Explanations*, pp. 363–393, might supplement Socrates' view. Even if retributive punishment effects no further change in a person, it is better for that person to be connected (via punishment for wrongs done) to correct values than to be completely disconnected. Best is to act on correct values, second best to repent oneself for flouting them, third best to be (even unwillingly) connected to correct values, and worst is to be completely disconnected.

19. Some of Socrates' tactics seem unfair. A person is asked a question, little suspecting what lies ahead. He might have answered differently, or expressed hesitation, if he knew which aspects of the issues Socrates was concerned with. Unsuspectingly he answers, and then is pushed, not to an unwelcome consequence of what he really does believe, but to an unbelieved consequence of what he literally and uncarefully has said. No wonder that often Socrates' interlocutors were annoyed.

Yet Socrates is not merely a crafty lawyer who traps people into contradictions no matter what they believe or start out saying. For his questioning often is illuminating, and drives a reader to a deeper view even when he disagrees with Socrates' view.

20. Escape would injure the state, and injury is not to be caused. But may it not be caused in (legitimate) self-defense—Socrates did serve as a soldier, after all—and is not Socrates under unjust attack? By his actions and acceptance of the benefits of the legal system and the city, Socrates has consented to the city's laws and procedures. How do we know, though, the extent of implicit consent or commitment? Apparently Socrates had not consented to carrying out orders to inflict injustices upon others. Suppose I am told I've implicitly consented to being killed unjustly; mightn't I answer that my actions and receipt of benefits hadn't said *that*? How can the detailed content of an agreement, including whatever exception-clauses it contains, be read off actions performed in circumstances that did not exhibit any of the exceptional conditions? And *is* Socrates trying to kill the city, merely because the city would be destroyed if no one obeyed its edicts in any circumstances? Even if a generalization argument is appropriate here, was "No one should ever obey any edict of the city" really the maxim of Socrates' action? Socrates has received benefits, but is there no limit to what one must do (or accept) in gratitude for benefits received from parents or from one's city?

21. It is not a coincidence that Socrates developed this notion of a beautifully ordered soul while growing up and living in Athens at the very time the Parthenon was being constructed. Did Phidias's building influence Socrates' view, or was Athenian culture the common cause that influenced them both?

7. Experience, Theory, and Language

1. *Word and Object*, p. 5.

2. We need not worry here whether some scattered sentences might have it, e.g., "red here now."

3. Could a person deductively connect his body of beliefs B with experience E by adding to B the belief: if B then E will occur? He couldn't formulate his total body of beliefs so as to place it in the antecedent of this conditional; anything he could state in the antecedent would be only a tiny fragment of his beliefs, yielding something much smaller than a total theory as having experiential consequences.

4. Does Duhem's thesis have even the consequence that sentences don't have some experiential content of their own, even if this does not exhaust them? To derive this consequence one would have to add to Duhem's thesis that individual statements are not disconfirmed by experience, the additional claim that they also are not confirmed by experience.

This is an appropriate place to note that Quine's notion of stimulus meaning does not delineate separate content, in the sense of Duhem. For due to a person's assumptions and other current beliefs, much will be in the negative (or affirmative) stimulus meaning of a sentence for him at a time, which Duhem would hold is not part of the sentence's isolated content. (And wouldn't Quine follow Duhem here?)

5. Compare Quine on dispositions as underlying mechanisms, in *The Roots of Reference*, pp. 10–12; "Natural Kinds," 130–138.

6. Hilary Putnam, "The Meaning of 'Meaning,'" in K. Gunderson, ed., *Minnesota Studies in the Philosophy of Science*, vol. 7 (Minneapolis: University of Minnesota Press, 1975).

7. As remarks on pp. 37, 48 of *Word and Object* hint Quine might do.

8. Yet the facts of scientific agreement to be explained can be specified, I believe, so as not to run afoul of this. Note also that within a psychological theory of spoken utterances of the sort to be discussed below (in terms of past conditioning and three term contingencies), nothing special would ride on the question of whether a particular sound was a "sign of assent" or not.

Quine uses the notions of assent and dissent to develop the notion of a *verdict function*, and notes that conjunction and disjunction are, though truth-functional, not (completely) verdict-functional (*Roots of Reference*, pp. 77–78). We can further delimit conjunction and disjunction by special verdict tables which use negation, which *is* verdict-functional as well as truth-functional. In Quine's verdict tables (p. 77), let q be not-p; we get six cases which don't arise, but we also get dissent as the center entry for conjunction and assent as the center entry for disjunction. *If* to learn *and* and *or* is also to learn these special verdict tables, we have the law of non-contradiction and excluded middle centrally bound up with the very learning of these notions. (Contrast Quine's remarks on p. 80 of *Roots of Reference*.)

9. *Word and Object*, p. 39. A more limited view of stimulus meaning as individuating what can be learned in ostension is taken by Quine in "Replies," p. 313.

10. I take the following listing of 'facts' to be explained by semantic theory from Jerrold Katz, *Semantic Theory* (New York: Harper and Row, 1972), pp. 5–6, who goes on to say (p. 7) "that the phenomena cited . . . are semantic in nature and that together they provide us with a reasonable conception of what phenomena the subject of semantics is concerned with seems to me beyond serious doubt."

11. See Katz, p. 24, for this description of communication.

12. Noam Chomsky, "Formal Properties of Grammars," in R. D. Luce, R. Bush, and E. Galanter (eds.), *Handbook of Mathematical Psychology*, vol. 2 (New York: John Wiley and Sons, 1963), p. 330.

13. The standard position within the philosophy of science would have it be the simplest linguistics plus psychology that is desired, just as it is the simplest geometry plus physics. A partial focus on the simplest linguistics corresponds to Poincaré's commitment to the simplest geometry. On the view to be described below, in which linguistics disappears within psychology, what would be desired is the simplest total psychology.

14. Chomsky, *Aspects*, p. 4.

15. Katz, *Semantic Theory*, pp. 16–17, in a section entitled "Theories about the objective reality of language," takes this view of language. See also de Saussure, *Course in General Linguistics* (New York: McGraw Hill, 1959), p. 9; and Louis Hjelmslev, *Prolegomena to a Theory of Language* (Madison: University of Wisconsin Press, 1963), pp. 5–6.

16. Quine, *Philosophy of Logic*, pp. 15–16; "The Problem of Meaning in Linguistics," in *From a Logical Point of View*, pp. 49, 51–54.

17. Quine asks, "What is the rationale behind that infinite additional membership of K, over and above the finite part J?" and answers that the linguist rounds off. ("Problem of Meaning in Linguistics," p. 54). But wouldn't this Quinean linguist reject a rounding off which failed to fit a complicated utterance he could produce yet hadn't (with none like it being in J already)? "Without this notion (of significant sequence or possible normal utterance) or something to somewhat the same effect, we cannot say what the grammarian is trying to do" (p. 52). This should not be too worrisome if, even with the notion, we can't say why he's trying to do it.

18. There is no objection to describing patterns among the actual products of a process when this serves to explain some further facts identifiable *apart* from the theory which describes the patterns, *viz.,* biologists doing taxonomy or describing the functions of organs or the physiology of organisms.

Shall the set of sentences of the language be delineated in order to specify the output the psychological theory must have, thus serving as an eternal condition of adequacy on the psychological theory rather than as a component of it? But for that purpose, one would not (contra linguistics) offer a specification which goes far beyond anything we know an actual person can do.

19. As Quine, I think, would agree. I discuss it briefly here only because it would provide a rationale for the grammarian's task as Quine states that task; and I see no other rationale.

20. "Problem of Meaning in Linguistics," pp. 55–56.

21. We cannot distinguish circumstances which trigger an existing disposition to utter a sentence from those which teach the language and create such a disposition by the duration of circumstances C; consider sentences such as "I have been ——ing for n years," where presently you have been ——ing for a far shorter time. And any acquisition of a disposition to say will itself be based

upon a pre-existing disposition (neurological condition) to acquire the first disposition. In what way is this pre-existing disposition ruled out as the requisite disposition to utter *S*?

22. *The Roots of Reference*, p. 15.

23. B. F. Skinner, *Verbal Behavior* (New York: Appleton-Century-Crofts, 1957).

24. "The behaviors of speaker and listener together compose what may be called a total verbal episode. There is nothing in such an episode which is more than the combined behavior of two or more individuals. Nothing 'emerges' in the social unit. The speaker can be studied while assuming a listener, and the listener while assuming a speaker. The separate accounts which result exhaust the episode in which both participate." Skinner, *Verbal Behavior*, p. 2.

25. "Propositional Objects," in *Ontological Relativity*, p. 158; see also *Roots of Reference*, p. 41.

26. *Words and Objections*, p. 284.

27. "The idioms of propositional attitudes have uses in which they are not easily supplanted" (*Philosophy of Logic*, p. 34).

28. A view of realist philosophy of science as an explanatory theory is presented by Richard Boyd in an unpublished manuscript.

29. Within his theory, Quine thinks "we give content to the ontological issue when we regiment the language of science strictly within the framework of the logic of truth functions and objectual quantification." Otherwise, saying constructions are innocent of referential intent "would be meaningless for want of a standard of referential intent" (*Roots of Reference*, p. 136). But what *content* does the ontological issue have when given content? What we quantify over; but what is that standard a standard of? What (we think) there is; what our speech commits us to there being. But then Quine's remarks about why we shouldn't assess our referential intent via seeing what we quantify over with *branched quantifiers* are puzzling. For why should the fact that ordinary quantification theory "determines an integrated domain of logical theory with bold and significant boundaries," "enjoys an extraordinary combination of depth and simplicity, beauty and utility," and admits of complete proof procedures for validity and inconsistency, whereas branched quantification theory doesn't (see *Philosophy of Logic*, pp. 89–91; "Existence and Quantification," pp. 111–113), recommend it over branched quantifiers as our criterion of ontological commitment? If these virtues are relevant to "referential intent," then either we need a sharper discussion to show why, or "referential intent" doesn't mean what we thought it did. When the choice of criterion is so delicate, what is the value or purpose of the ontologist's (standing on the best current theory and) telling us what exists?

30. See Skinner, *Verbal Behavior*, epilogue 1, "The Validity of the Author's Verbal Behavior," pp. 453–456.

31. See Skinner, pp. 114–115.

32. In the long interim between the writing of this essay in 1975 and its publication in 1986, a piece was detached and published elsewhere instead. See "Simplicity as Fall-Out," originally published in 1983, reprinted here as Essay 8.

References for Essay 7

Quine, W. V. "Epistemology Naturalized." In J. R. Royce and
W. W. Roozeboom (eds.), *The Psychology of Knowing* (London: Gordon and Breach, 1972). Also in R. M. Chisholm and R. S. Swartz (eds.), *Empirical Knowledge* (New York: Prentice Hall, 1973).

—— "Existence and Quantification." In *Ontological Relativity and Other Essays.*

—— *From a Logical Point of View* (Cambridge, MA: Harvard University Press, 1953; new ed., 1980).

—— "Natural Kinds." In *Ontological Relativity and Other Essays.*

—— *Ontological Relativity and Other Essays* (New York: Columbia University Press, 1969).

—— *Philosophy of Logic* (Englewood, NJ: Prentice Hall, 1970; rev. ed., Cambridge, MA: Harvard University Press, 1986).

—— "Replies [to Critics]." In Donald Davidson and Jaakko Hintikka (eds.), *Words and Objections: Essays on the Work of W. V. Quine* (Dordrecht: D. Reidel, 1969).

—— *The Roots of Reference* (La Salle, IL: Open Court, 1974).

—— *Word and Object* (Cambridge, MA: MIT Press, 1960; paperback edition, 1964).

8. Simplicity as Fall-Out

This essay was part of a larger one written in 1975 (see Essay 7) and was deleted from that one in order to appear in a volume of essays in honor of Sidney Morgenbesser in 1983 (*How Many Questions?*, ed. Leigh Cauman et al.). Its publication in that volume was especially appropriate because it was in Morgenbesser's classes that I first encountered the writings of Quine and issues about simplicity.

1. W. V. Quine, "On Simple Theories of a Complex World," in his *The Ways of Paradox* (Cambridge, Mass.: Harvard University Press, 1976), p. 255.

2. *The Web of Belief* (New York: Random House, 1970), p. 47.

3. I doubt whether Quine is correct in his particular claims about how simplicity might artifactually be favored by our procedures. Some experimental setups allow us to get evidence for similarities but not for differences. Do none work in the reverse direction? And Quine's claim that if we add a parameter we have modified a hypothesis whereas if we change a parameter the hypothesis is refuted, seems merely verbal (is it "refuted" or "altered"?), and too fragile to support or produce even an artifact of the procedures.

4. See Hilary Putnam, "'Degree of Confirmation' and Inductive Logic," in P. A. Schilpp (ed.), *The Philosophy of Rudolf Carnap* (La Salle, Ill.: Open Court, 1963), esp. pp. 770–774. Refinements of our approach to simplicity, I hope, would apply to more complicated and intricate versions of this simple model.

5. It is an oversimplification to say that only data gathered *after* a hypothesis is formulated support it. (Even the oversimplification should be put more accurately so that it ignores *when* the hypothesis was formulated, and concentrates on whether or not the hypothesis was *designed* to fit the data.) A newly accepted hypothesis (accepted on the basis of independent data gathered after its formulation) will *inherit* as support the data of the hypothesis it supplants, even though the new hypothesis was geared to explain the previously known data. So there is a historical *change* in whether data support a hypothesis; data that don't at one time support a hypothesis (because the hypothesis was dreamed up to fit those data) may come later to support it, when that hypothesis is accepted because it also fits new data that refute the previously reigning hypothesis. This phenomenon of inherited support makes it (even more) likely that the method of tenacity will yield much of the maxim of conservatism about theory change.

6. More accurately, that subset of the original batch containing all those as simple as H_S, including H_S itself.

7. Note that we have presented, thus far, an *invisible-hand explanation* of simplicity. [See my *Anarchy, State, and Utopia* (New York: Basic Books, 1974), pp. 18–22.] There may be still another connection between simplicity and underdetermination of theories. Underdetermination of theories makes it too easy to find a hypothesis that fits the data, and so the fact that one fits isn't (much) support for it. Whereas being a hypothesis that data gathered afterwards fit is harder. But there might be yet other hard conditions to fulfill. Is a hypothesis supported if it fulfills *any* hard-to-fulfill previously formulated condition *C*, or must something independently be said for *C* as connected with truth? To whatever extent the former gives support, then, having a certain degree of simplicity will count for a hypothesis, if it is not easy to find a simple hypothesis that fits the data.

8. If "simpler than" was not merely some structural relationship between hypotheses or theories, but also depended upon the way the hypotheses handled the data at hand, then the argument would not go through. For in *this* case

$H_1, \ldots, H_m$ might each be simpler than *any* other hypothesis to explain data D_1, yet at the second stage still another hypothesis could be simpler than any one of these in relation to the data $D_1 + D_2$. (I owe this observation to Walter Gilbert.) Thus the argument applies only to notions of simplicity which satisfy 5. Note also that the conditions do not mention or require multiple generation of T's at any stage. Though presumably the more there are, the quicker there will be convergence to the D-est.

9. Might the *whole* truth about simplicity be that standards of simplicity change to fit what we believe? No, for we still think some hypotheses that were rejected earlier (e.g., circular planetary orbits) are simpler than what we currently believe. There is no psychological process that creates a simplicity gradient that peaks at our current beliefs.

10. Gilbert Harman, "The Inference to the Best Explanation," *Philosophical Review* 74, 1 (January 1965), 88–95.

11. When we seek simplicity in this way, the total process whereby we end up with simplicity is no longer merely an invisible-hand process, though it is based on one. The invisible-hand character of even the original fall-out process would be undermined if part of the explanation of why (in that process) we think up the hypotheses we do is that they are simple; that is, if we tend to think them up *because* they're simple. On the view we have presented, we think them simple because we tend to think them up.

I need hardly mention that I do not claim that the view presented here is the *complete* story about simplicity. But so intractable is the topic of the real connection between simplicity and truth that it is progress, I think, to chip away at simplicity, reducing what remains for a (metaphysical?) theory to explain.

9. Invisible-Hand Explanations

This essay is dedicated to the memory of Raymond Lubitz, 1937–1984, A.B. Columbia (1959), B. Phil. Oxford (1961), Ph.D. in Economics, Harvard University (1967), Assistant and Associate Professor of Economics, Columbia University (1967–1973), Federal Reserve Board, Washington, D.C. (1973–1984), and Chief of its World Payments Economic Activities Section, Division of International Finance; coauthor of Kenen and Lubitz (1971).

1. Daniel Dennett (1991) proposes such a disaggregated theory of the self. Question: what decentralized competing processes *within* an individual would give rise to a (relatively) coherent decision-maker?

2. For instance, a theory would be interesting if it showed that, although everyone *was* aiming at a pattern, either their actions animated by that aim were not what produced the pattern, or if they did, that the pattern did not

arise by the route everyone imagined—it was a side effect of their envisioned plans.

3. The evidentially expected utility of an action is the weighted sum of the utilities of its (exclusive) possible outcomes, weighted by their conditional probabilities given the actions. The causally expected utility of an act replaces these conditional probabilities by probabilities (of outcomes on actions) reflecting some direct causal influence.

4. Notice that, on this view, decision theory is not a theory of rational action, but of best or optimal action. An action would be rational if it were given rise to by a process that reliably yields optimal or maximizing actions. However, a person might happen to stumble confusedly upon doing such a maximizing action. In performing it, he would not be acting rationally, for his action would not be generated by a process that reliably produces optimal actions.

5. Invisible-hand explanations need not be a subclass of methodological individualist ones. Suppose that some pattern arises at random in particular societies, and also that there exists an irreducible filter (not susceptible to individualist explanation) that eliminates all societies that do not fit that pattern. Then there would be an invisible-hand (but not an individualist) explanation of why all societies fit that pattern (see Nozick, 1974, p. 22). (I sharpen and discuss the notion of methodological individualism in Nozick, 1977.)

In his Ely lecture, Kenneth Arrow (1994) refers to common information in the public domain as raising problems for methodological individualist explanation, but it is not evident why either the existence or the consequences of such information (or of *books!*) must elude such explanations.

References for Essay 9

Arrow, Kenneth J. 1994. "Methodological Individualism and Social Knowledge." *American Economic Review* 84(2): 1–9.

Becker, Gary. 1981. *A Treatise on the Family.* Cambridge, MA: Harvard University Press.

Cambell, Richmond, and Lanning Sowden. 1985. *Paradoxes of Rationality and Cooperation: Prisoner's Dilemma and Newcomb's Problem.* Vancouver: University of British Columbia Press.

Dennett, Daniel. 1991. *Consciousness Explained.* Boston: Little, Brown.

Kenen, Peter B., and Raymond Lubitz. *International Economics,* 3d ed. Englewood Cliffs, NJ: Prentice-Hall.

Nozick, Robert. 1969. "Newcomb's Problem and Two Principles of Choice." [See Essay 2.]

———— 1974. *Anarchy, State, and Utopia.* New York: Basic Books.

———— 1977. "On Austrian Methodology." [See Essay 5.]

———— 1993. *The Nature of Rationality*. Princeton, NJ: Princeton University Press.
Ullmann-Margalit, Edna. 1978. "Invisible-Hand Explanations." *Synthese* 39(2): 263–291.

10. Moral Complications and Moral Structures

Parts of this essay were delivered in an address given to the twelfth annual meeting of the Board of Editors of the *Natural Law Forum*, September 29, 1967.

    1. An especially clear and self-conscious example of attempting to carry out this task is Henry Sidgwick's *Methods of Ethics* (1907).

    2. Goodman (1955), chap. III.

    3. He might not say "because it has features $T_1, \ldots, T_m$," but rather "because it has features ————" and fill in the blank with some though not all of the m T-features. The task of accounting for the shortening of the answer is similar to that faced by an adherent of the deductive-nomological model as an adequate account of a certain kind of explanation (or as presenting necessary conditions for one important kind of explanation) in explaining why when one says "Event E happens because ————" one does not normally fill in the blank with *all* of the things that the model says forms part of the explanation, not even with all of the initial conditions. For a discussion of the kinds of principles underlying the shortening of explanation answers (which is relevant to the point with which this footnote begins), cf. S. Bromberger, "An Approach to Explanation," in Butler (1965); "Why Questions," in Colodny (1966); and Hart and Honoré (1959), chaps. I–II. On the deductive-nomological model of explanation, see Hempel (1965). Though I shall later in the text be discussing a model of the structure of moral views other than the deductive one, this alternative model also faces the task of accounting for shortened answers. The literature cited here is also relevant to that task for the alternative model, which I shall not attempt in this paper.

    4. That is, principles of the form of (3) and (4) where it can be decided, with little room for fiddling, on nonmoral grounds whether the features mentioned in the principle apply to an action. For other sorts of features the persons I am considering might be willing to assent to exceptionless principles, e.g., "any action which shows lack of love of one's neighbor is morally impermissible."

    5. Cf. The American Law Institute (1962), sec. 3.02. No rules are provided whereby it is to be determined whether "the harm or evil sought to be avoided by such conduct is greater than that sought to be prevented by the law defining the offense charged," and presumably this is to be decided by a jury.

6. It is worth briefly noting one kind of theoretical solution to this particular reason for desiring judicial discretion. ("Theoretical" because it ignores limitations upon the time and energy of legislators and legislatures.) In those cases, which are not constitutional cases and which needn't be decided immediately, where, under the doctrine of judicial discretion, the judge should *use* his discretion (e.g., an obvious injustice is worked by the law as it "clearly" stands, the legislature did not foresee such a case and would not, one thinks, have intended the consequence required by the law in such a case, etc.), the judge finds the person guilty and throws the case back to the legislature. That is, he notifies the legislature that here is a case where he believes an obvious injustice is worked by the law as it "clearly" stands, and the legislature has a specified amount of time to pass new legislation in this area. If under the new law, the defendant's act is no longer an offense, he is then found innocent. If some act performed by someone prior to the promulgation of the new law is an offense (only according to the new law), he is not tried.

In the preceding paragraph, I consider only those cases where, under the doctrine of judicial discretion, the judge should use his discretion to avoid the defendant's being found guilty of an offense. In the cases where the law "clearly" holds the person innocent, many of the objections to ex post facto legislation would apply to a judge's using his discretion to find the person guilty. (Though perhaps one would sometimes wish it to be done. Cf. e.g., *Riggs v. Palmer*, 115 N.Y. 506, 22 N.E. 188 [1889].) Similarly, though less strongly, for cases where no particular finding is "clearly" required by the law as written. In cases where two parties are opposing litigants, a more complicated procedure would be needed.

Many detailed questions arise about the operation of a system such as the one sketched above which, in view of the theoretical character of the solution, are not worth pursuing here. The reason for mentioning such a "solution" is to point out that no analogous procedure is even theoretically available to us in the moral case. For, putting it roughly, our task of accounting for an individual's moral judgments is like the one of formulating the rules and principles by which, under the scheme, the legislature decides the cases thrown back to it, or the judge decides when an injustice would be worked by the nondiscretionary application of the law.

7. See his books, *The Right and the Good* (Ross, 1930) and *Foundations of Ethics* (Ross, 1939).

8. Whether the *R*-list should contain (and contain only) features such that an action having some of these features, and none on the *W*-list, is morally required, is a question that requires much discussion. What is important is that it contain features which may override features on the *W*-list. The host of complicated questions about how to state this, and its consequences, will be considered later.

9. This seems an appropriate place to informally explain some symbols which sometimes are used at different places in the text, with which some readers may be unfamiliar. $X \cup Y$ (the union of set X and set Y) is that set containing as members just those things which are members of X, or Y, or both. ϕ is the set without any members, and is referred to as the null set. "$X \subset Y$" is read "X is a (proper) subset of Y" and is true if and only if each member of set X is also a member of set Y, and some member of set Y is not a member of set X. "$X \subseteq Y$" is read "X is a subset of Y" and is true if and only if $X \subset Y$ or X and Y have exactly the same members. A selection set from a group of sets is a set containing exactly one member from each set in the group. "$x \in X$" is read "x is a member of the set X." "$(\exists x)$ (... x ...)" is read "There is an x such that (... x ...)," e.g., "$(\exists x)$ (green x)" is read "There is an x such that x is green" or "There is something which is green." "(x) (... x ...)" is read "For all x, (... x ...)," e.g., "(x) (green x)" is read "For all x, x is green." "——— → ... " is read "if ——— then ... " As an example of how things fit together

$$(X)(X \text{ is a set} \rightarrow (\exists y)(y \in X) \text{ or } X = \phi)$$

is read: For all X, if X is a set then there is a y such that y is a member of X, or X is equal to the null set.

10. If an action with members of R and no members of W may be morally permissible though not morally required, it is not clear how to interpret $\phi < R_i$.

11. I shall ignore in this paper any need for variables ranging over all the rationals or reals.

12. In this section "features" shall refer to features on the lists without variables, or specifications of features, with variables, on the lists (i.e., with constants substituted for each variable). If certain conditions are met, features with bounded variables (the bounds being represented by equations) may be included also. I shall not pursue here the obvious way to do this.

13. The metaphor of balancing and outweighing leads one to want to consider a notion of exactly balancing, and to want to distinguish moral views which hold that in exact balancing situations the action is morally permissible, from those that hold that in exact balancing situations the action is morally impermissible. Though our explanation of the inequality sign does not leave room for this distinction, it may be desirable to pursue the possibility of other structures which allow it.

14. Strictly speaking, since (2) is not imposed upon our fragmentary moral views, this intuitive argument for (3) should be put somewhat differently.

15. In the absence of (3), one might wish to define $X \gg Y$ as (Z) $(Y > Z \rightarrow X > Z)$ & $(Z)(Z > X \rightarrow Z > Y)$ & $(\exists Z)$ $(X > Z$ & $Z > Y)$.

16. For an explanation of this and other ordering terminology, see Suppes (1957), pp. 220–223.

17. Very difficult issues arise here, related to some about explaining the notion of "intrinsically valuable" when there are causal or probability connections between features, which must be considered in a full exposition of the theory.

18. It does not matter whether you agree with my moral conclusions about these particular two situations. What is important is that you can find two situations with structures parallel to these which you would view as I view these: e.g., in (1) the only way to stop P is to shoot him; in (2) you can also stop him by lying to him.

19. I am here assuming the truth of condition (5) of section III. If this condition or some of the others accepted in section III are inadequate then more complicated principles must be formulated here. But even if the conditions in the previous section are inadequate and must be replaced, we can adequately raise the issues we are concerned with here by using them.

20. One does not need a scale of measurement stronger than that gotten in section III, to state condition V. For $(W_A - W_B) > 0$ can be stated, using the notation of section III, as $W_A \gg W_B$. Similarly, one may state condition VI below without assuming such a stronger scale of measurement. However, the statement of VII, below, *does* require the assumption of a stronger scale of measurement than we yet have available.

21. We might consider the stronger principle
(VII') If $(\exists B)$ (B is an alternative available to the person & $W_A \gg W_B$ & $(W_A - W_B) \geq (R_A - R_B)$), then it is impermissible to do A.
This principle, unlike (VII), covers the case where $(W_A - W_B) = (R_A - R_B)$. Given a scale of measurement we might be able to interpret this, but we could not, if my remarks in section III were correct, offer an intuitive argument for (VII') similar to that offered for (VII). For the action C which took up the difference between B and A would have to be such that $W_C = R_C$. And we have not seen any way to interpret this.

22. Paralleling the economists' notion of opportunity cost, one may deny this. My claim, to be elaborated below, is that all morally relevant opportunity cost of an action is already implicitly built into its W-features.

23. I am not claiming that it is always permissible to lie to someone to save oneself personal expense and inconvenience, or that it always is permissible when the R-features outweigh the W-features, but that it sometimes is in this latter case. No doubt, the pursuer's performing a wrongful act makes it especially clear in this case.

24. That is, are there cases where C does *not* stand in the relation described by (VII) to A, yet it is impermissible to do A (if B is available) and if so, how are

these to be marked off from the cases where B stands in the relation described by (VII) to A, yet—because of the personal costs which B involves—it is not impermissible to do A?

25. This First Asymmetry thesis has the consequence that there is no duality which involves only the substitution of "permissible" for "impermissible," and "$<$" for "$>$," as there is in the simple structure with which we began in section II. Talk of asymmetries brings to mind the famous asymmetry between good and bad; *viz,* that all good things must come to an end.

26. Note that it does not follow from this that in every possible situation there is at least one action available to a person which is morally permissible. It *may* be that a person can (wrongfully) intentionally put himself into a situation such that none of the alternatives in the situation he got himself into are morally permissible for him to do.

27. Notice that we are here speaking of whether something *about the alternatives* to A can prevent A from being impermissible even though $W_A > R_A$. In section VI we shall consider whether A can be morally permissible, even though $W_A > R_A$, because of something about larger courses of action of which A is a part.

28. I owe this example, which led to a rewriting of an earlier version of this part of this section, to Professor Judith Thomson of the Massachusetts Institute of Technology.

29. This is not the same as saying that if the train were proceeding along a side track it would be permissible to switch it to the center track because avoiding the death of 40 persons outweighs killing 20 persons.

30. We might say that a feature of an act, for our purposes, is about *that* act, and not about, even implicitly, others. Of course, the problems in explaining *this* are immense.

31. Cf. Von Neumann and Morgenstern (1953), appendix; Luce and Raiffa (1957), chap. II; G. Debreu, "Cardinal Utility for Even-Chance Mixtures of Pairs of Sure Prospects," *Review of Economic Studies* 26 (1959), 174–177. For weakening of the strong conditions, relevant to attempts to parallel them in the moral case, see M. Hausner, "Multidimensional Utilities," in Thrall, Coombs, and Davis (1954), and R. J. Aumann, "Utility Theory without the Completeness Axiom," *Econometrica* 29 (1962), 445–462.

32. Throughout (a)–(d′) the labels of the form F_X and W_X are merely labels for sets of features and do not say anything more than this. I have used these labels, in a notation which is by now familiar, because I shall soon discuss the sets of features for situations where the here-arbitrary labels mean what they have meant previously.

33. Perhaps the person could reasonably judge that, under the described circumstances, a particular A is impermissible if B is available for reasons quite

different from the sort we are here considering. One should incorporate conditions excluding such reasons into the antecedent of the principle. (I assume there are a small number of kinds. One does not want to require in the antecedent of the principles the proper kind of reason unless there is a way of specifying it which does not require reference to an apparatus beyond the one we had before numbers were introduced.) In this way one can hope to eliminate any counter-examples to the principle which there may be, which are irrelevant to our concern here.

34. This is all put roughly. For detailed discussions of Representation and Uniqueness theorems, see P. Suppes and J. L. Zinnes, "Basic Measurement Theory," in Luce, Bush, and Galanter (1963).

35. On structural conditions, see P. Suppes, "Some Open Problems in the Foundations of Subjective Probability," in Machol (1960), and D. Scott and P. Suppes, "Foundational Aspects of Theories of Measurement," *Journal of Symbolic Logic* 23 (1958), 113–128.

36. For further details on the sort of existing system I am thinking of, see S. Siegel, "A Method for Obtaining and Ordered Metric Scale," *Psychometrika* 21 (1956), 207–216; P. Suppes and M. Winet, "An Axiomatization of Utility Based on the Notion of Utility Differences," *Journal of Management Science* 1 (1955), 259–270; and especially R. D. Luce and J. D. Tukey, "Simultaneous Conjoint Measurement: A New Type of Fundamental Measurement," *Journal of Mathematical Psychology* 1 (1964), 1–27.

37. If we let W_A'' be the set-theoretic difference $(W_A - W_A')$ then, given an addivity assumption which is not unreasonable for these cases, one will get (for the case where $W_A > R_A$) the result that $W_A'' > R_A - W_A'$. And by using this, we may get a measure of the weight of the "features" which refer to the suitable alternative acts.

38. I have already argued that because of considerations about *alternative* courses of action taking up the same time interval as A does, $R_A > W_A$ is not a sufficient condition for A's being permissible.

39. Suppose, for simplicity, a finite number of possible larger courses of action of which A is a part, $A^1, A^2, \ldots, A^n$. Then if "is part of an act which ——" *is* a feature of an act, then A would have as a W-feature "must be part of an act with features $W_A 1$ or with features $W_A 2$ or . . . or with features $W_A n$."

40. Strictly, no part of measure non-zero. I shall omit this in what follows.

41. One can define an apparently weaker notion: A is *weakly undercut$_t$* = df. (X) (X is an act over t containing $A \rightarrow (\exists Y)$ (Y does not contain A & Y undercuts$_0$ X)). Similarly one can get definitions paralleling the ones which follow by using "weakly undercuts" rather than "strongly undercuts" (and other obvious changes). Interesting questions arise about the relation of the "weak" notions to the "strong" ones.

42. (2) is equivalent to: If $W_A > R_A$ then [A is permissible if and only if ($\exists C$) (C is available to the person & A is part of C & $R_C > W_C$ & C is not ruled impermissible by (1))].

43. In this case, principles (1) and (2) above.

44. Here, as below, I ignore the issues raised in sections IV and VI, and momentarily suppose that permissibility or impermissibility is determined by the way some general inequality goes. Such a simplification is useful as a first step in an intuitive explanation of the different ways.

45. As in the case where you don't go to a dinner to which you promised to go, in order to minister to an accident victim whom you encounter on the way to the dinner. You must call your hostess "as soon as possible" (compatible with your best ministering), make explanations, etc.

46. Though perhaps the person saved is so required. This raises the question of whether in all such cases *someone* (though perhaps not the person who did the act) is morally required, if it is possible, to make amends or reparations to those harmed by overridden W-features of an act. Pursuing this issue leads one to issues similar to some discussed by welfare economists; see Little (1960), chap. VI.

47. When one reaches the point where one can make amends or reparations or offer explanations, some features override or overcome "not making amends or reparations and not offering explanations after a I situation" which do not override or overcome "not making amends or reparations and not offering explanations after a II situation," and the second outweighs or overshadows some R-features that the first does not.

48. Take the first person who T-ed someone else. If his action is morally impermissible, he is from that time forth, a *T-person*. If his action was morally permissible, take the next person to T someone. The first one who does it impermissibly becomes the first T-person. (I ignore here the possibility that two persons simultaneously and impermissibly T each other.) The only way to become a T-person is by T-ing someone who is not a T-person, where the W-features of this act of T-ing are not overridden, overcome, etc. On the view we are considering, it is permissible to T a T-person; that is, the W-feature, T, of an action has no moral weight when the action is done to a T-person.

I do not wish to discuss here whether, for some feature T on the W-list, such a view is correct. It is a possible view, and an adequate account of the sort of moral structures we are discussing must be able to handle it.

49. I shall not pause to consider the different views that fall under the retributivists' view that it's good that someone who has committed a wrong suffer; e.g., is it good that he suffer, or is it good that he suffer *because* he's committed the wrong (that his suffering be due to his having committed the wrong),

or is it good (that his suffering be due to his having committed the wrong, and he know that his suffering is due to having committed the wrong)? And if more than one of these is held to be good, do they differ in degree of goodness?

50. V–VIII have only been sketched. The details needed to state them correctly would take us away from our major concern here.

51. To be sure, the lawyers must write something down completely, without open-ended lists. (Though perhaps section 3.02 of the Model Penal Code is meant to open the ends.) I should note that nothing I say here depends upon a claim that, given its content, section 3.04 of the Model Penal Code cannot plausibly be reduced to a simpler structure.

52. Distinctions analogous to those discussed, for example, in R. Chisholm, "Supererogation and Offense: A Conceptual Scheme for Ethics," *Ratio* 5 (1963), 1–14, and R. Chisholm and E. Sosa, "Intrinsic Preferability and the Problem of Supererogation," *Synthese* 16 (1966), 321–331.

53. Suggestive material can be found in Levi (1967), chap. VIII.

54. I ignore the complications introduced by section IV about alternative courses of action, and also ignore the complications introduced in section VI about longer courses of action. These extra complications just reinforce the point to be made here, and would unduly complicate my exposition.

55. Persons who hold that if someone is to have made a moral judgment that an action is impermissible, then he must have certain kinds of moral reasons in *support* of the judgment, must deny that in this case the person has made a moral judgment.

56. See Chomsky (1965), chap. I, secs. 1 and 2; and for some critical remarks, G. Harman, "Psychological Aspects of the Theory of Syntax," *Journal of Philosophy* 64 (1967), 75.

57. One year after the completion of this essay, I am led to add a gnomic footnote, which I hope to explain elsewhere. It now (September, 1968) seems to me that if one were completely successful in carrying through the program of this paper (which is *far* from having been done here), one would have produced a *Tractatus Logico-Ethicus*. What is needed, perhaps, is an Ethical Investigations.

References for Essay 10

American Law Institute. 1962. *Model Penal Code: Proposed Official Draft.*
Butler, R. J., ed. 1965. *Analytical Philosophy*, second series. Oxford: Basil Blackwell.
Chomsky, Noam. 1965. *Aspects of the Theory of Syntax.* Cambridge, MA: MIT Press.

Colodny, R. G., ed. 1966. *Mind and Cosmos*. Pittsburgh: University of Pittsburgh Press.

Goodman, Nelson. 1955. *Fact, Fiction, and Forecast*. Cambridge, MA: Harvard University Press.

Hare, R. M. 1963. *Freedom and Reason*. Oxford: Clarendon Press.

Hart, H. L. A., and A. M. Honoré. 1959. *Causation in the Law*. Oxford: Clarendon Press.

Hempel, Carl G. 1965. *Aspects of Scientific Explanation*. New York: Free Press.

Levi, Isaac. 1967. *Gambling with Truth*. New York: Alfred A. Knopf.

Little, I. M. D. 1960. *A Critique of Welfare Economics*, 2d ed. Oxford: Oxford University Press.

Luce, R. D., R. Bush, and E. Galanter, eds. 1963. *Handbook of Mathematical Psychology*, vol 1. New York: Wiley and Sons.

Luce, R. D., and H. Raiffa. 1957. *Games and Decisions*. New York: Wiley and Sons.

Machol, R. E., ed. 1960. *Information and Decision Processes*. New York: McGraw-Hill.

Ross, W. D. 1930. *The Right and the Good*. Oxford: Clarendon Press.

———— 1939. *Foundations of Ethics*. Oxford: Clarendon Press.

Sidgwick, Henry. 1907. *The Methods of Ethics*. 7th ed. London: Macmillan.

Suppes, Patrick. 1957. *Introduction to Logic*. Princeton, N.J.: D. Van Nostrand Co., Inc.

Thrall, R. M., C. H. Coombs, and R. L. Davis, eds. 1954. *Decision Processes*. New York: Wiley and Sons.

Von Neumann, J., and Oscar Morgenstern. 1953. *Theory of Games and Economic Behavior*, 3d ed. Princeton, N.J.: Princeton University Press.

11. On the Randian Argument

1. The main sources are *Atlas Shrugged*, especially Galt's long speech, and the essay "The Objectivist Ethics" in her book of essays, *The Virtue of Selfishness*. The other essays in this book are helpful also (later references to some of her other essays will be to essays in this book), as are her other books, including *Introduction to Objectivist Epistemology*, in understanding her views.

Since I shall be quite critical of Miss Rand's argument in the remainder of this essay, I should here note (especially since she has been given a largely vituperative and abusive hearing in print) that I have found her two major novels exciting, powerful, illuminating, and thought-provoking. These virtues, even combined with a "sense of life" that is worthy of man, do not, of course, guarantee that her conclusions are true, and even if we suppose they are true, all this does not, of course, guarantee that the actual *arguments* offered will be cogent, that they will prove their conclusions. Nothing I say in this essay is meant to deny that Miss Rand is an interesting thinker, worthy of attention.

2. Note in passing that persons may have innate preferences unconnected with their own welfare and survival. There is a natural selection argument that, in the evolutionary process, preferences that tend to help keep you alive to the reproductive age will be selected for, but also there are natural selection arguments that innate preferences for behavior which is reproductive behavior, and for behavior after reproduction which enhances the chances of the progeny's survival, even to destroying oneself to guard one's young, will be selected for in the evolutionary process. So beings may be preprogrammed or predisposed to do things which lessen their *individual* chances of survival.

3. Nathaniel Branden, "Rational Egoism: A Reply to Professor Emmons," *The Personalist*, Spring 1970, p. 201.

4. It may seem a necessary truth that "right," "ought," "should," etc. are to be explained in terms of what is (intended to be) productive of the greatest good. So, it is often thought, that what is wrong with utilitarianism (which *is* of this *form*) is that its conception of good is too narrow. It doesn't, for example, take rights and their nonviolation into account in the proper way, but leaves them a derivative status. (Hence many of the counterexample cases to utilitarianism: punishing an innocent man, to save a neighborhood from a vengeful rampage, etc.) But even if one includes the nonviolation of rights into a theory in a primary way (and those of us for whom there is some desirable society in which we would choose to live, even though in it some of our rights are sometimes violated, rather than move to an island on which we could survive, alone, do not think that it is the sole greatest good), one may include it in the wrong place, in the wrong manner. For suppose we build into the desirable end-state to be achieved some condition about minimizing the amount and significance of the violation of rights which takes place in the society. We then have something like a utilitarianism of rights, which could still require us to violate someone's rights if this act of violation leads to a minimizing of the amount of violation of rights in society. It might do this perhaps by deflecting others from their intended action of gravely violating people's rights, removing their motive for doing it, diverting their attention, and so on. (A mob rampaging through a part of town, killing and burning, *will* be violating the rights of those living there, and so one might try to justify one's act of punishing someone you know to be innocent of the crime which enraged the mob, on the grounds that this action will lead to a minimizing of the weight of the violations of rights in the society.)

As against this conception, which builds rights into the end-state to be achieved, one might say that their proper place is as a constraint upon the actions to be done. So the structure of the view is: Among those acts available to you which don't violate constraints C, act so as to maximize goal G.

This differs from one which says: act so as to maximize G, and which tries to build the side-constraints C *into* the goal G. For the view with the side-constraints forbids your violating having the minimizing of the violation of these constraints in the goal, allows you to violate the constraints in order to lessen the total amount of violation of such constraints in the society. I ignore questions about finding a way of putting the side-constraint view into the form of the goal-without-side-constraints view, e.g., perhaps by having a distinction made, in the goal, between *your* violating the constraint, and someone else's doing it, where the former is given infinite weight in the goal, so that no amount of stopping someone else's doing it can outweigh your violating the constraints. Even with this possibility, notice that indexical expressions ("*my* doing something") appear in the goal. I also ignore questions about whether sometimes you are allowed to violate rights of innocents in order to prevent monstrous deeds by others. For example, suppose that the only way to have stopped the Nazis from conquering all was to have used some weapon on them which would have also killed innocent people in the city attacked who couldn't leave and weren't choosing to stay there. *Perhaps* avoiding great moral horror *swamps* people's rights, so that one would be justified in doing something one knew would kill innocent people, in order to stop the horror. (See Michael Walzer's paper "World War II: Why Was This War Different?" delivered before the American Political Science Association, September 1970 meeting.)

The possibility of "swamping" of rights may lead one to think that it is the goal structure, with a weighting of constraints inside the goals, which is appropriate, rather than the structure with absolute side-constraints. But other structures are possible, e.g., a side-constraint structure with principles governing the setting aside of that whole structure. (But since many of the set-aside structure's features will have to reappear again in its replacement, is this the proper way to view things?) These issues, connecting with some discussed in "Moral Complications and Moral Structures" (Essay 10), are very complex, and I hope to discuss them in detail on another occasion.

These considerations enable us to clarify a difficulty with the classical conception of the night-watchman state, which limits the legitimate functions of the state to the protection of its citizens against violence, theft, fraud, and to the enforcement of contracts, etc., but specifically excludes redistributive tasks. The difficulty (which I first presented in a paper, "A Framework for Utopia," delivered at the APA Eastern Division Meeting in 1969, with Sidney Hook as commentator) is that the protection of people in this way costs money (for detectives, police to bring criminals into custody, courts, prisons). How is it to be paid for, and, in particular, is there some non-redistributive way of financing it? We might imagine a system in which the state provides these protective services only to those who specifically pay for them, with perhaps different packages of protective services offered for different fees. People who don't buy a protection contract don't get protected. Now consider this system of individuals purchasing protection from the state *combined with* a voucher system (cf. Milton Friedman's school vouchers, which, of course, allow the people a choice of schools) funded by taxation, under which all people, or those in need, etc., are given vouchers, backed by the funds collected by taxation, which can be used only for the purchase of a protection policy from the state. It is clear that the latter system is redistributive (compare it to the former), yet this latter system is equivalent to the system of the night-watchman state. So, unless some other nonredistributive method of financing protection for everyone can be found (and, on the face of it, it is difficult to see how it can be), the night-watchman state itself performs some redistributive functions (*viz.*, having some people pay for the protection of others). And, it might well be asked, if this redistributive function of the state (redistribution in order to protect everyone) is legitimate, why is redistribution for other attractive and desirable purposes not legitimate as well? On the other hand, if the nonredistributionist accepts something like the first system described, then his position will seem to many to be inconsistent, as well as monstrous.

I wish here to focus only on the first of these charges. The proponent of the night-watchman state is greatly concerned with the violation of rights and with protecting these rights; so that he makes the protection the only legitimate function of the state, protesting that other functions are illegitimate because their performance will itself involve the violation of rights. How can he then, given his paramount placing of the protection and nonviolation of rights, move to the first position which would, it seems, leave some persons' rights unprotected or ill-protected; how can he do this *in the name* of the nonviolation of rights? This objection assumes that the proponent of the first system is a "utilitarian of rights," whose goal is, say, the minimization of the amount and significance of the violation of rights in the society, and who will pursue this goal, even through using means which themselves violate people's rights. But if he places the nonviolation of rights as a constraint upon action, rather than building it into the end-state to be realized (it may, let me hasten to add, occur in *both* places), and his conception of rights is such that your being forced to contribute to another's welfare violates your rights, and is such that someone else's not providing you with something you need greatly, essential to the protection of your rights, does not *itself* violate your rights (though it may facilitate, or avoid making more difficult, someone else's doing so) then this theorist will be led to something like the first system of individuals purchasing protection for themselves (and those others they voluntarily choose to do so for). And this will be a consistent position. (That it is a consistent position does not, of course, show that it is an acceptable position.)

Given the subject of this essay, we do well here to mention Ayn Rand's proposal, in her essay entitled "Government Financing in a Free Society." Briefly put, her suggestion is that the government enforce the contracts of only those who have paid a special fee (others may sign contracts backed by trust, desire to continue their good reputation etc., but not by government's powers of force) and that the government's other legitimate functions be financed out of the funds so collected from those who voluntarily choose to make use of (and pay for) the government's contract-enforcing powers. But it is difficult to see why she finds this a legitimate solution to the problem. For the government has a legal monopoly on the use of force, and the proposal involves the government charging *extra* to enforce contracts, in order to cover the costs of its other protective functions. (Compare what it would charge for enforcing contracts if it did not take on these other protective functions.) Why is this not illegitimate forcible redistribution, and isn't talk of people voluntarily dealing with the legal monopoly (and voluntarily paying the higher fees to cover the legal monopoly's other functions?) too quick? If in the United States today, the post office, with a legal monopoly on the right to carry the mails, charged one dollar per letter, in order to cover the costs of other redistributive activities (and thus charged more than even a monopolistic post office, covering its costs, which was singlemindedly devoted to delivering the mail), would Miss Rand think that a legitimate means had been found to finance redistributive activities, say the educational costs of college students? Could anyone who otherwise thought that there was a problem with governmental redistributive activities feel that problem avoided by tying redistributive activities to the provision of some service *protected by a legal monopoly?* To be sure, there are powerful arguments for the state's having a legal monopoly on the use of violence (rather than allowing, e.g., private contract-enforcing firms to use force to enforce contracts they have been hired to enforce), as there are not for the post office's having a legal monopoly to deliver the mails. But since the arguments for the state's having a monopoly on the use of violence do not involve redistributive considerations, it is difficult to see why it is legitimate to allow the monopoly thus established to exploit its monopolisitic position in order to pursue redistributive aims. These considerations are not addressed to and will have, perhaps, little interest for those who find no problem with the state's forcible redistributive activities; they are meant merely to point out that those who do find a problem cannot avoid it by slipping the state's redistributive activities in through the (only) back door, in the fashion of Miss Rand.

5. Rand, "The Objectivist Ethics," p. 27.

6. See also our discussion in section V, which considers a case where John Galt seems not to act on (1).

7. If rights are explained as "conditions of existence required by man's nature for his proper survival," then we can reconstruct the Randian argument for a right to life, but this argument will not answer the question: why should I not violate another's right to life; why should I not intervene by force to eliminate one of the conditions of another man's existence required by his nature for his

proper survival? That is, with this explanation of rights, argument is needed for (6) above. If we assume that rights are not to be violated, and others should not forcibly intervene in the exercise of someone's rights, then argument is needed to the conclusion that a person does have a right to his own life, that is, that *others* shouldn't forcibly intervene in it, even granting that its maintenance is *his* highest value. Taking either approach, we face the question of why one person shouldn't intervene by force to thwart the conditions of another man's existence.

A similar question is raised by Mortimer Adler's argument in his *The Time of Our Lives: The Ethics of Common Sense* (1970), where there is a transition (chap. 14, sec. 2) from an individual's moral obligation to pursue his own real good to an individual's moral right (entailing obligations of others not to interfere) to pursue his own real good. He attempts to bridge this gap (chap. 16) by grounding our moral obligations not to violate the rights of others on our obligation to make a good life for ourselves. He argues as follows:

(1) Each of us needs civil peace as a means of making a good life for ourselves. Every universal act which injures other men or the community is a breach of civil peace. "Hence when I act unjustly toward others or act in any way that is contrary to the good of the community, I am injuring myself. It may not appear to be so in the short run; I may gain apparent goods by my injustice toward others or by criminal activities that injure the community itself. But in the long run, I *may* have gained these apparent goods only at the loss of a real good that I need—the civil peace of the community in which I live. It is only in the short run that injustice can appear to be expedient. In the long run, which is the omen of my whole life, the just *tends* to be the expedient" (p. 173, my italics).

Note that my individual conduct breaches the peace; it does not destroy it. And it is an undestroyed peace (rather than an unbreached one) that it is said I need.

(2) Under ideal conditions "when an individual seeks only those things which are really good for him, he does not infringe on or interfere with the pursuit of happiness on the part of others through their seeking the same real goods for themselves" (p. 174). For Adler says, consider that one man's pursuit of real self-improvement (which is the greatest good) cannot interfere with another's similar pursuit. But if there are scarce (in the economist's sense, which does *not* entail that the situation is non-ideal, in Adler's sense; cf. pp. 177–178) resources of self-improvement (books, musical instruments), then such interference is possible; similarly, with teachers, with the added possibility of *forcing* one of the few able people in a subject (who would rather be improving *himself*) to instruct you. It is even easier to see how this might happen with the goods other than self-improvement that Adler discusses.

(3) Under non-ideal conditions, men may not obtain the privileges which enable them to lead good lives by force or fraud (footnote 3, pp. 309–310).

No reason connecting this constraint to an individual's obligation to pursue a good life for himself is offered by Adler. (Nor is any other reason offered.) It would be interesting to hear what reasons he would produce, in view of his statement (pp. 171–172): "If it could be shown, as I think it cannot be shown, that the individual's obligations to others and to the community are independent of his obligation to make a good life for himself, then the discharge of such obligations would impose a burden on him that might interfere with or even frustrate the pursuit of his own happiness. I would like to add, in passing, that those who regard their duties to others or to the community as independent of their obligation to make a good life for themselves are either sentimentalists or thoughtless do-gooders"!!

8. Or, to go to a case which is merely meant to caution one about how one formulates the harmony condition, each of two boxers, who have promised to win the fight, and who each have contracted with different outside parties to win, should win, and furthermore, it is permissible for one to thwart the other's attempt to do what he should do.

9. I say "stronger" realizing that she would deny that it is a stronger claim, because she thinks that there is no additional step needed to get from something being in one's interests to its being something one should and ought to do.

10. We should notice here a slide many writers in and readers of this tradition make, from X is a (morally) better act than Y, to one is (morally) better doing X than Y, to one is better off doing X than Y. An argument that right conduct and self-interest don't diverge requires independent ways of identifying each, plus an argument that these two independently identified things always go together; at any rate, so it must go if the ordinary view that *self-interest* and *rightness* are distinct notions is to be adhered to. Alternatively, it might be argued that they don't diverge because there are not two independent notions, but rather one of them is primary and the other one can be explained in a coherent fashion only in terms of the first (in such a manner as to yield their nondivergence). So, one might explain "morally right" or "morally ought" in terms of "self-interest," or against such a background (Rand). Or, one might attempt to argue that the notion of *self-interest* itself cannot be coherently explained except in terms of *morally right* (with a particular form, and perhaps content) in such a fashion that they don't diverge. This latter possibility is an exciting and tantalizing one, which should be pursed.

11. See her essay, "The Conflicts of Men's Interests," in *The Virtue of Selfishness*.

12. It is sometimes assumed that the unconstrained (constrained) egoist can give no weight to the interests of others except as they are reflected in his own interests (and the constraints). But a theoretically possible egoist position could require: Maximize self-interest (subject to constraints) and among those actions which *tie* so far as (constrained) self-interest is concerned, pick that one which

best satisfies condition C (where C may be any condition, e.g., the utilitarian one). Here we would have a lexicographic ordering, with the (constrained) egoistic score occupying the first place in the vector, so that nothing can override considerations of self-interest, *and* other things are given some weight later on in the vector. I use "constraint" here as it is used in linear programming, to mean bound on another maximizing or goal-directed process.

13. And not a path that Miss Rand would follow, I think. (See "The Objectivist Ethics," pp. 28–30.) But one cannot merely say, to use Miss Rand's terminology, that happiness is the *purpose* of ethics, but not the *standard*. For the problem here is that it is known that the action will *not* achieve *this* purpose, when it is guided by Galt's valuing Dagny Taggart's life above his own. And in the science fiction case below, the purpose of happiness is achieved by his *not* following the standard, *without* his making whims or irrational desires his guide to conduct.

What the egoist condition on desires is which allows non-self-centered valuing of another's life above one's own, or the valuing of the triumph of justice and right above one's own life, but rules out other, *altruistic,* desires as incompatible with rational egoism is a puzzle.

I discuss the position in the text because when the components of Miss Rand's view, assumed to be indissolubly intertwined, part company, it is *one* path that can be taken to reconstruct the position (and has been taken in conversation with me by persons who term themselves followers of Miss Rand, for whose intellectual meanderings she is, of course, not responsible). As I have said, it is not a path that the preponderant thrust of her view (the components of her view which, I assume, have major weight for her) would lead her to take, I think. But in that case, it is unclear what alternative teleological argument she would offer for a life lived in accordance with the virtues of rationality, honesty, integrity, pride, productiveness, justice, and independence.

14. If "happy" is what it is. More likely terribly sad, hoping that they'll reach safety.

15. Privacy invasions raise an interesting problem for libertarian theory, for it seems that we can imagine such invasions without any of the particular sorts of physical invasions which libertarians tend to focus upon. For example, suppose that there is one telepath who picks up emanations from you which can't be screened in. He knows exactly what you are doing, and thinking, at any given moment. Perhaps he broadcasts you on a particular T.V. wavelength. Anyone can tune in, any time, to see what you are doing and thinking at that moment. On Saturday night, after you are asleep, there are the highlights of your week. No thought or action of yours is private, yet the telepath has not *invaded* you or your property in any way (as libertarians speak of invasion). Are there any grounds to legally forbid the telepath from so operating, which the libertarian can formulate? Would we wish to forbid it in this case?

It might be said that such cases are impossible, and it is not a difficulty with a view that it does not handle some impossible case as we would wish. But it is, I think, an objection to a view *if* it does not handle *this* kind of case correctly (as it would be to show that a consequence of a moral view was that if there were anyone who could travel faster than the speed of light, then it would be morally permissible for him to murder whomever he wished), even though the task of marking off *which* kind of impossibilities cause trouble for a moral theory still requires doing.

16. By inadequacy I mean that the view does not handle some particular cases as the reader, in his considered judgment, would wish to see them handled. Of course, if the reader insists on seeing each example through the principles he accepts ("Well, since it doesn't violate principle *P*, it's o.k.") then it will be impossible to produce what he will accept as a counterexample to the principles. Issues about how nondogmatically to hold principles so that they're open to counterexamples (as well as to counterarguments: but even here, one sufficiently attached to a consistent principle *P* could deny any statement *Q* from which not-*P* follows), but still to hold and accept them rather than merely contemplating them, are of great interest and merit extended discussion.

Followers of Miss Rand should not scorn holding principles in this fashion, if I am right in thinking that:

(a) They do not possess a knock-down deductive demonstration of their principles.

(b) A large part of the attraction of the Randian view for people is the way it handles particular cases, the kind of considerations it brings to bear, its "sense of life." For many, the first time they encounter a libertarian view saying that a rational life (with individual rights) is possible and justified is in the writings of Miss Rand, and their finding such a view attractive, right, etc., can easily lead them to think that the particular *arguments* Miss Rand offers for the view are conclusive or adequate. Here it is not the argument which has led them to accept the view, but rather the way the view codifies, integrates, unifies, extends many of the judgments they want to make, feel are right, and supports their aspirations. If this is so, then one should hold the view so that it is open to challenge from just that sort of data that has provided its main support.

Here we do well to mention a problem which has received little discussion in the literature on ethics. Some writers on ethics have viewed their task as offering moral principles which would unify and account for the particular moral judgments we make, often adding that the reciprocal process of formulating such principles, and modifying particular judgments, itself is the process of moral justification. We may ask the philosopher of science's question: Does the data uniquely determine one theory which accounts for it, or are there alternative theories which equally well account for all the data we have or could have? Asking this question forces us to clarify the notion of all possible moral data: is it, for *each* act in each situation, a pairing of the act in the situation with a judgment of moral permissibility? Here it seems plausible to think that alternative different theories will equally well account for all this data (as plausible as to think that alternative physical theories can account for all possible observational data). Perhaps adding into the data other types of particular judgments (e.g., of persons' characters) will help, but, one suspects, not much. More promising is the claim that in the data we have not only particular judgments of particular actions but also, often, some (partial) reason offered for the judgment. And so the theory must not only yield the particular judgment but also, when we have them, certain sorts of reasons for the judgment. (I say "certain sorts" to mark a problem: if we offered as our reason for a judgment, "because it follows from T" where T is a complete fundamental moral theory, then any theory which accounted for our judgments would have to be, contain, or yield T. So it is a more delimited sort of reason which is needed.) Placing this into the data, is it still the case that there are alternative theories which equally well account for the data, where no one theory accounts for and reduces all the others. If so, the various well-known positions in the philosophy of science as to the content of theories become available as options, and one may pick an option in ethics different from the one one holds with regard to a particular theory of physics. The whole area is open, and would repay detailed investigation.

17. Independently, Thomas Nagel argues against the principle of experiential ethics in his paper "Death," *Nous*, 1970.

12. Weighted Voting and "One-Man, One-Vote"

My comments in this essay refer to a paper by William H. Riker and Lloyd S. Shapley given at the 1965 meeting of the Society for Political and Legal Philosophy. The published version of their talk appeared as "Weighted Voting: A Mathematical Analysis for Instrumental Judgments" in *Representation*, edited by J. Roland Pennock and John W. Chapman (New York: Atherton Press, 1968), pp. 199–216.

1. "One wants to equalize" shall in this paper mean "one must equalize in order to conform to one reasonable interpretation of the Court's decisions." I shall not here be concerned with the desirability of this equalization, and shall not discuss whether in constructing a system of representative institutions one should, under all circumstances, build into it such equalization. Nor shall I discuss the question of under what circumstances one should reconstruct an existing system of representative institutions in order to achieve such equalization.

2. The situation is somewhat more complicated, as is pointed out in John F. Banzhof III, "Multi-member Electoral Districts: Do They Violate the 'One Man, One Vote' Principle?" *Yale Law Journal*, 75 (1966), 1309. Questions paralleling those I raise arise for the more complicated formulation.

3. To say that important purposes are served by representation by geographical districts is not to say that one never should want to modify such a system. For example, if persons working in New York City but residing elsewhere must pay some income tax to New York City, and one takes seriously the slogan "No taxation without representation," then one may think it desirable to give such persons some vote (weighted less than one) for the representatives in the New York City Council of the districts in which they work.

4. Interesting questions arise about whether in this situation the legislator's power should be proportional to the number of eligible voters, the number of registered voters, or the number of actual voters in his district. I shall not pause to discuss these questions, nor shall I discuss the claim that the legislator's power should be proportional to the number of votes he has received, which presumably would require something like a system of proportional representation. Though I shall not discuss systems of proportional representation, I should mention that they seem to me to raise very important questions for and perhaps about political philosophy. I conjecture that one can list conditions on representative institutions which are jointly satisfied only by a system of proportional representation, and which are such that each seems reasonable and desirable and indeed required by justice. But political science books tell us that systems of proportional representation work out terribly and so we reject such systems. Still, it may be that when we go back to our conditions, though we see which must be rejected to avoid a system of proportional representation and keep (an idealization of) our current system, we will feel that these conditions, which must be rejected if we are to avoid proportional representation, are conditions of fairness and justice. Yet we are reluctant to conclude that we should sometimes choose unfair and unjust institutions over fair and just ones. I do not claim that there can be no adequate theory of justice to resolve this difficulty, but merely that it poses a problem for and perhaps about a theory of justice.

5. A legislator might wish to split his votes on an issue, if this is permitted by the system, to reflect deep divisions within his district.

6. As I understand it, there are two (related) rationales for the Shapley power measure:

(1) The three conditions which only the Shapley measure satisfies. For a statement and discussion of these conditions, which raise some questions about the adequacy of the third condition, see R. Duncan Luce and Howard Raiffa, *Games and Decisions* (New York: Wiley, 1957), pp. 245–250.

(2) The rationale in terms of random coalition formation.

Does the Shapley measure yield intuitive results for all systems of voting, e.g., for the system in which the legislators are ordered, and each may vote for a bill, against it, or abstain. If a legislator votes for (against) a bill, and all legislators before him in the order abstain, then the bill passes (is defeated). If no one votes for the bill, it is defeated. Under this arrangement, it seems that (a) each legislator has more power than anyone who follows him in the order, and (b) the first legislator could not have more power. I believe the Shapley measure cannot yield both (a) and (b), and it would, I think, lead to the rejection of (b), thus not giving the first legislator the maximal amount of power. This may lead one to question the imposition of Shapley's second condition (that the individual values of the game form an additive partition of the value of the whole game) in measuring the power of legislators in legislative bodies.

7. If one ignored everything but voting power on the floor of the legislature, e.g., that some districts would be represented on committees less than proportionally to their size.

8. It is of some interest to formulate the conditions which a gerrymandered system of districts violates. If the *intention* of the person forming the districts isn't relevant (but rather the effects of certain districting) and the geographical and population-density conditions formulated by political scientists are not desirable in themselves but are meant to make unlikely the violation of further conditions, then one wants to know what these further conditions are. One suspects that these further conditions may naturally tie in with systems of proportional representation.

9. For this example, I assume that all the legislators must vote, and that each must cast his votes as a bloc.

10. When m is the total number of legislators, $x = m!$.

11. Where $x = m!$.

12. One actually wants something more than this; namely, that a legislator's power be between zero and one (excluding the endpoints) if he has associated with him some though not all of the persons associated with the legislators.

13. It is not, I think, clear what facts may legitimately be included in the relevant structure for determining measures of power. Should one include the fact that certain methods of election make it more likely that the two representatives of a multimember district will vote in the same way than that two randomly selected representatives will, that the number of political parties and the degree of party discipline affects the likelihood of different permutations, that some representatives look to others for guidance on specific sorts of issues, that some legislative committees' recommendations are rarely rejected, and so forth.

15. Why Do Intellectuals Oppose Capitalism?

An earlier version of this essay was given as part of a lecture series at Trinity College, Connecticut. This (revised) version was submitted in 1984 for publication in the volume of essays from that lecture series but, by some accident, it was the earlier manuscript that got published in *The Future of Private Enterprise*, ed. Craig Aronoff et al. (Atlanta: Georgia State University Business Press, 1986).

1. See B. Bruce-Biggs, ed., *The New Class?* (New York: McGraw-Hill, 1981).

2. See Mancur Olson, *The Logic of Collective Action* (Cambridge, MA: Harvard University Press, 1965).

3. Ludwig von Mises, *The Anti-Capitalistic Mentality* (Princeton, NJ: Van Nostrand, 1956).

4. It is ironic that we see anti-capitalist feeling as a consequence of the schooling system, when recent radical writers see that system as molding people *for* capitalism, to be docile and obedient instruction followers, acceptors of hierarchy, keepers of schedules, etc. A school system, of course, *could* have both effects, whether intended or not, molding some to fit into the economic system and others to resent it.

5. We now can see why school athletes do not tend disproportionately to turn against the capitalist system, even though they too may experience a drop in social position after the school years. It was the informal social system which earlier treated them so well, and while they later may regret or resent the preferences of the consumers in the market, they will not have a prior attachment to any mode of distribution other than through the aggregate of individuals' preferences.

6. Paul Goodman, *Compulsory Mis-Education and the Community of Scholars* (New York: Vintage Books, 1966).

7. Not restricting his point to schools, Joseph Schumpeter discusses how "a capitalist-bourgeois society will find it difficult to bring the intellectuals to heel . . . In defending the intellectuals as a group . . . the bourgeoisie defends itself and its scheme of life. Only a government of non-bourgeois nature and non-bourgeois creed—under modern circumstances only a socialist or fascist one—is strong enough to discipline them. In order to do that it would have to change typically bourgeois institutions and drastically reduce the individual freedom of *all* strata of the nation. And such a government is not likely—it would not even be able—to stop short of private enterprise. From this follows both the unwillingness and the inability of the capitalist order to control its intellectual sector effectively"; *Capitalism, Socialism and Democracy* (New York: Harper, 1950), 150–151.

16. The Characteristic Features of Extremism

1. Geula Cohen, "The Passion of the True Believer," *Congress Monthly* 54, no. 5 (July/August 1987), 10–11.

CREDITS

12. "Weighted Voting and 'One-Man, One-Vote,'" from *Representation: Nomos X*, ed. J. R. Pennock and J. W. Chapman (New York: Atherton Press, 1968), 217–225.

13. "Goodman, Nelson, on Merit, Aesthetic," *Journal of Philosophy* 69 (1972): 783–785.

14. "Who Would Choose Socialism?" *Reason*, May 1978, 22–23.

15. "Why Do Intellectuals Oppose Capitalism?" a revised version of an essay first published in *The Future of Private Enterprise*, ed. Craig Aronoff et al. (Atlanta: Georgia State University Business Press, 1986).

16. "The Characteristic Features of Extremism," *Congress Monthly* 54 (July/August 1987): 12–13.

17. "War, Terrorism, Reprisals—Drawing Some Moral Lines," originally appeared as "Total War, Nuclear Deterrence, Terrorism, Reprisals—Drawing Some Moral Lines," *Reason*, December 1978, 19.

18. "Do Animals Have Rights?" originally appeared as "About Mammals and People," *New York Times Book Review*, November 27, 1983, 11; copyright © 1983 by The New York Times Company. Reprinted by permission.

19. "Fiction" originally appeared in *Ploughshares* 6, no. 3 (Fall 1980): 74–77.

20. "R.S.V.P.—A Story," *Commentary*, March 1972, 66-68.

21. "Testament," from "Two Philosophical Fables," *Mosaic* 12, no. 1 (Spring 1971): 24–28; published by the Harvard-Radcliffe Hillel Society.

22. "Teleology," from "Two Philosophical Fables," *Mosaic* 12, no. 1 (Spring 1971): 24–28; published by the Harvard-Radcliffe Hillel Society.

NAME INDEX

SUBJECT INDEX